— chapter 7 —

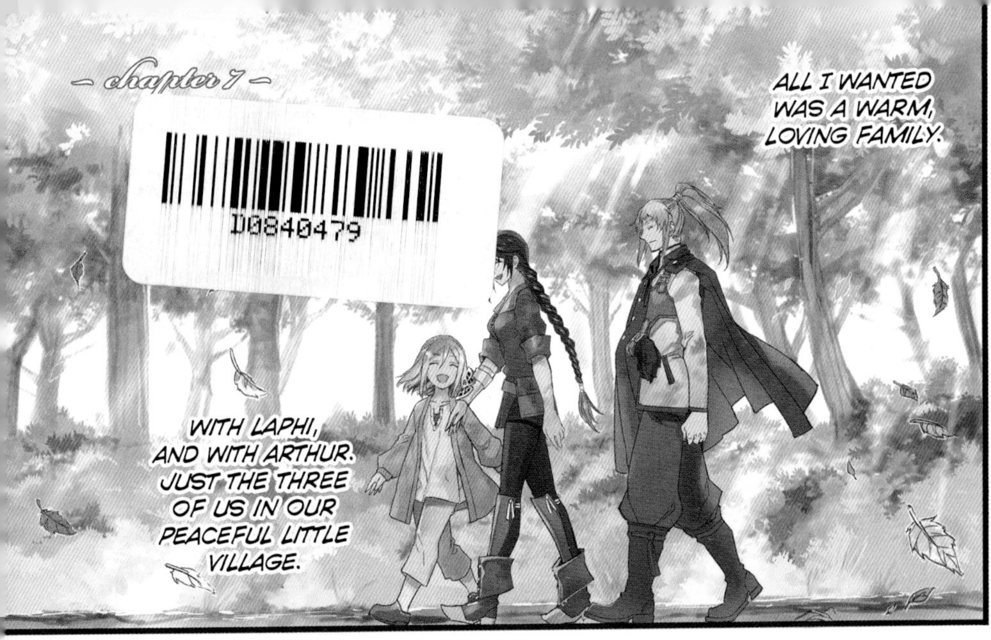
ALL I WANTED WAS A WARM, LOVING FAMILY.
WITH LAPHI, AND WITH ARTHUR. JUST THE THREE OF US IN OUR PEACEFUL LITTLE VILLAGE.

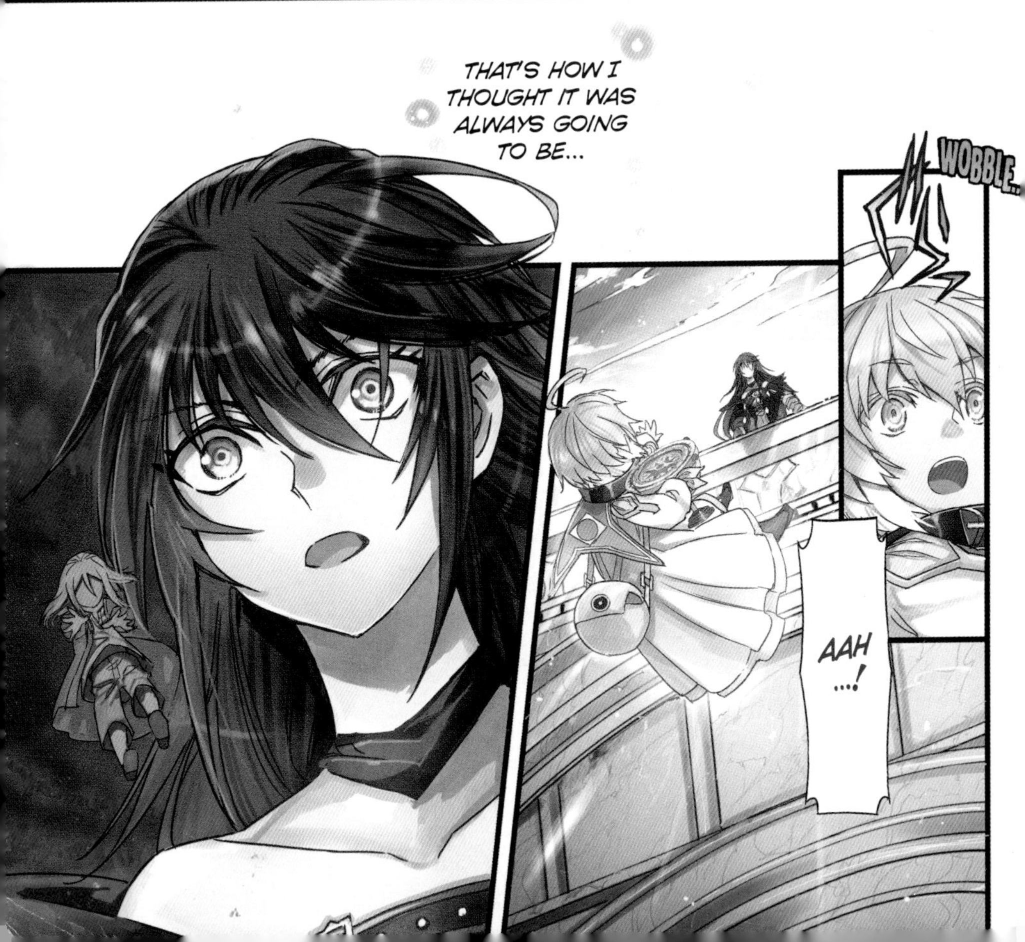
THAT'S HOW I THOUGHT IT WAS ALWAYS GOING TO BE...
WOBBLE...
AAH ...!

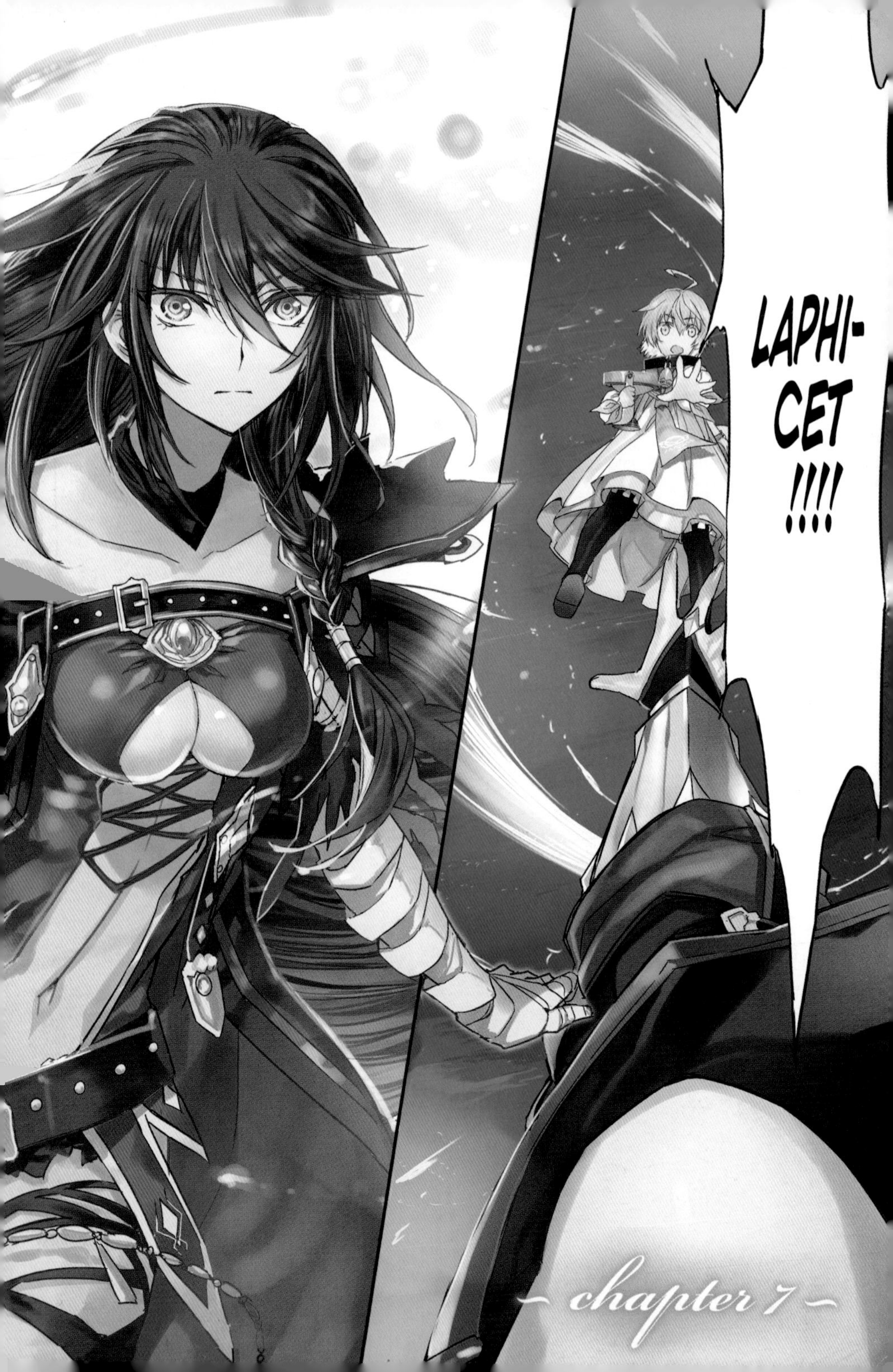
LAPHI-
CET
!!!!
chapter 7

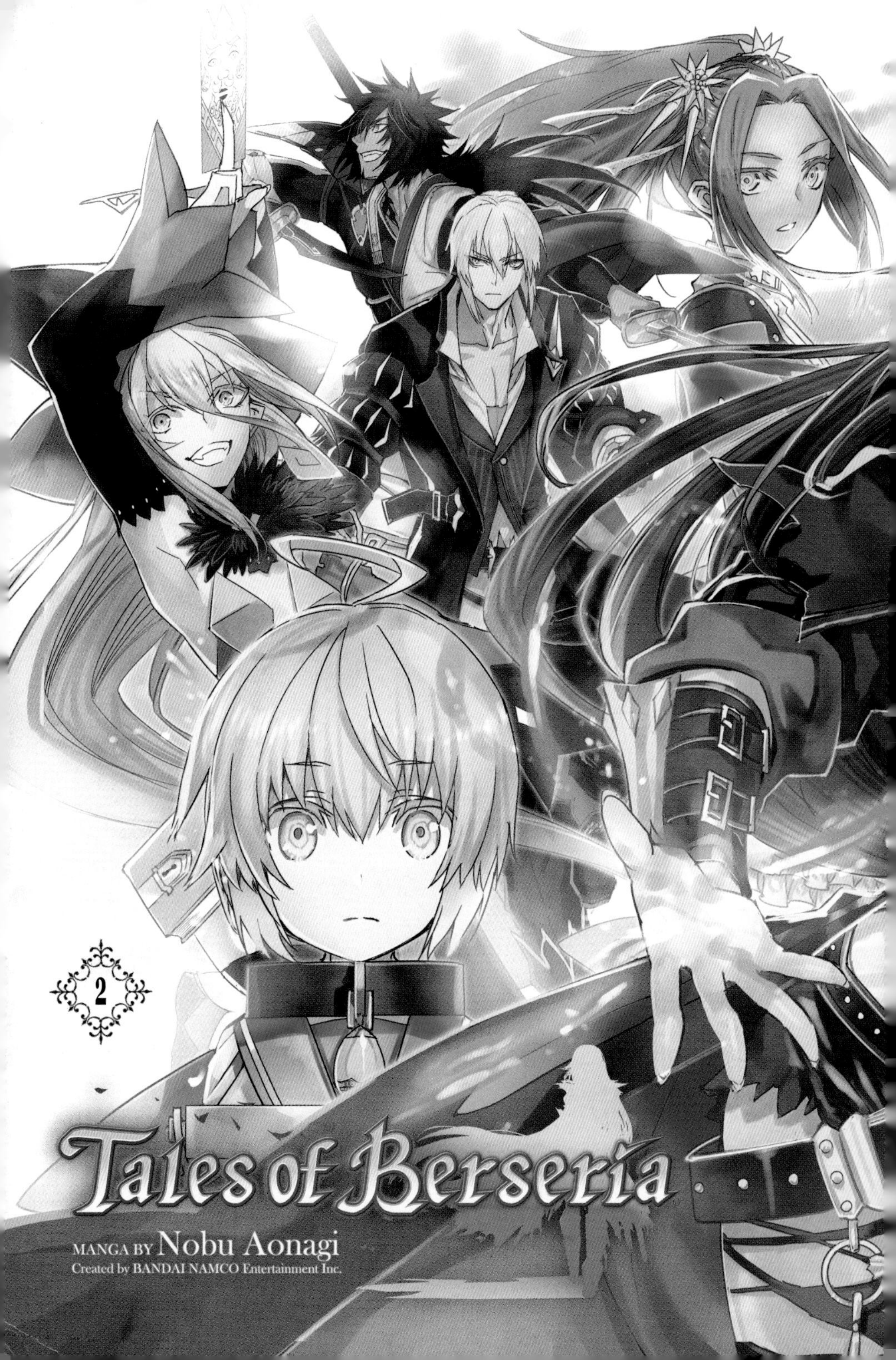
2
Tales of Berseria
MANGA BY Nobu Aonagi
Created by BANDAI NAMCO Entertainment Inc.

Contents

2

Tales of Berseria

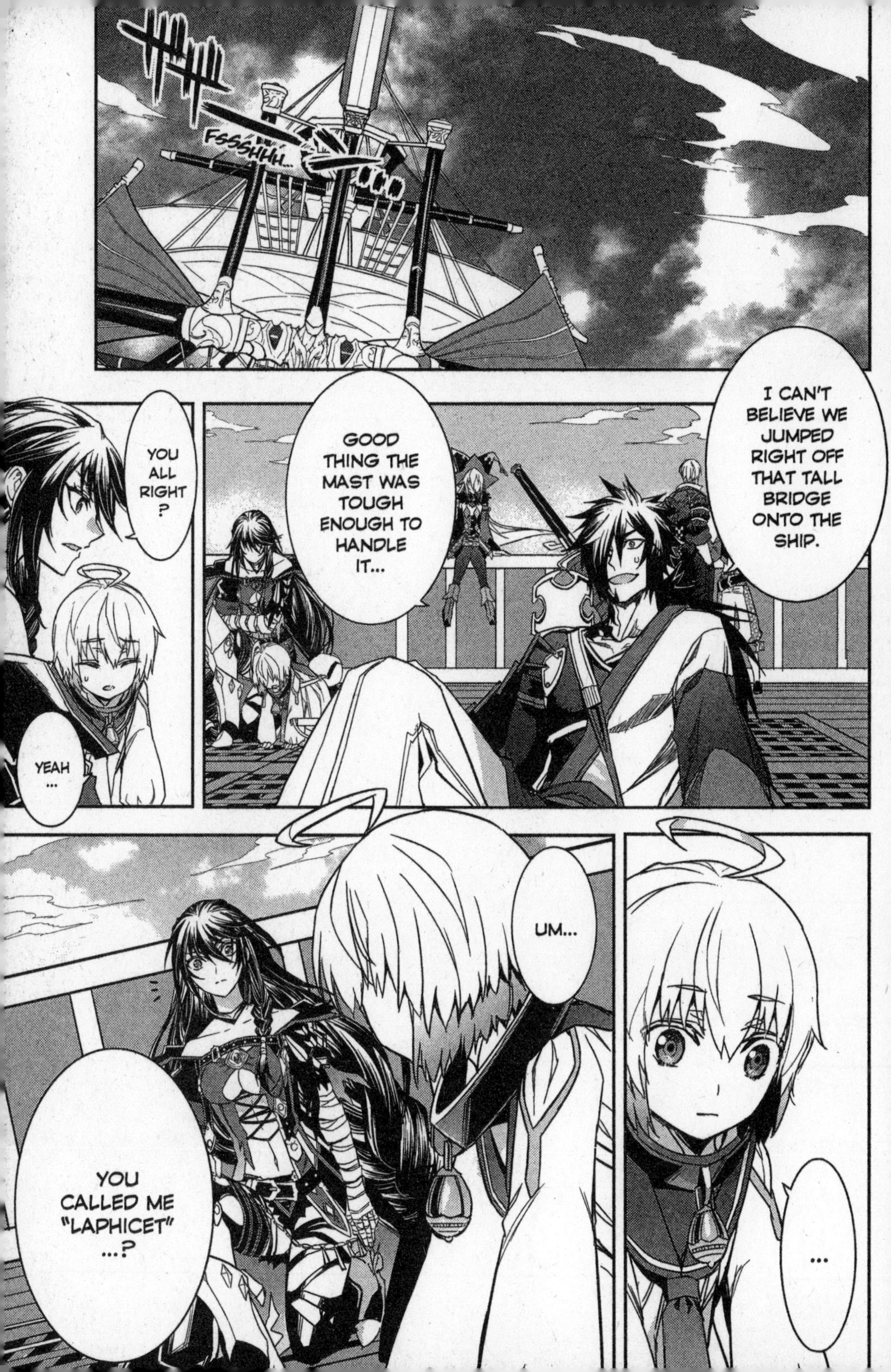
FSSSHHH...
I CAN'T BELIEVE WE JUMPED RIGHT OFF THAT TALL BRIDGE ONTO THE SHIP.
GOOD THING THE MAST WAS TOUGH ENOUGH TO HANDLE IT...
YOU ALL RIGHT?
YEAH...
...
UM...
YOU CALLED ME "LAPHICET"...?

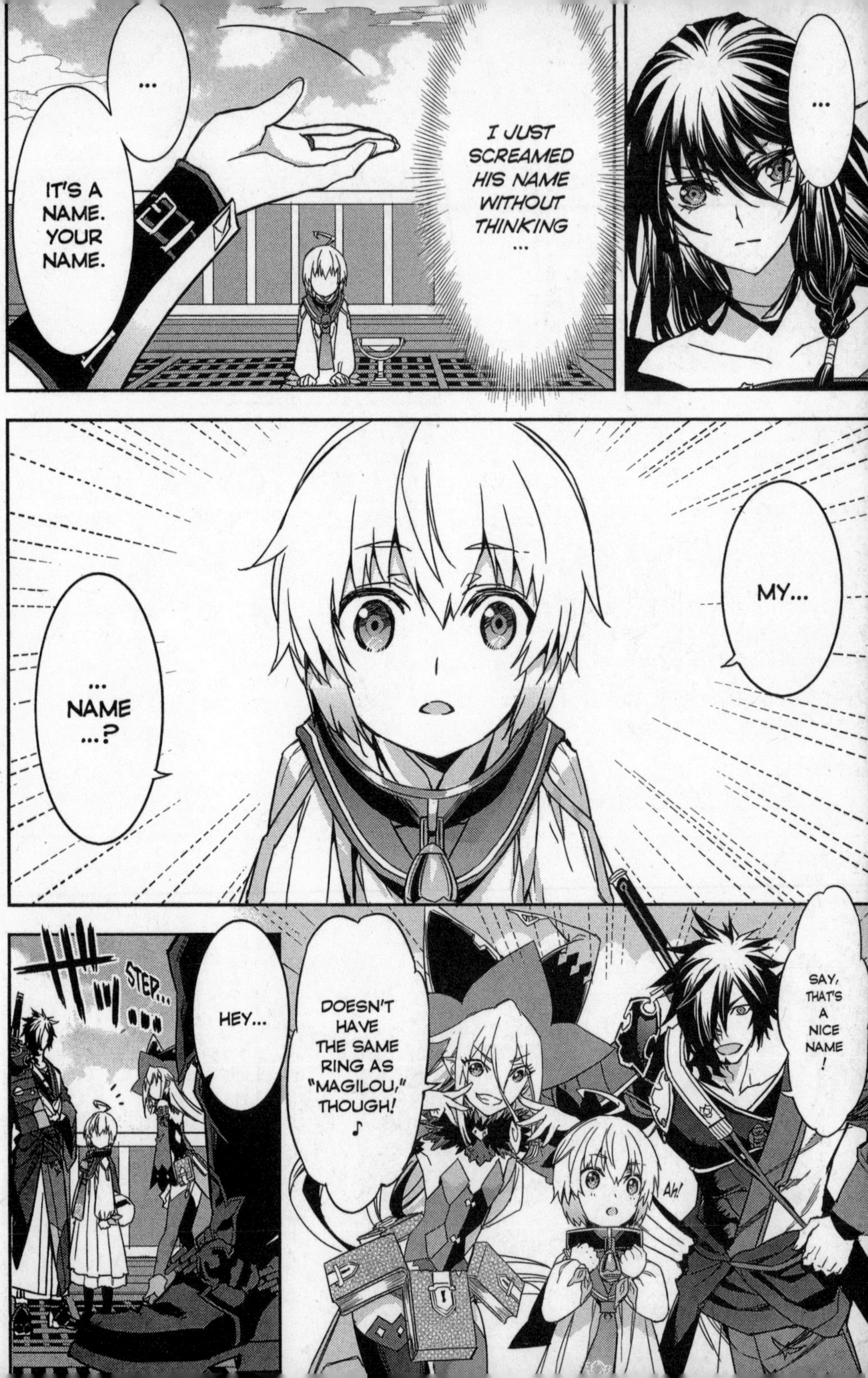
...
I JUST SCREAMED HIS NAME WITHOUT THINKING ...
...
IT'S A NAME. YOUR NAME.
MY...
... NAME ...?
SAY, THAT'S A NICE NAME!
DOESN'T HAVE THE SAME RING AS "MAGILOU," THOUGH! ♪
AH!
HEY...
STEP...

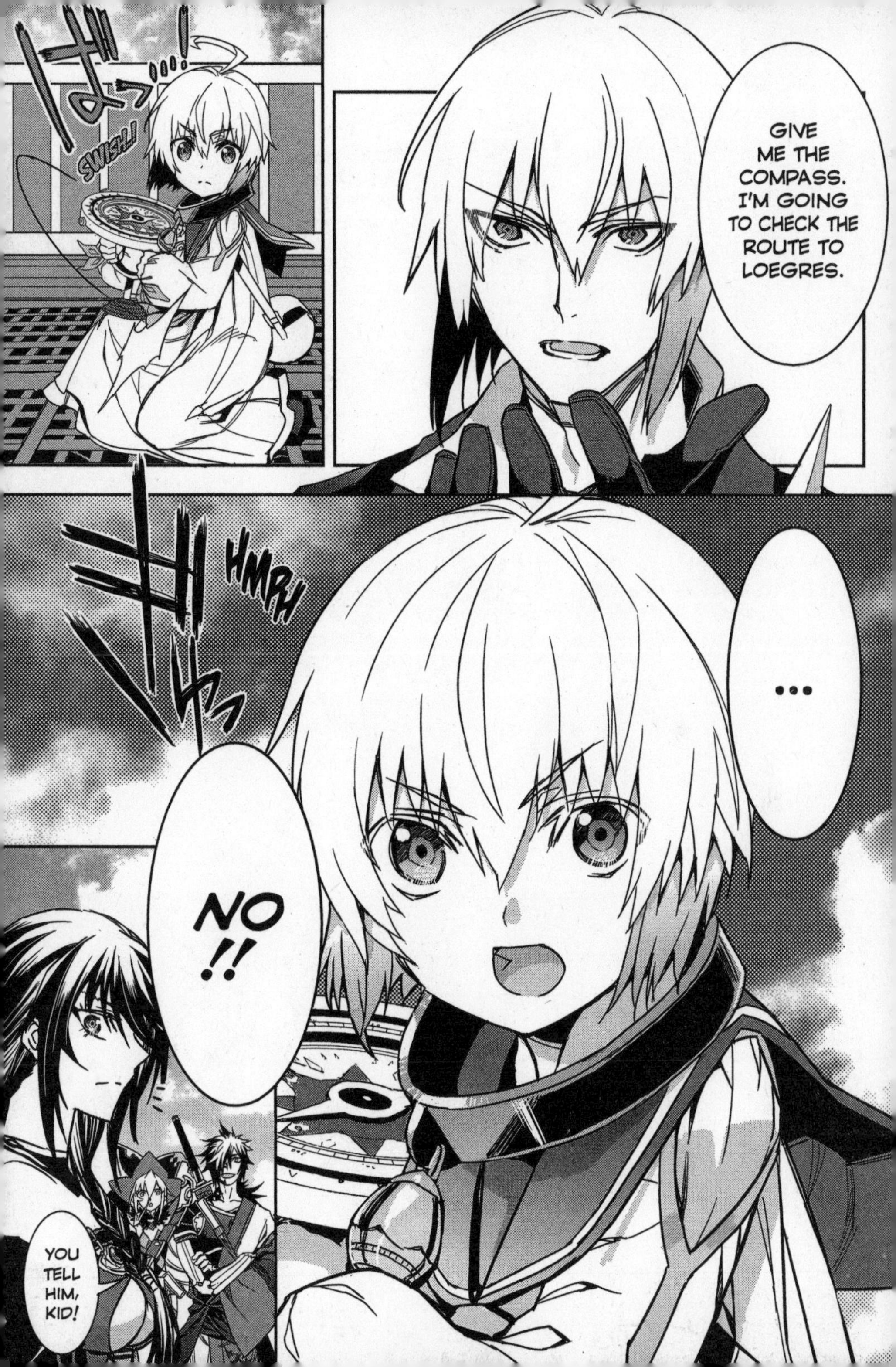

GIVE ME THE COMPASS. I'M GOING TO CHECK THE ROUTE TO LOEGRES.
ばっ
SWISH!
...
HMPH
NO!!
YOU TELL HIM, KID!

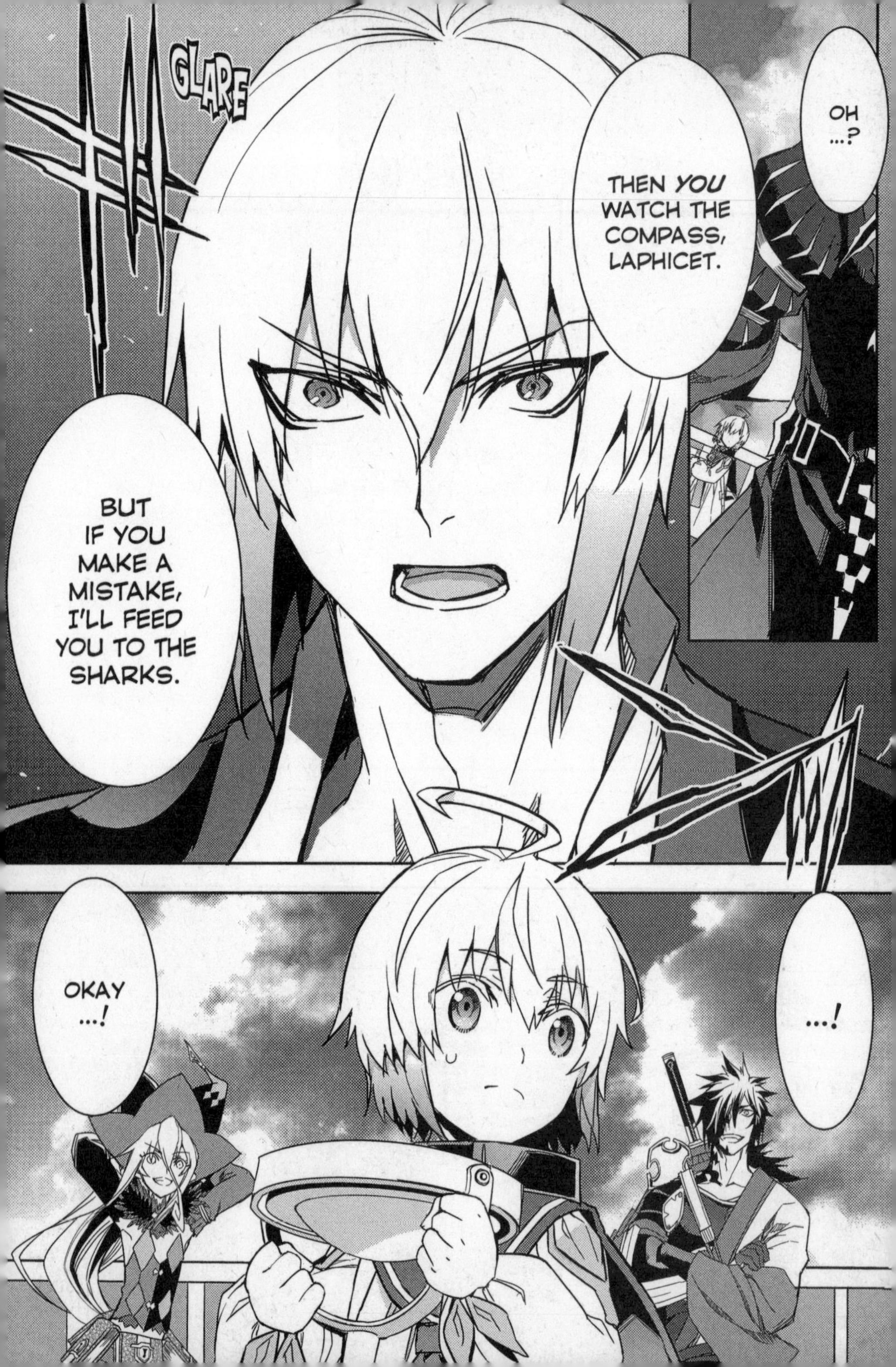
OH ...?
THEN YOU WATCH THE COMPASS, LAPHICET.
GLARE
BUT IF YOU MAKE A MISTAKE, I'LL FEED YOU TO THE SHARKS.
...!
OKAY ...!

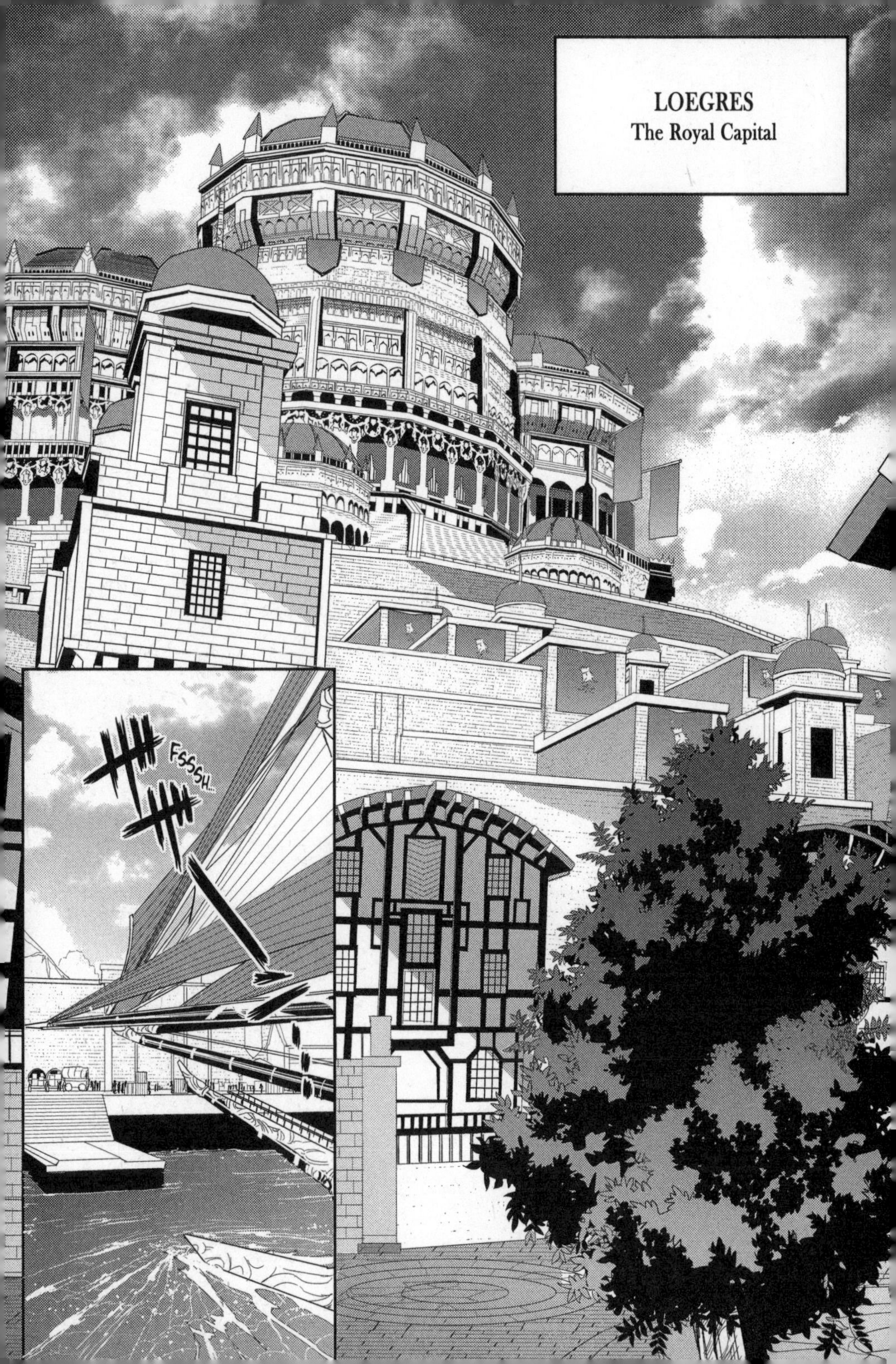
LOEGRES
The Royal Capital
FSSSH...

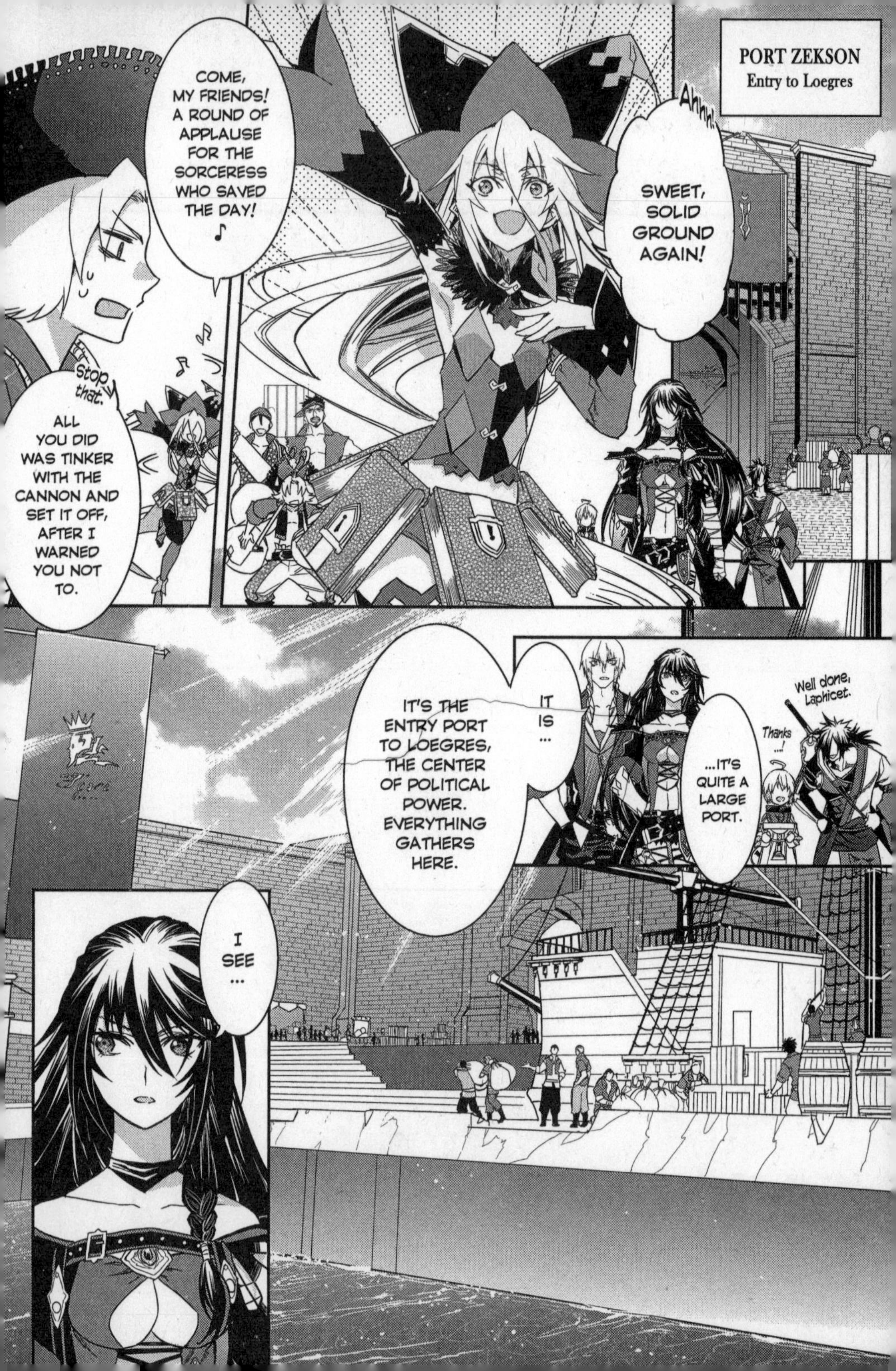

PORT ZEKSON
Entry to Loegres
Ahhh!
SWEET, SOLID GROUND AGAIN!
COME, MY FRIENDS! A ROUND OF APPLAUSE FOR THE SORCERESS WHO SAVED THE DAY! ♪
Stop that.
ALL YOU DID WAS TINKER WITH THE CANNON AND SET IT OFF, AFTER I WARNED YOU NOT TO.
Well done, Laphicet.
Thanks...!
...IT'S QUITE A LARGE PORT.
IT IS...
IT'S THE ENTRY PORT TO LOEGRES, THE CENTER OF POLITICAL POWER. EVERYTHING GATHERS HERE.
I SEE...

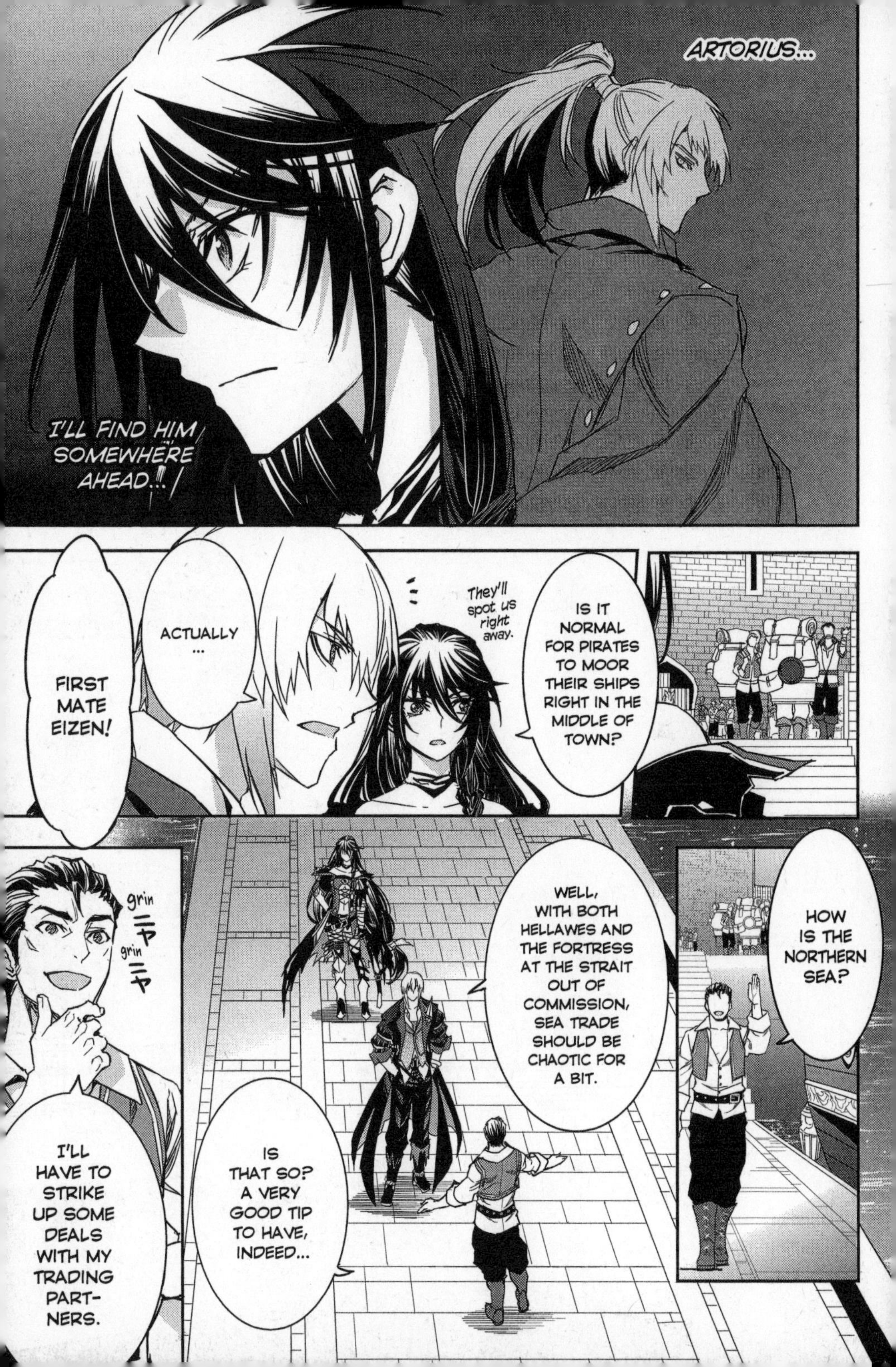
ARTORIUS...
I'LL FIND HIM SOMEWHERE AHEAD...!
IS IT NORMAL FOR PIRATES TO MOOR THEIR SHIPS RIGHT IN THE MIDDLE OF TOWN?
They'll spot us right away.
ACTUALLY...
FIRST MATE EIZEN!
HOW IS THE NORTHERN SEA?
WELL, WITH BOTH HELLAWES AND THE FORTRESS AT THE STRAIT OUT OF COMMISSION, SEA TRADE SHOULD BE CHAOTIC FOR A BIT.
IS THAT SO? A VERY GOOD TIP TO HAVE, INDEED...
grin ニヤ
grin ニヤ
I'LL HAVE TO STRIKE UP SOME DEALS WITH MY TRADING PARTNERS.

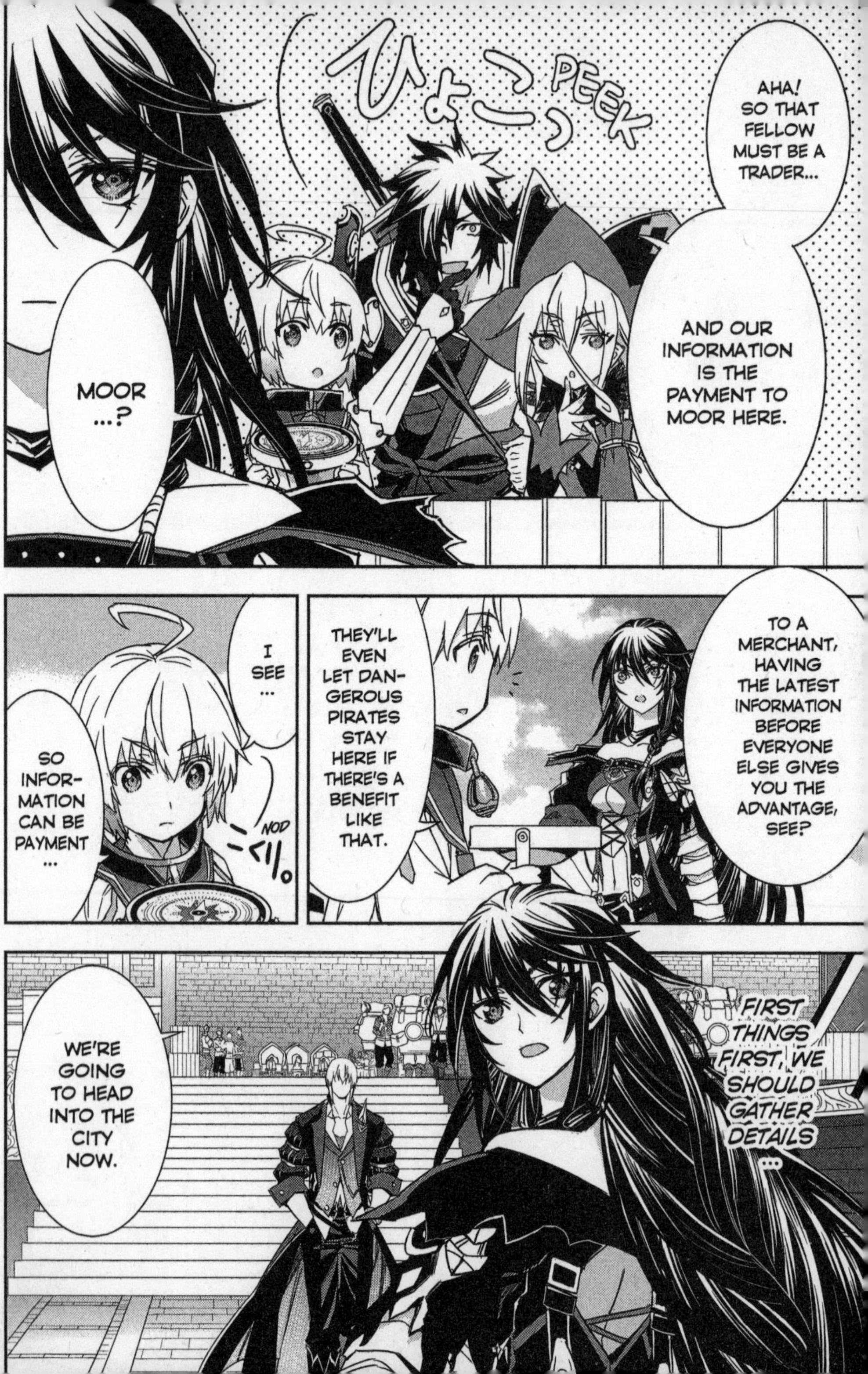
AHA! SO THAT FELLOW MUST BE A TRADER...
ひょこっ PEEK
AND OUR INFORMATION IS THE PAYMENT TO MOOR HERE.
MOOR ...?
TO A MERCHANT, HAVING THE LATEST INFORMATION BEFORE EVERYONE ELSE GIVES YOU THE ADVANTAGE, SEE?
THEY'LL EVEN LET DAN-GEROUS PIRATES STAY HERE IF THERE'S A BENEFIT LIKE THAT.
I SEE ...
SO INFOR-MATION CAN BE PAYMENT ...
こくり NOD
FIRST THINGS FIRST, WE SHOULD GATHER DETAILS ...
WE'RE GOING TO HEAD INTO THE CITY NOW.

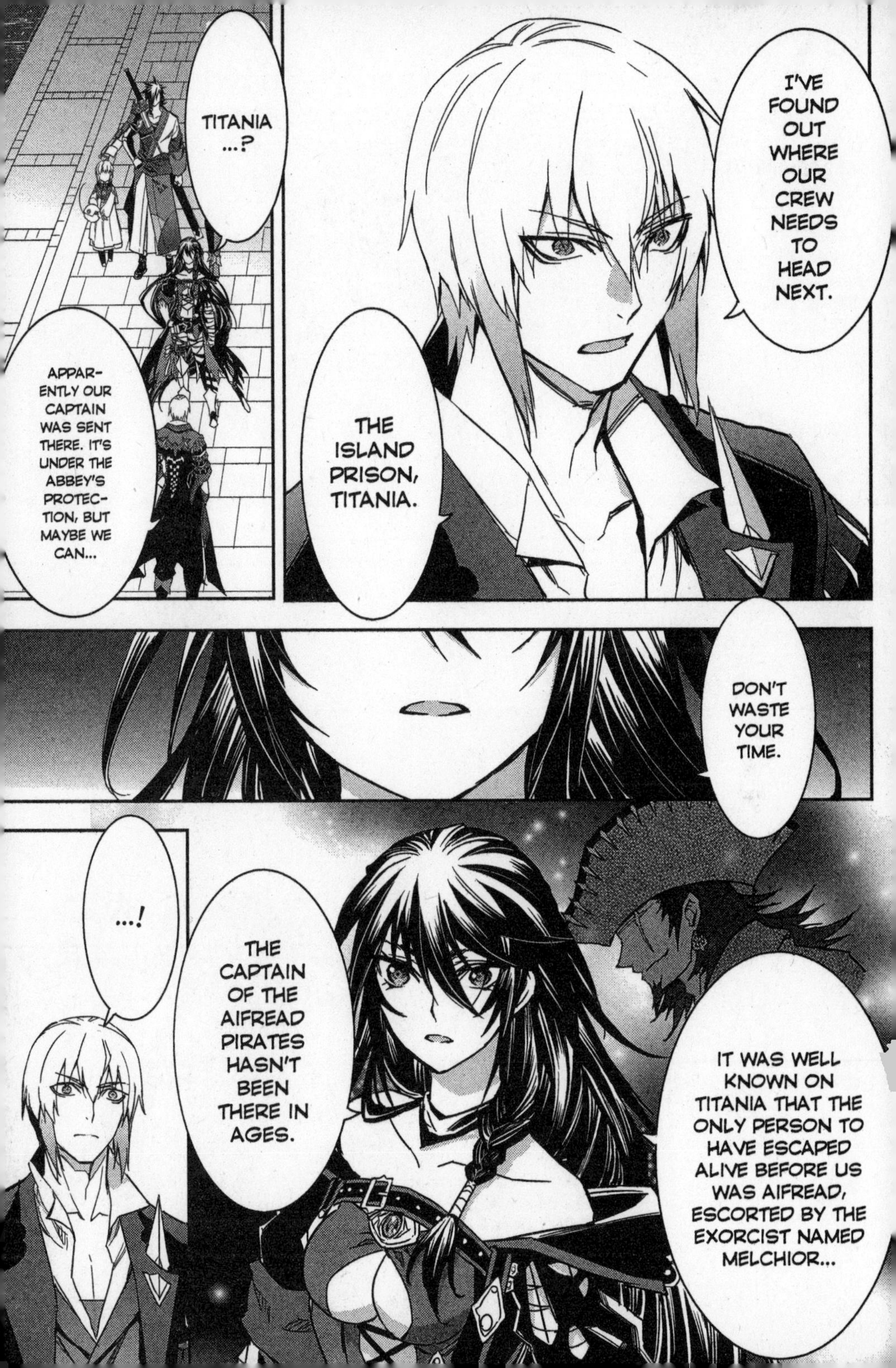
I'VE FOUND OUT WHERE OUR CREW NEEDS TO HEAD NEXT.
THE ISLAND PRISON, TITANIA.
TITANIA ...?
APPARENTLY OUR CAPTAIN WAS SENT THERE. IT'S UNDER THE ABBEY'S PROTECTION, BUT MAYBE WE CAN...
DON'T WASTE YOUR TIME.
THE CAPTAIN OF THE AIFREAD PIRATES HASN'T BEEN THERE IN AGES.
IT WAS WELL KNOWN ON TITANIA THAT THE ONLY PERSON TO HAVE ESCAPED ALIVE BEFORE US WAS AIFREAD, ESCORTED BY THE EXORCIST NAMED MELCHIOR...
...!

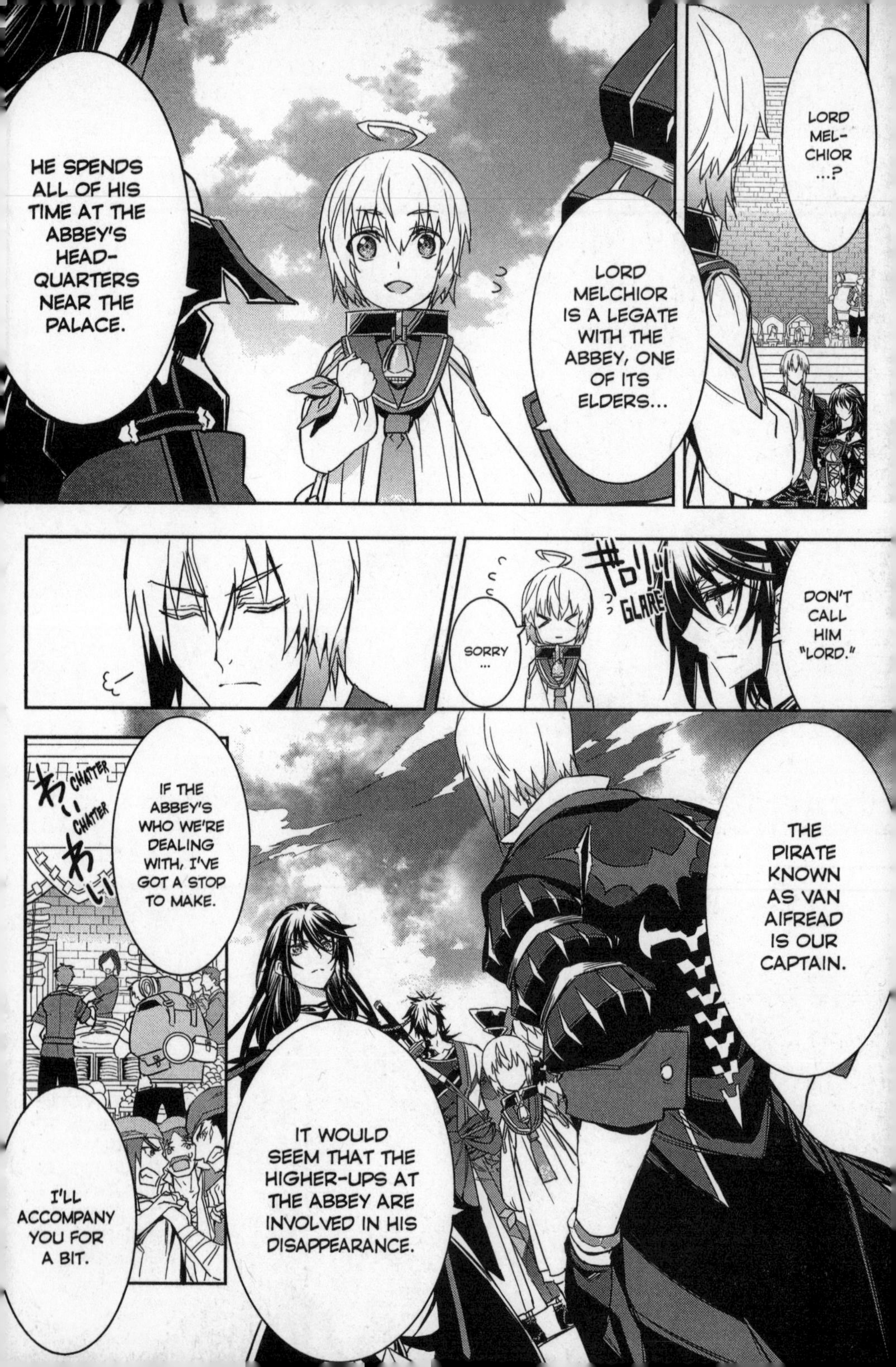
LORD MEL-CHIOR ...?
LORD MELCHIOR IS A LEGATE WITH THE ABBEY, ONE OF ITS ELDERS...
HE SPENDS ALL OF HIS TIME AT THE ABBEY'S HEAD-QUARTERS NEAR THE PALACE.
DON'T CALL HIM "LORD."
GLARE
SORRY ...
THE PIRATE KNOWN AS VAN AIFREAD IS OUR CAPTAIN.
IT WOULD SEEM THAT THE HIGHER-UPS AT THE ABBEY ARE INVOLVED IN HIS DISAPPEARANCE.
IF THE ABBEY'S WHO WE'RE DEALING WITH, I'VE GOT A STOP TO MAKE.
CHATTER CHATTER
I'LL ACCOMPANY YOU FOR A BIT.

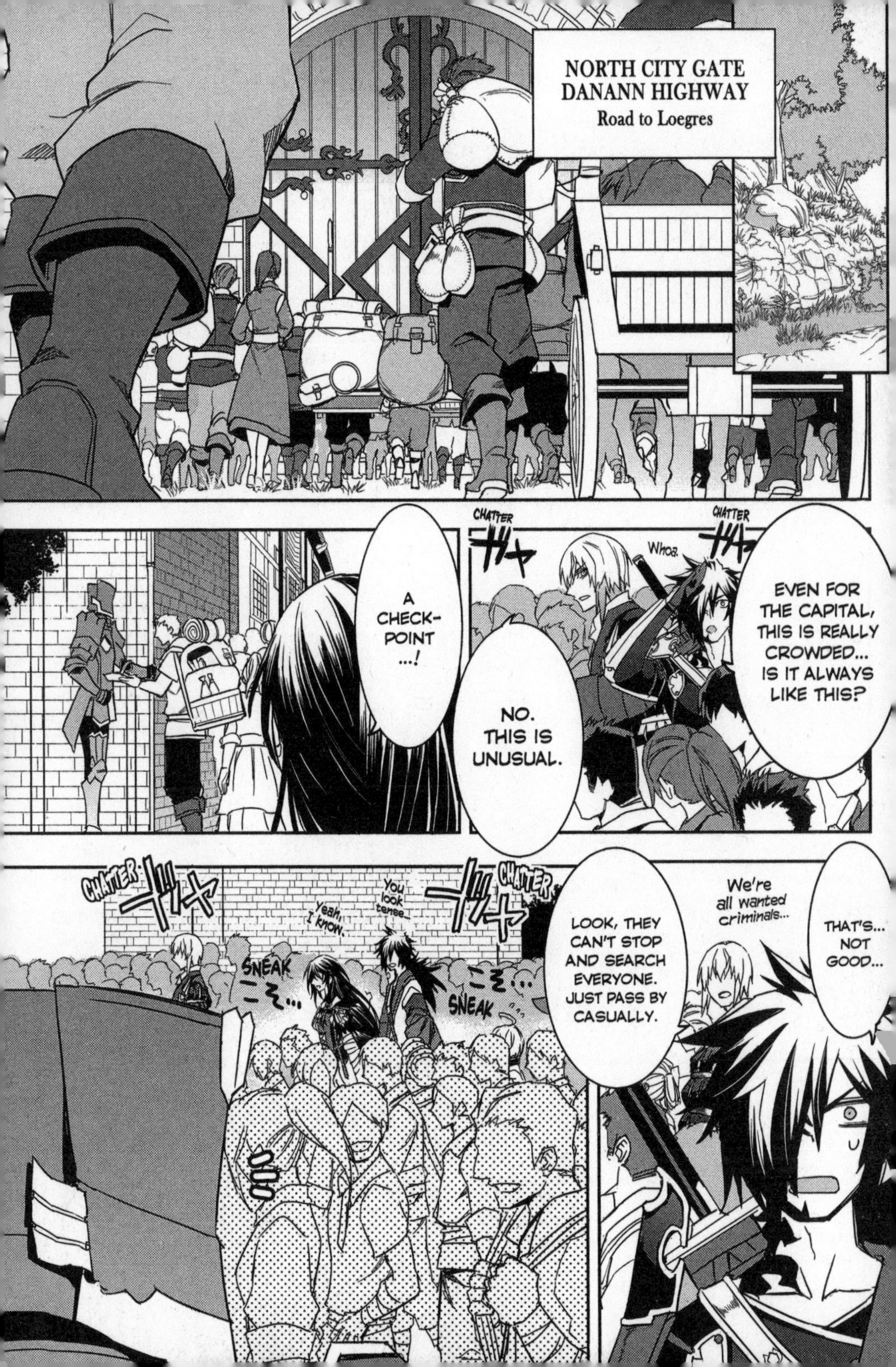
NORTH CITY GATE
DANANN HIGHWAY
Road to Loegres
CHATTER
EVEN FOR THE CAPITAL, THIS IS REALLY CROWDED... IS IT ALWAYS LIKE THIS?
Whoa.
CHATTER
NO. THIS IS UNUSUAL.
A CHECK-POINT ...!
THAT'S... NOT GOOD...
We're all wanted criminals...
LOOK, THEY CAN'T STOP AND SEARCH EVERYONE. JUST PASS BY CASUALLY.
CHATTER
You look tense...
Yeah, I know.
SNEAK
SNEAK
CHATTER

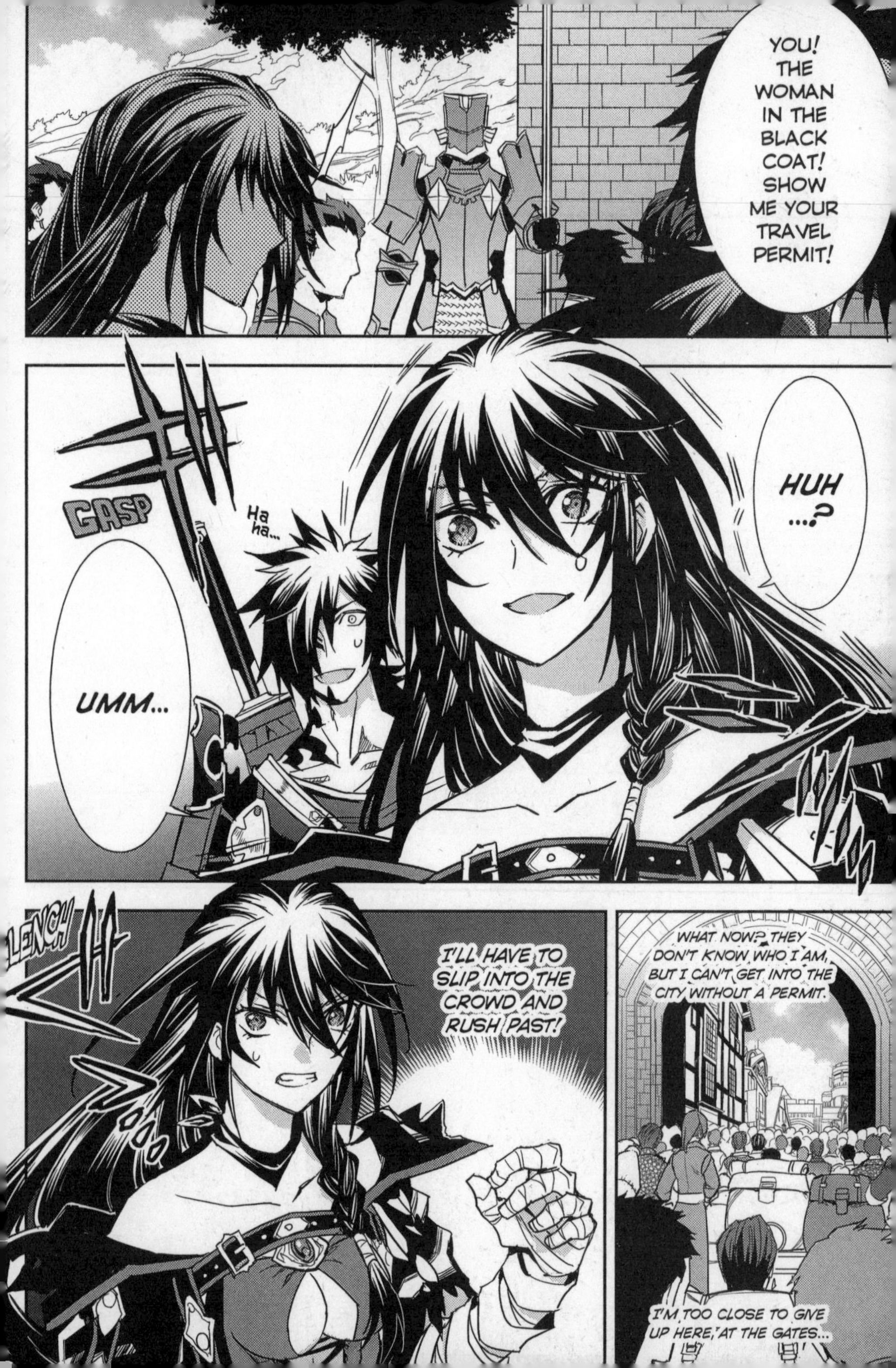
YOU! THE WOMAN IN THE BLACK COAT! SHOW ME YOUR TRAVEL PERMIT!
HUH ...?
Ha ha...
GASP
UMM...
WHAT NOW? THEY DON'T KNOW WHO I AM, BUT I CAN'T GET INTO THE CITY WITHOUT A PERMIT.
I'M TOO CLOSE TO GIVE UP HERE, AT THE GATES...
I'LL HAVE TO SLIP INTO THE CROWD AND RUSH PAST!
LENCH

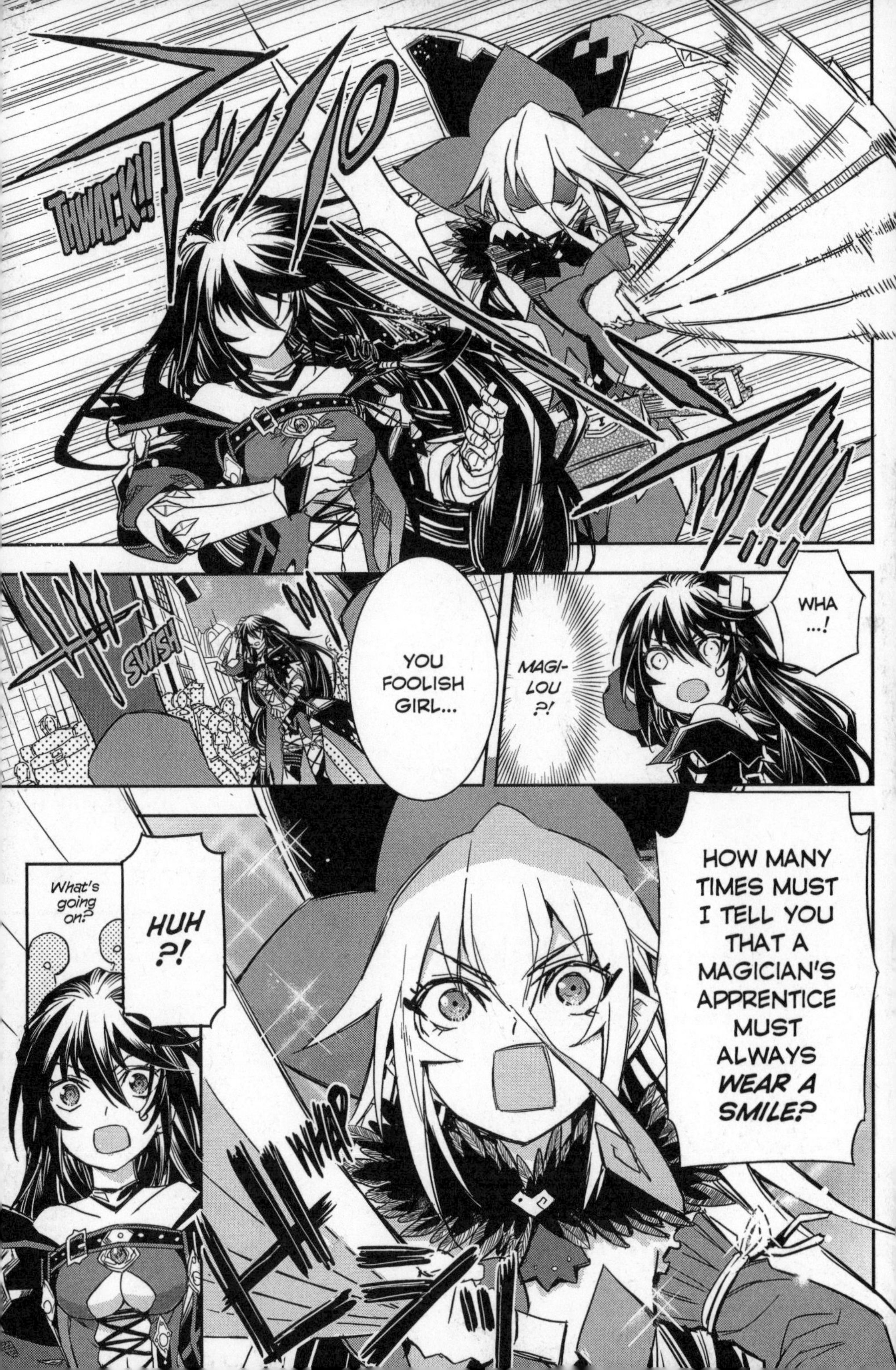
THWACK!!
WHA ...!
MAGI-LOU ?!
YOU FOOLISH GIRL...
SWISH
HOW MANY TIMES MUST I TELL YOU THAT A MAGICIAN'S APPRENTICE MUST ALWAYS *WEAR A SMILE?*
WHAP
HUH ?!
What's going on?

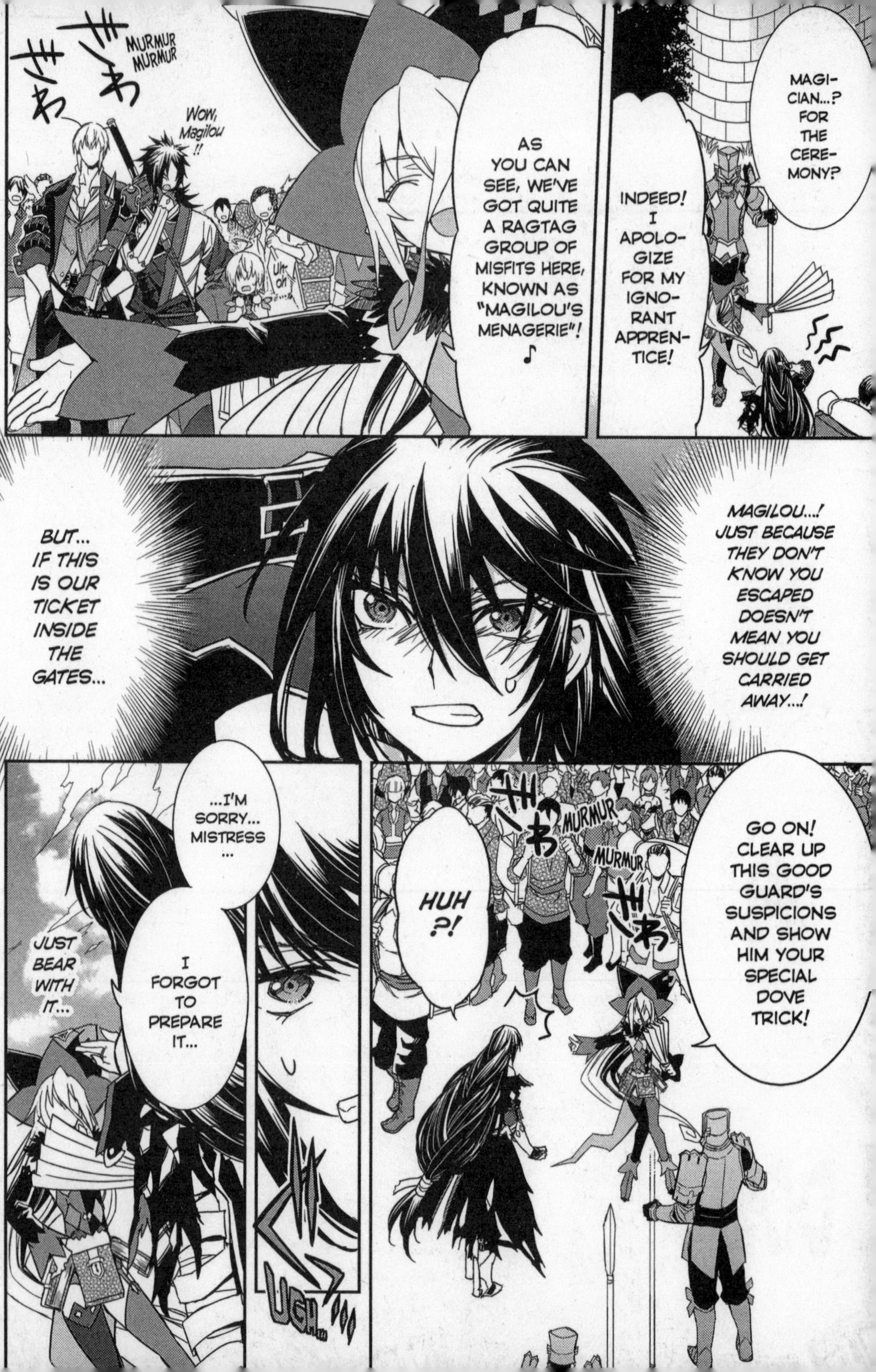
MAGI-CIAN...? FOR THE CEREMONY?
INDEED! I APOLOGIZE FOR MY IGNORANT APPRENTICE!
AS YOU CAN SEE, WE'VE GOT QUITE A RAGTAG GROUP OF MISFITS HERE, KNOWN AS "MAGILOU'S MENAGERIE"! ♪
MURMUR MURMUR
Wow, Magilou!!
Uh-oh
MAGILOU...! JUST BECAUSE THEY DON'T KNOW YOU ESCAPED DOESN'T MEAN YOU SHOULD GET CARRIED AWAY...!
BUT... IF THIS IS OUR TICKET INSIDE THE GATES...
GO ON! CLEAR UP THIS GOOD GUARD'S SUSPICIONS AND SHOW HIM YOUR SPECIAL DOVE TRICK!
MURMUR
MURMUR
HUH?!
...I'M SORRY... MISTRESS...
I FORGOT TO PREPARE IT...
JUST BEAR WITH IT...
UGH...

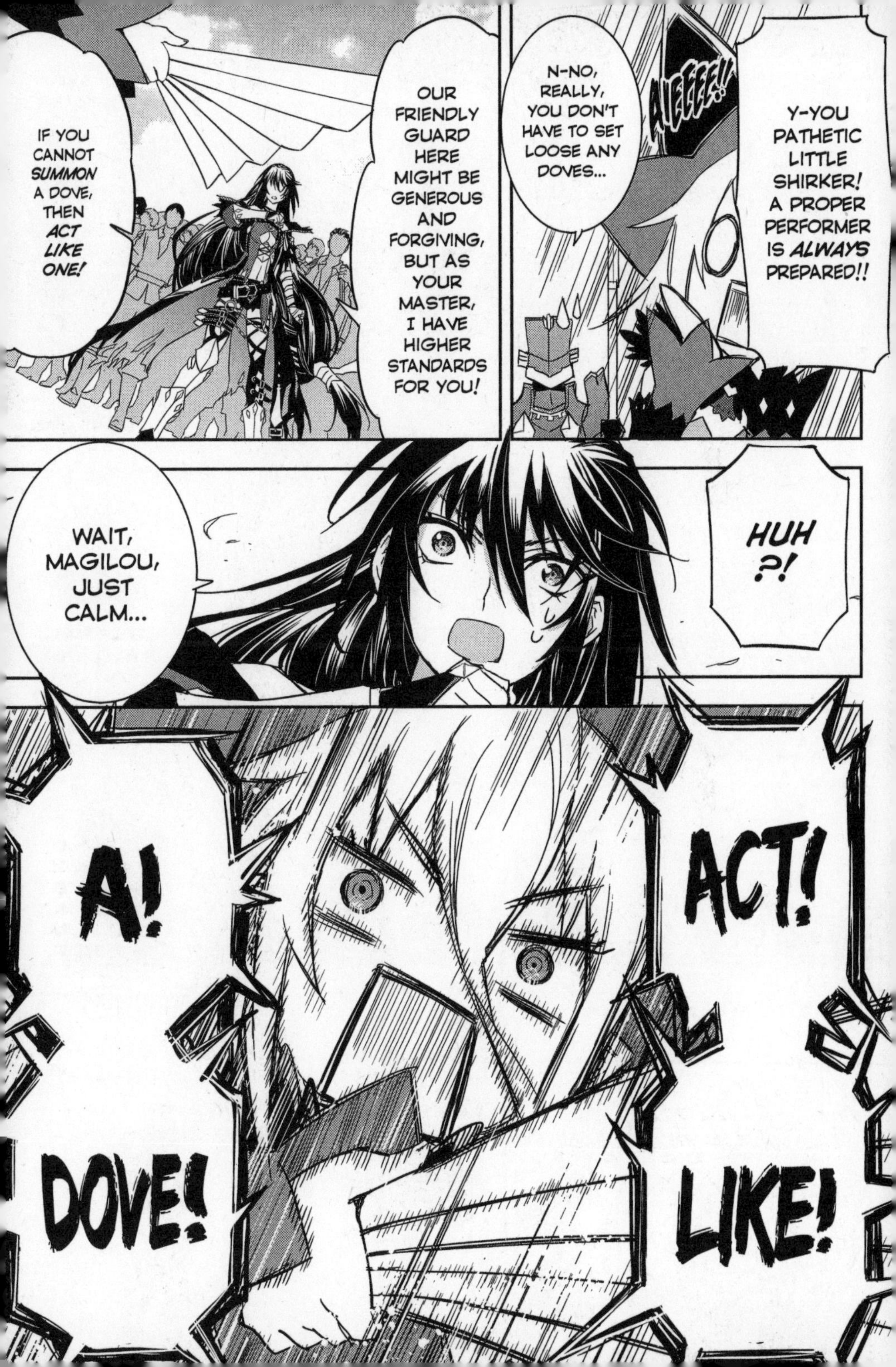

Y-YOU PATHETIC LITTLE SHIRKER! A PROPER PERFORMER IS ALWAYS PREPARED!!
AIEEEE!!
N-NO, REALLY, YOU DON'T HAVE TO SET LOOSE ANY DOVES...
OUR FRIENDLY GUARD HERE MIGHT BE GENEROUS AND FORGIVING, BUT AS YOUR MASTER, I HAVE HIGHER STANDARDS FOR YOU!
IF YOU CANNOT SUMMON A DOVE, THEN ACT LIKE ONE!
HUH ?!
WAIT, MAGILOU, JUST CALM...
ACT!
LIKE!
A!
DOVE!

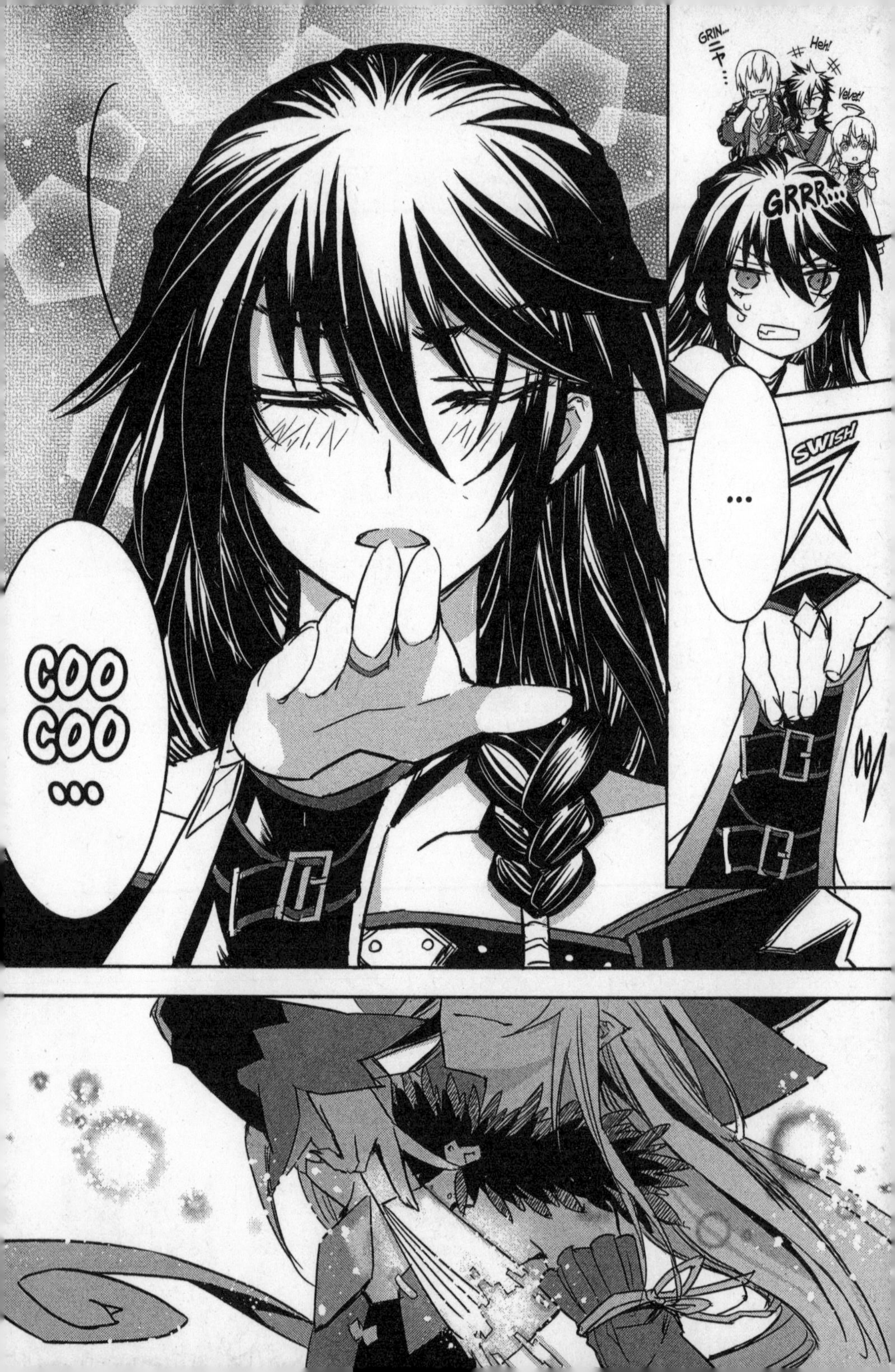
Heh!
GRIN... ニヤ…
Velvet!
GRRR...
...
SWISH
COO COO...

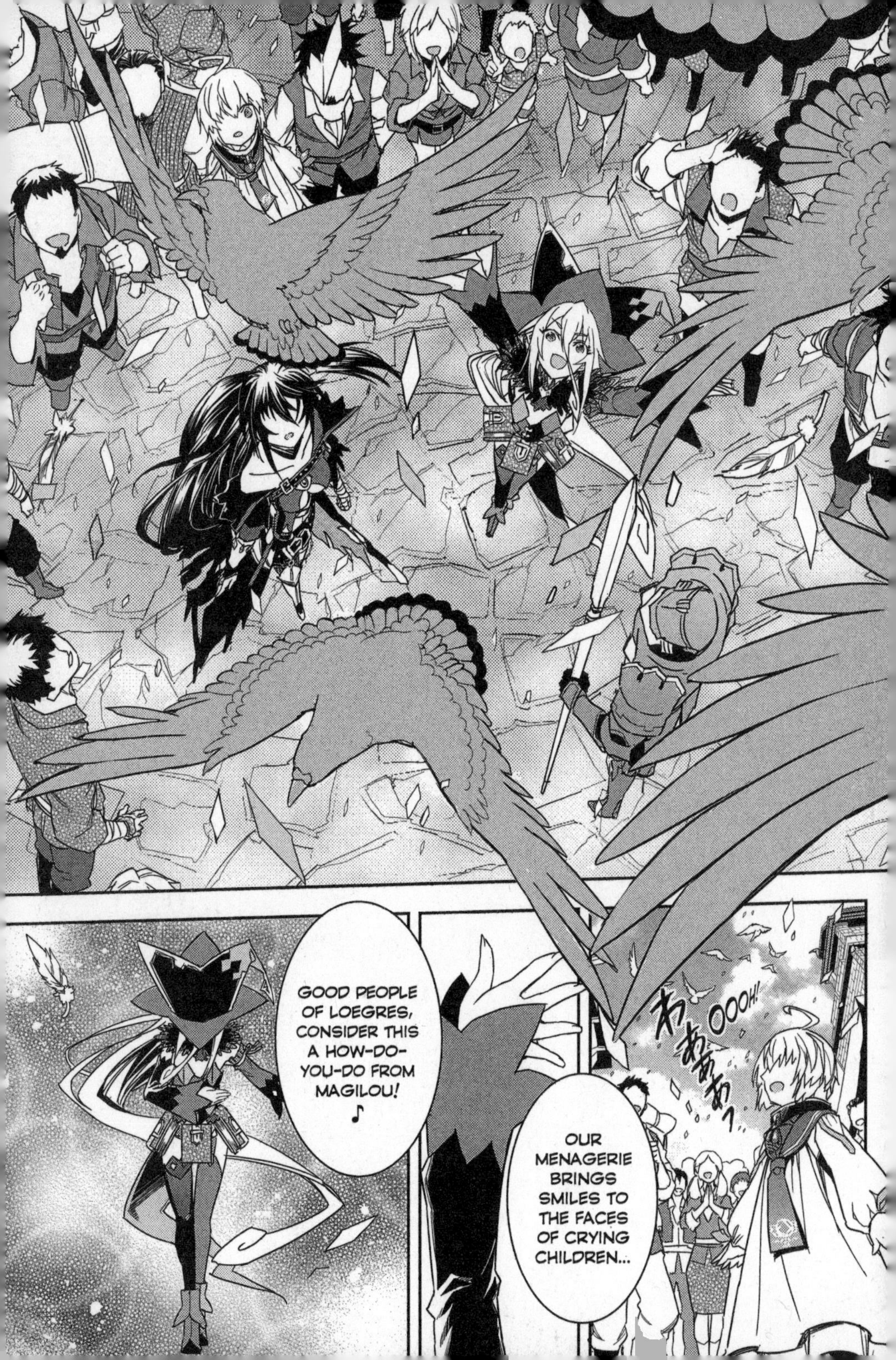
OOOH!
OUR MENAGERIE BRINGS SMILES TO THE FACES OF CRYING CHILDREN...
GOOD PEOPLE OF LOEGRES, CONSIDER THIS A HOW-DO-YOU-DO FROM MAGILOU! ♪

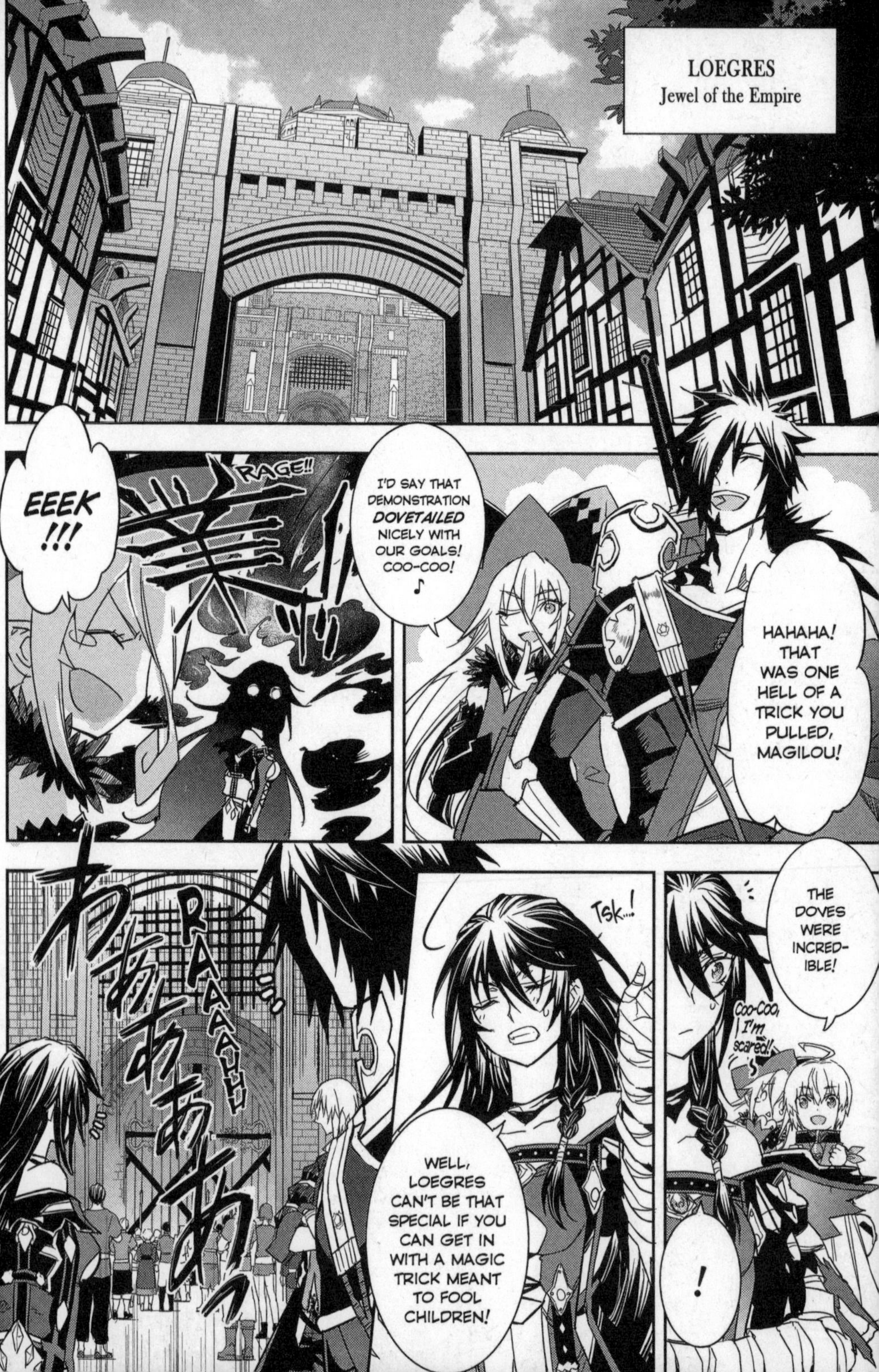
LOEGRES
Jewel of the Empire
HAHAHA! THAT WAS ONE HELL OF A TRICK YOU PULLED, MAGILOU!
I'D SAY THAT DEMONSTRATION DOVETAILED NICELY WITH OUR GOALS! COO-COO! ♪
RAGE!!
EEEK!!!
THE DOVES WERE INCREDIBLE!
Coo-Coo, I'm scared!!
!
Tsk...!
WELL, LOEGRES CAN'T BE THAT SPECIAL IF YOU CAN GET IN WITH A MAGIC TRICK MEANT TO FOOL CHILDREN!
RAAAAH!!

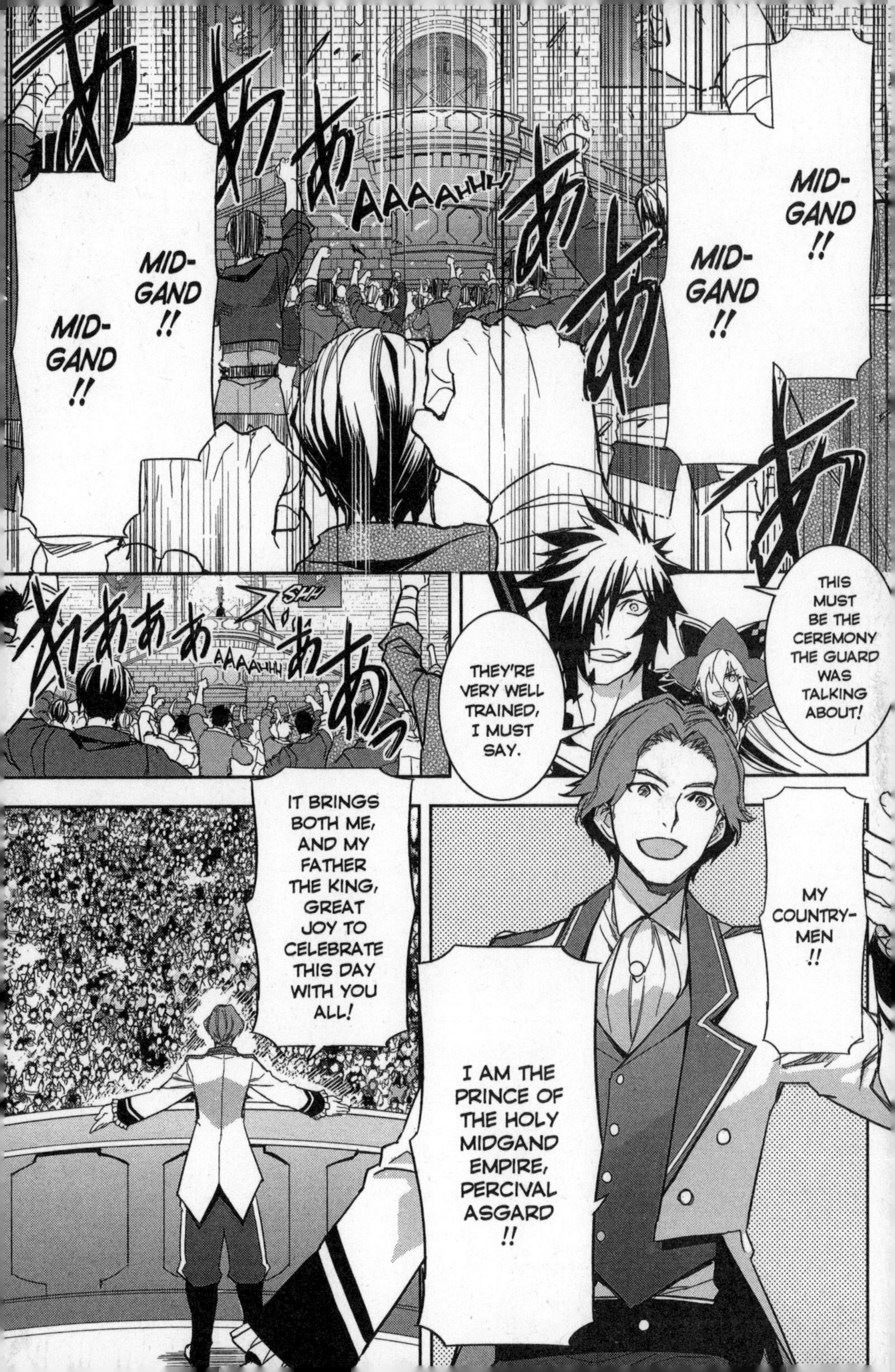
MID-GAND!!
MID-GAND!!
AAAAHHH
MID-GAND!!
MID-GAND!!
THIS MUST BE THE CEREMONY THE GUARD WAS TALKING ABOUT!
THEY'RE VERY WELL TRAINED, I MUST SAY.
SHH
AAAAHHH
MY COUNTRYMEN!!
I AM THE PRINCE OF THE HOLY MIDGAND EMPIRE, PERCIVAL ASGARD!!
IT BRINGS BOTH ME, AND MY FATHER THE KING, GREAT JOY TO CELEBRATE THIS DAY WITH YOU ALL!

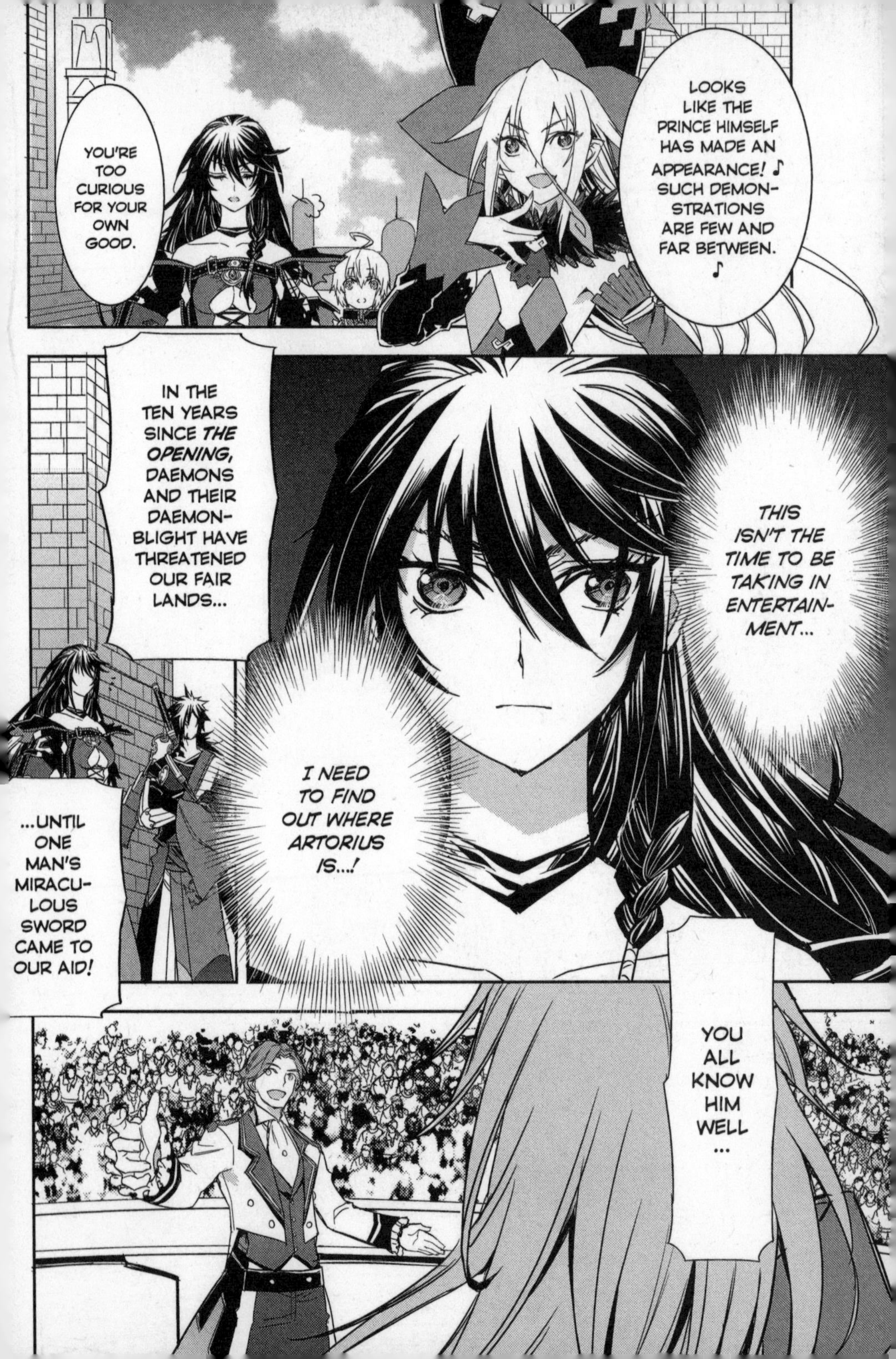
LOOKS LIKE THE PRINCE HIMSELF HAS MADE AN APPEARANCE! ♪ SUCH DEMONSTRATIONS ARE FEW AND FAR BETWEEN. ♪
YOU'RE TOO CURIOUS FOR YOUR OWN GOOD.
THIS ISN'T THE TIME TO BE TAKING IN ENTERTAINMENT...
I NEED TO FIND OUT WHERE ARTORIUS IS...!
IN THE TEN YEARS SINCE *THE OPENING*, DAEMONS AND THEIR DAEMONBLIGHT HAVE THREATENED OUR FAIR LANDS...
...UNTIL ONE MAN'S MIRACULOUS SWORD CAME TO OUR AID!
YOU ALL KNOW HIM WELL...

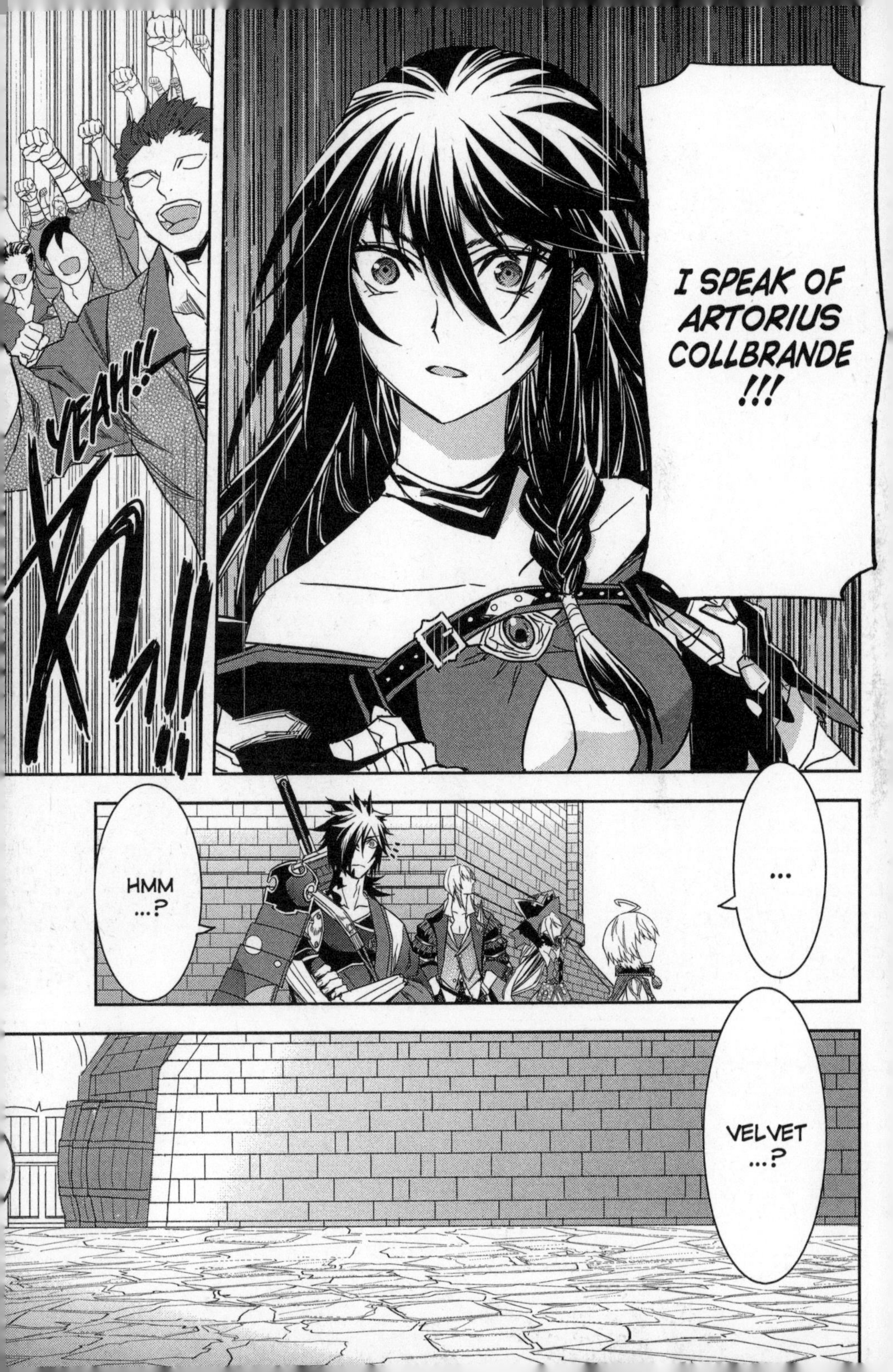
I SPEAK OF ARTORIUS COLLBRANDE !!!
YEAH!!
...
HMM ...?
VELVET ...?

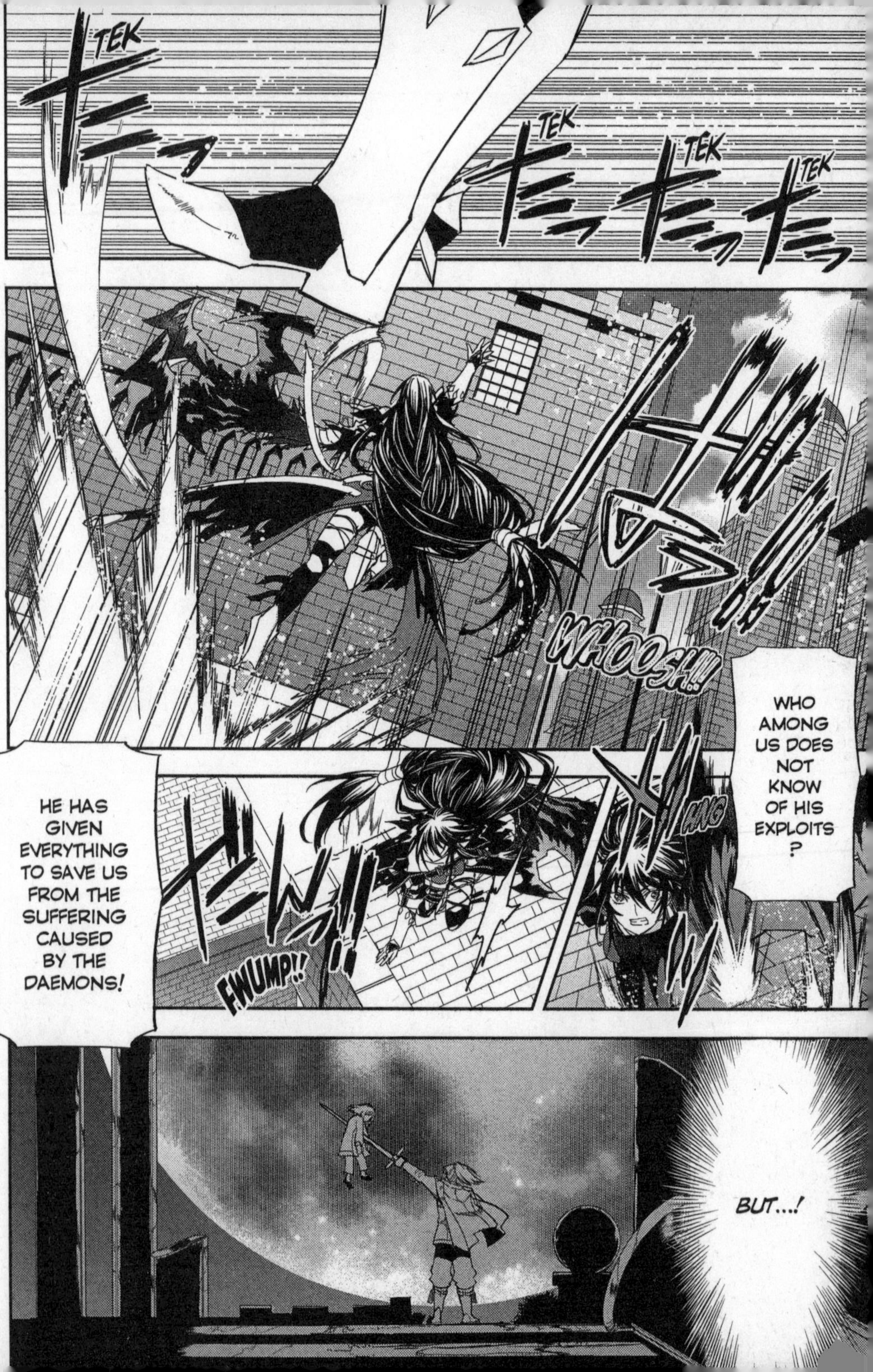
TEK
TEK
TEK
TEK
WHOOSH!!
WHO AMONG US DOES NOT KNOW OF HIS EXPLOITS?
HE HAS GIVEN EVERYTHING TO SAVE US FROM THE SUFFERING CAUSED BY THE DAEMONS!
FWUMP!!
BUT...!

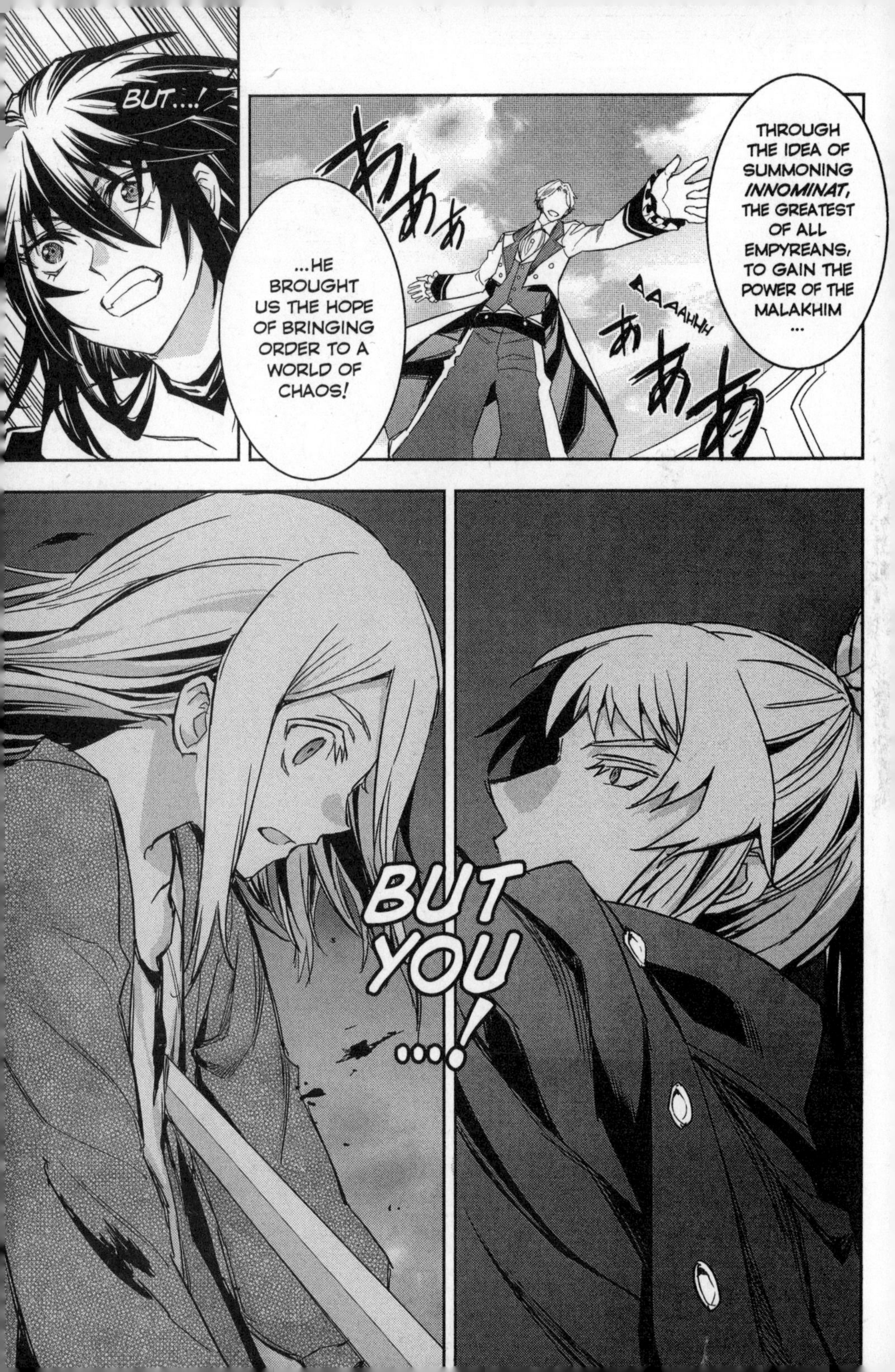
THROUGH THE IDEA OF SUMMONING *INNOMINAT*, THE GREATEST OF ALL EMPYREANS, TO GAIN THE POWER OF THE MALAKHIM ...
AAAAAHHH
...HE BROUGHT US THE HOPE OF BRINGING ORDER TO A WORLD OF CHAOS!
BUT...!
BUT YOU ...!

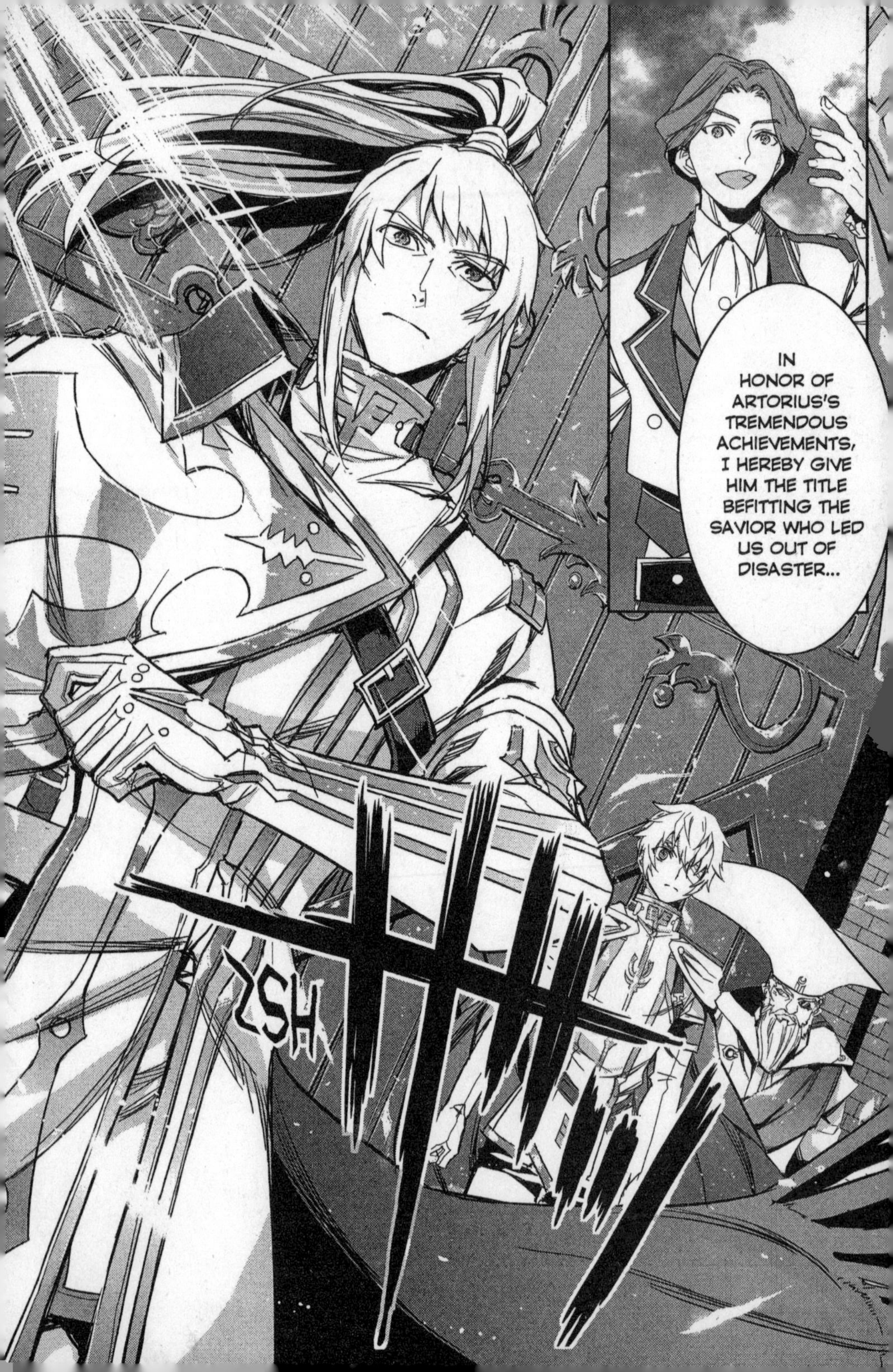
IN HONOR OF ARTORIUS'S TREMENDOUS ACHIEVEMENTS, I HEREBY GIVE HIM THE TITLE BEFITTING THE SAVIOR WHO LED US OUT OF DISASTER...
ZSH

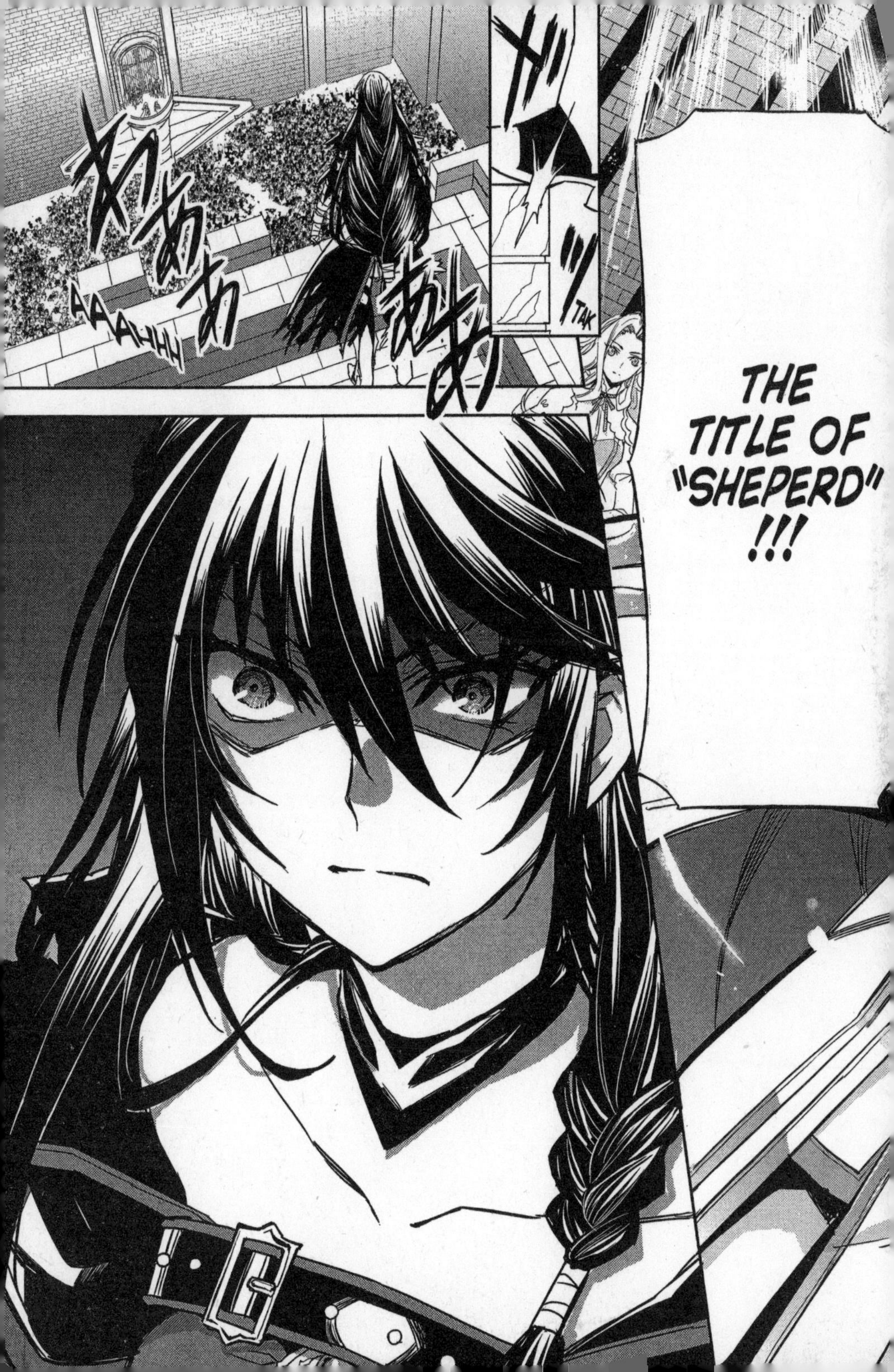
TAK
AAAAHHH
THE TITLE OF "SHEPERD" !!!

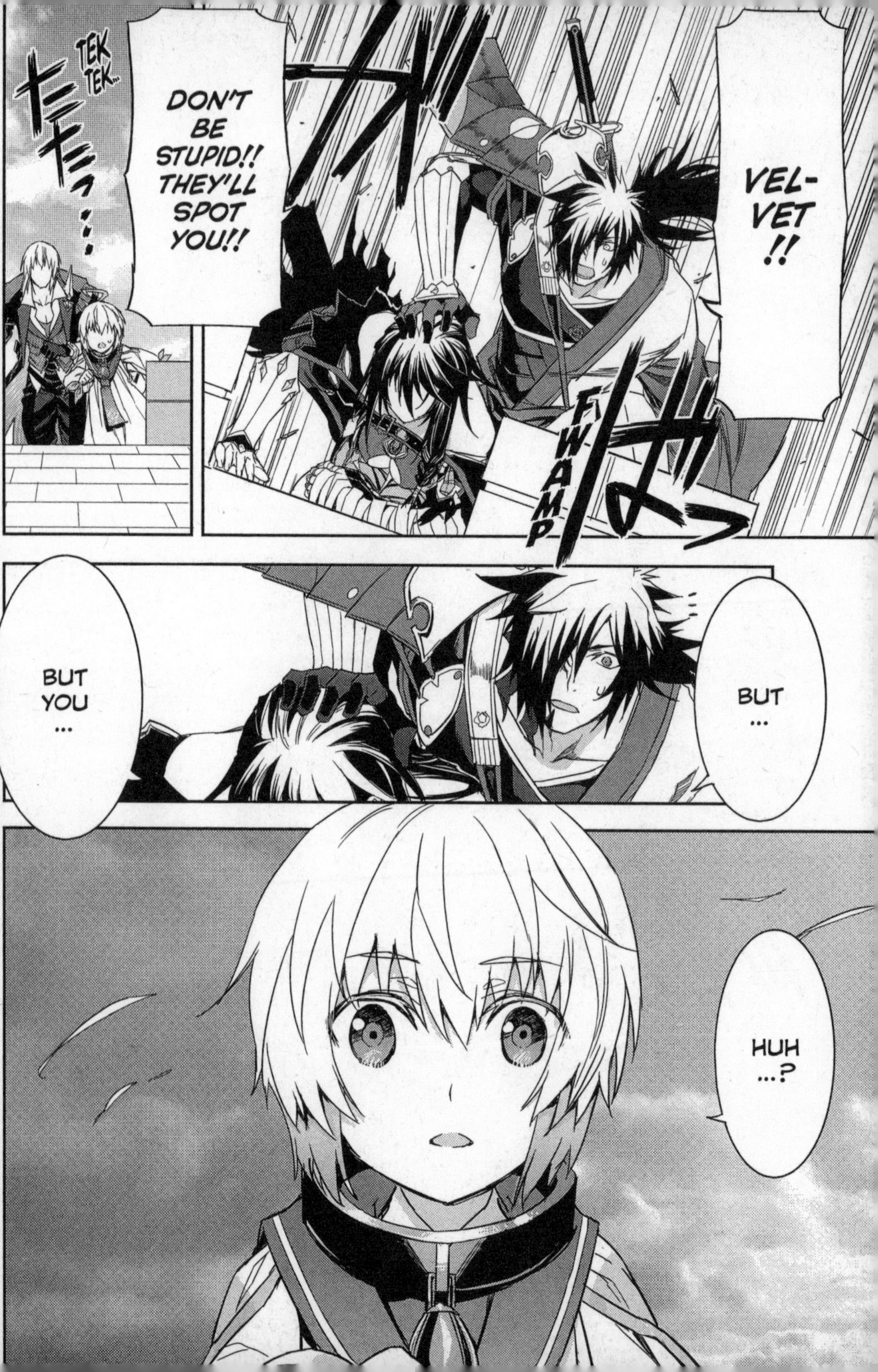
VEL-VET!!
FWAMP
DON'T BE STUPID!! THEY'LL SPOT YOU!!
TEK TEK...
BUT...
BUT YOU...
HUH...?

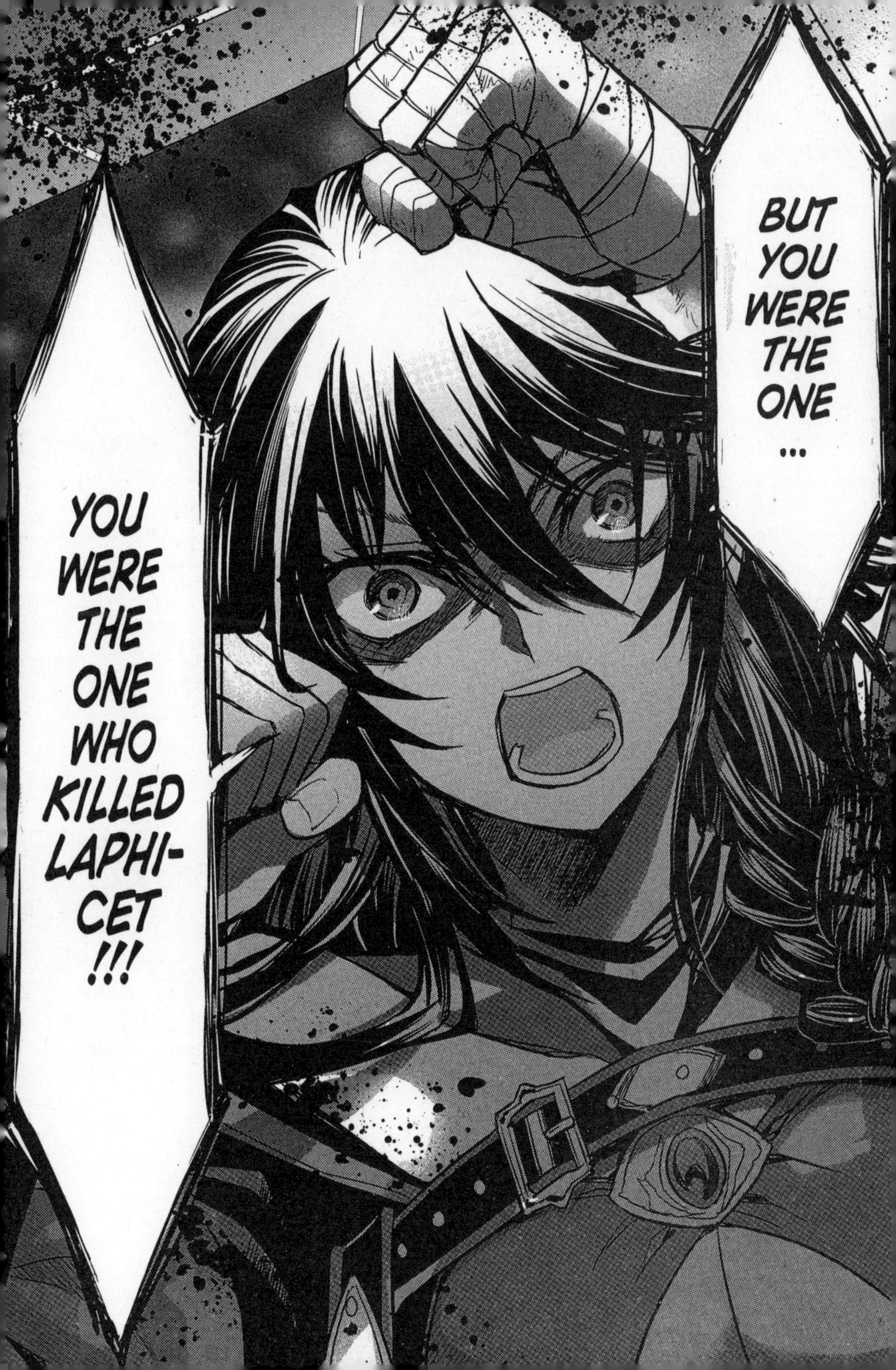
BUT YOU WERE THE ONE ...
YOU WERE THE ONE WHO KILLED LAPHI-CET !!!

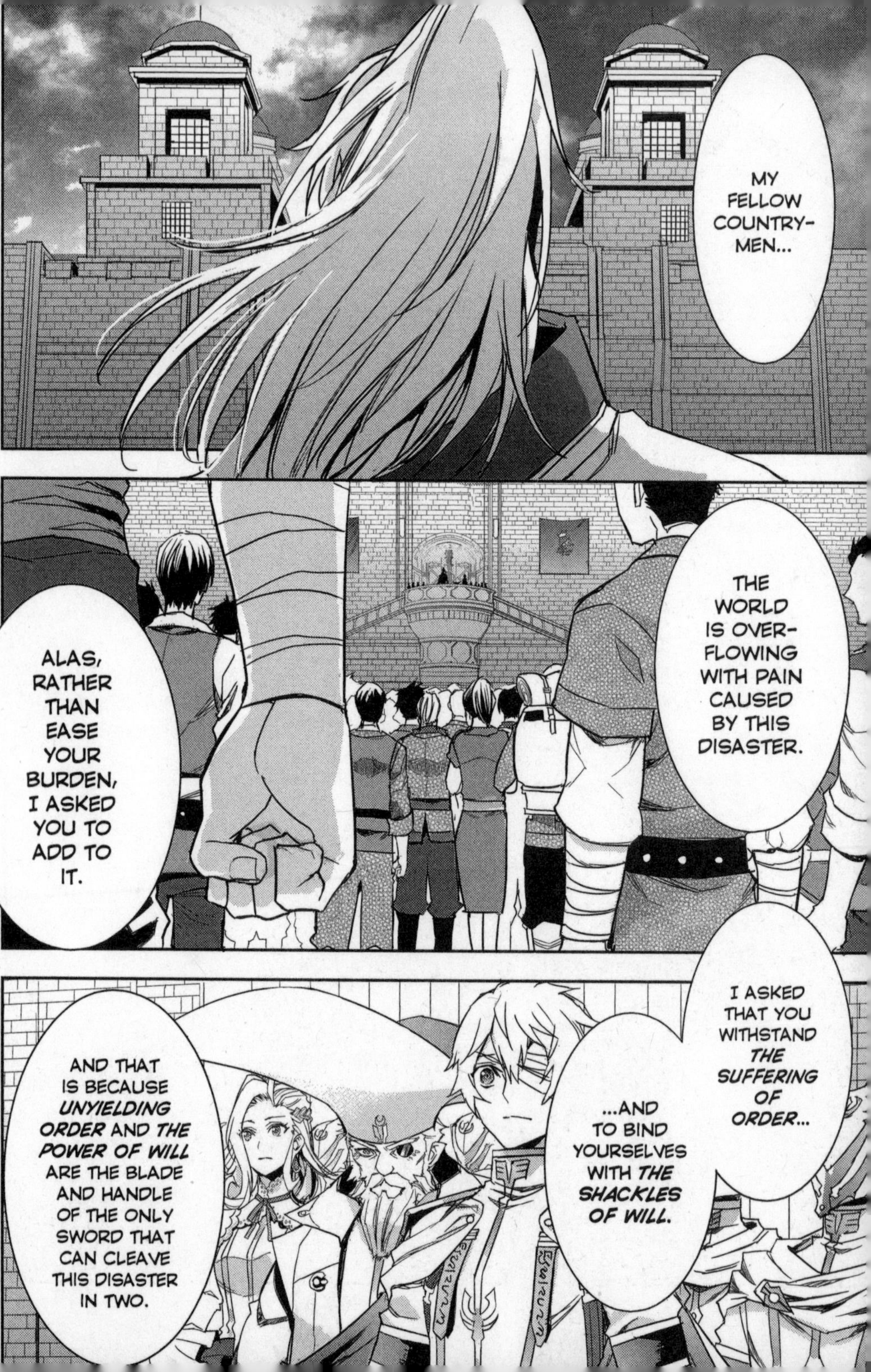
MY FELLOW COUNTRY-MEN...
THE WORLD IS OVER-FLOWING WITH PAIN CAUSED BY THIS DISASTER.
ALAS, RATHER THAN EASE YOUR BURDEN, I ASKED YOU TO ADD TO IT.
I ASKED THAT YOU WITHSTAND *THE SUFFERING OF ORDER*...
...AND TO BIND YOURSELVES WITH *THE SHACKLES OF WILL*.
AND THAT IS BECAUSE *UNYIELDING ORDER* AND *THE POWER OF WILL* ARE THE BLADE AND HANDLE OF THE ONLY SWORD THAT CAN CLEAVE THIS DISASTER IN TWO.

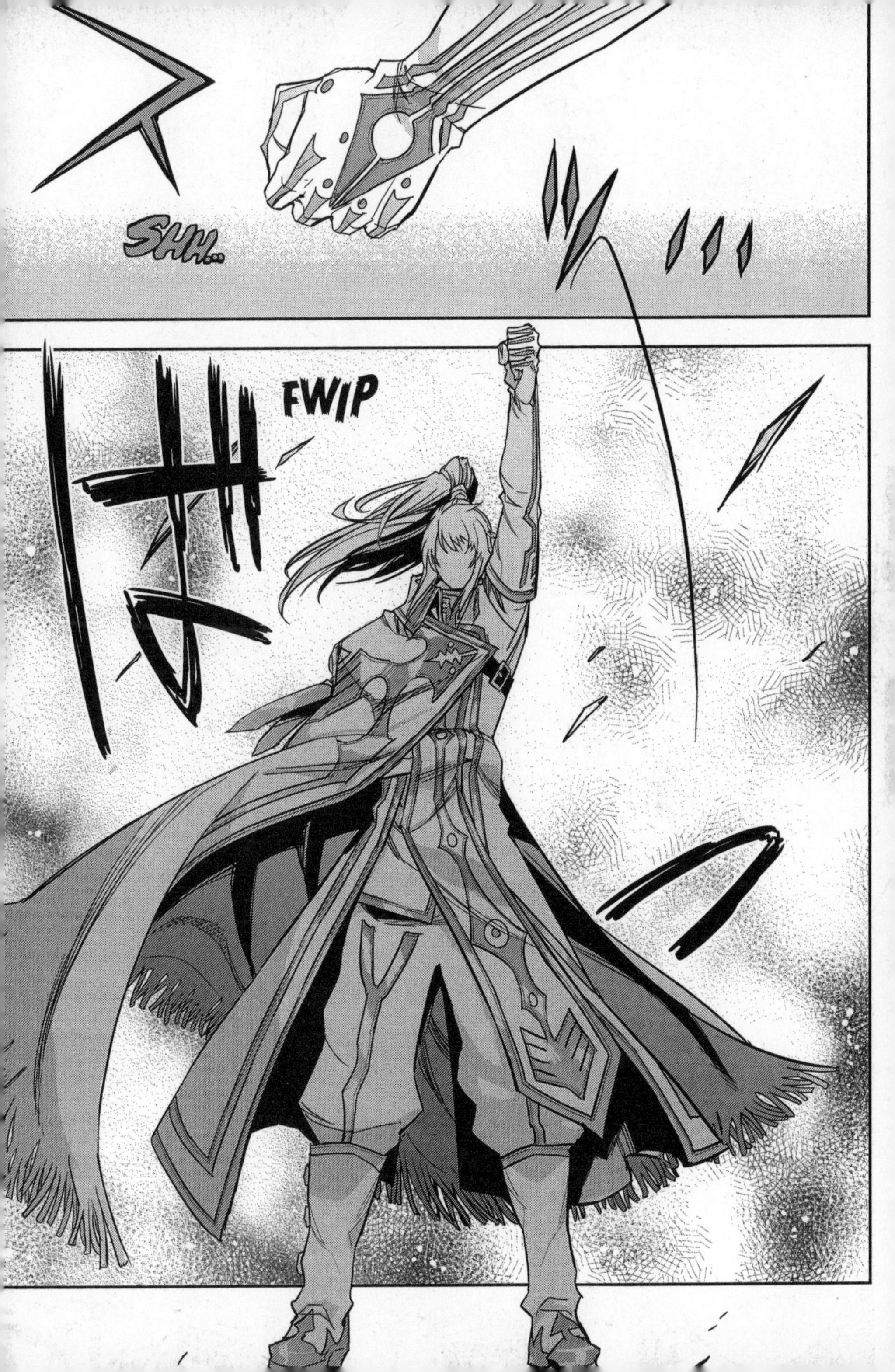
SHH...
FWIP

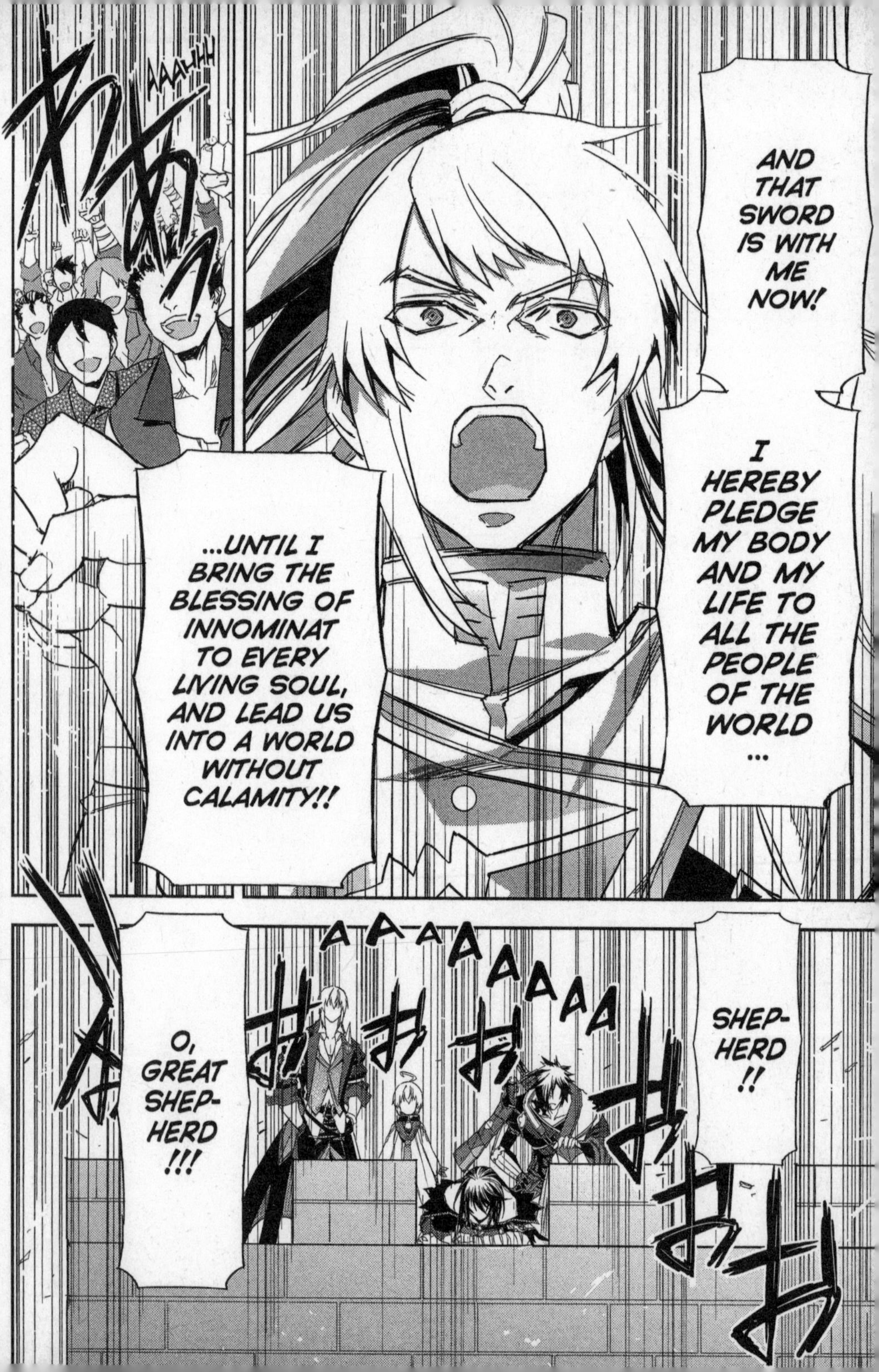
AND THAT SWORD IS WITH ME NOW!
I HEREBY PLEDGE MY BODY AND MY LIFE TO ALL THE PEOPLE OF THE WORLD ...
...UNTIL I BRING THE BLESSING OF INNOMINAT TO EVERY LIVING SOUL, AND LEAD US INTO A WORLD WITHOUT CALAMITY!!
AAAHHH
SHEP-HERD!!
O, GREAT SHEP-HERD!!!
AAAAAAAAAA

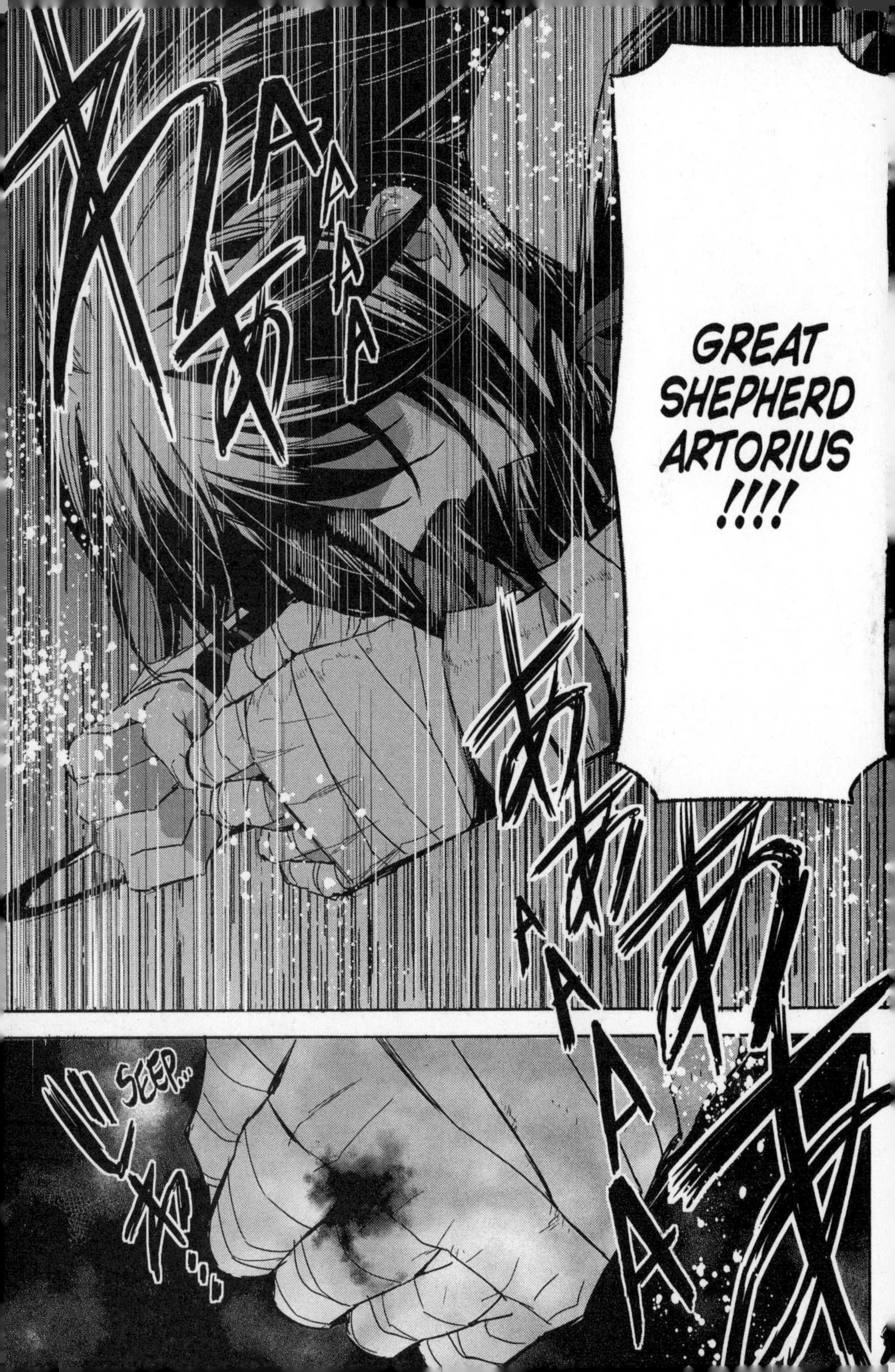
GREAT SHEPHERD ARTORIUS !!!!
SEEP...

☆ Magilou's Menagerie ☆

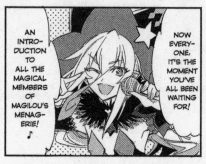

NOW EVERYONE, IT'S THE MOMENT YOU'VE ALL BEEN WAITING FOR!
AN INTRODUCTION TO ALL THE MAGICAL MEMBERS OF MAGILOU'S MENAGERIE! ♪
THE FEARSOME FIRST MATE OF THE AIFREAD PIRATES, WHO DRIES THE EYES OF CRYING CHILDREN...
EIZEN THE FREAKISHLY STRONG!!
WITH A SWORD IN HIS HANDS, NONE SHINES BRIGHTER!!
ROKUROU THE ACROBAT!!!
And you won't believe your ears!!
MANY HAVE TRIED, BUT NONE CAN OUTDO THE CALL OF VELVET THE DOVE-IMPERSONATOR...
ARE YOU STILL TRYING TO MAKE THAT A THING?!
GONG!!

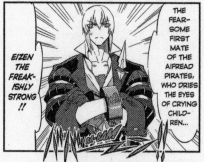

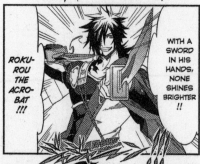

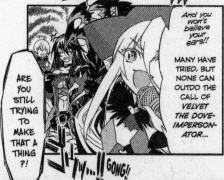

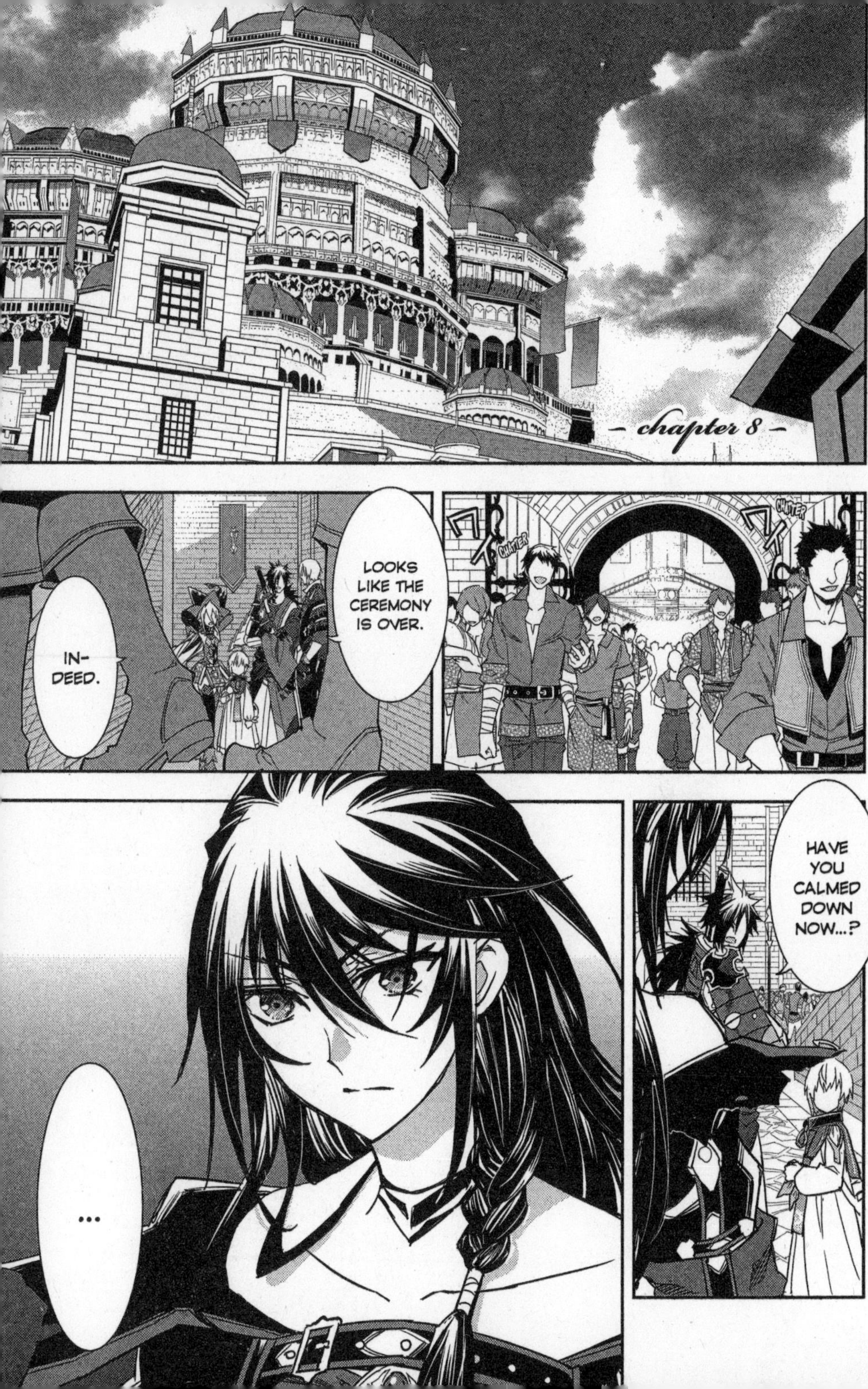

- chapter 8 -
CHATTER
CHATTER
LOOKS LIKE THE CEREMONY IS OVER.
IN-DEED.
HAVE YOU CALMED DOWN NOW...?
...

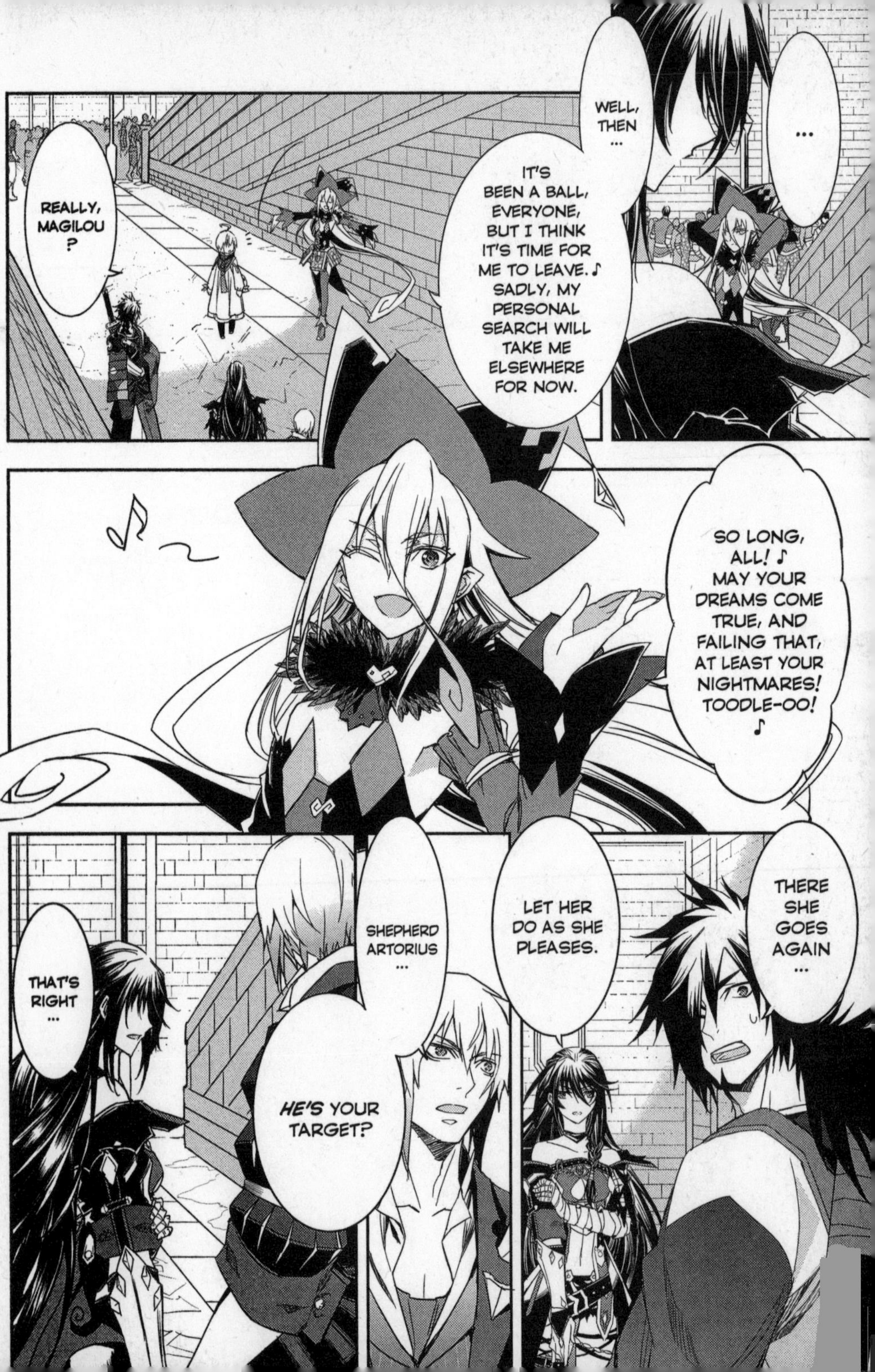
...
WELL, THEN ...
IT'S BEEN A BALL, EVERYONE, BUT I THINK IT'S TIME FOR ME TO LEAVE. ♪ SADLY, MY PERSONAL SEARCH WILL TAKE ME ELSEWHERE FOR NOW.
REALLY, MAGILOU?
SO LONG, ALL! ♪ MAY YOUR DREAMS COME TRUE, AND FAILING THAT, AT LEAST YOUR NIGHTMARES! TOODLE-OO! ♪
THERE SHE GOES AGAIN ...
LET HER DO AS SHE PLEASES.
SHEPHERD ARTORIUS ...
HE'S YOUR TARGET?
THAT'S RIGHT ...

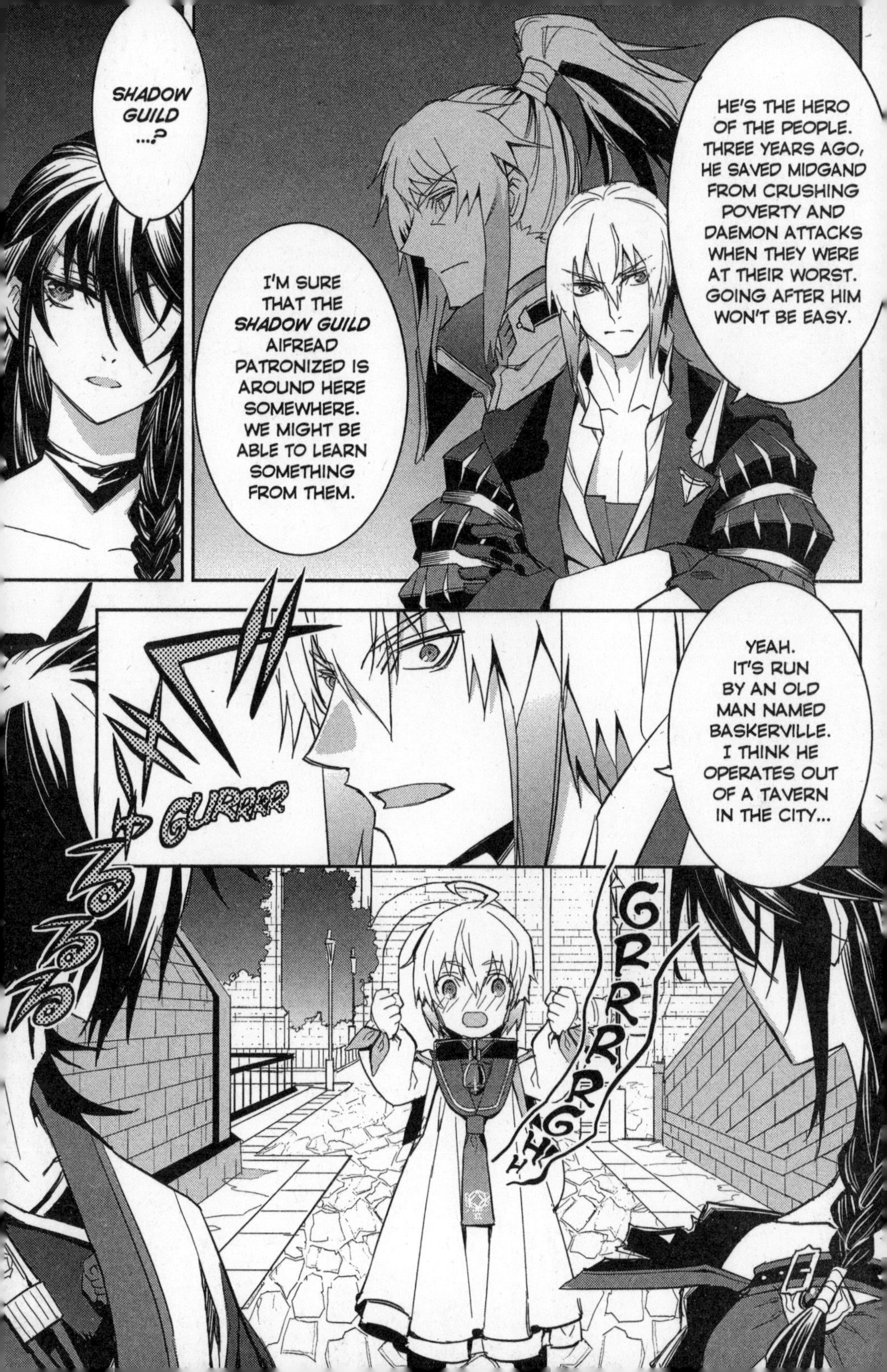
HE'S THE HERO OF THE PEOPLE. THREE YEARS AGO, HE SAVED MIDGAND FROM CRUSHING POVERTY AND DAEMON ATTACKS WHEN THEY WERE AT THEIR WORST. GOING AFTER HIM WON'T BE EASY.
I'M SURE THAT THE *SHADOW GUILD* AIFREAD PATRONIZED IS AROUND HERE SOMEWHERE. WE MIGHT BE ABLE TO LEARN SOMETHING FROM THEM.
SHADOW GUILD ...?
YEAH. IT'S RUN BY AN OLD MAN NAMED BASKERVILLE. I THINK HE OPERATES OUT OF A TAVERN IN THE CITY...
GURRRR
GRRRRRGH

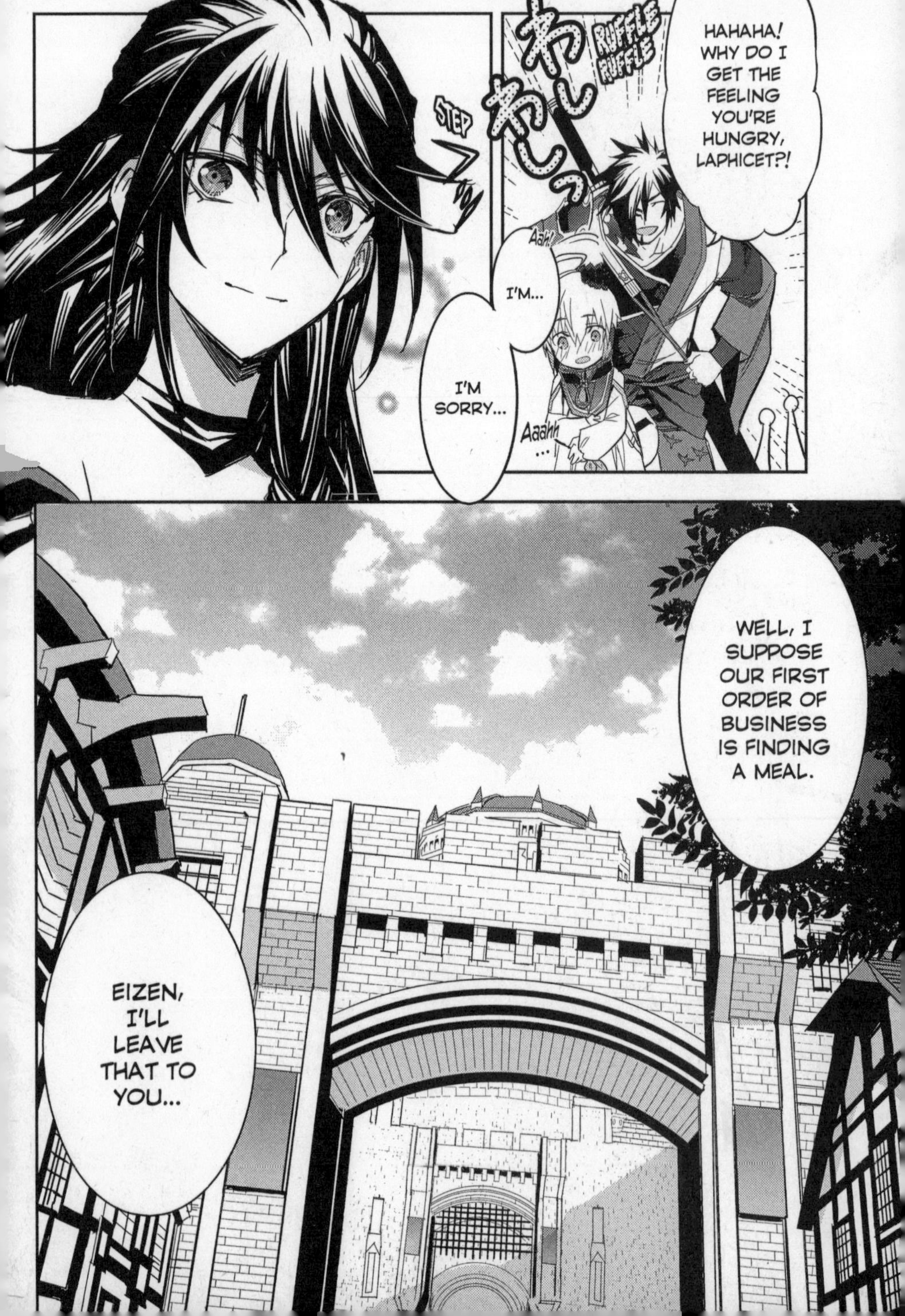
HAHAHA! WHY DO I GET THE FEELING YOU'RE HUNGRY, LAPHICET?!
わしわしっ
RUFFLE RUFFLE
Aah!
I'M...
I'M SORRY...
Aaahh...
STEP
WELL, I SUPPOSE OUR FIRST ORDER OF BUSINESS IS FINDING A MEAL.
EIZEN, I'LL LEAVE THAT TO YOU...

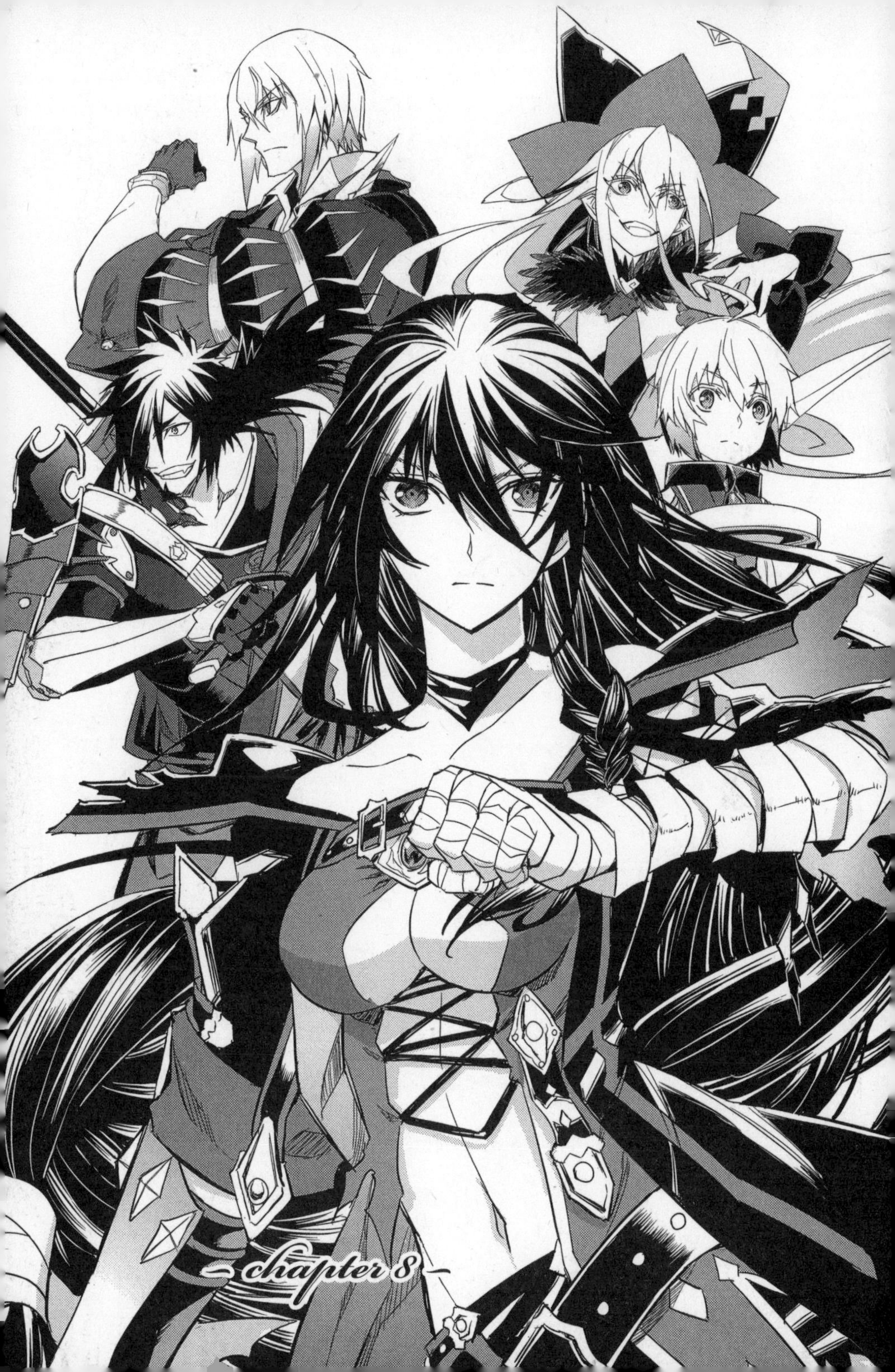
chapter 8

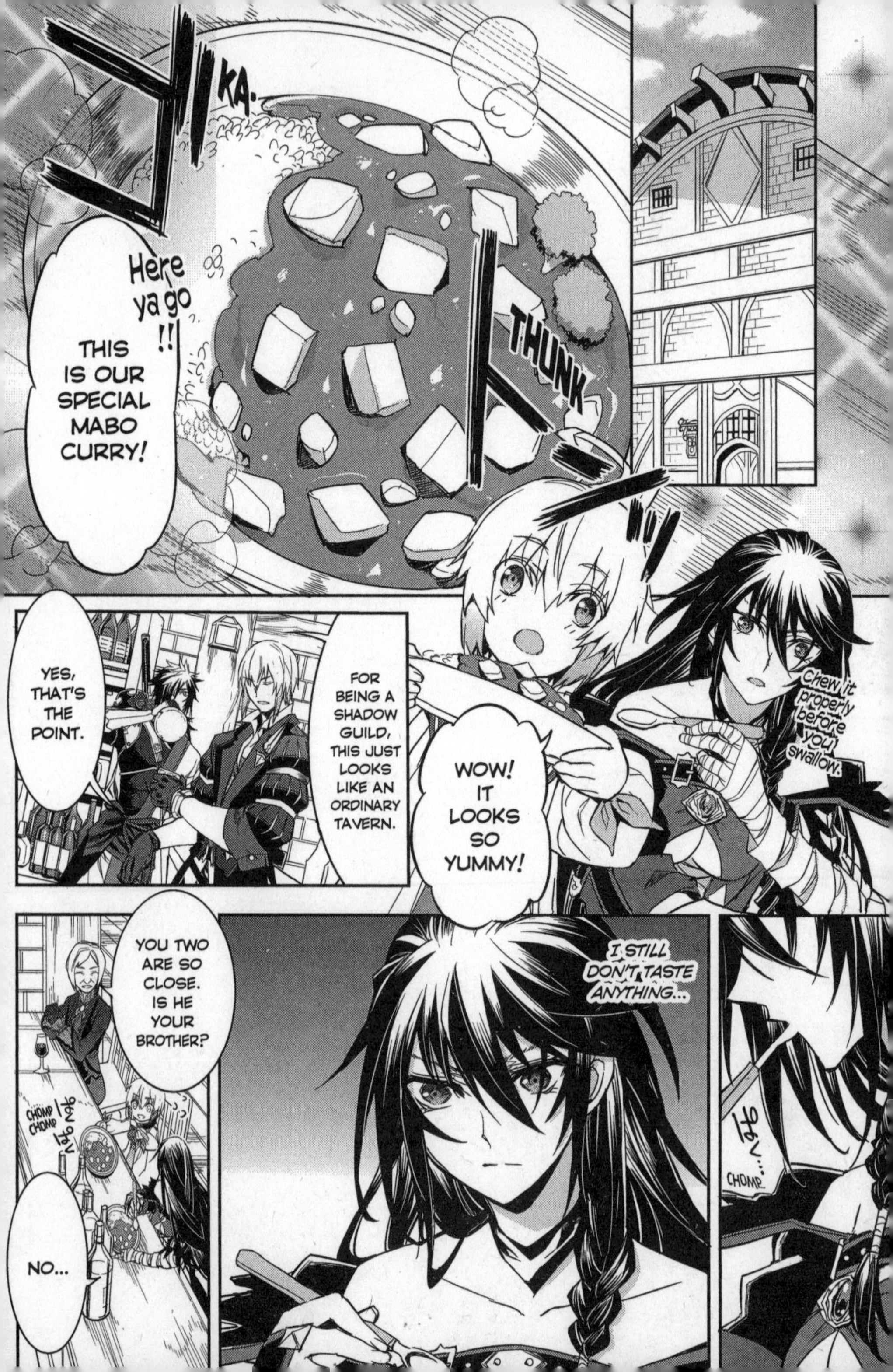
KA-
THUNK
Here ya go!!
THIS IS OUR SPECIAL MABO CURRY!
Chew it properly before you swallow.
WOW! IT LOOKS SO YUMMY!
FOR BEING A SHADOW GUILD, THIS JUST LOOKS LIKE AN ORDINARY TAVERN.
YES, THAT'S THE POINT.
CHOMP
I STILL DON'T TASTE ANYTHING...
YOU TWO ARE SO CLOSE. IS HE YOUR BROTHER?
CHOMP CHOMP
NO...

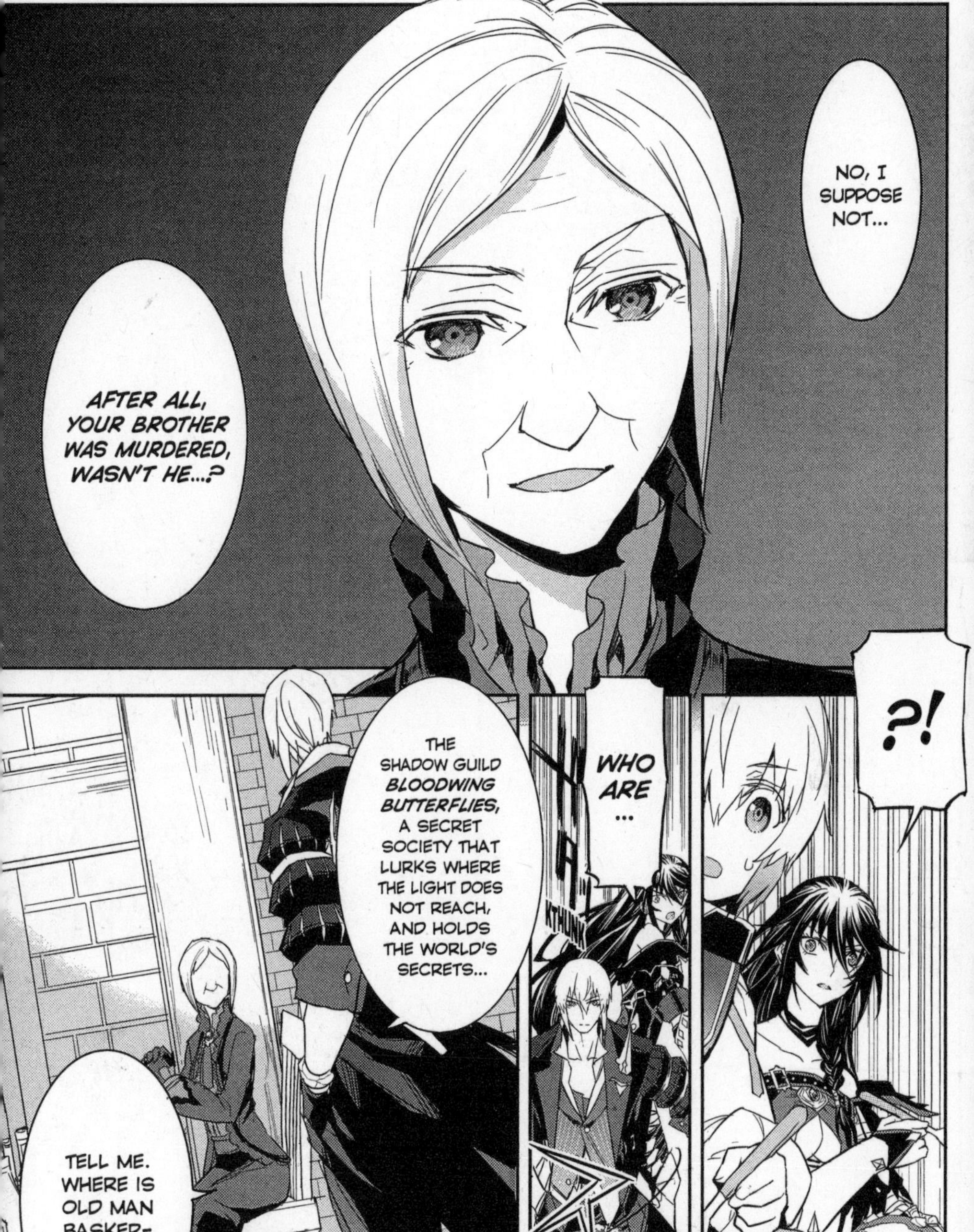
NO, I SUPPOSE NOT...
AFTER ALL, YOUR BROTHER WAS MURDERED, WASN'T HE...?
?!
WHO ARE ...
KTHUNK
SWISH
THE SHADOW GUILD BLOODWING BUTTERFLIES, A SECRET SOCIETY THAT LURKS WHERE THE LIGHT DOES NOT REACH, AND HOLDS THE WORLD'S SECRETS...
TELL ME. WHERE IS OLD MAN BASKER-VILLE?

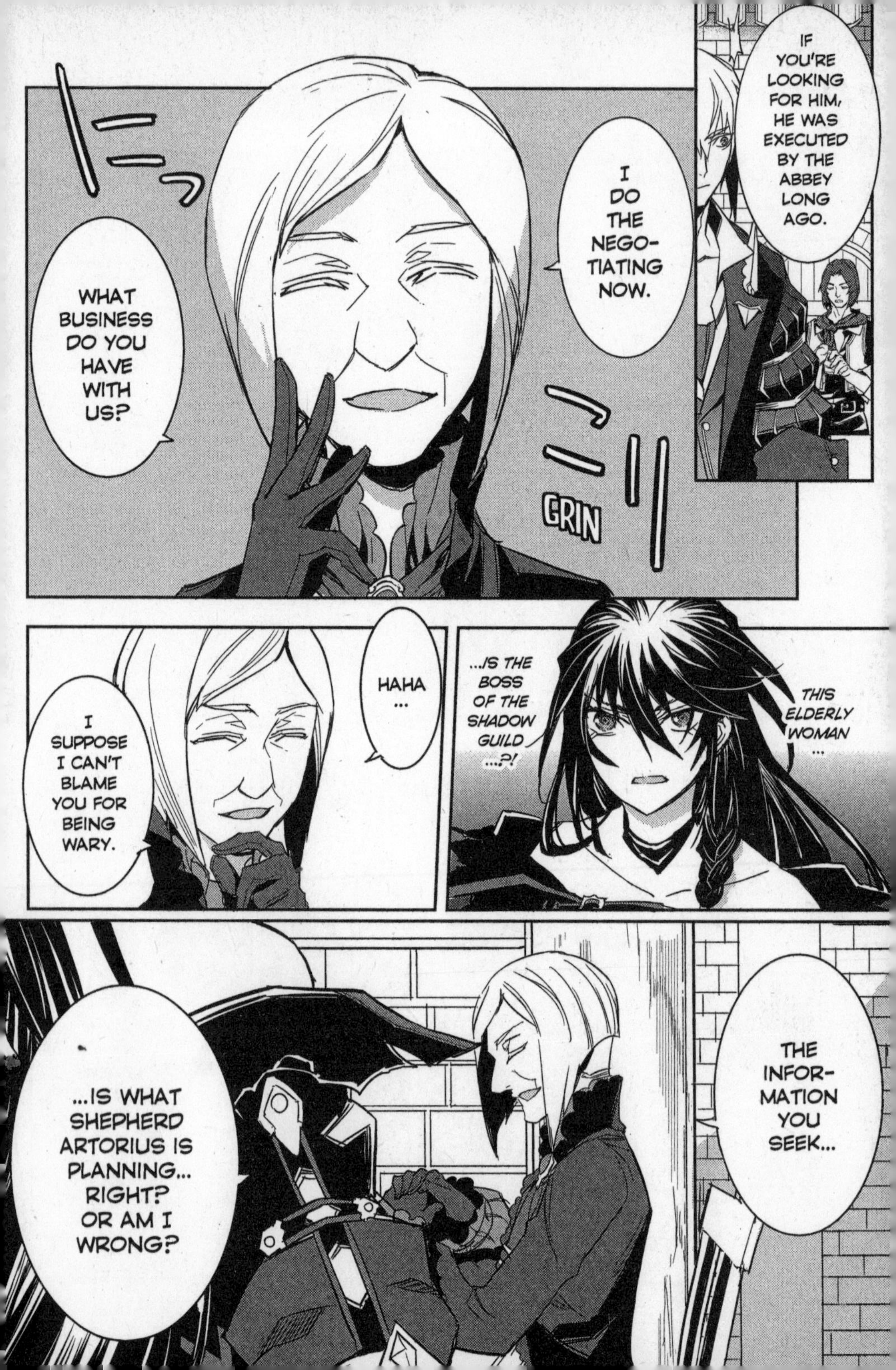
IF YOU'RE LOOKING FOR HIM, HE WAS EXECUTED BY THE ABBEY LONG AGO.
I DO THE NEGOTIATING NOW.
WHAT BUSINESS DO YOU HAVE WITH US?
GRIN
THIS ELDERLY WOMAN ...
...IS THE BOSS OF THE SHADOW GUILD ...?!
HAHA ...
I SUPPOSE I CAN'T BLAME YOU FOR BEING WARY.
THE INFORMATION YOU SEEK...
...IS WHAT SHEPHERD ARTORIUS IS PLANNING... RIGHT? OR AM I WRONG?

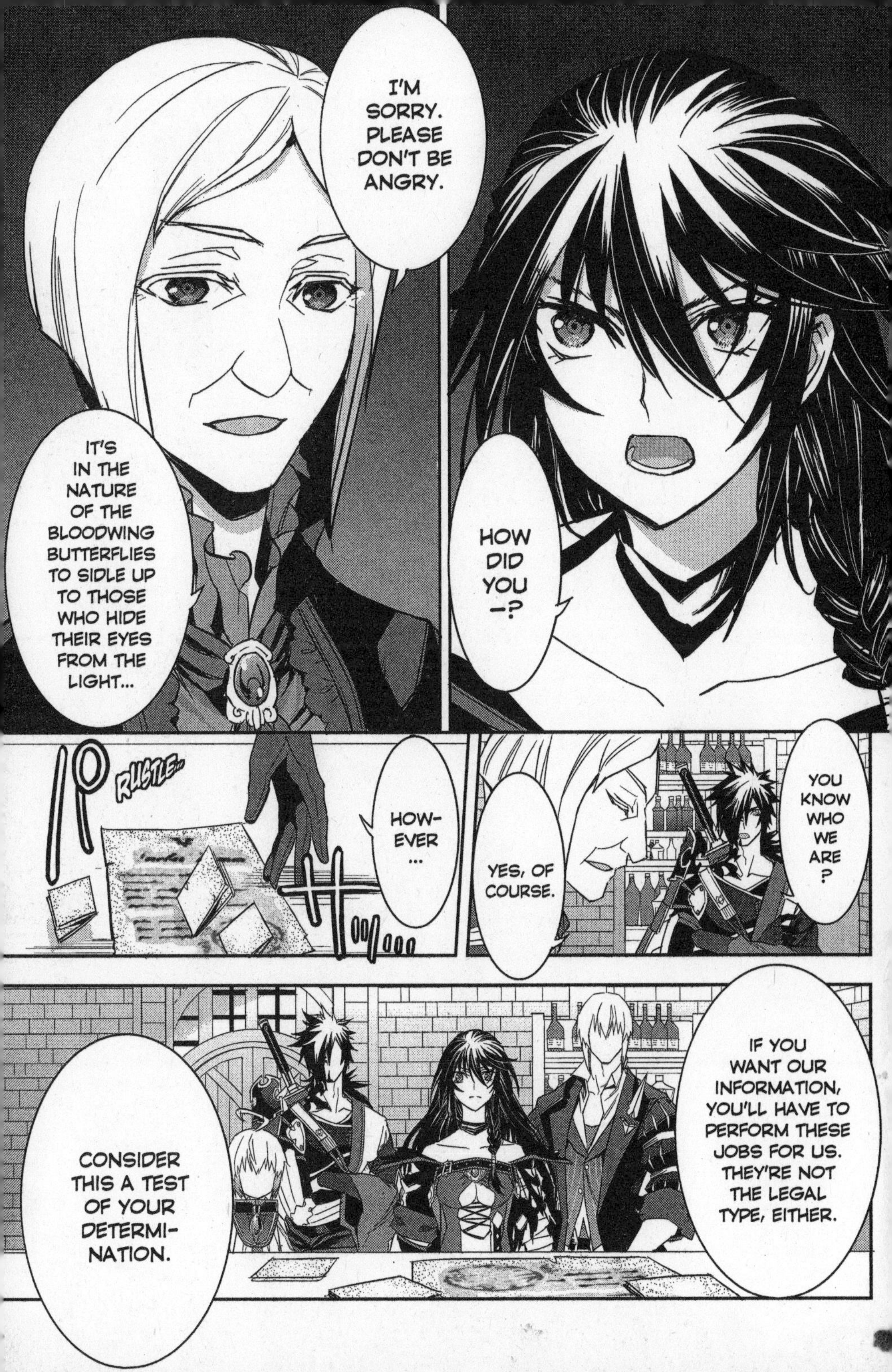
HOW DID YOU —?
I'M SORRY. PLEASE DON'T BE ANGRY.
IT'S IN THE NATURE OF THE BLOODWING BUTTERFLIES TO SIDLE UP TO THOSE WHO HIDE THEIR EYES FROM THE LIGHT...
YOU KNOW WHO WE ARE?
YES, OF COURSE.
HOW-EVER...
RUSTLE...
IF YOU WANT OUR INFORMATION, YOU'LL HAVE TO PERFORM THESE JOBS FOR US. THEY'RE NOT THE LEGAL TYPE, EITHER.
CONSIDER THIS A TEST OF YOUR DETERMI-NATION.

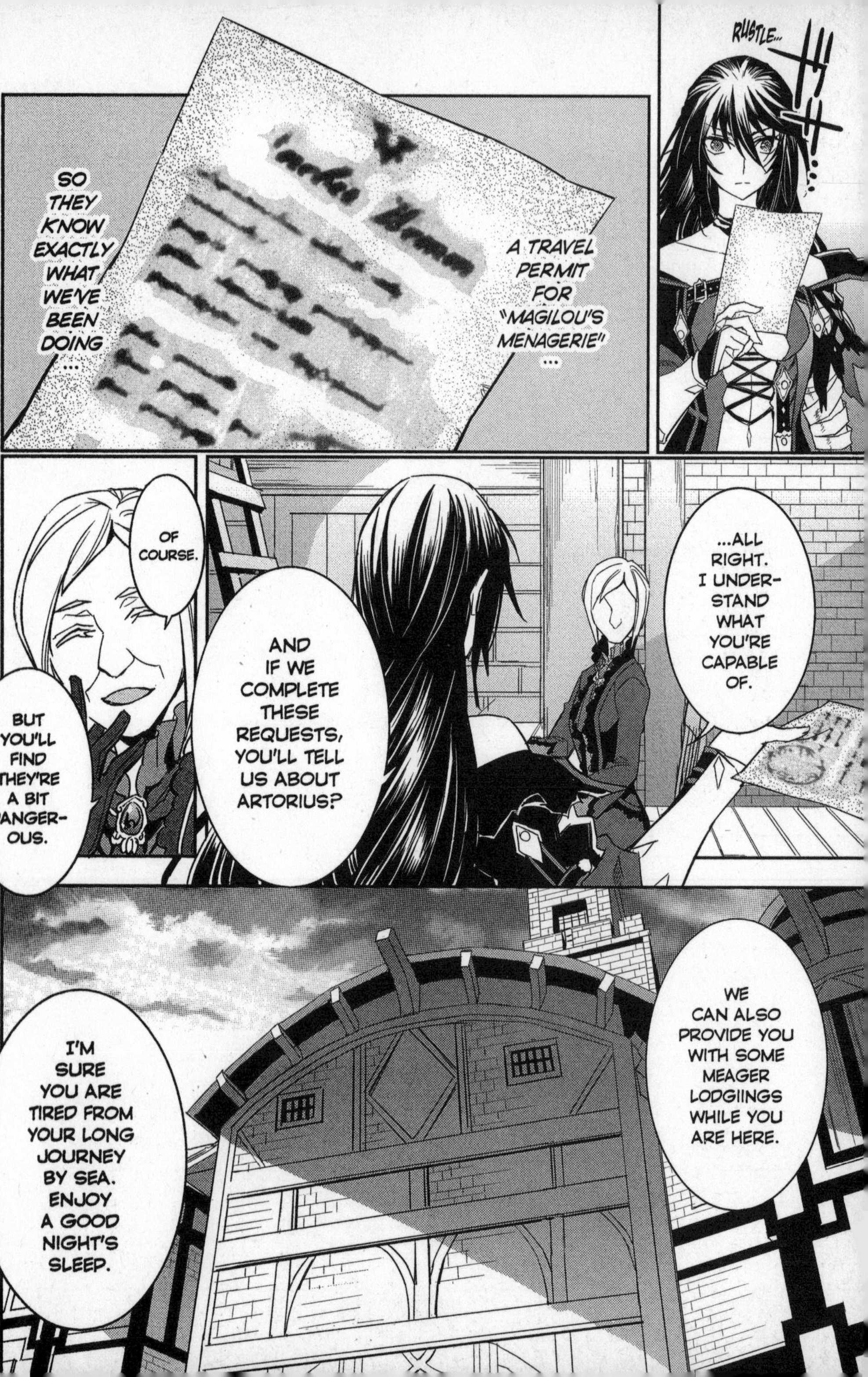
RUSTLE...
A TRAVEL PERMIT FOR "MAGILOU'S MENAGERIE"...
SO THEY KNOW EXACTLY WHAT WE'VE BEEN DOING...
...ALL RIGHT. I UNDERSTAND WHAT YOU'RE CAPABLE OF.
AND IF WE COMPLETE THESE REQUESTS, YOU'LL TELL US ABOUT ARTORIUS?
OF COURSE.
BUT YOU'LL FIND THEY'RE A BIT DANGEROUS.
WE CAN ALSO PROVIDE YOU WITH SOME MEAGER LODGIINGS WHILE YOU ARE HERE.
I'M SURE YOU ARE TIRED FROM YOUR LONG JOURNEY BY SEA. ENJOY A GOOD NIGHT'S SLEEP.

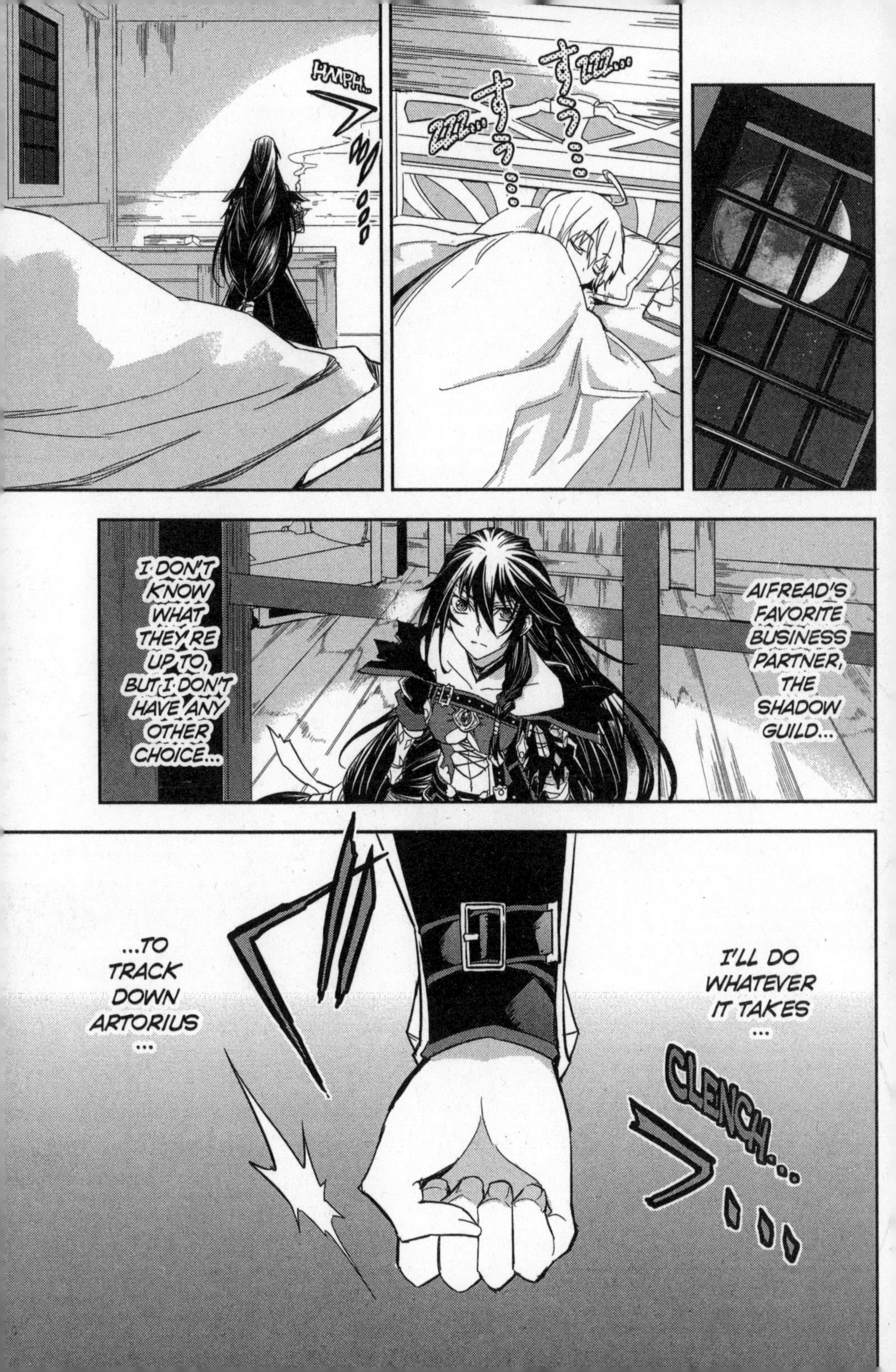
ZZZ...
ZZZ...
HMPH...
AIFREAD'S FAVORITE BUSINESS PARTNER, THE SHADOW GUILD...
I DON'T KNOW WHAT THEY'RE UP TO, BUT I DON'T HAVE ANY OTHER CHOICE...
I'LL DO WHATEVER IT TAKES ...
CLENCH...
...TO TRACK DOWN ARTORIUS ...

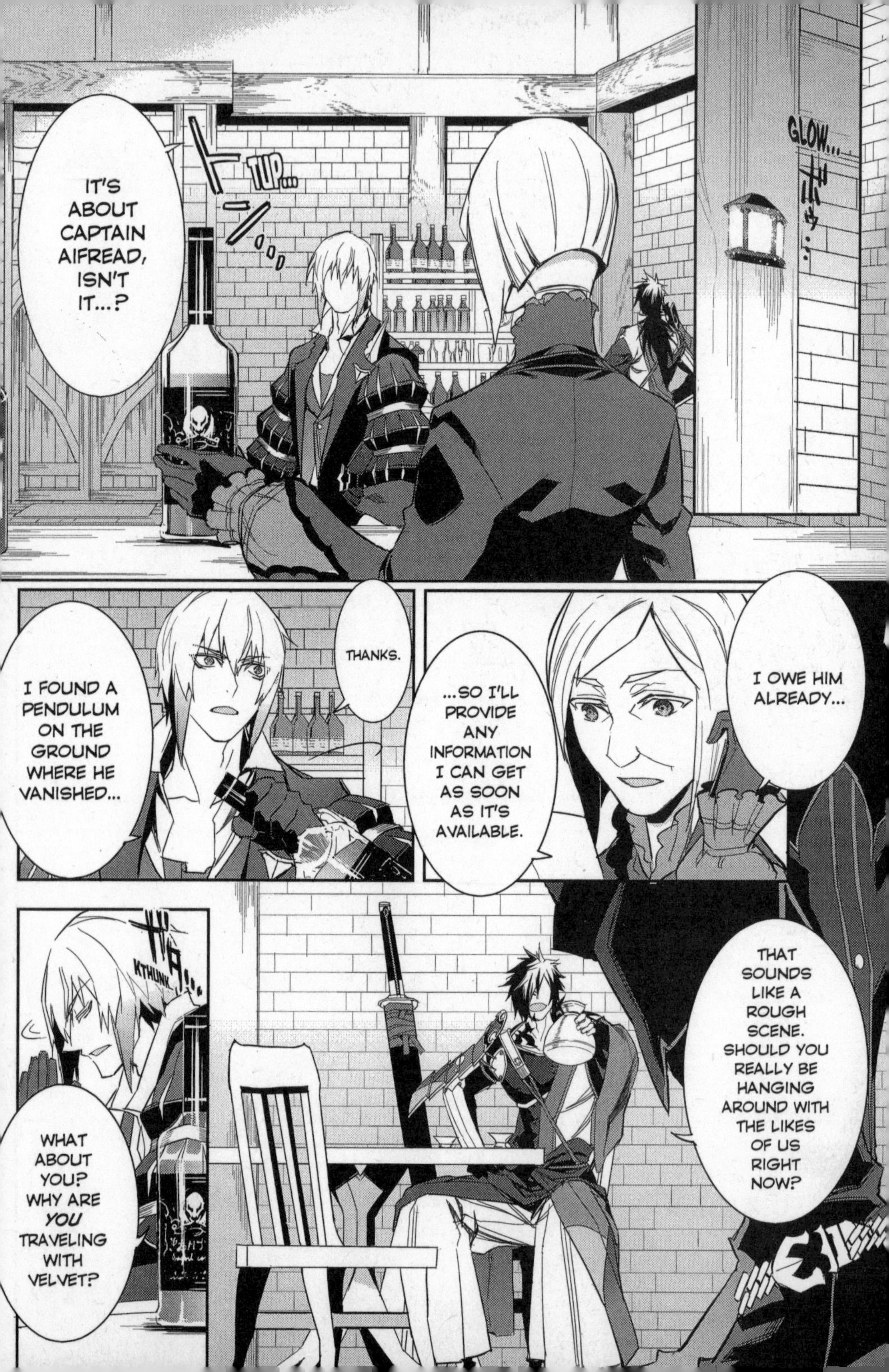
GLOW...
TUP...
IT'S ABOUT CAPTAIN AIFREAD, ISN'T IT...?
I OWE HIM ALREADY...
...SO I'LL PROVIDE ANY INFORMATION I CAN GET AS SOON AS IT'S AVAILABLE.
THANKS.
I FOUND A PENDULUM ON THE GROUND WHERE HE VANISHED...
THAT SOUNDS LIKE A ROUGH SCENE. SHOULD YOU REALLY BE HANGING AROUND WITH THE LIKES OF US RIGHT NOW?
KTHUNK...
WHAT ABOUT YOU? WHY ARE *YOU* TRAVELING WITH VELVET?

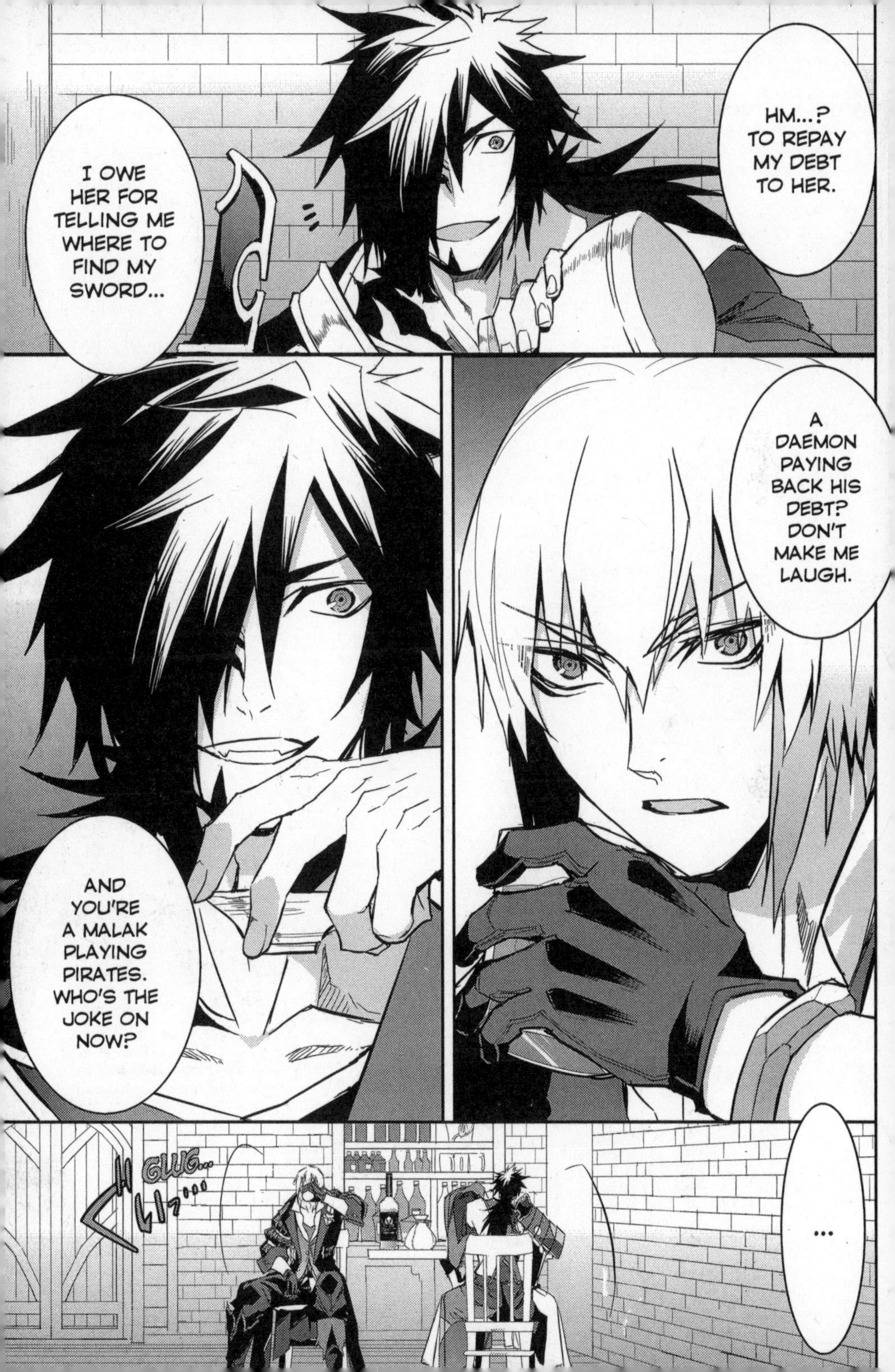
HM...? TO REPAY MY DEBT TO HER.
I OWE HER FOR TELLING ME WHERE TO FIND MY SWORD...
A DAEMON PAYING BACK HIS DEBT? DON'T MAKE ME LAUGH.
AND YOU'RE A MALAK PLAYING PIRATES. WHO'S THE JOKE ON NOW?
...
GLUG...

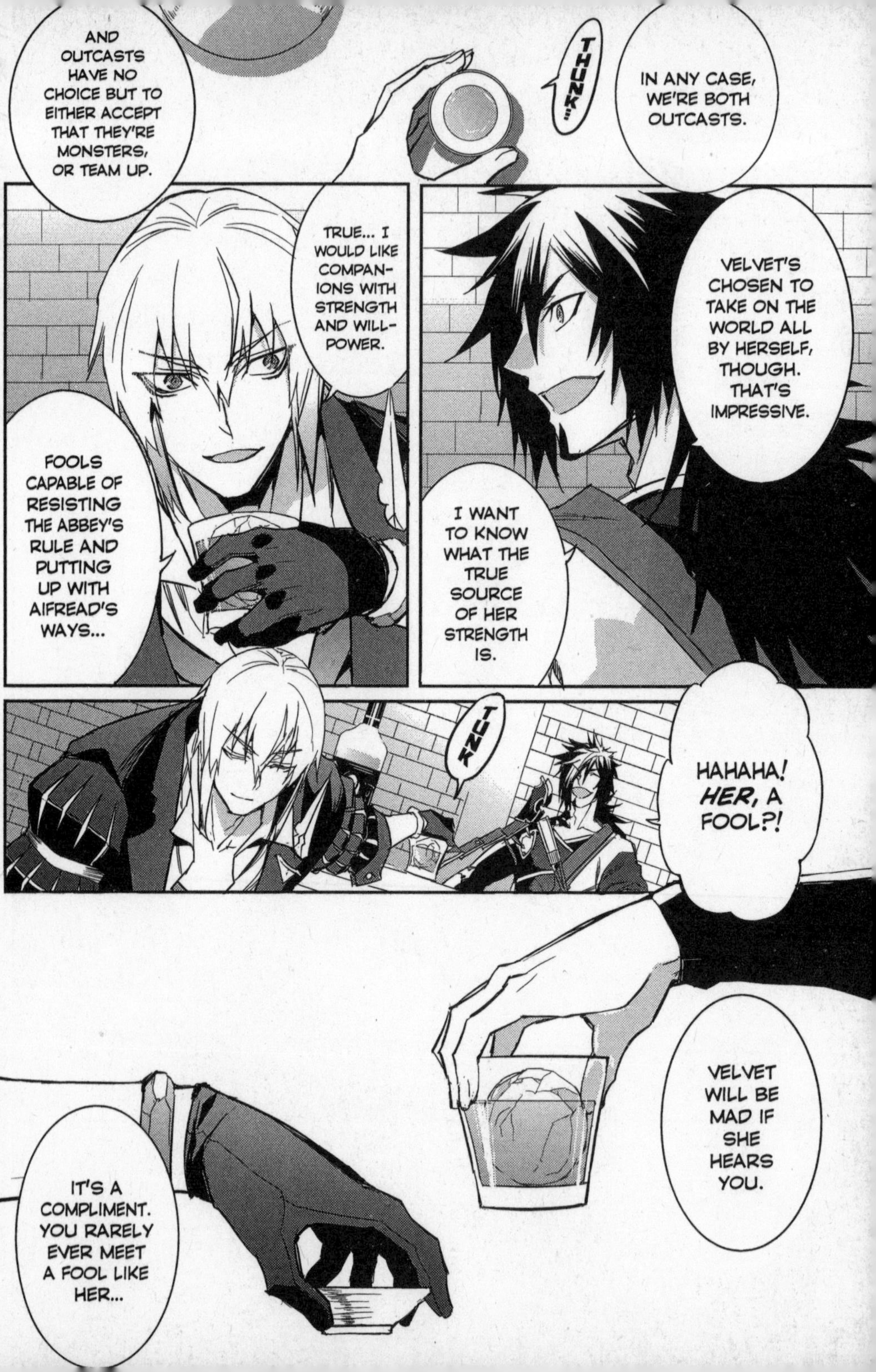
IN ANY CASE, WE'RE BOTH OUTCASTS.
THUNK!!
AND OUTCASTS HAVE NO CHOICE BUT TO EITHER ACCEPT THAT THEY'RE MONSTERS, OR TEAM UP.
VELVET'S CHOSEN TO TAKE ON THE WORLD ALL BY HERSELF, THOUGH. THAT'S IMPRESSIVE.
I WANT TO KNOW WHAT THE TRUE SOURCE OF HER STRENGTH IS.
TRUE... I WOULD LIKE COMPANIONS WITH STRENGTH AND WILL-POWER.
FOOLS CAPABLE OF RESISTING THE ABBEY'S RULE AND PUTTING UP WITH AIFREAD'S WAYS...
HAHAHA! ***HER***, A FOOL?!
TUNK
VELVET WILL BE MAD IF SHE HEARS YOU.
IT'S A COMPLIMENT. YOU RARELY EVER MEET A FOOL LIKE HER...

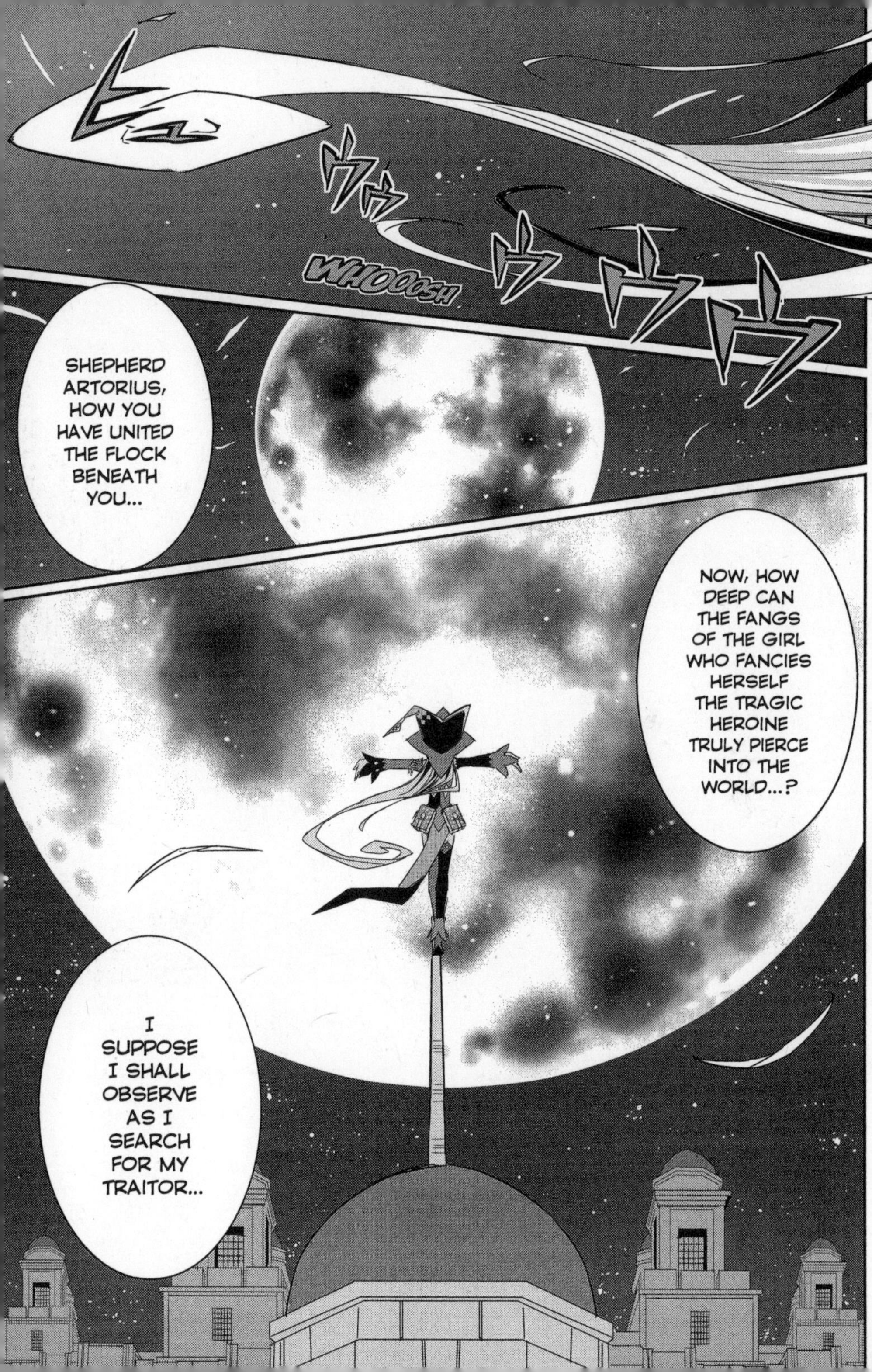
WHOOOSH
SHEPHERD ARTORIUS, HOW YOU HAVE UNITED THE FLOCK BENEATH YOU...
NOW, HOW DEEP CAN THE FANGS OF THE GIRL WHO FANCIES HERSELF THE TRAGIC HEROINE TRULY PIERCE INTO THE WORLD...?
I SUPPOSE I SHALL OBSERVE AS I SEARCH FOR MY TRAITOR...

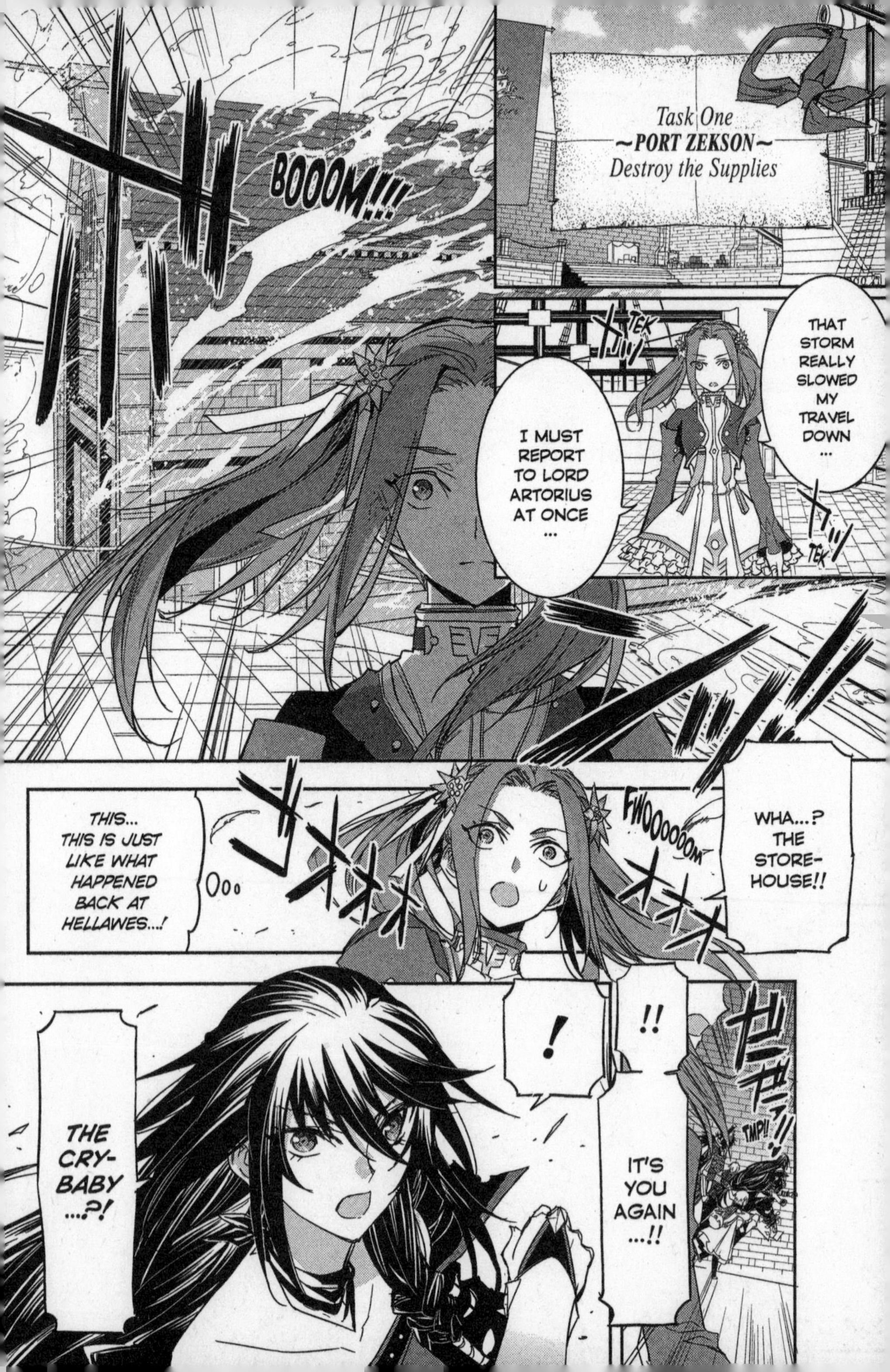

Task One
~PORT ZEKSON~
Destroy the Supplies
THAT STORM REALLY SLOWED MY TRAVEL DOWN ...
TEK
TEK
I MUST REPORT TO LORD ARTORIUS AT ONCE ...
BOOOM!!!
WHA...? THE STORE-HOUSE!!
FWOOOOOOM
THIS... THIS IS JUST LIKE WHAT HAPPENED BACK AT HELLAWES...!
Ooo
TMP!!
IT'S YOU AGAIN ...!!
!!
!
THE CRY-BABY ...?!

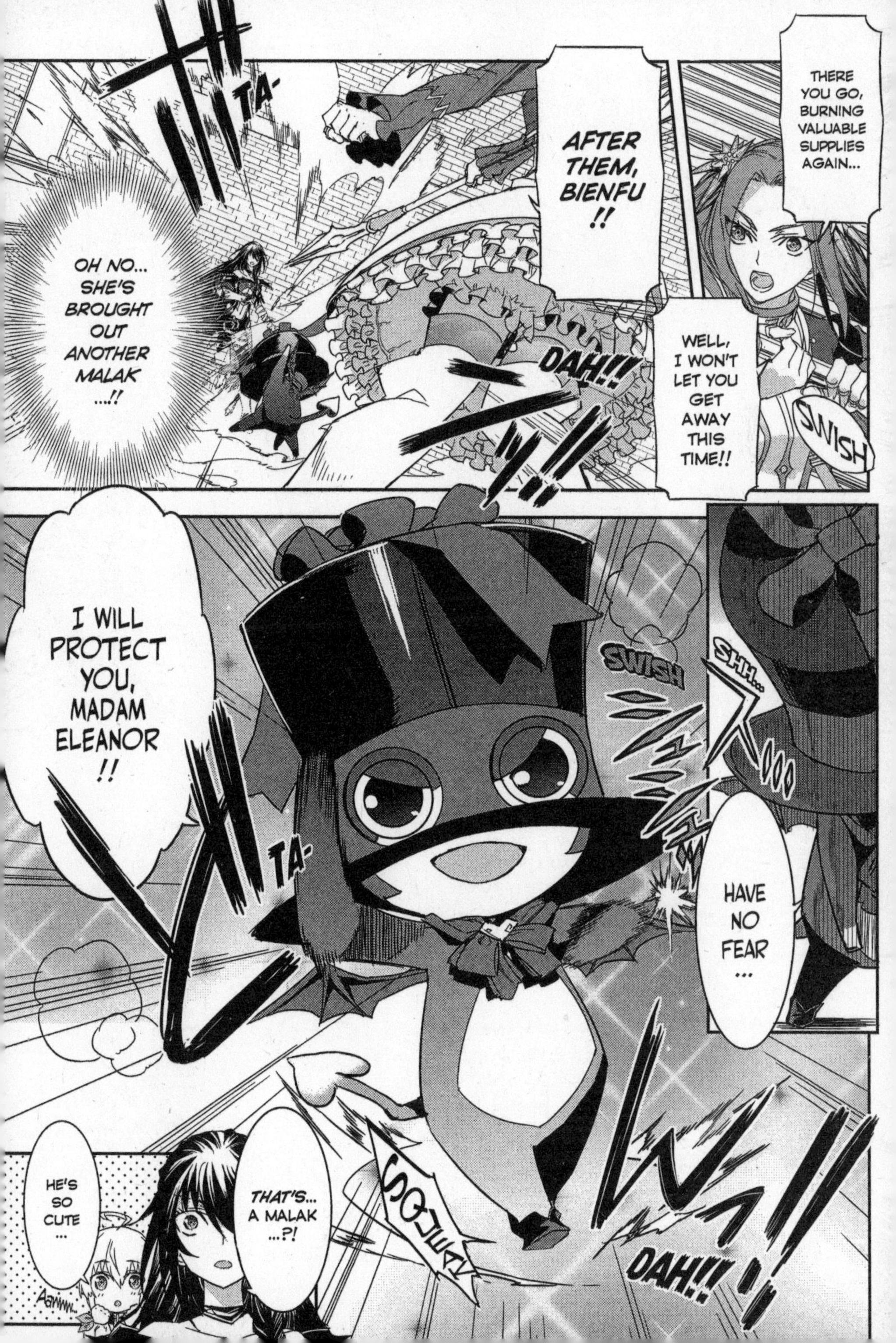

THERE YOU GO, BURNING VALUABLE SUPPLIES AGAIN...
WELL, I WON'T LET YOU GET AWAY THIS TIME!!
SWISH
AFTER THEM, BIENFU!!
TA-
DAH!!
OH NO... SHE'S BROUGHT OUT ANOTHER MALAK...!!
SHH...
HAVE NO FEAR...
SWISH
I WILL PROTECT YOU, MADAM ELEANOR!!
TA-
DAH!!
THAT'S... A MALAK...?!
HE'S SO CUTE...

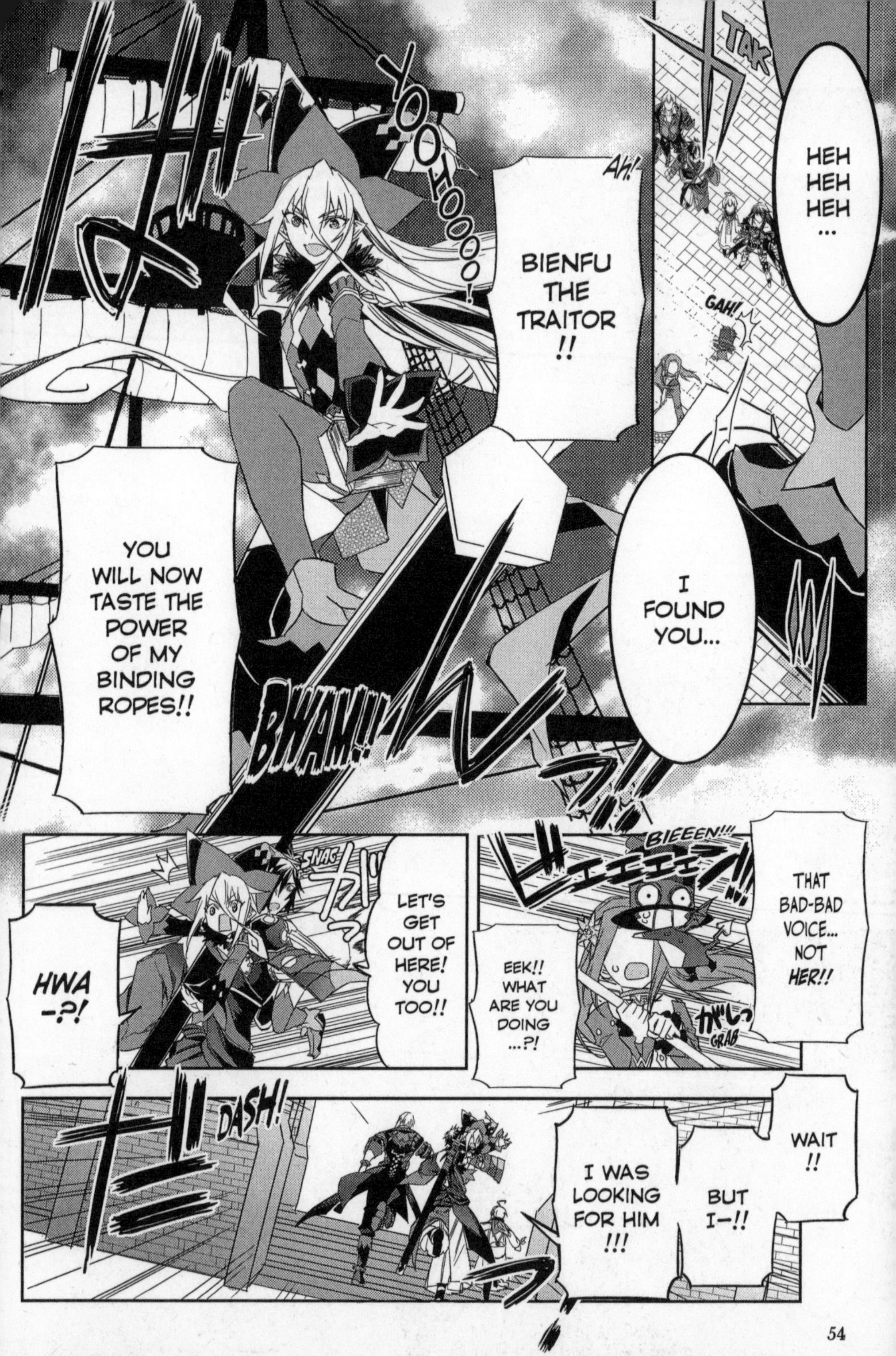
TAK
HEH HEH HEH ...
GAH!
I FOUND YOU...
YOOHOOOOO!
Ah!
BIENFU THE TRAITOR !!
YOU WILL NOW TASTE THE POWER OF MY BINDING ROPES!!
BWAM!!
BIEEEN!!!
THAT BAD-BAD VOICE... NOT HER!!
GRAB
EEK!! WHAT ARE YOU DOING ...?!
SNAG
LET'S GET OUT OF HERE! YOU TOO!!
HWA-?!
WAIT !!
BUT I-!!
I WAS LOOKING FOR HIM !!!
DASH!

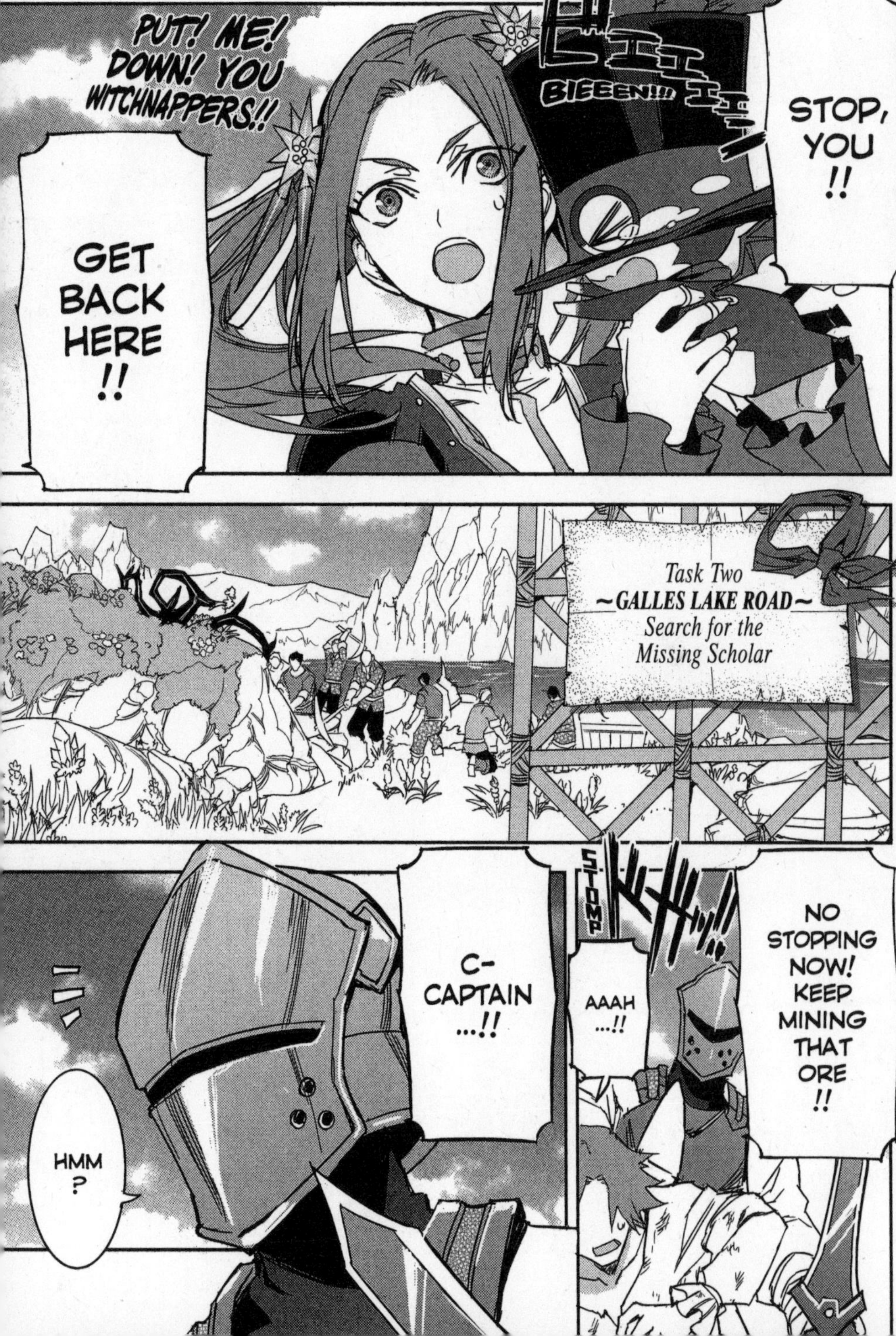
STOP, YOU !!
BIEEEN!!!
PUT! ME! DOWN! YOU WITCHNAPPERS!!
GET BACK HERE !!
Task Two
~GALLES LAKE ROAD~
Search for the Missing Scholar
NO STOPPING NOW! KEEP MINING THAT ORE !!
STOMP
AAAH ...!!
C-CAPTAIN ...!!
HMM ?

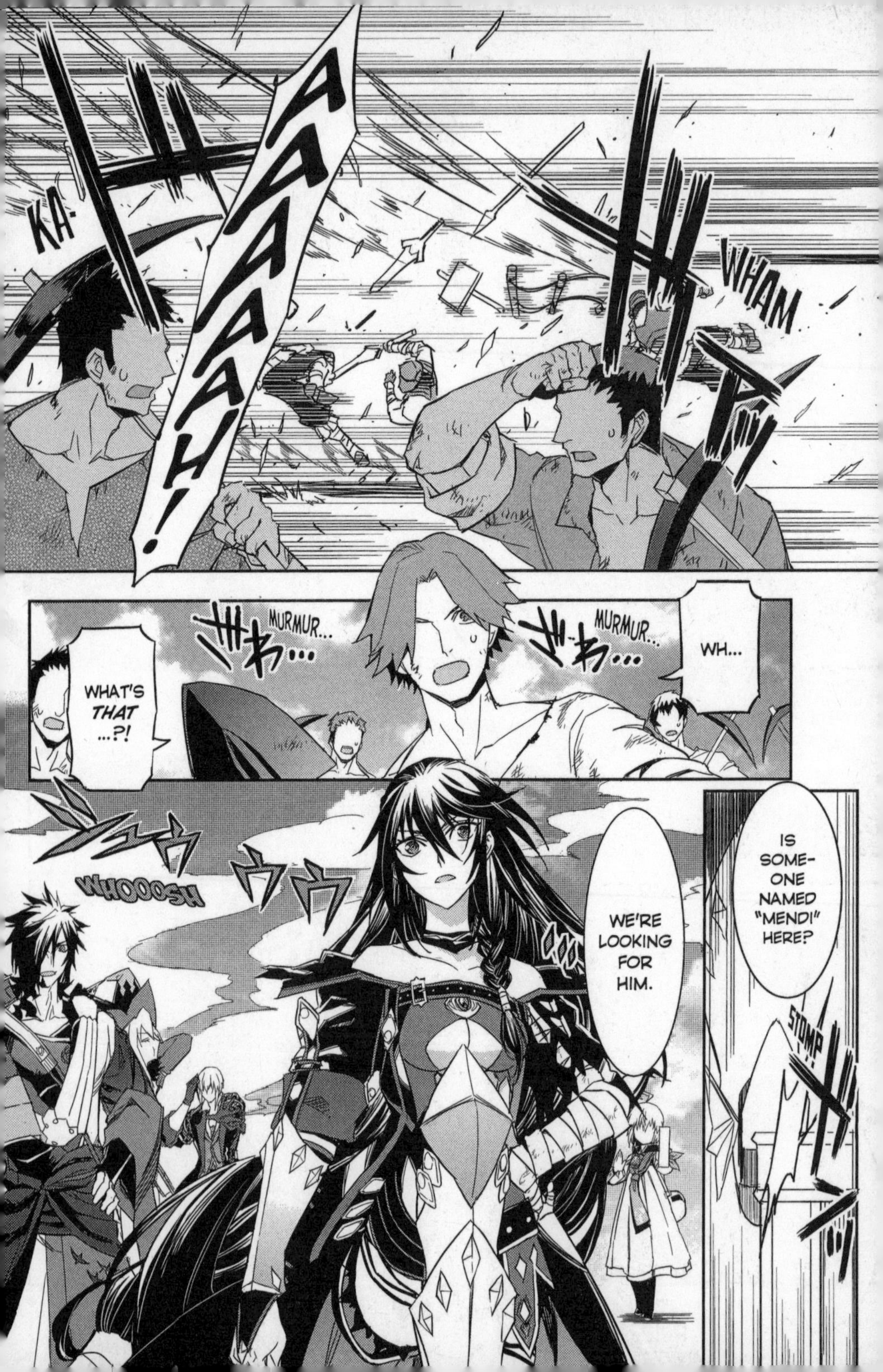
WHAM
AAAAAH!
KA-
WH...
MURMUR...
MURMUR...
WHAT'S *THAT* ...?!
IS SOME-ONE NAMED "MENDI" HERE?
STOMP
WE'RE LOOKING FOR HIM.
WHOOOSH

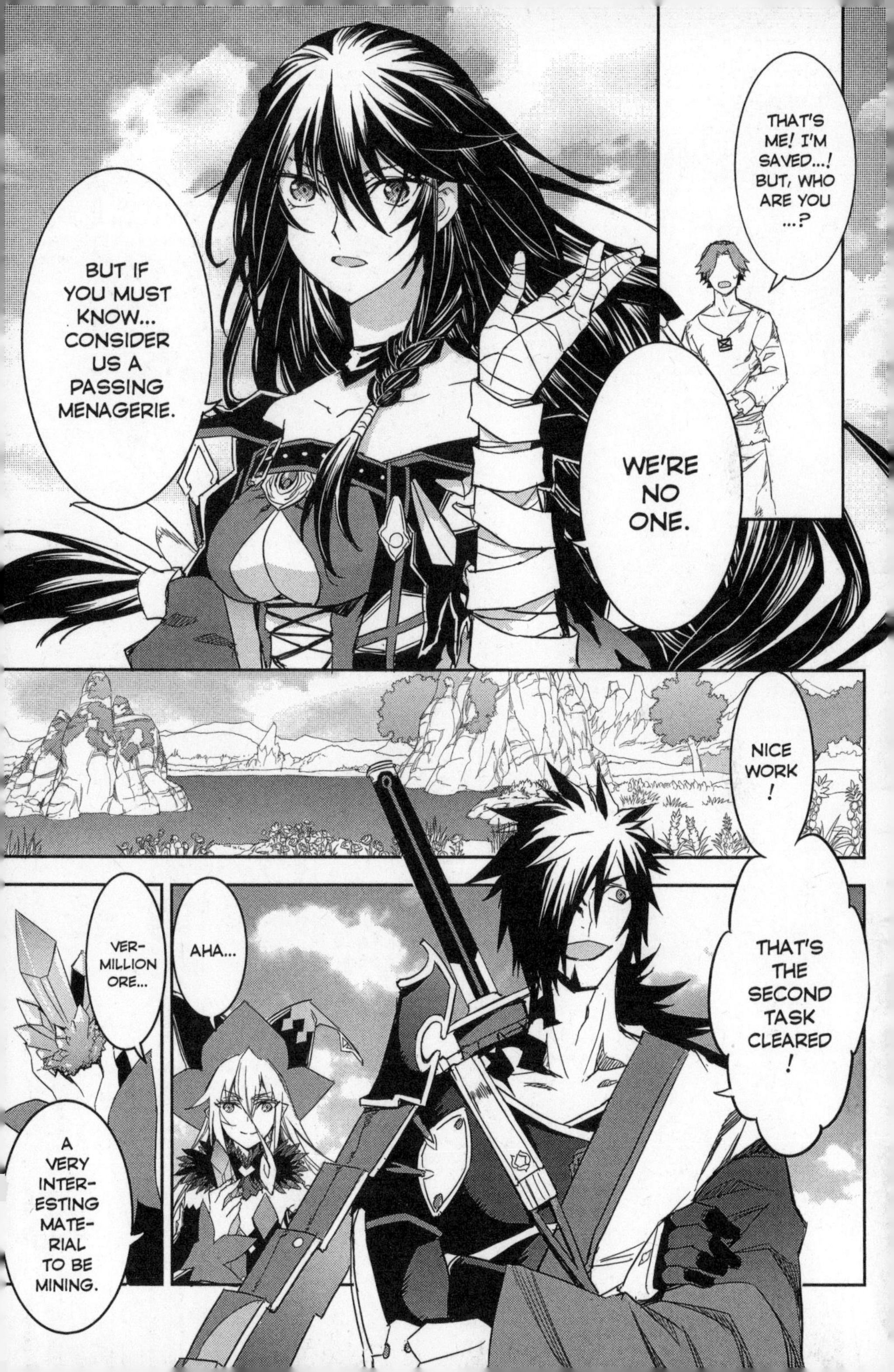
THAT'S ME! I'M SAVED...! BUT, WHO ARE YOU ...?
WE'RE NO ONE.
BUT IF YOU MUST KNOW... CONSIDER US A PASSING MENAGERIE.
NICE WORK!
THAT'S THE SECOND TASK CLEARED!
AHA...
VER-MILLION ORE...
A VERY INTER-ESTING MATE-RIAL TO BE MINING.

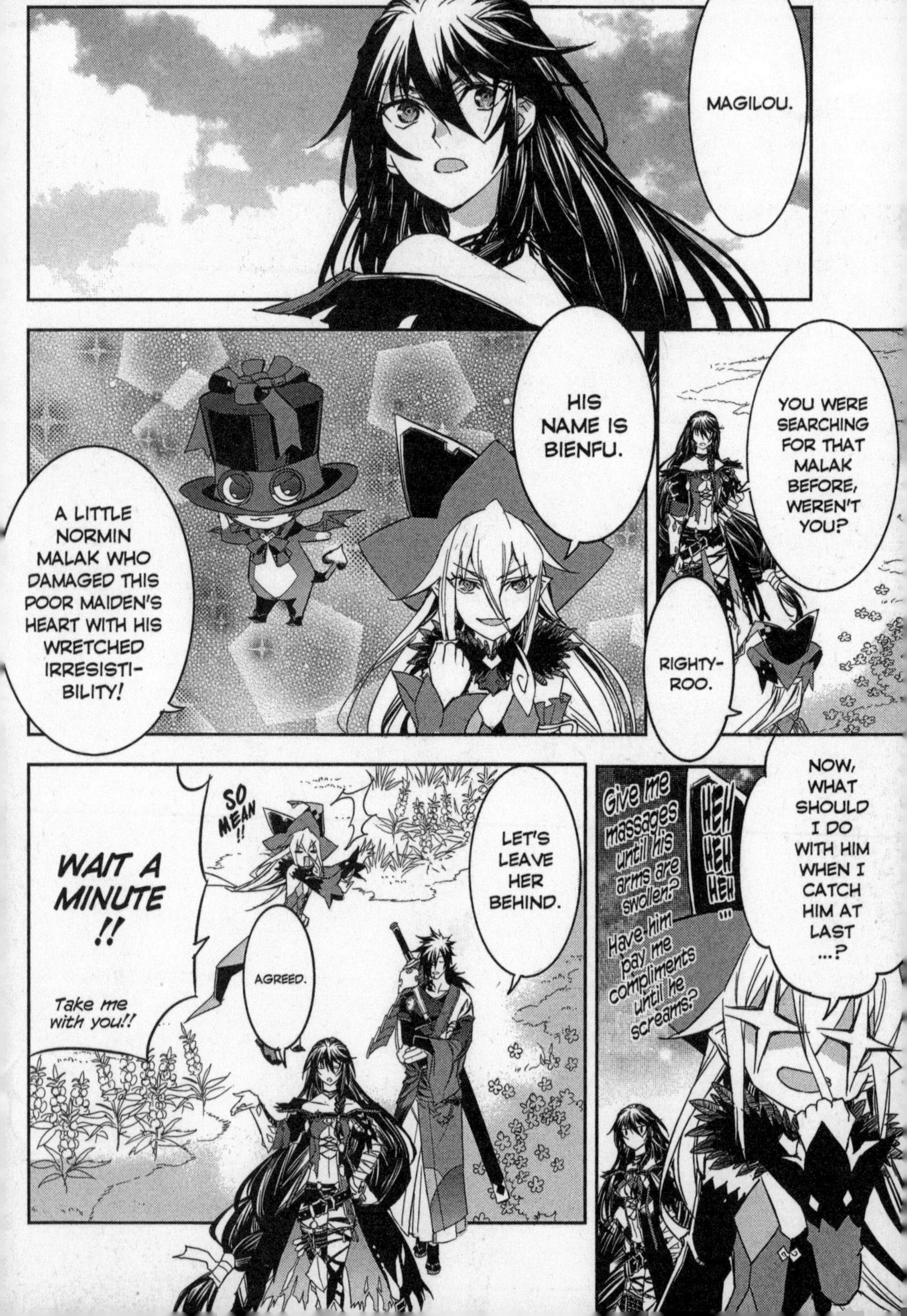
MAGILOU.
YOU WERE SEARCHING FOR THAT MALAK BEFORE, WEREN'T YOU?
RIGHTY-ROO.
HIS NAME IS BIENFU.
A LITTLE NORMIN MALAK WHO DAMAGED THIS POOR MAIDEN'S HEART WITH HIS WRETCHED IRRESISTI-BILITY!
NOW, WHAT SHOULD I DO WITH HIM WHEN I CATCH HIM AT LAST ...?
HEH HEH HEH ...
Give me massages until his arms are swollen? Have him pay me compliments until he screams?
LET'S LEAVE HER BEHIND.
AGREED.
SO MEAN !!
WAIT A MINUTE !!
Take me with you!!

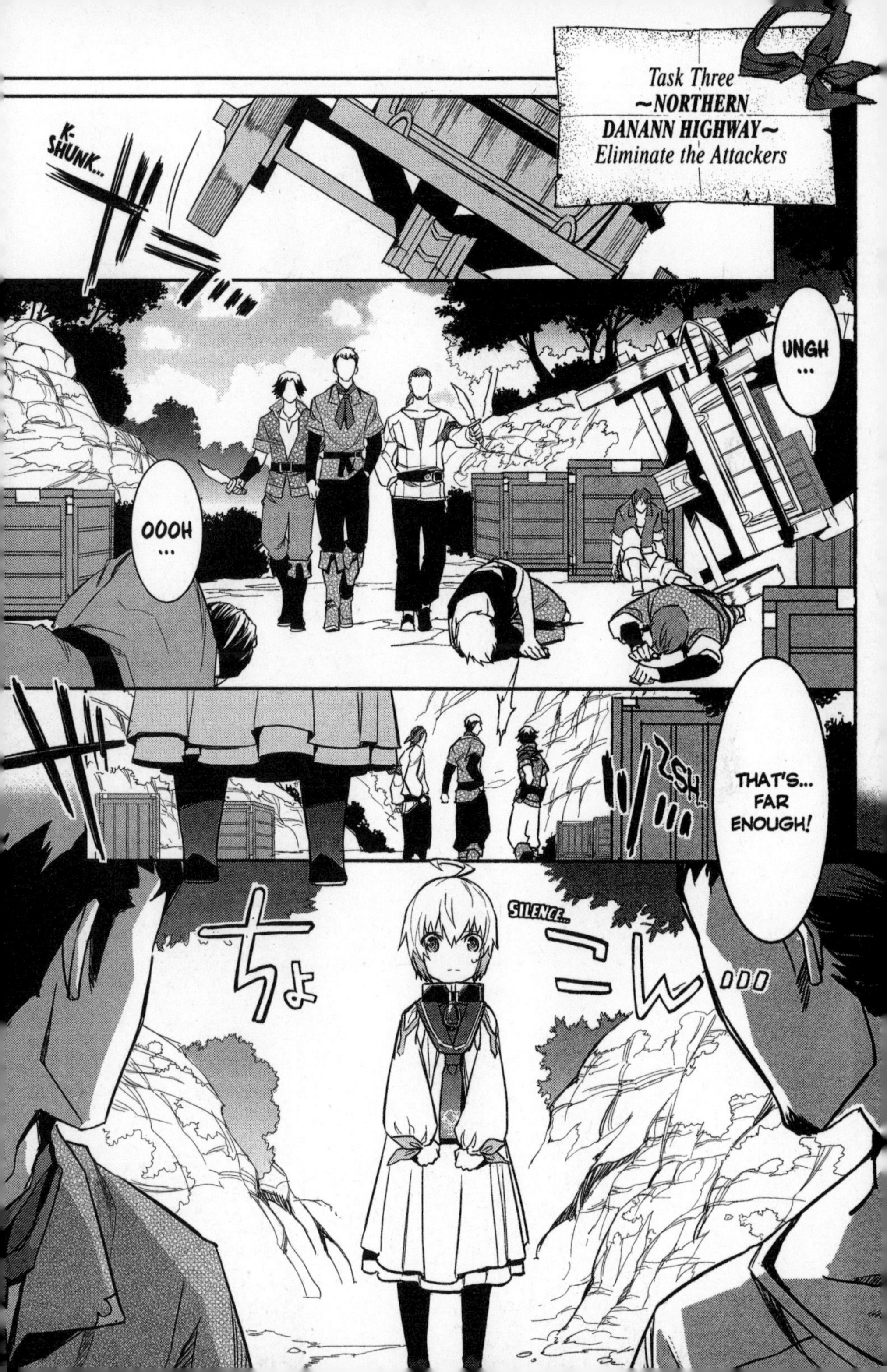
Task Three
~NORTHERN DANANN HIGHWAY~
Eliminate the Attackers
K-SHUNK...
UNGH...
OOOH...
THAT'S... FAR ENOUGH!
ZSH...
SILENCE...

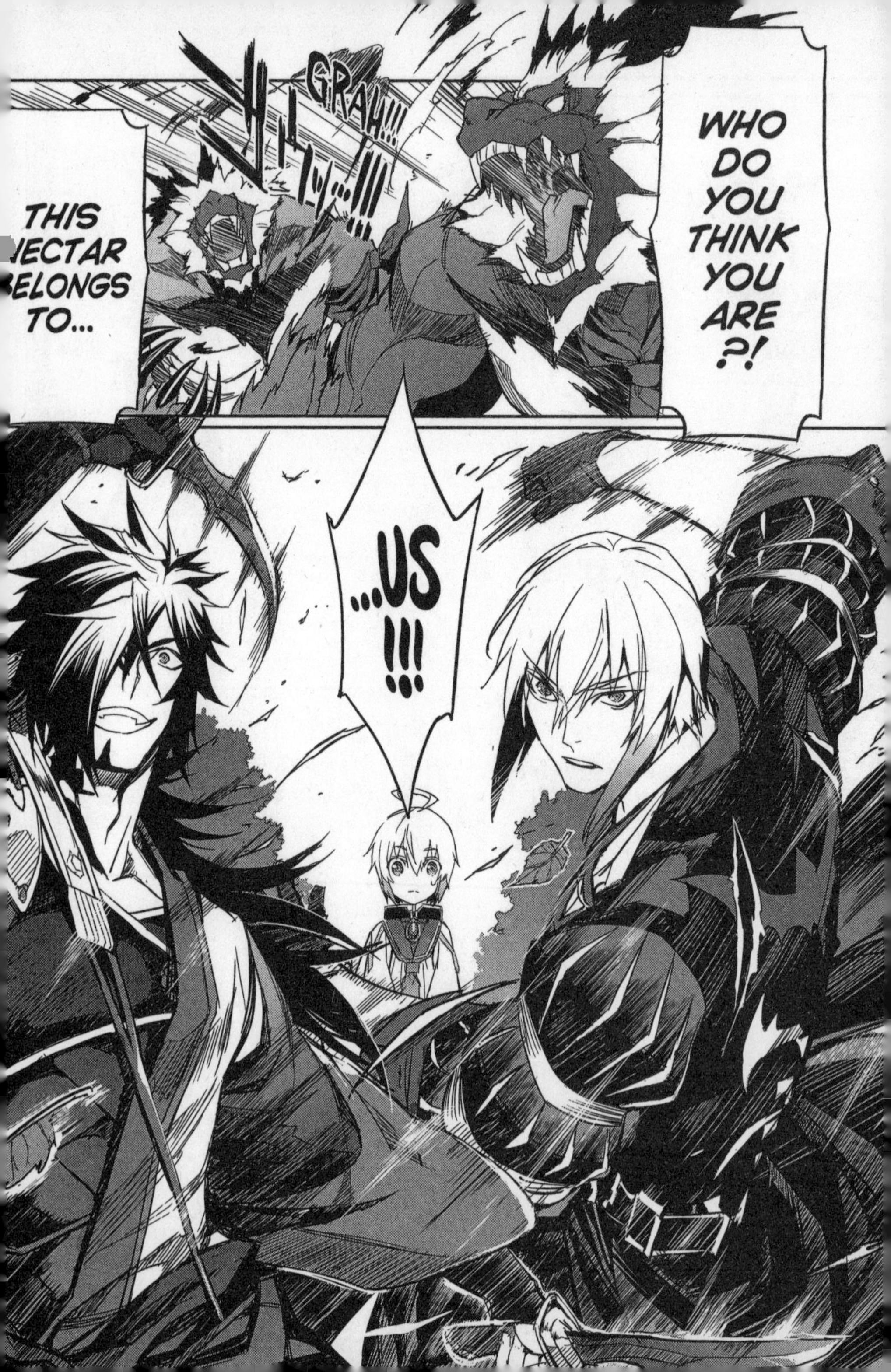
WHO DO YOU THINK YOU ARE?!
GRAH!!!
THIS NECTAR BELONGS TO...
...US!!!

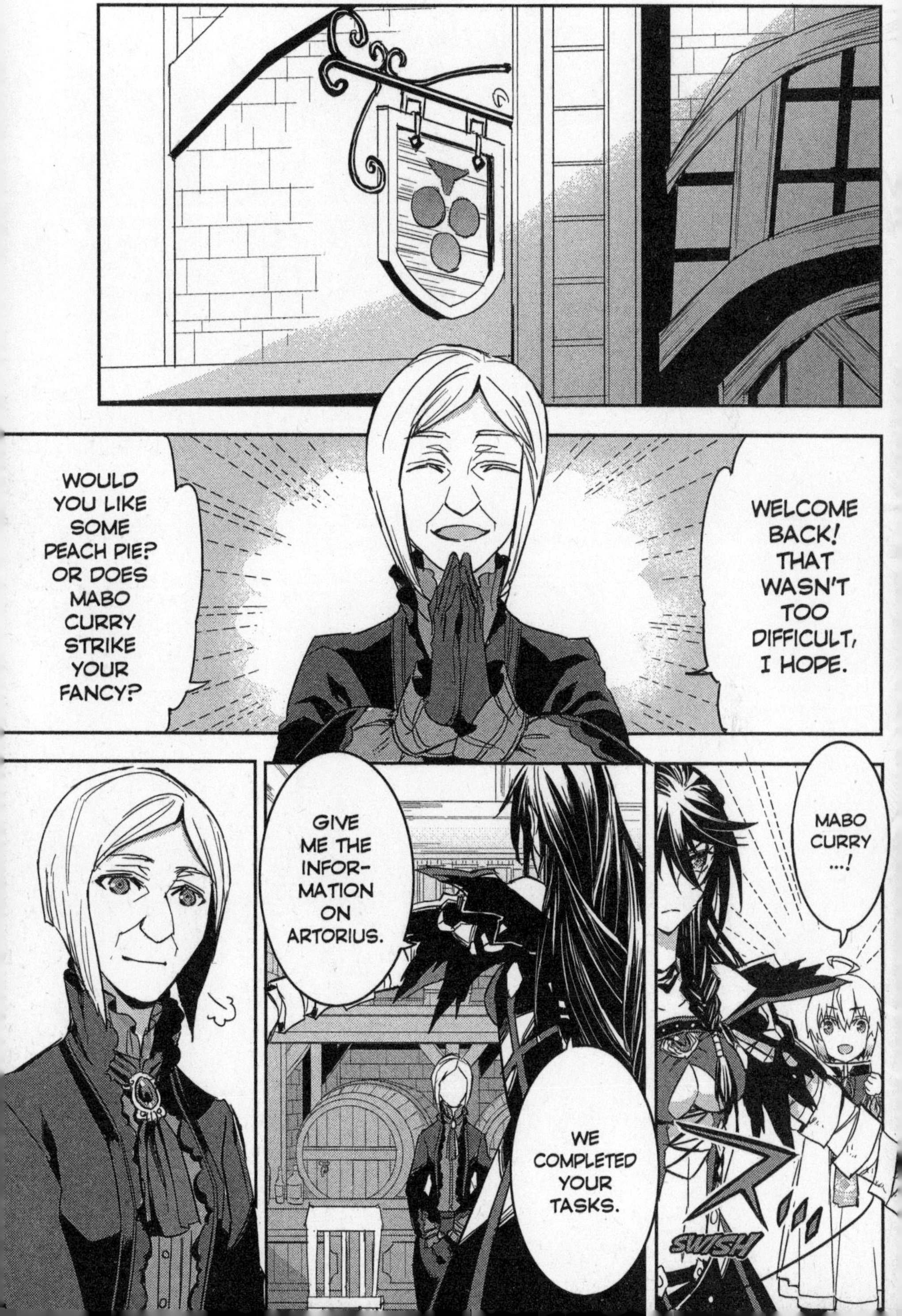
WELCOME BACK! THAT WASN'T TOO DIFFICULT, I HOPE.
WOULD YOU LIKE SOME PEACH PIE? OR DOES MABO CURRY STRIKE YOUR FANCY?
MABO CURRY ...!
SWISH
GIVE ME THE INFORMATION ON ARTORIUS.
WE COMPLETED YOUR TASKS.

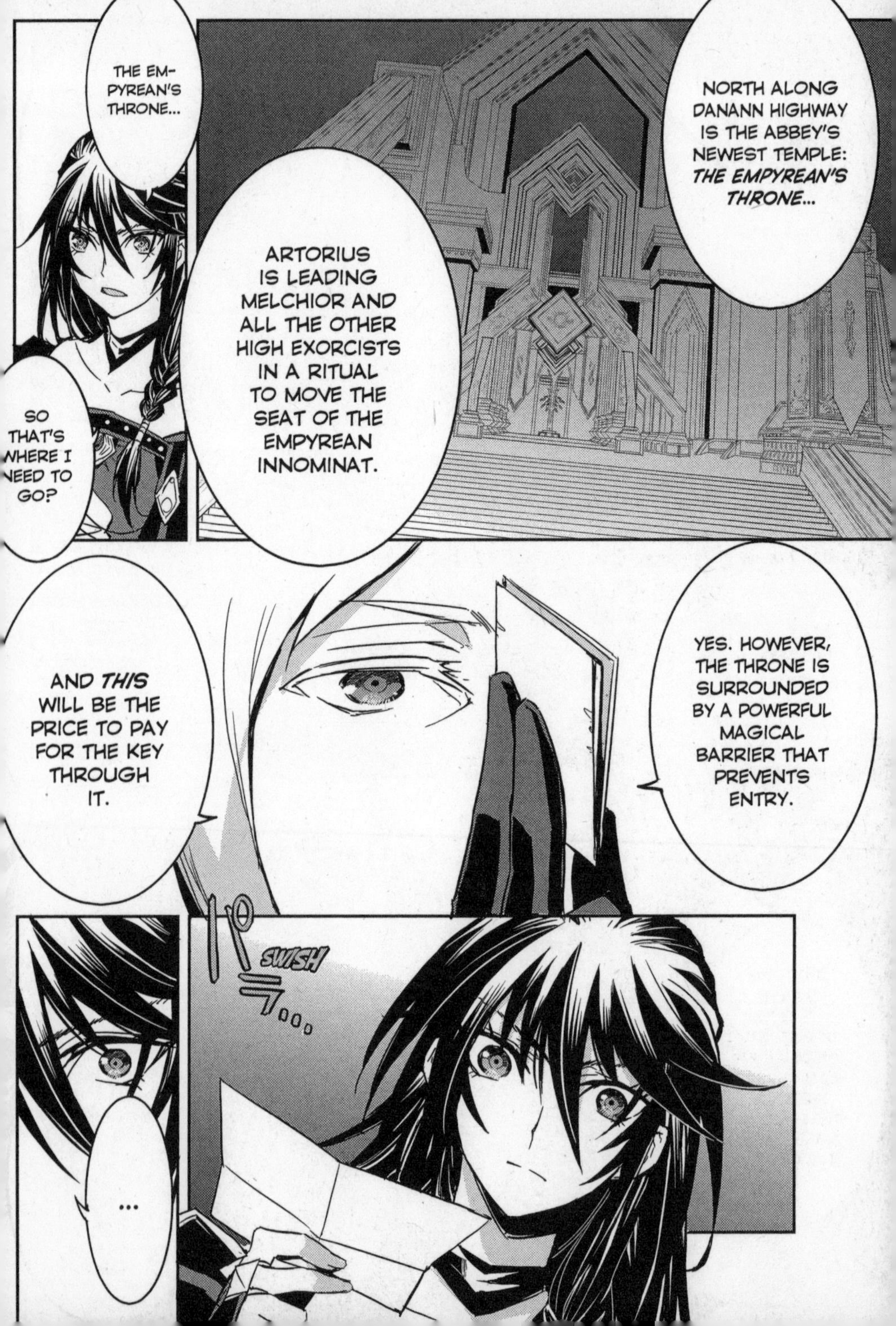
NORTH ALONG DANANN HIGHWAY IS THE ABBEY'S NEWEST TEMPLE: *THE EMPYREAN'S THRONE*...
ARTORIUS IS LEADING MELCHIOR AND ALL THE OTHER HIGH EXORCISTS IN A RITUAL TO MOVE THE SEAT OF THE EMPYREAN INNOMINAT.
THE EM-PYREAN'S THRONE...
SO THAT'S WHERE I NEED TO GO?
YES. HOWEVER, THE THRONE IS SURROUNDED BY A POWERFUL MAGICAL BARRIER THAT PREVENTS ENTRY.
AND *THIS* WILL BE THE PRICE TO PAY FOR THE KEY THROUGH IT.
SWISH
...

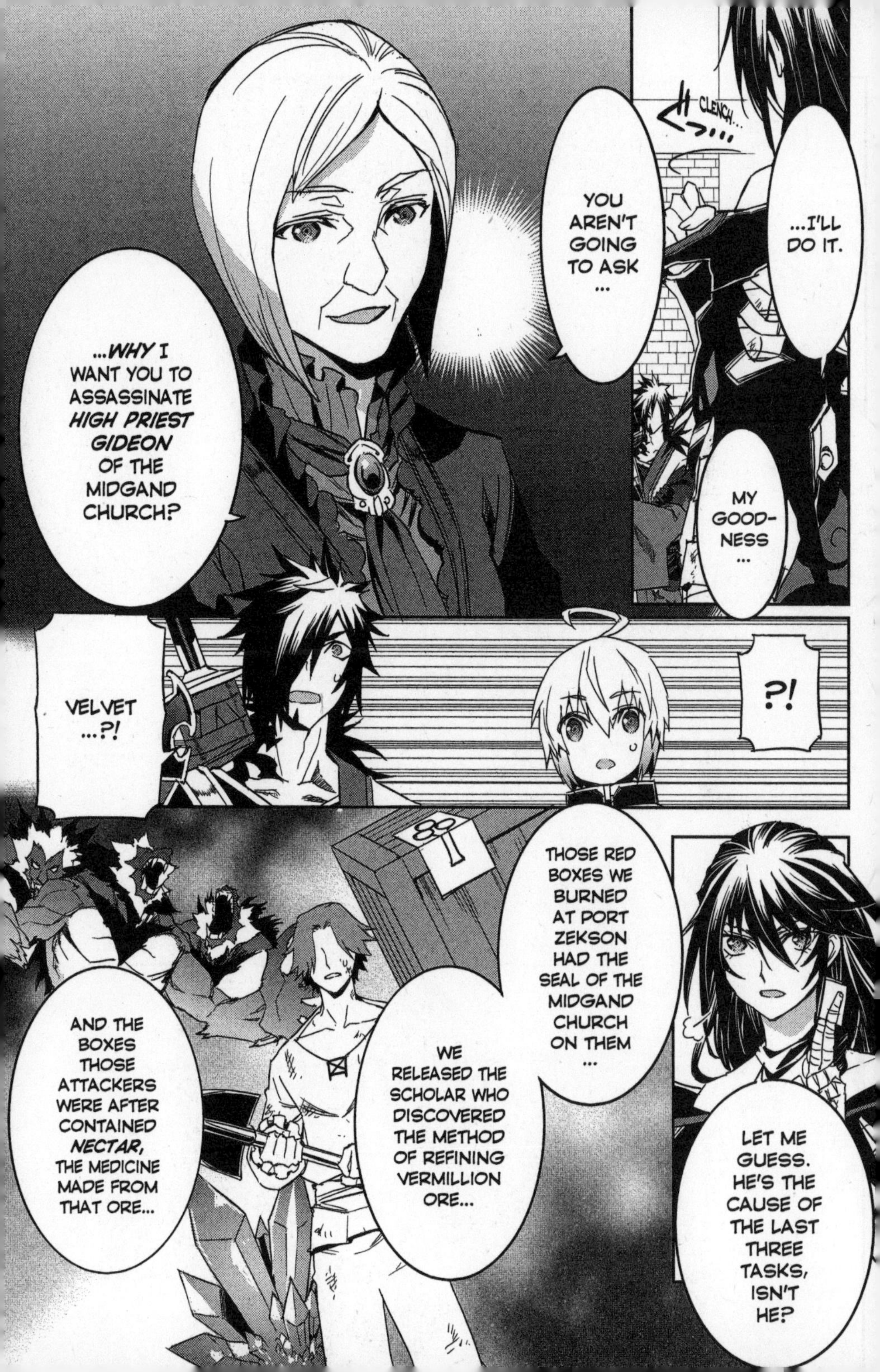
CLENCH...
...I'LL DO IT.
YOU AREN'T GOING TO ASK ...
MY GOOD-NESS ...
...*WHY* I WANT YOU TO ASSASSINATE *HIGH PRIEST GIDEON* OF THE MIDGAND CHURCH?
?!
VELVET ...?!
THOSE RED BOXES WE BURNED AT PORT ZEKSON HAD THE SEAL OF THE MIDGAND CHURCH ON THEM ...
WE RELEASED THE SCHOLAR WHO DISCOVERED THE METHOD OF REFINING VERMILLION ORE...
AND THE BOXES THOSE ATTACKERS WERE AFTER CONTAINED *NECTAR*, THE MEDICINE MADE FROM THAT ORE...
LET ME GUESS. HE'S THE CAUSE OF THE LAST THREE TASKS, ISN'T HE?

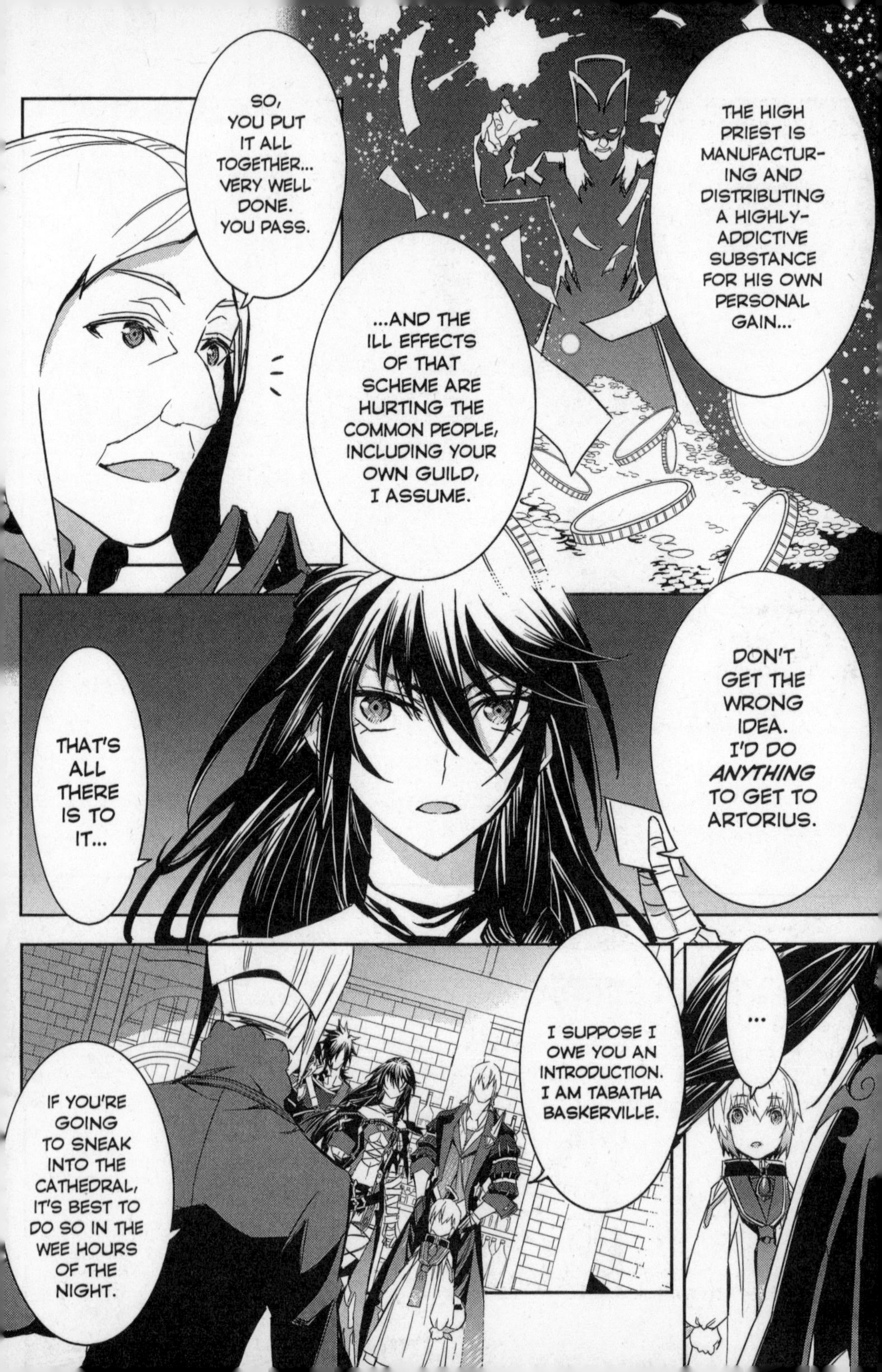
THE HIGH PRIEST IS MANUFACTURING AND DISTRIBUTING A HIGHLY-ADDICTIVE SUBSTANCE FOR HIS OWN PERSONAL GAIN...
...AND THE ILL EFFECTS OF THAT SCHEME ARE HURTING THE COMMON PEOPLE, INCLUDING YOUR OWN GUILD, I ASSUME.
SO, YOU PUT IT ALL TOGETHER... VERY WELL DONE. YOU PASS.
DON'T GET THE WRONG IDEA. I'D DO *ANYTHING* TO GET TO ARTORIUS.
THAT'S ALL THERE IS TO IT...
...
I SUPPOSE I OWE YOU AN INTRODUCTION. I AM TABATHA BASKERVILLE.
IF YOU'RE GOING TO SNEAK INTO THE CATHEDRAL, IT'S BEST TO DO SO IN THE WEE HOURS OF THE NIGHT.

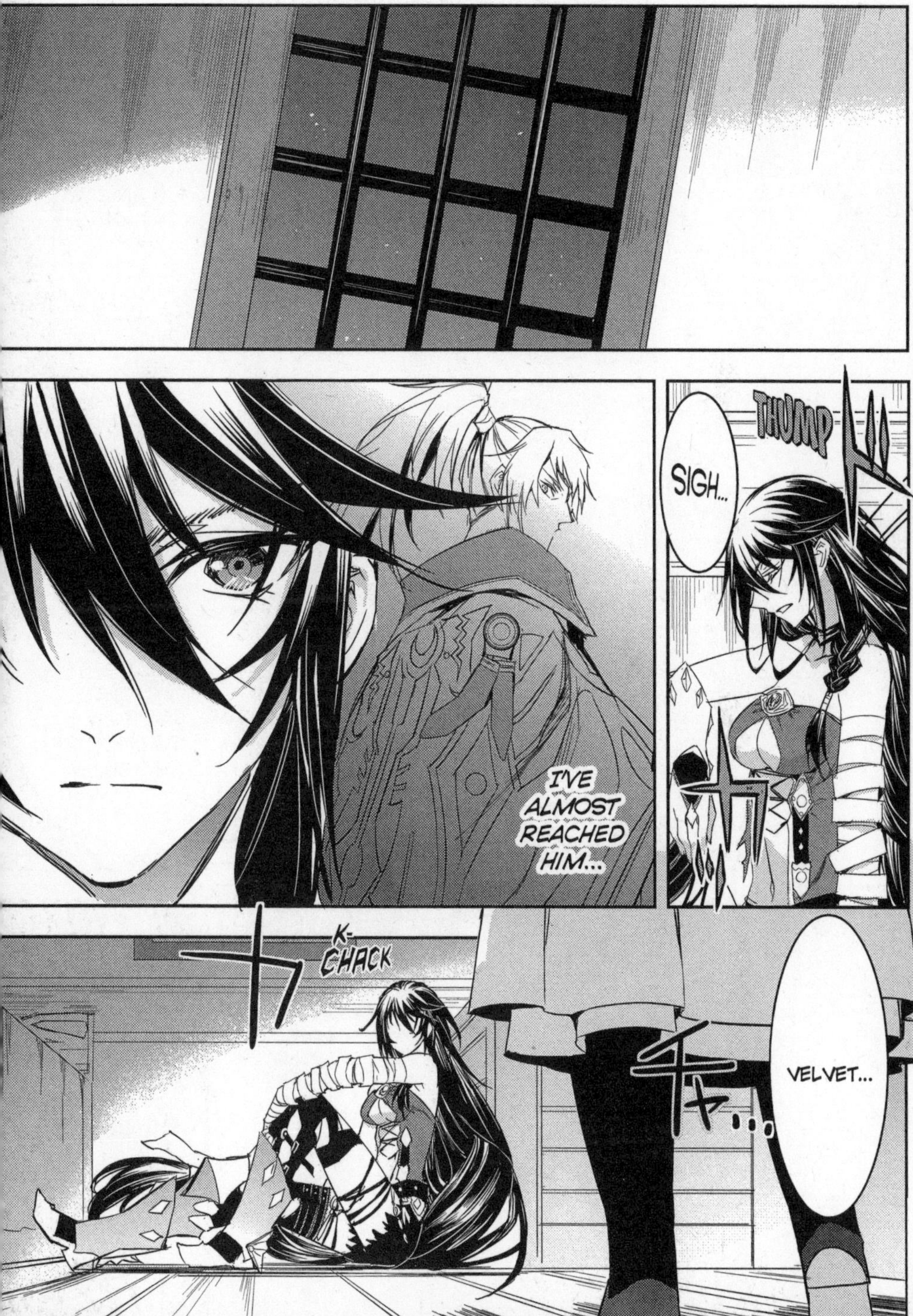
THUMP
SIGH...
I'VE ALMOST REACHED HIM...
VELVET...
K-CHACK

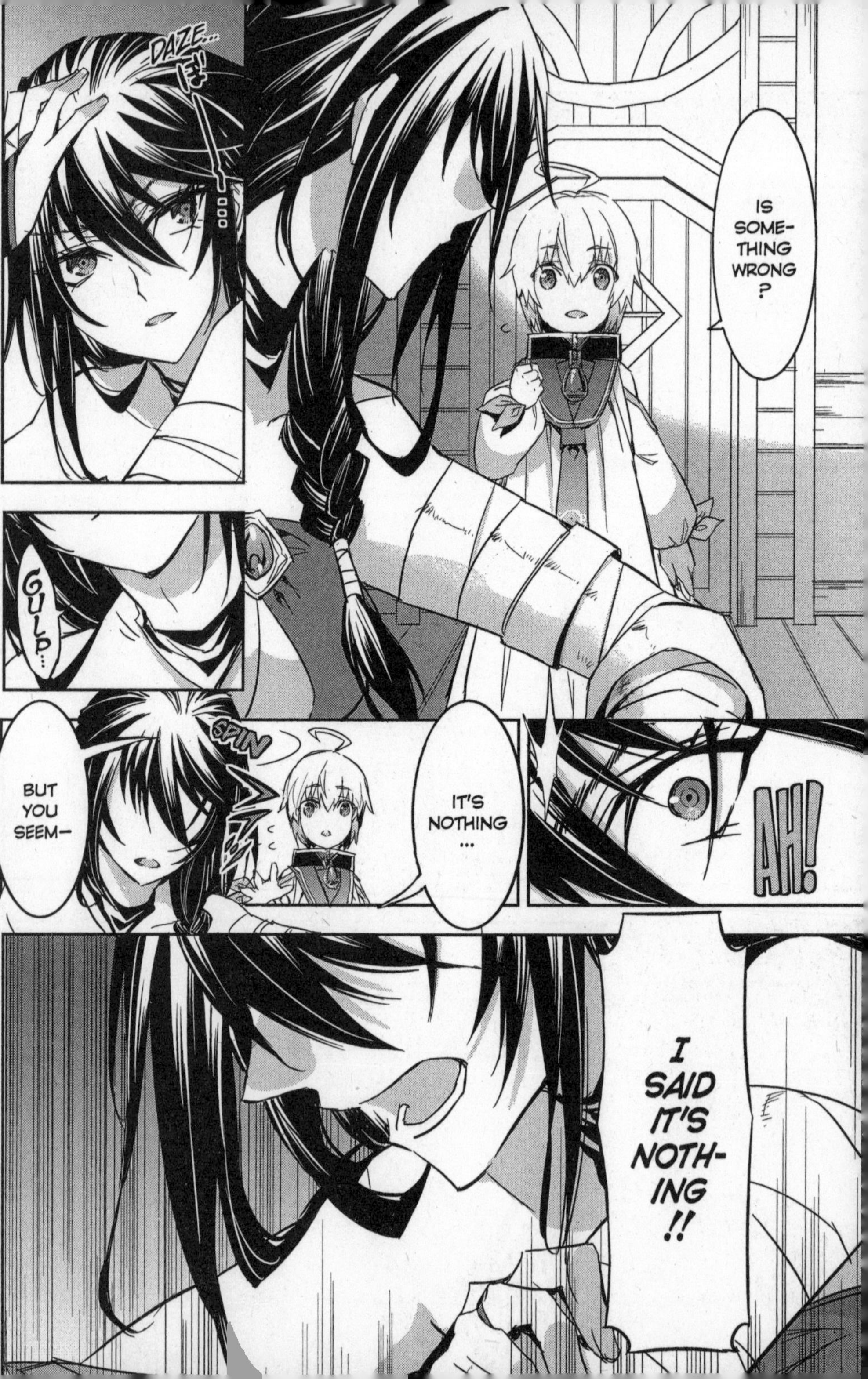
IS SOME-THING WRONG?
DAZE...
GULP...
AH!
IT'S NOTHING...
SPIN
BUT YOU SEEM—
I SAID IT'S NOTH-ING!!

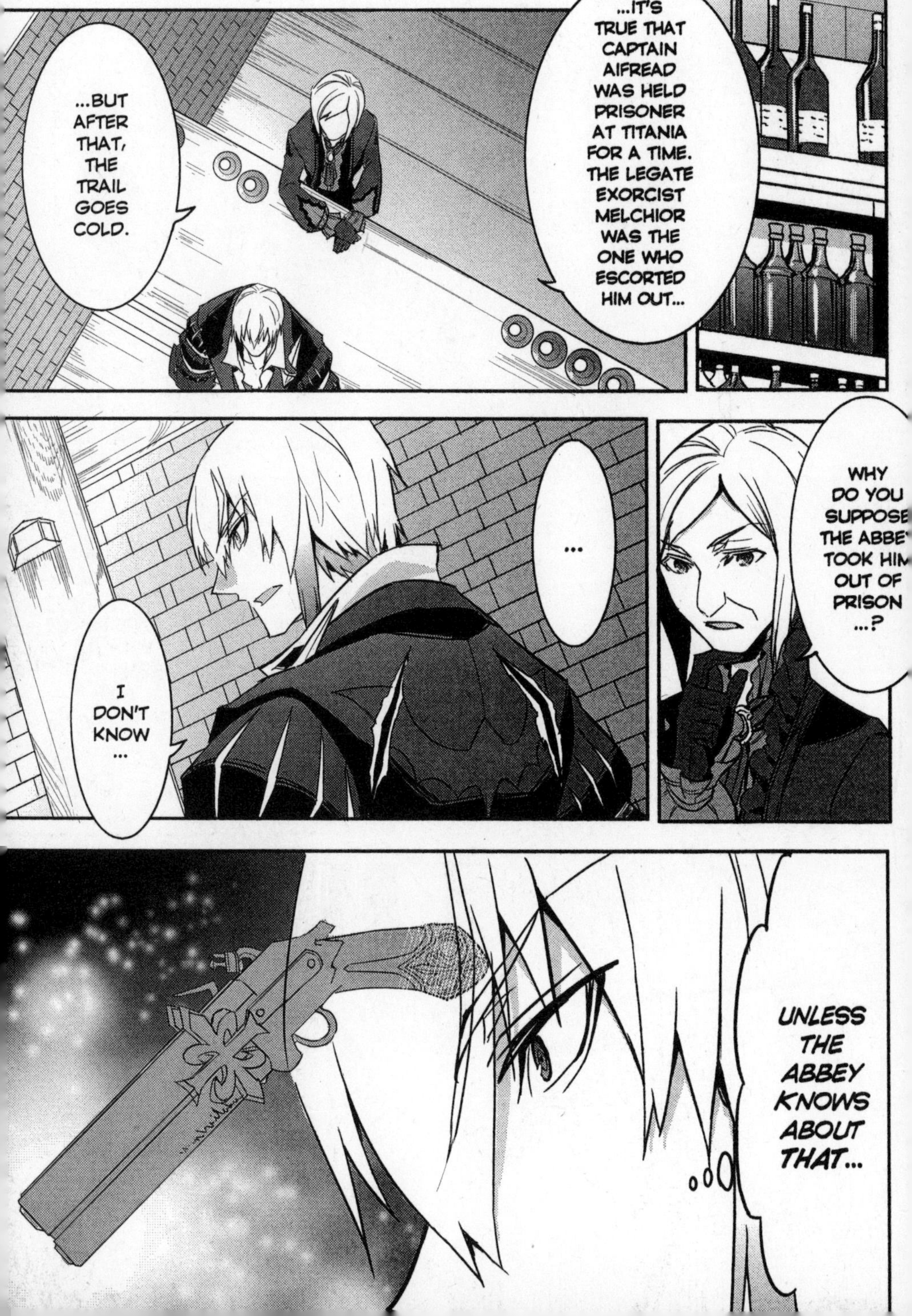

...IT'S TRUE THAT CAPTAIN AIFREAD WAS HELD PRISONER AT TITANIA FOR A TIME. THE LEGATE EXORCIST MELCHIOR WAS THE ONE WHO ESCORTED HIM OUT...
...BUT AFTER THAT, THE TRAIL GOES COLD.
WHY DO YOU SUPPOSE THE ABBEY TOOK HIM OUT OF PRISON ...?
...
I DON'T KNOW ...
UNLESS THE ABBEY KNOWS ABOUT THAT...

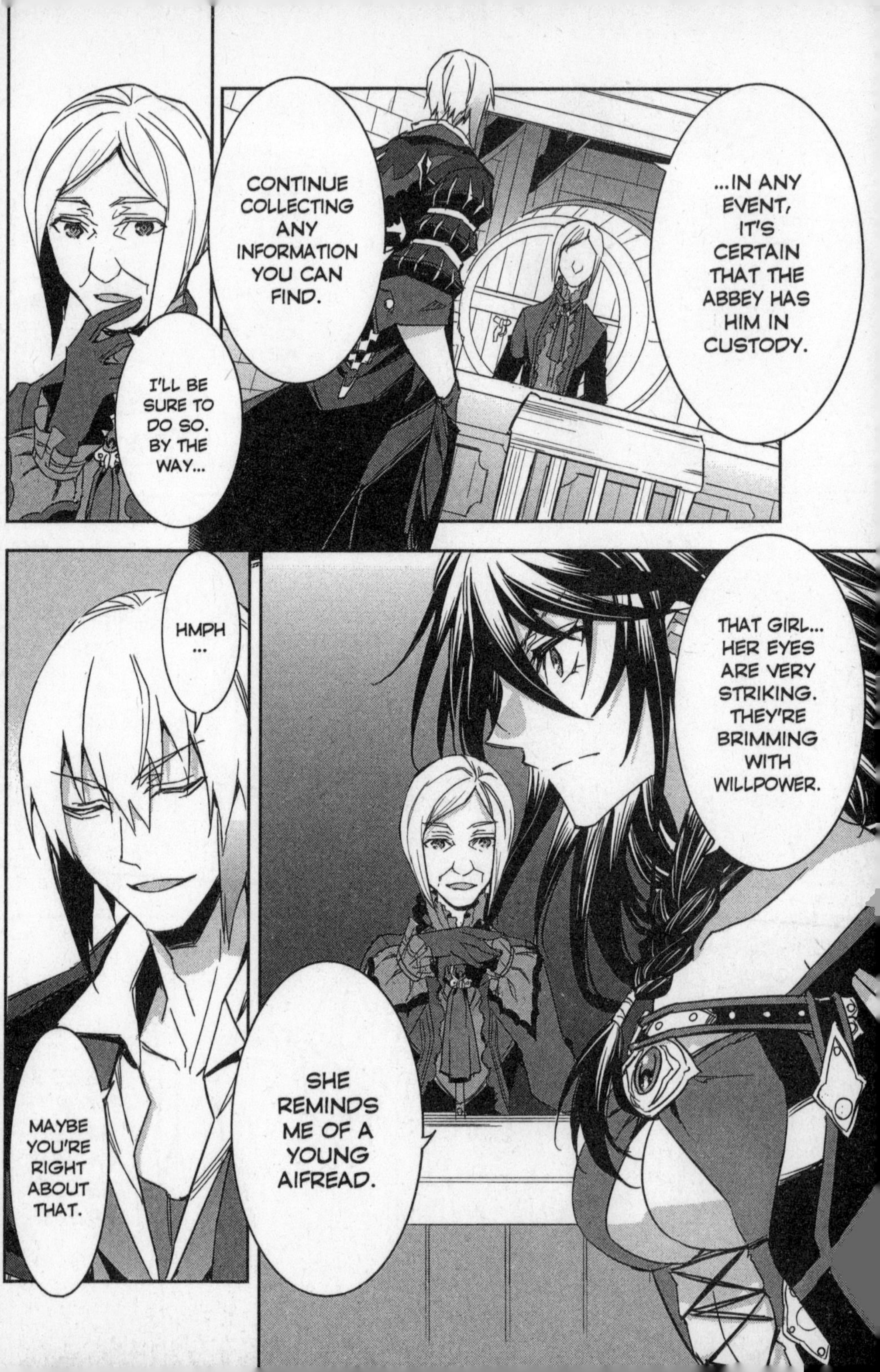
...IN ANY EVENT, IT'S CERTAIN THAT THE ABBEY HAS HIM IN CUSTODY.
CONTINUE COLLECTING ANY INFORMATION YOU CAN FIND.
I'LL BE SURE TO DO SO. BY THE WAY...
THAT GIRL... HER EYES ARE VERY STRIKING. THEY'RE BRIMMING WITH WILLPOWER.
SHE REMINDS ME OF A YOUNG AIFREAD.
HMPH ...
MAYBE YOU'RE RIGHT ABOUT THAT.

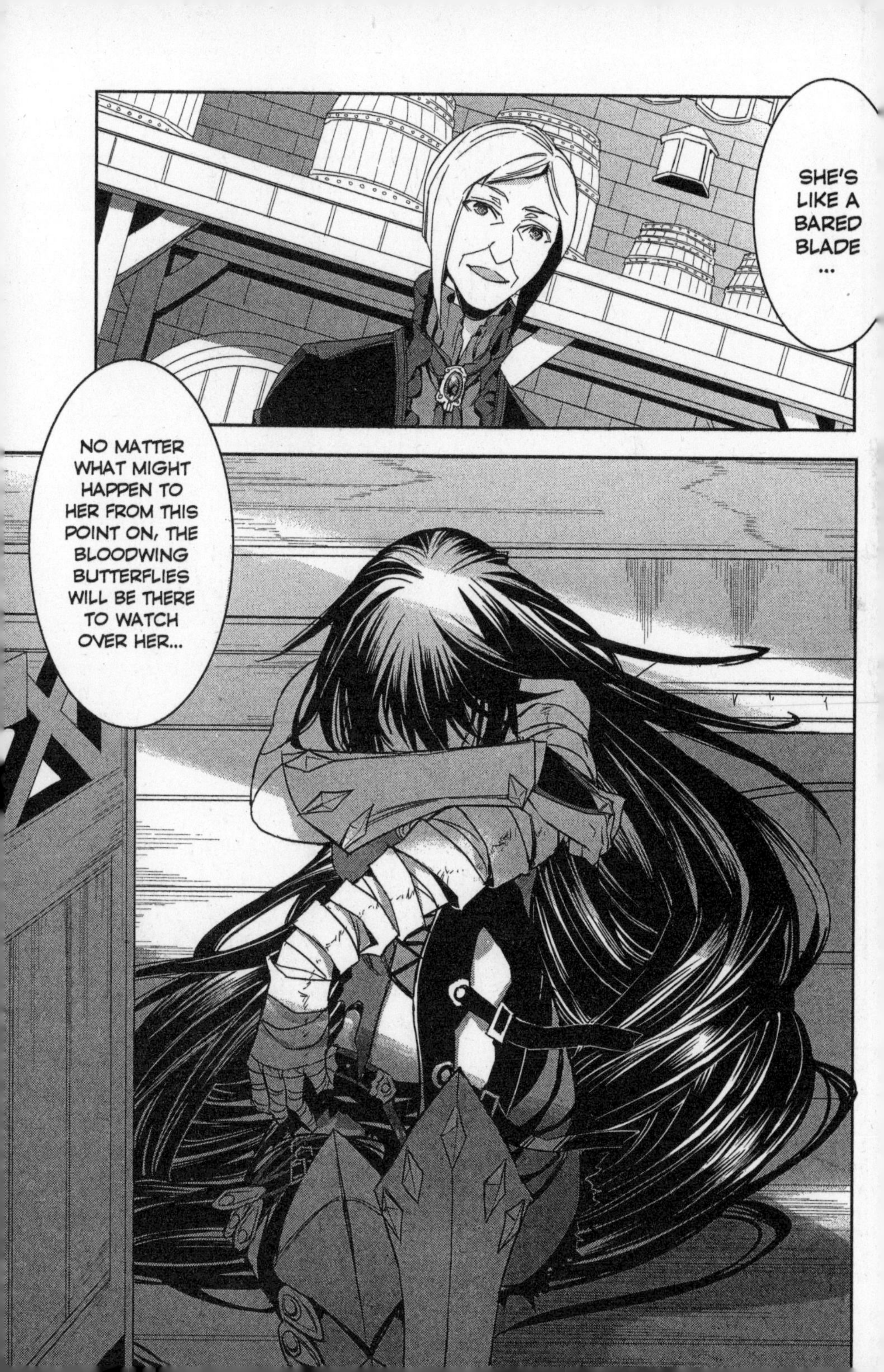
SHE'S LIKE A BARED BLADE ...
NO MATTER WHAT MIGHT HAPPEN TO HER FROM THIS POINT ON, THE BLOODWING BUTTERFLIES WILL BE THERE TO WATCH OVER HER...

He Really Seems to Enjoy It

SO THIS IS MABO CURRY!
IT'S SO GOOD!!
THIS IS RISOTTO AND MEAT PIE?!
IT'S SO GOOD!!
IT'S SO GOOD!!!
NEXT YOU'LL WANT TO TRY THESE SPIRITS...
NO, YOU'LL WANT TO TRY THIS RED WINE INSTEAD.
STOP THAT.

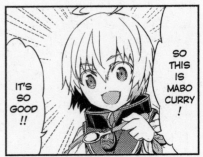

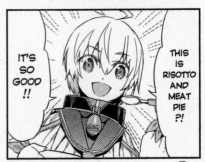

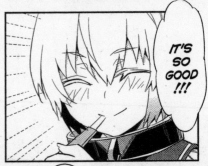

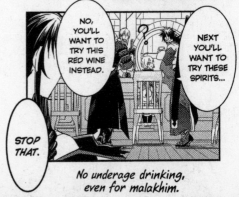

No underage drinking, even for malakhim.

– chapter 9 –

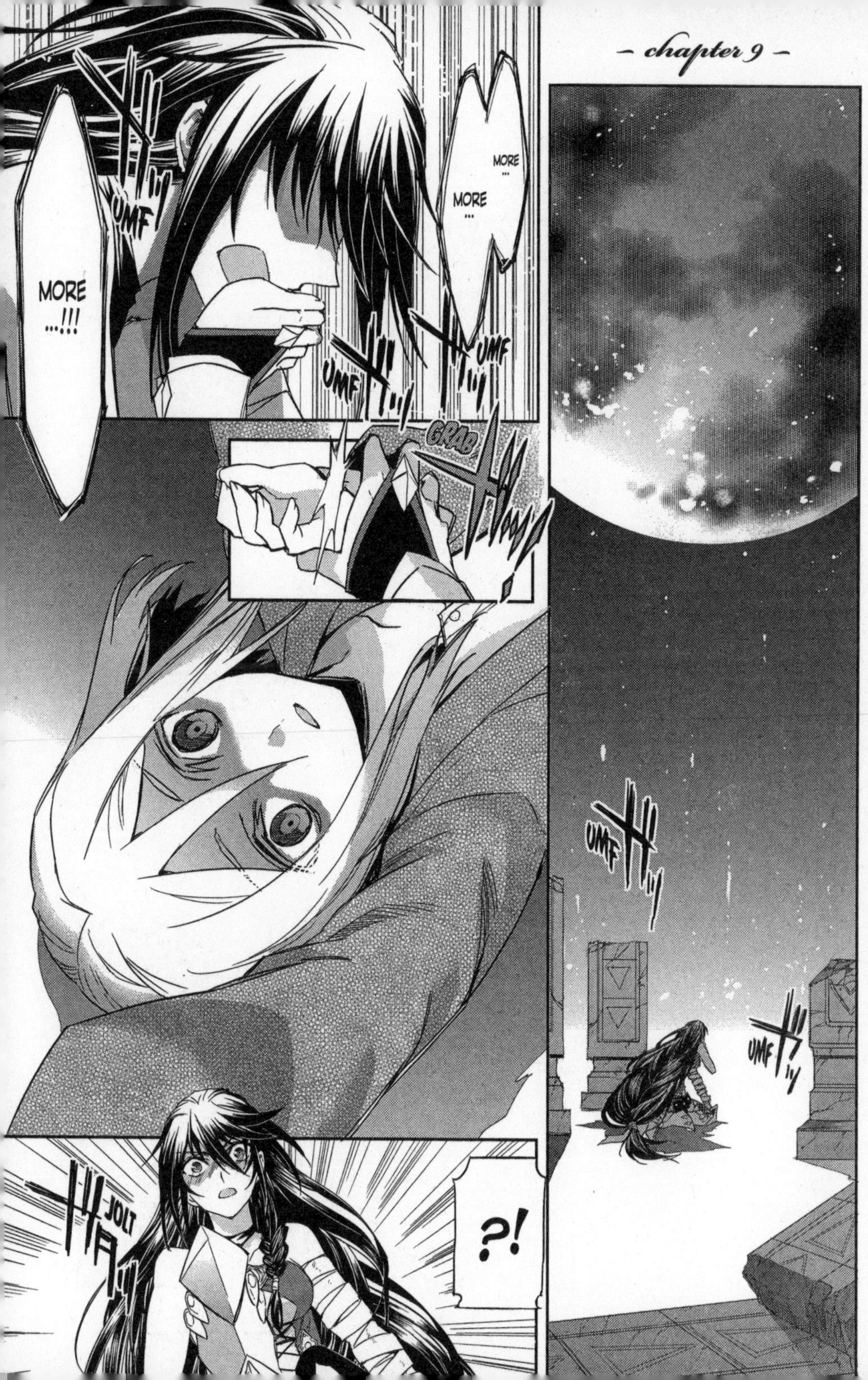
UMF
UMF
MORE ...
MORE ...
UMF
UMF
UMF
MORE ...!!!
GRAB
?!
JOLT

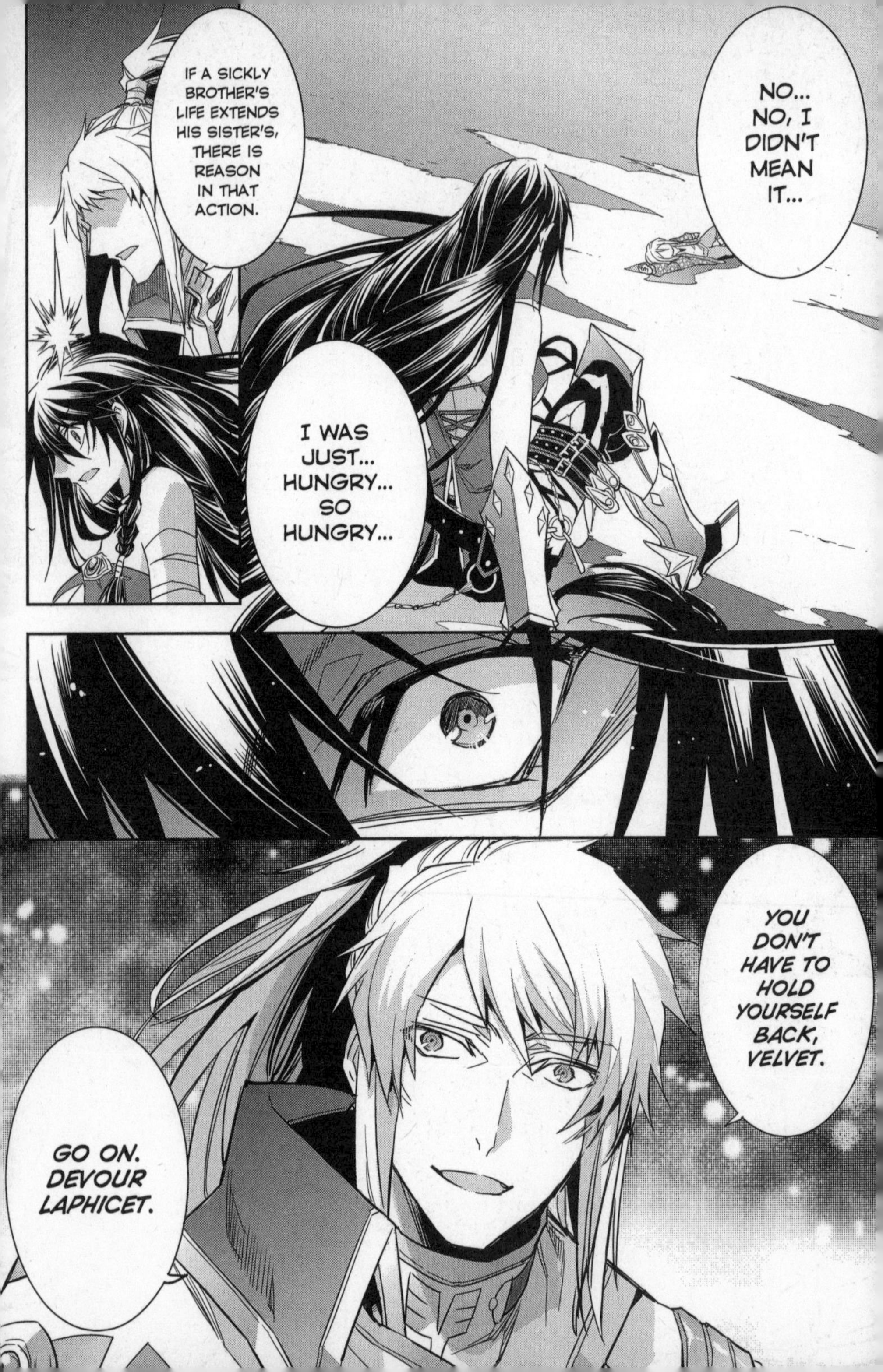
NO... NO, I DIDN'T MEAN IT...
I WAS JUST... HUNGRY... SO HUNGRY...
IF A SICKLY BROTHER'S LIFE EXTENDS HIS SISTER'S, THERE IS REASON IN THAT ACTION.
YOU DON'T HAVE TO HOLD YOURSELF BACK, VELVET.
GO ON. DEVOUR LAPHICET.

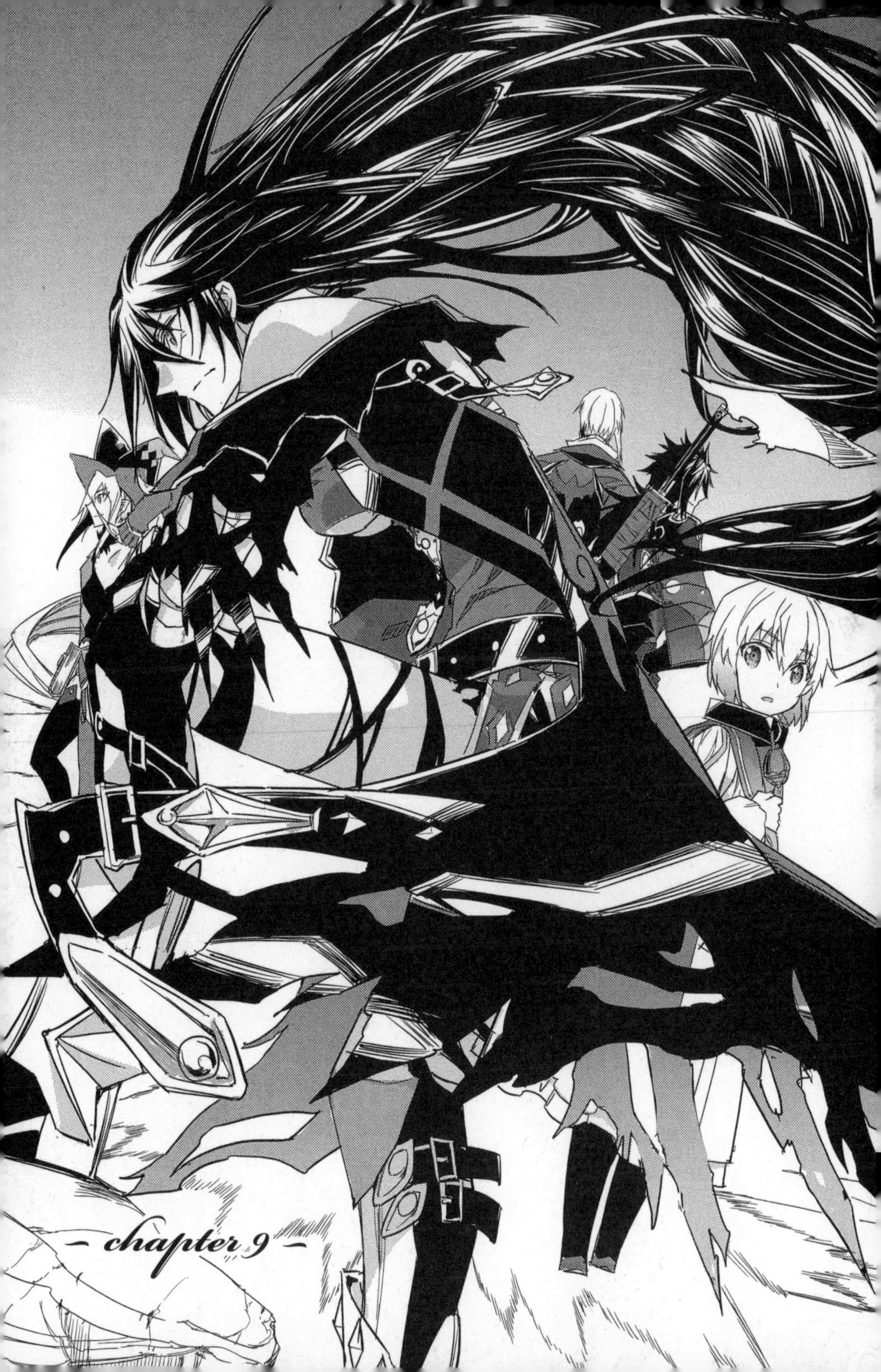
-chapter 9-

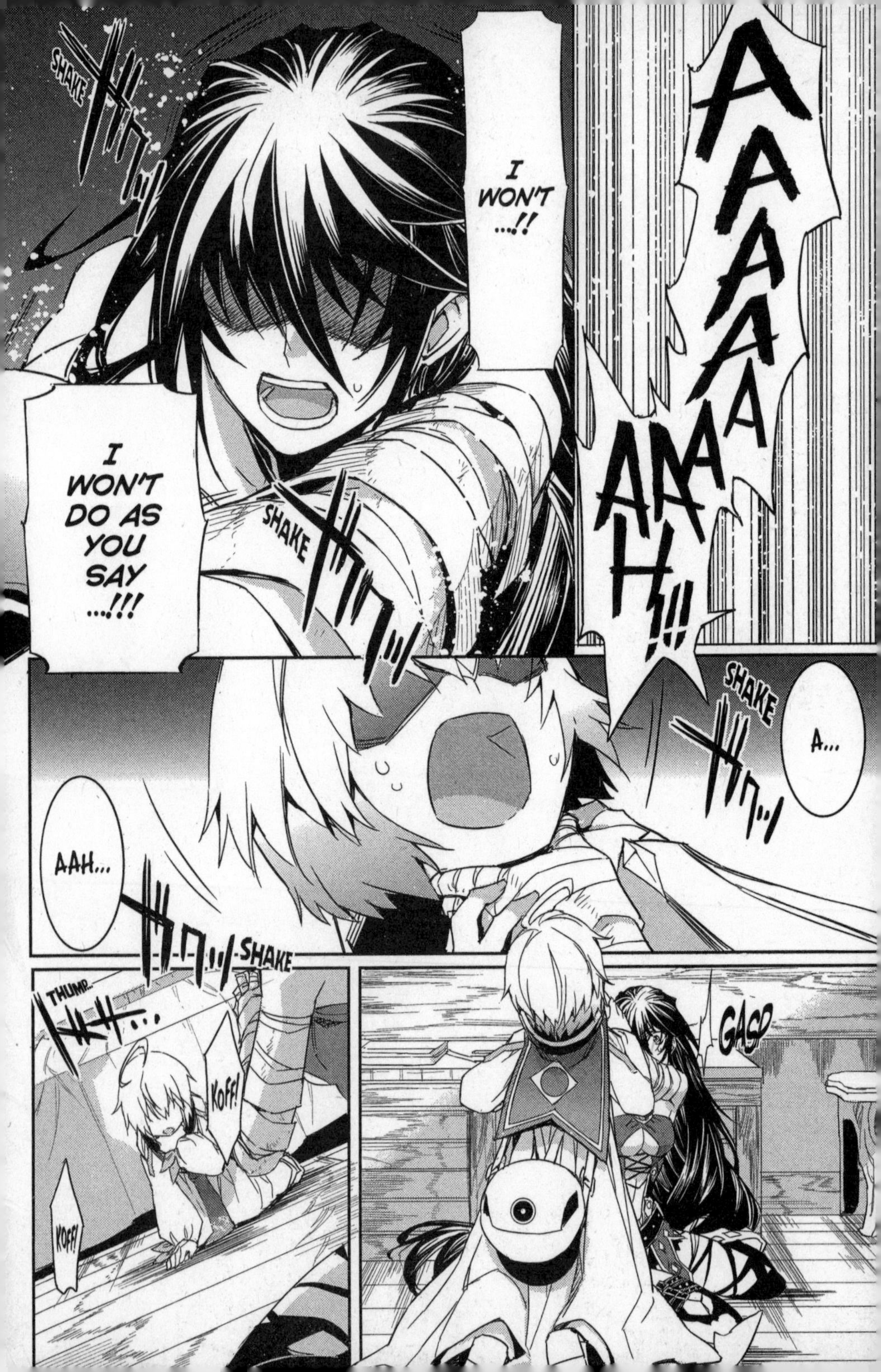
AAAAAAAAH!!!
I WON'T ...!!
SHAKE
I WON'T DO AS YOU SAY ...!!!
SHAKE
SHAKE
A...
AAH...
SHAKE
GASP
THUMP...
KOFF!
KOFF!

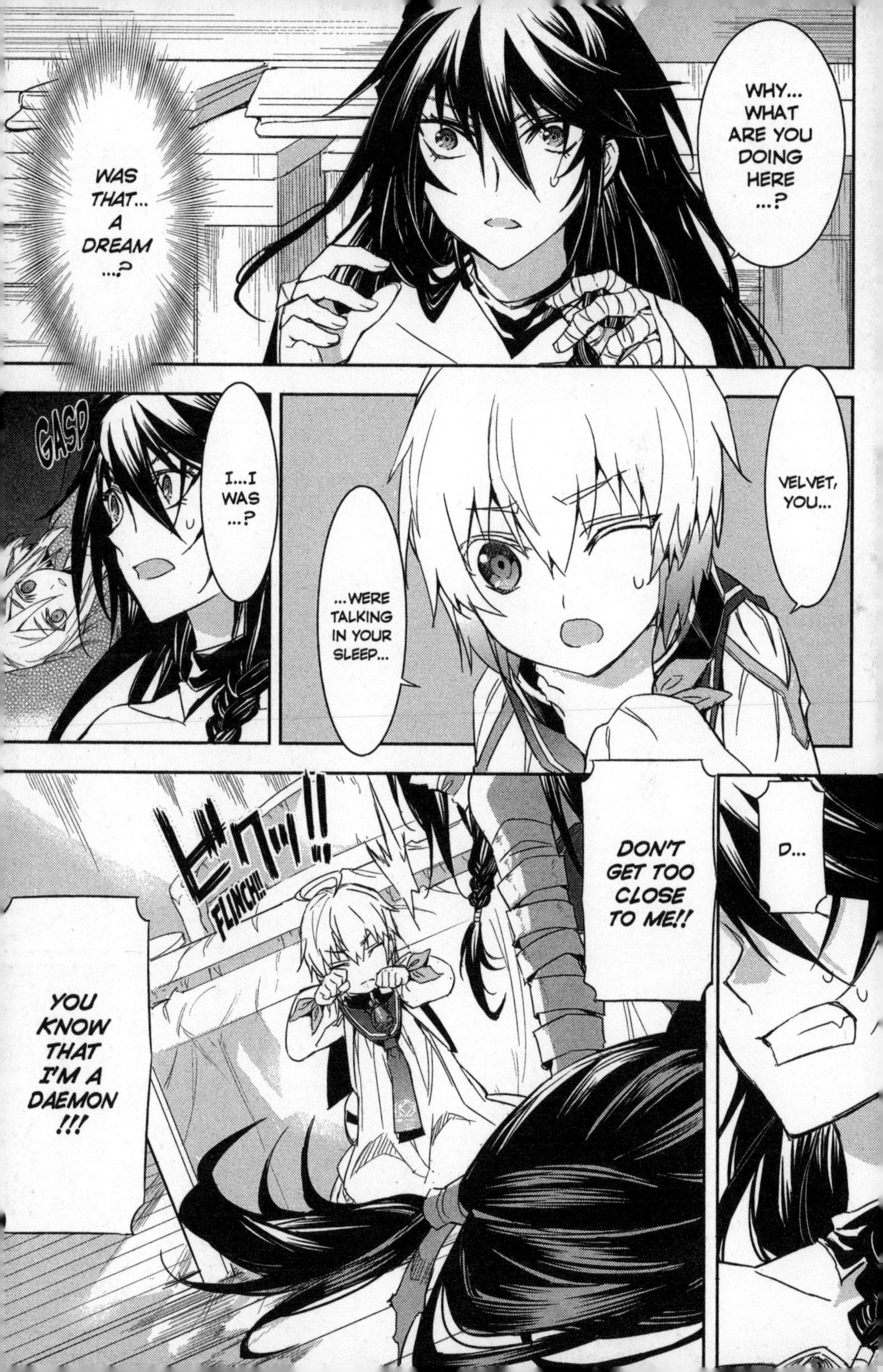
WHY... WHAT ARE YOU DOING HERE ...?
WAS THAT... A DREAM ...?
VELVET, YOU...
...WERE TALKING IN YOUR SLEEP...
GASP
I...I WAS ...?
D...
DON'T GET TOO CLOSE TO ME!!
ビクッ!!
FLINCH!!
YOU KNOW THAT I'M A DAEMON !!!

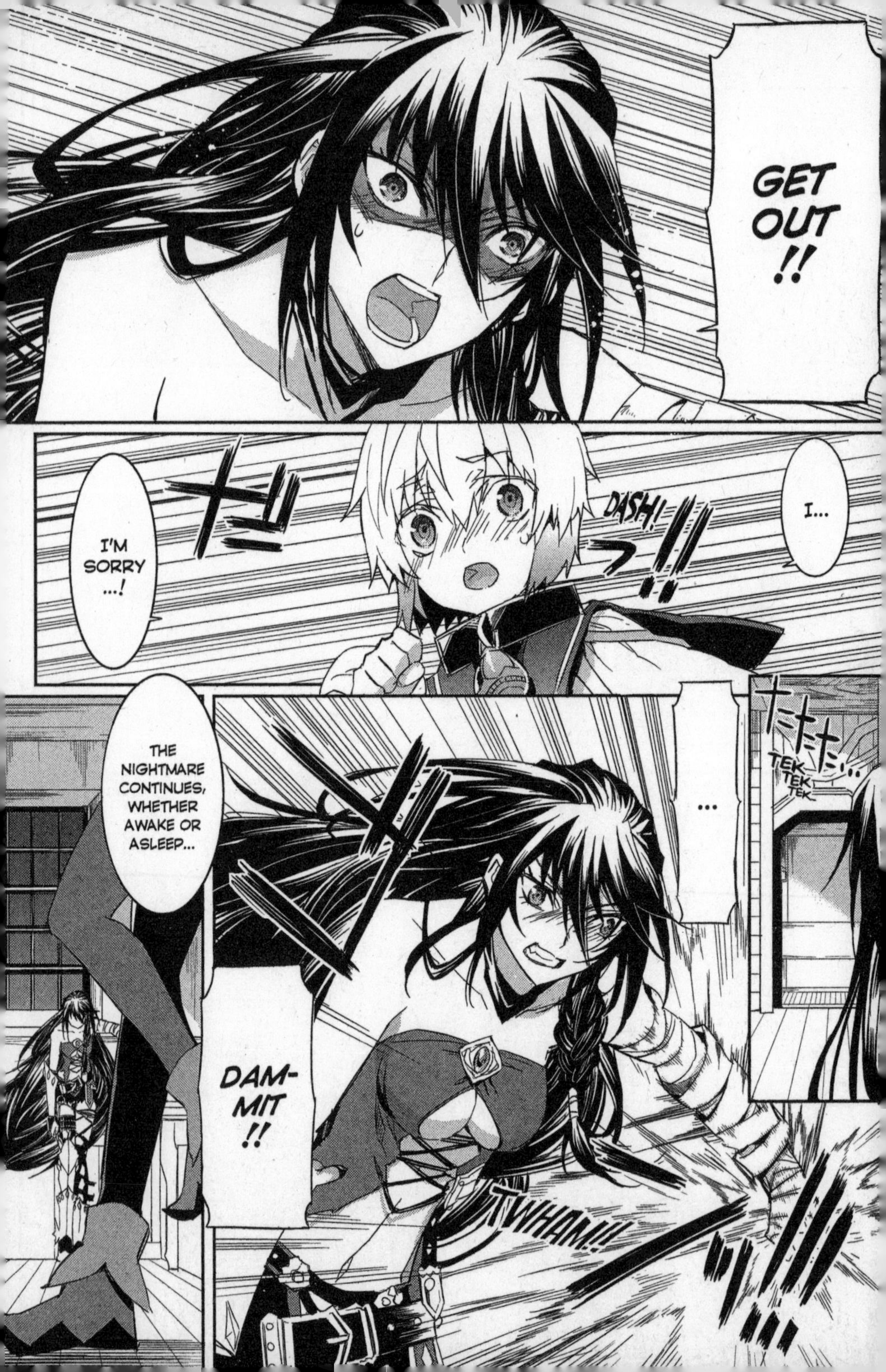
GET OUT!!
I...
DASH!
I'M SORRY...!
TEK TEK TEK
...
DAM-MIT!!
TWHAM!!!
THE NIGHTMARE CONTINUES, WHETHER AWAKE OR ASLEEP...

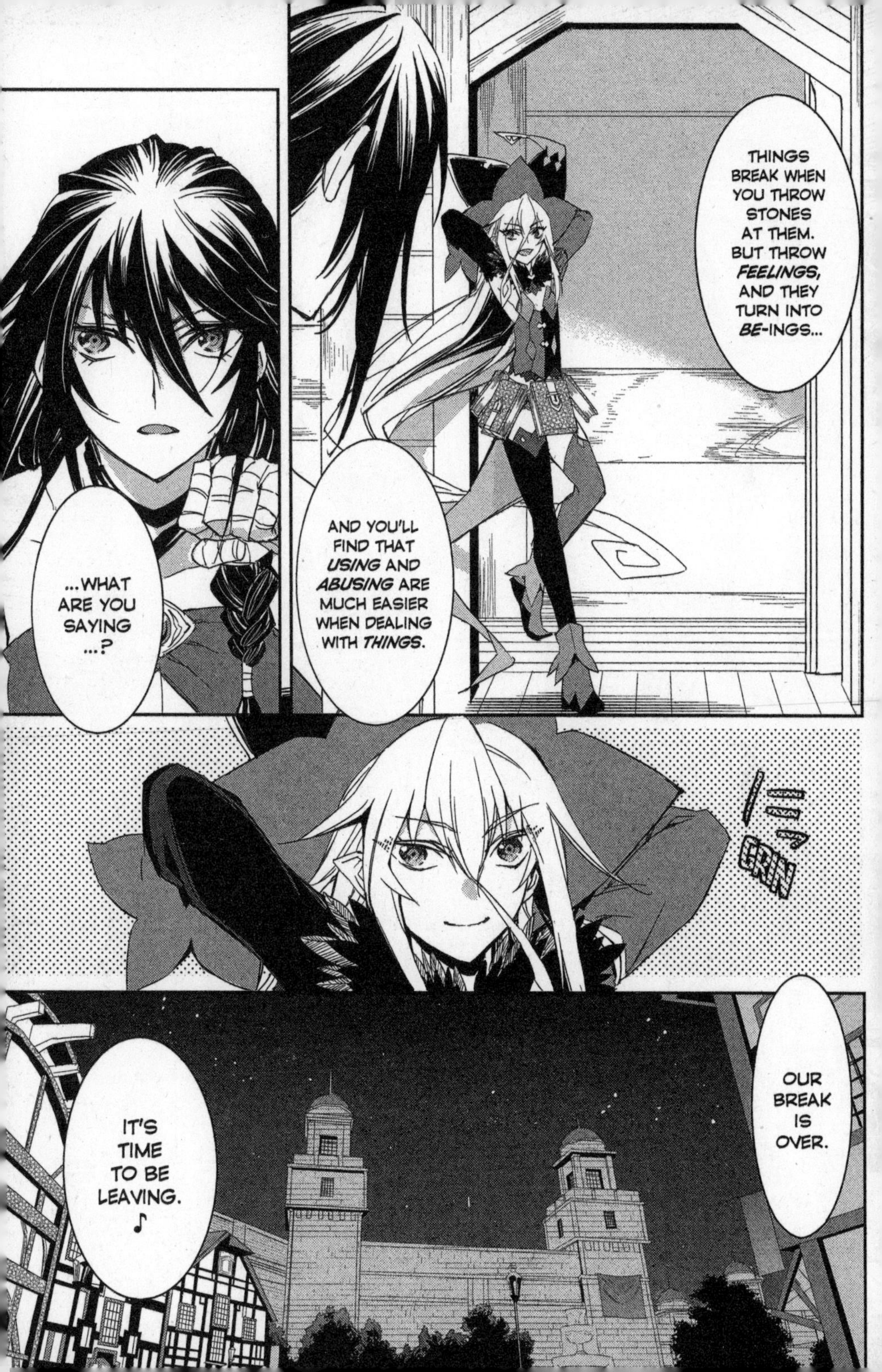
THINGS BREAK WHEN YOU THROW STONES AT THEM. BUT THROW *FEELINGS,* AND THEY TURN INTO *BE*-INGS...
AND YOU'LL FIND THAT *USING* AND *ABUSING* ARE MUCH EASIER WHEN DEALING WITH *THINGS.*
...WHAT ARE YOU SAYING ...?
GRIN
OUR BREAK IS OVER.
IT'S TIME TO BE LEAVING. ♪

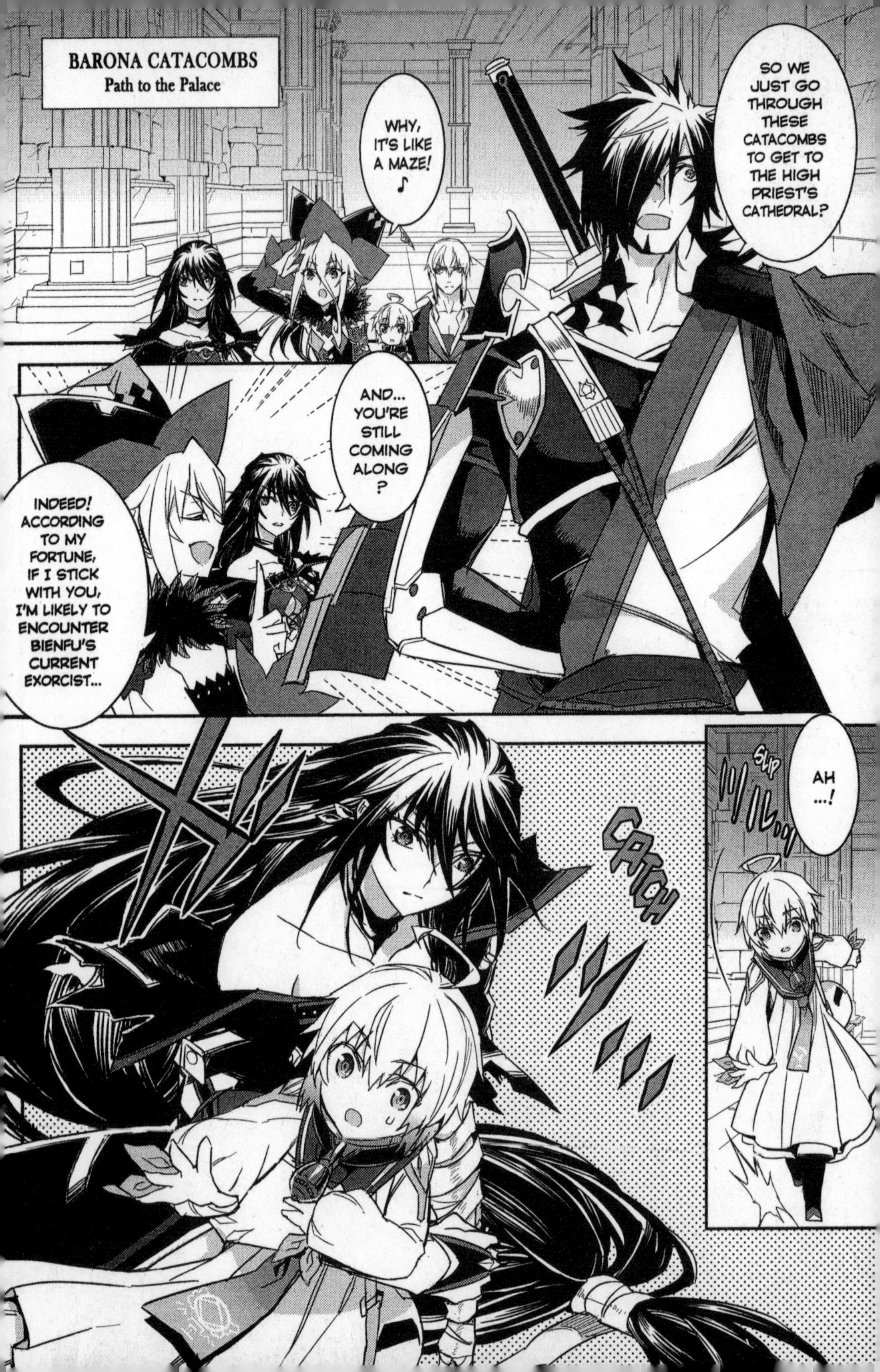
SO WE JUST GO THROUGH THESE CATACOMBS TO GET TO THE HIGH PRIEST'S CATHEDRAL?
WHY, IT'S LIKE A MAZE! ♪
BARONA CATACOMBS
Path to the Palace
AND... YOU'RE STILL COMING ALONG?
INDEED! ACCORDING TO MY FORTUNE, IF I STICK WITH YOU, I'M LIKELY TO ENCOUNTER BIENFU'S CURRENT EXORCIST...
AH ...!
SLIP
CATCH

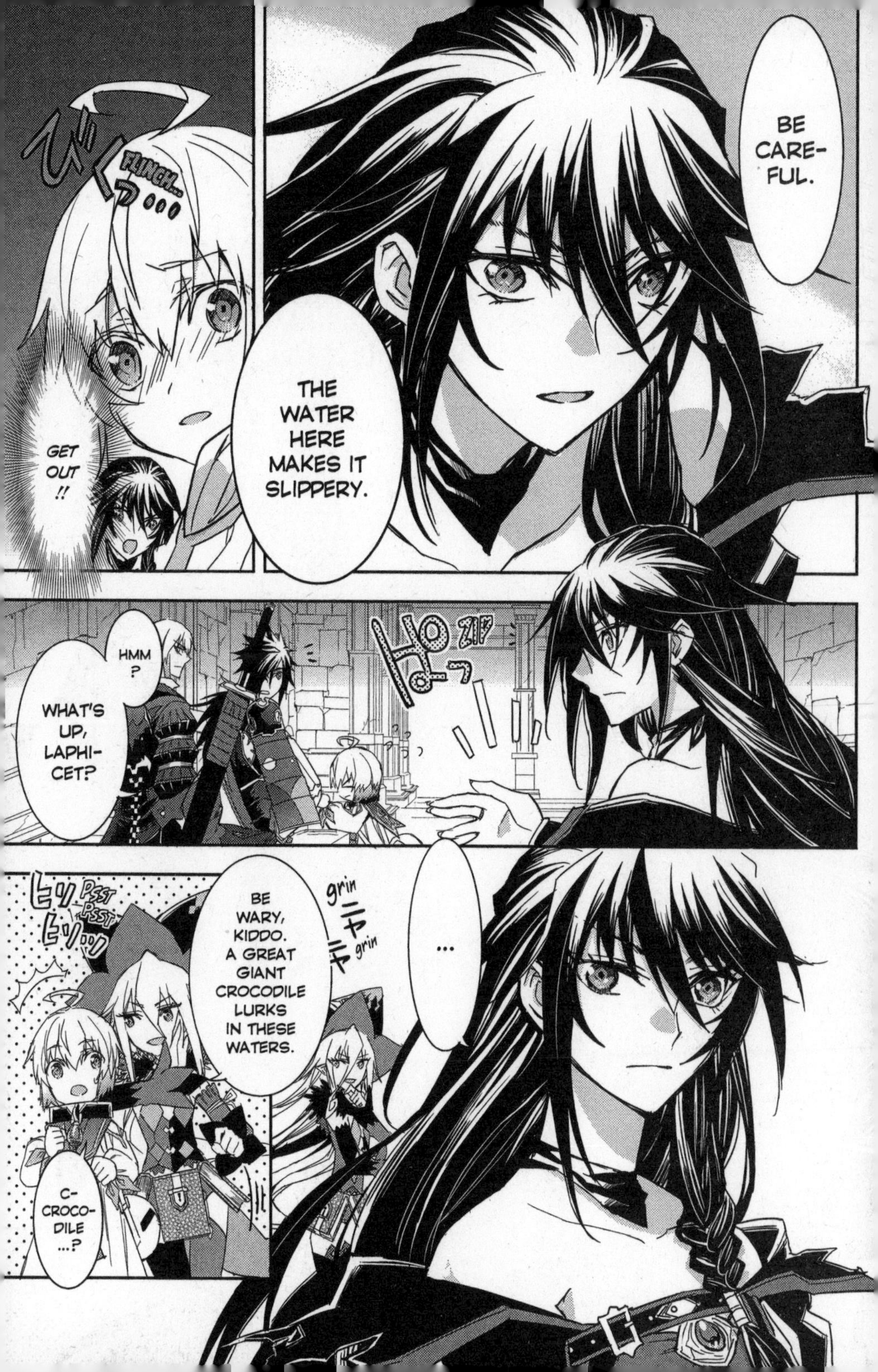
BE CARE-FUL.
THE WATER HERE MAKES IT SLIPPERY.
FLINCH...
GET OUT!!
ZIP
HMM?
WHAT'S UP, LAPHICET?
...
grin grin
BE WARY, KIDDO. A GREAT GIANT CROCODILE LURKS IN THESE WATERS.
PSST PSST
C-CROCODILE...?

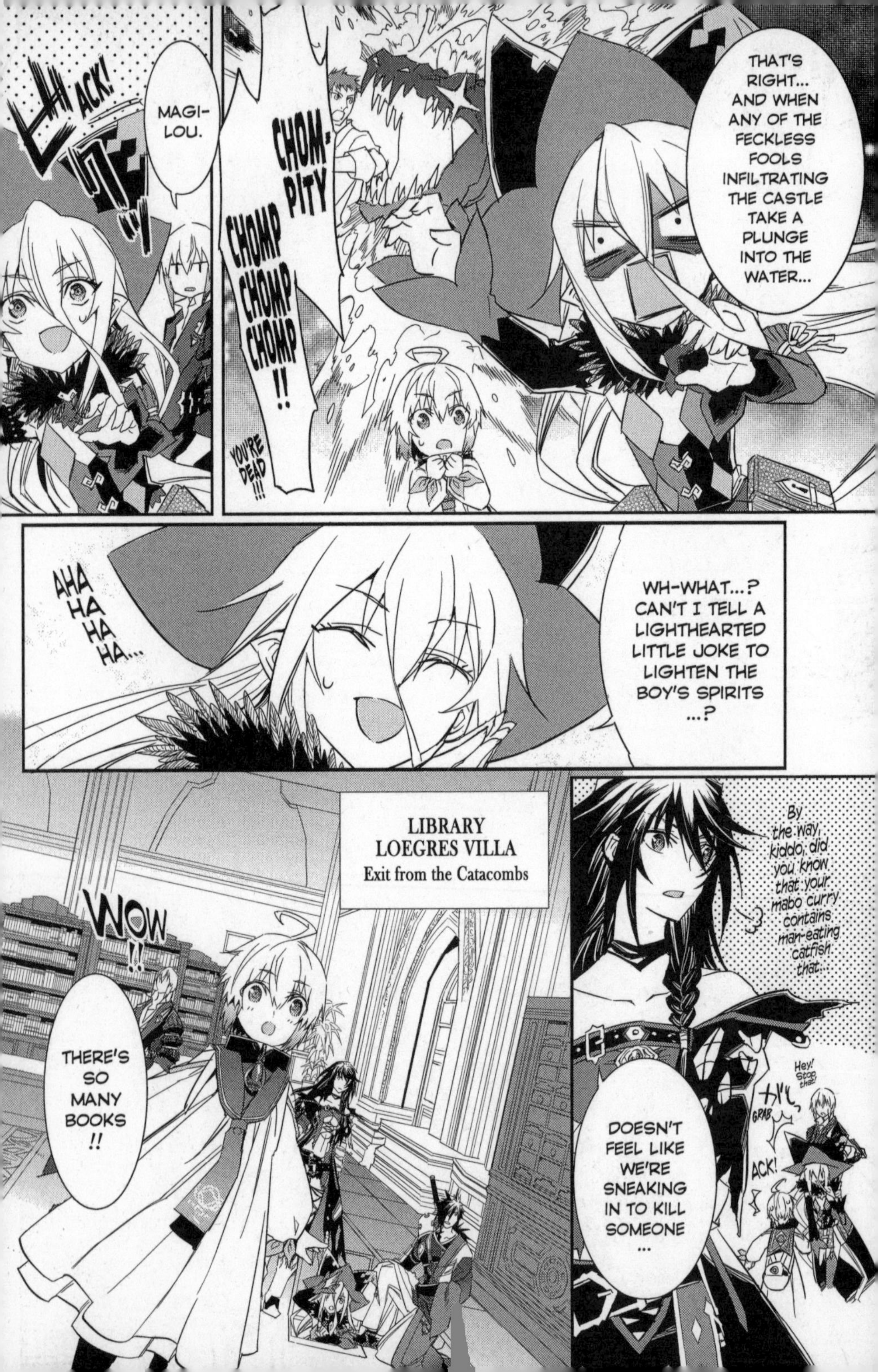
THAT'S RIGHT... AND WHEN ANY OF THE FECKLESS FOOLS INFILTRATING THE CASTLE TAKE A PLUNGE INTO THE WATER...
CHOMPITY
CHOMP CHOMP CHOMP!!
YOU'RE DEAD!!!
WHACK!
MAGI-LOU.
WH-WHAT...? CAN'T I TELL A LIGHTHEARTED LITTLE JOKE TO LIGHTEN THE BOY'S SPIRITS...?
AHA HA HA HA...
By the way, kiddo, did you know that your mabo curry contains man-eating catfish that...
DOESN'T FEEL LIKE WE'RE SNEAKING IN TO KILL SOMEONE...
Hey! Stop that.
GRAB
ACK!
LIBRARY
LOEGRES VILLA
Exit from the Catacombs
WOW!!
THERE'S SO MANY BOOKS!!

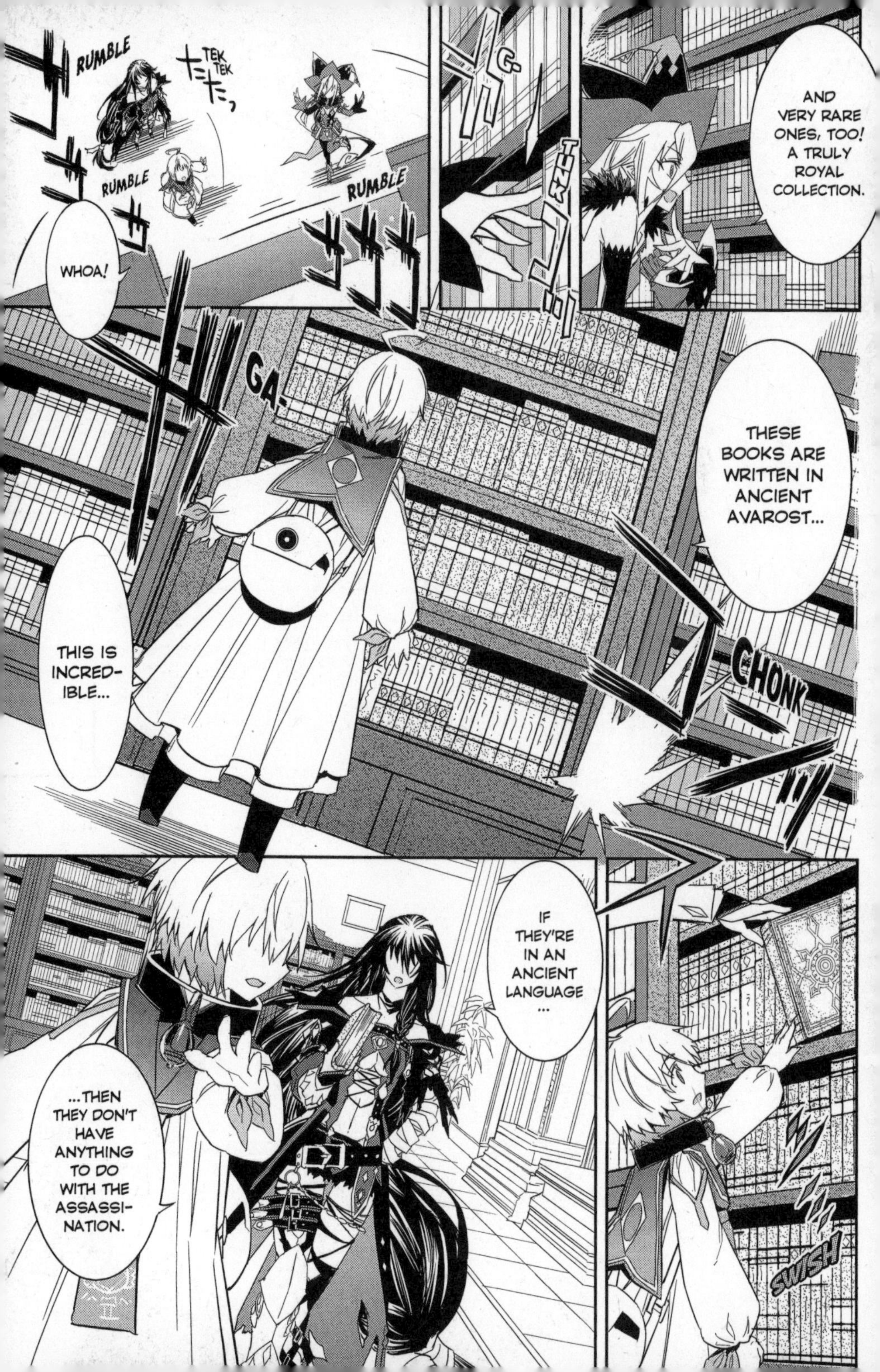
G-
TUNK
AND VERY RARE ONES, TOO! A TRULY ROYAL COLLECTION.
RUMBLE
TEK TEK
RUMBLE
RUMBLE
WHOA!
GA
THESE BOOKS ARE WRITTEN IN ANCIENT AVAROST...
CHONK
THIS IS INCREDIBLE...
SWISH
IF THEY'RE IN AN ANCIENT LANGUAGE ...
...THEN THEY DON'T HAVE ANYTHING TO DO WITH THE ASSASSINATION.

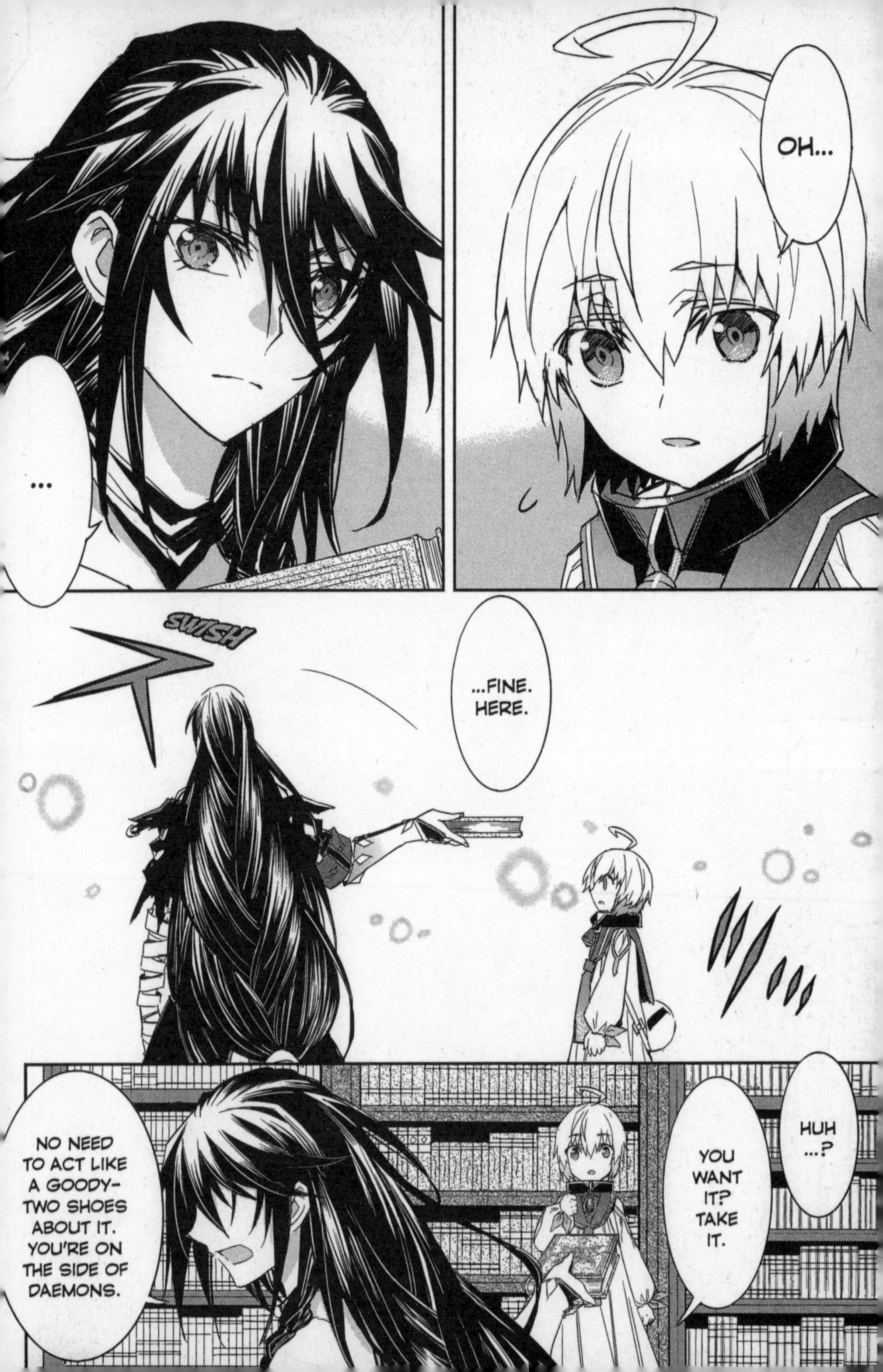
OH...
...
...FINE. HERE.
SWISH
HUH ...?
YOU WANT IT? TAKE IT.
NO NEED TO ACT LIKE A GOODY-TWO SHOES ABOUT IT. YOU'RE ON THE SIDE OF DAEMONS.

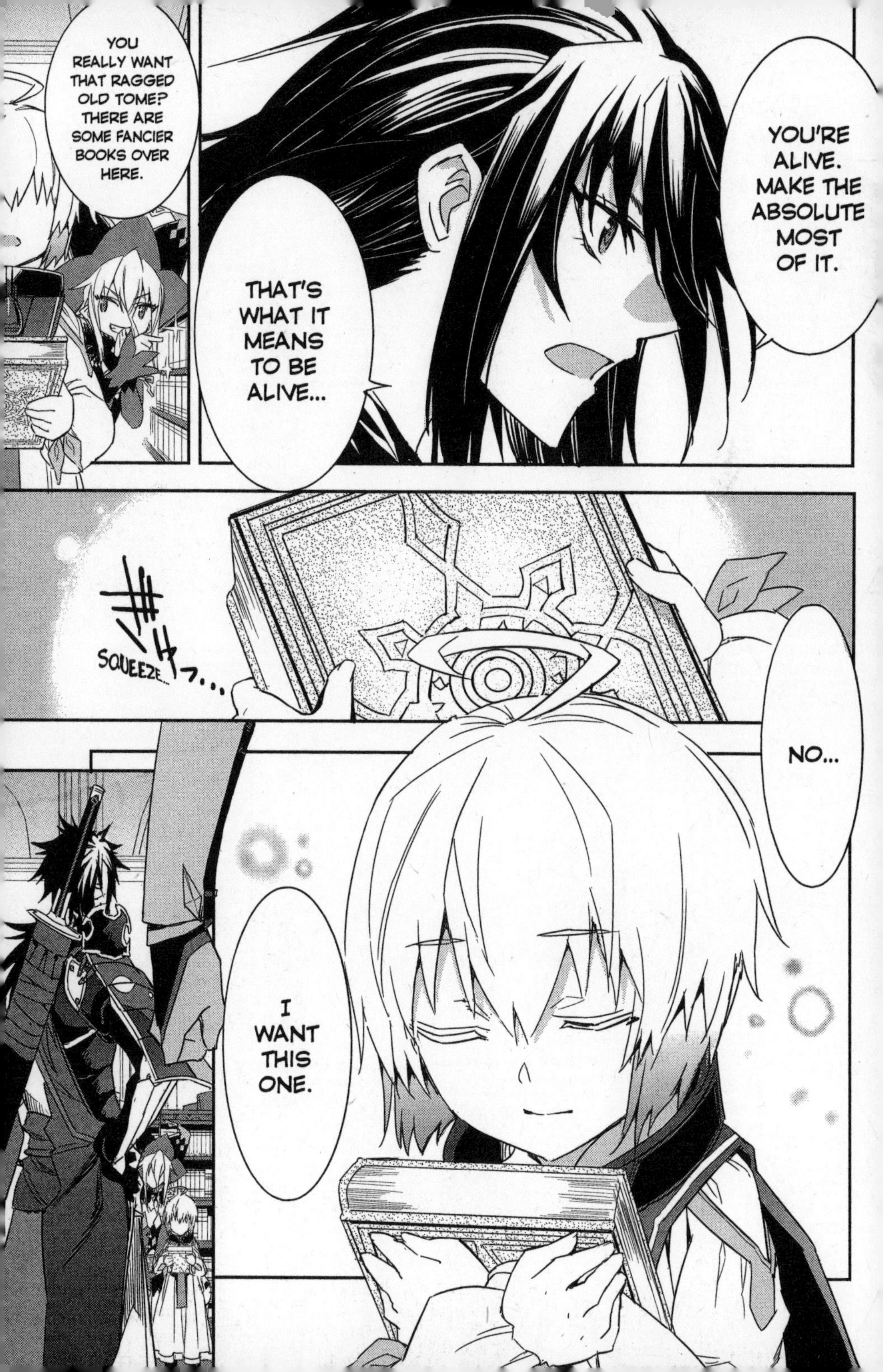
YOU'RE ALIVE. MAKE THE ABSOLUTE MOST OF IT.
THAT'S WHAT IT MEANS TO BE ALIVE...
YOU REALLY WANT THAT RAGGED OLD TOME? THERE ARE SOME FANCIER BOOKS OVER HERE.
SQUEEZE...
NO...
I WANT THIS ONE.

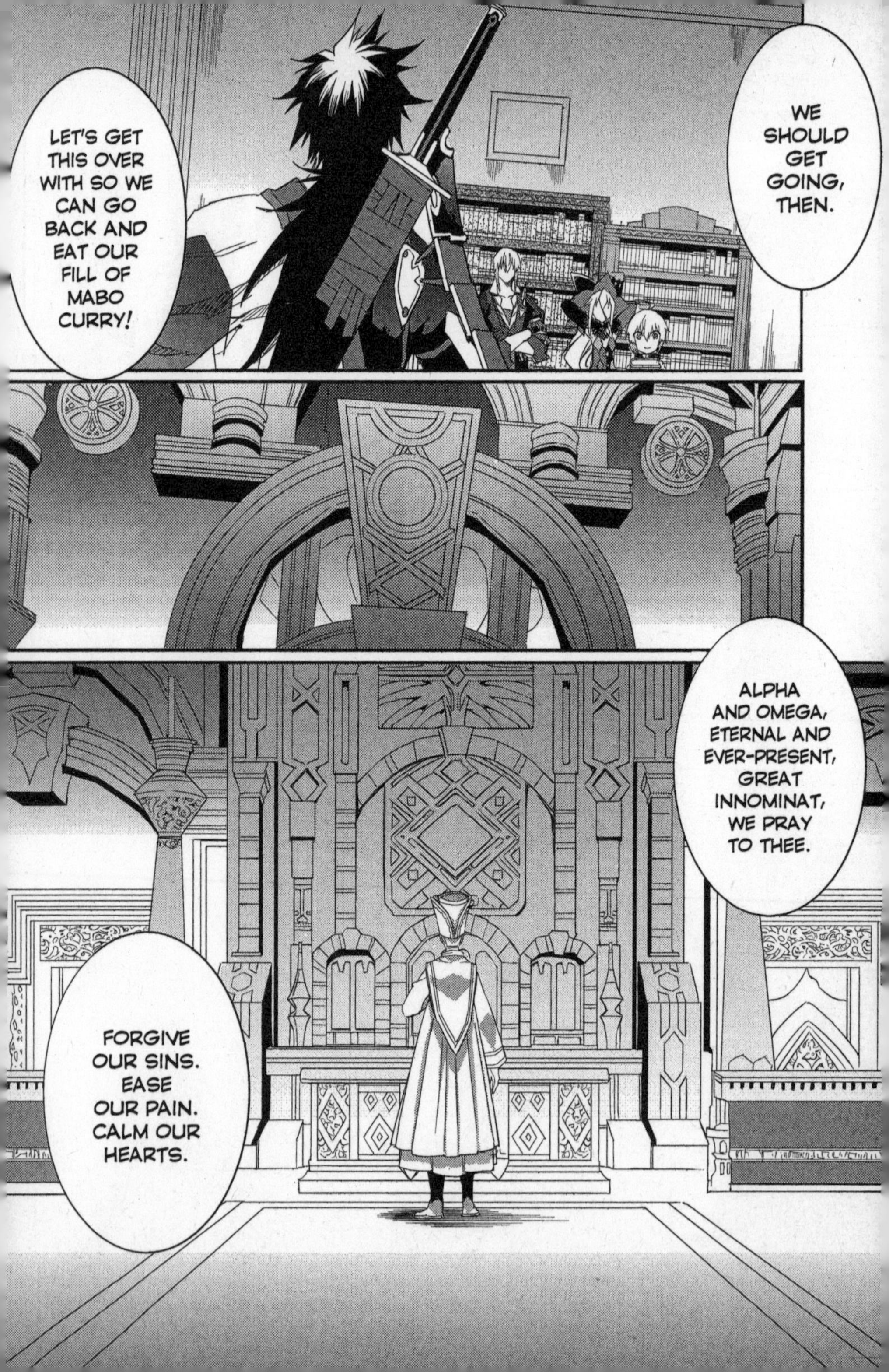
WE SHOULD GET GOING, THEN.
LET'S GET THIS OVER WITH SO WE CAN GO BACK AND EAT OUR FILL OF MABO CURRY!
ALPHA AND OMEGA, ETERNAL AND EVER-PRESENT, GREAT INNOMINAT, WE PRAY TO THEE.
FORGIVE OUR SINS. EASE OUR PAIN. CALM OUR HEARTS.

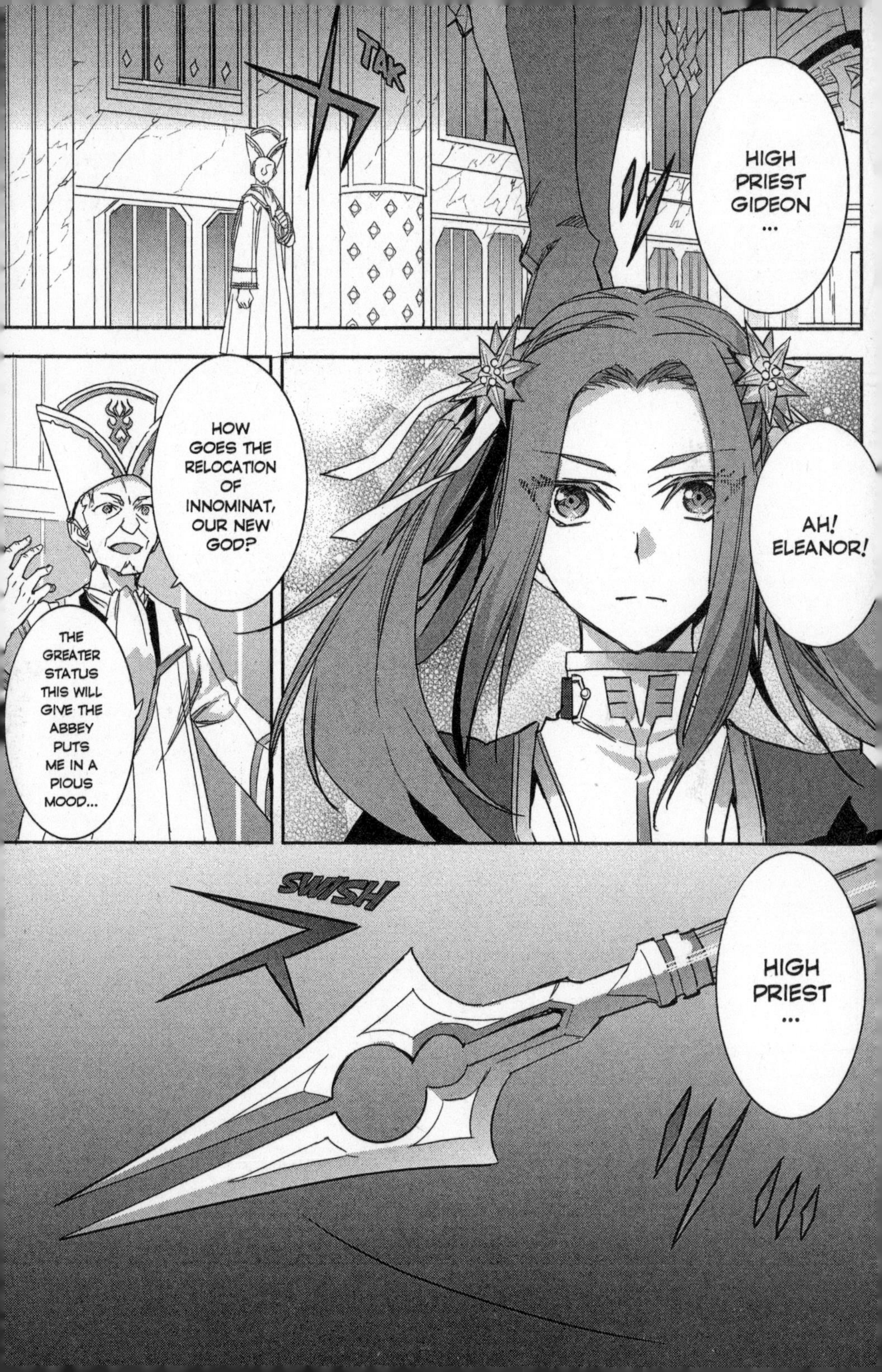
HIGH PRIEST GIDEON ...
TAK
AH! ELEANOR!
HOW GOES THE RELOCATION OF INNOMINAT, OUR NEW GOD?
THE GREATER STATUS THIS WILL GIVE THE ABBEY PUTS ME IN A PIOUS MOOD...
SWISH
HIGH PRIEST ...

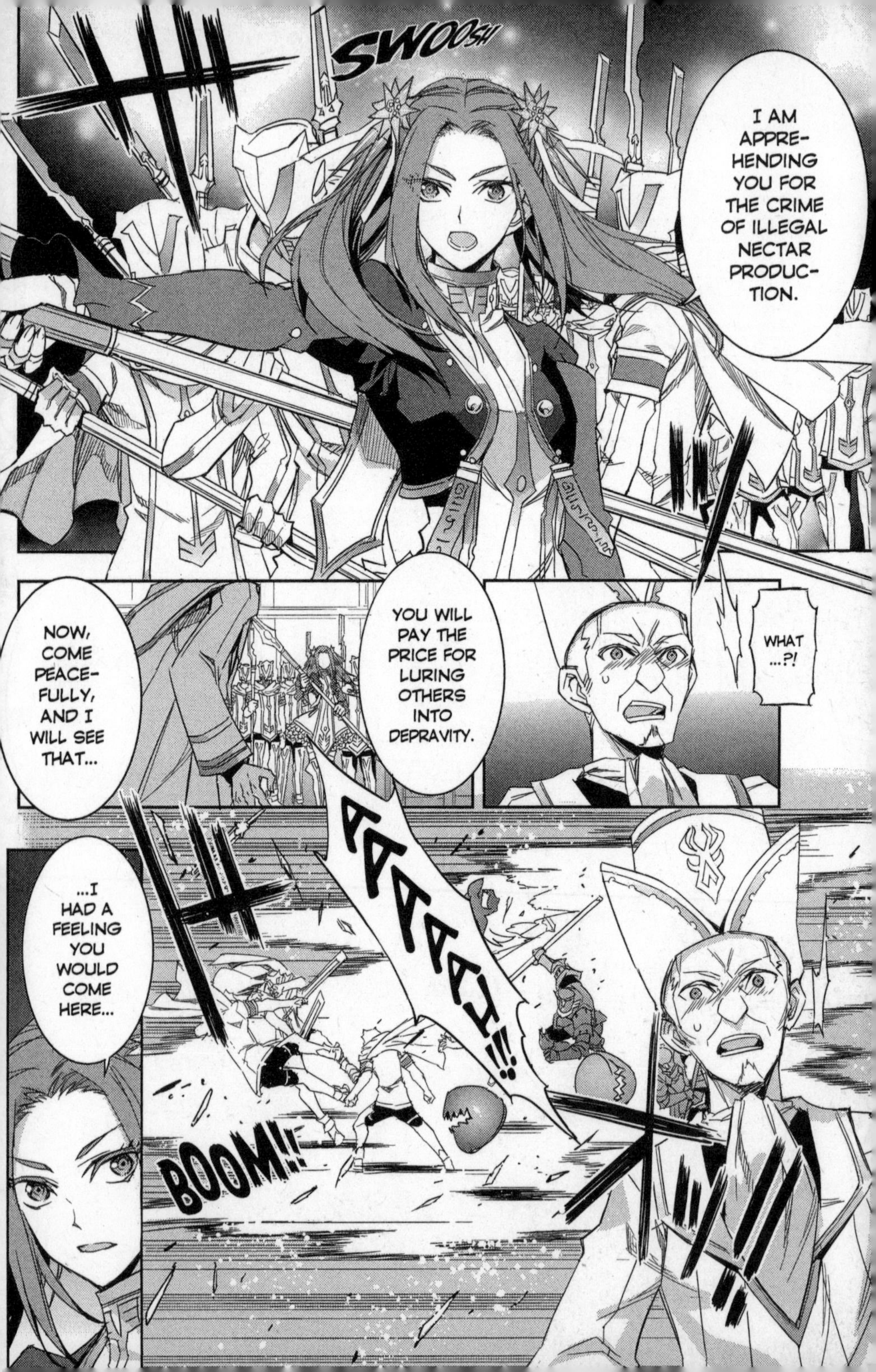
SWOOSH
I AM APPREHENDING YOU FOR THE CRIME OF ILLEGAL NECTAR PRODUCTION.
WHAT ...?!
YOU WILL PAY THE PRICE FOR LURING OTHERS INTO DEPRAVITY.
NOW, COME PEACEFULLY, AND I WILL SEE THAT...
AAAAAH!!!
BOOM!!
...I HAD A FEELING YOU WOULD COME HERE...

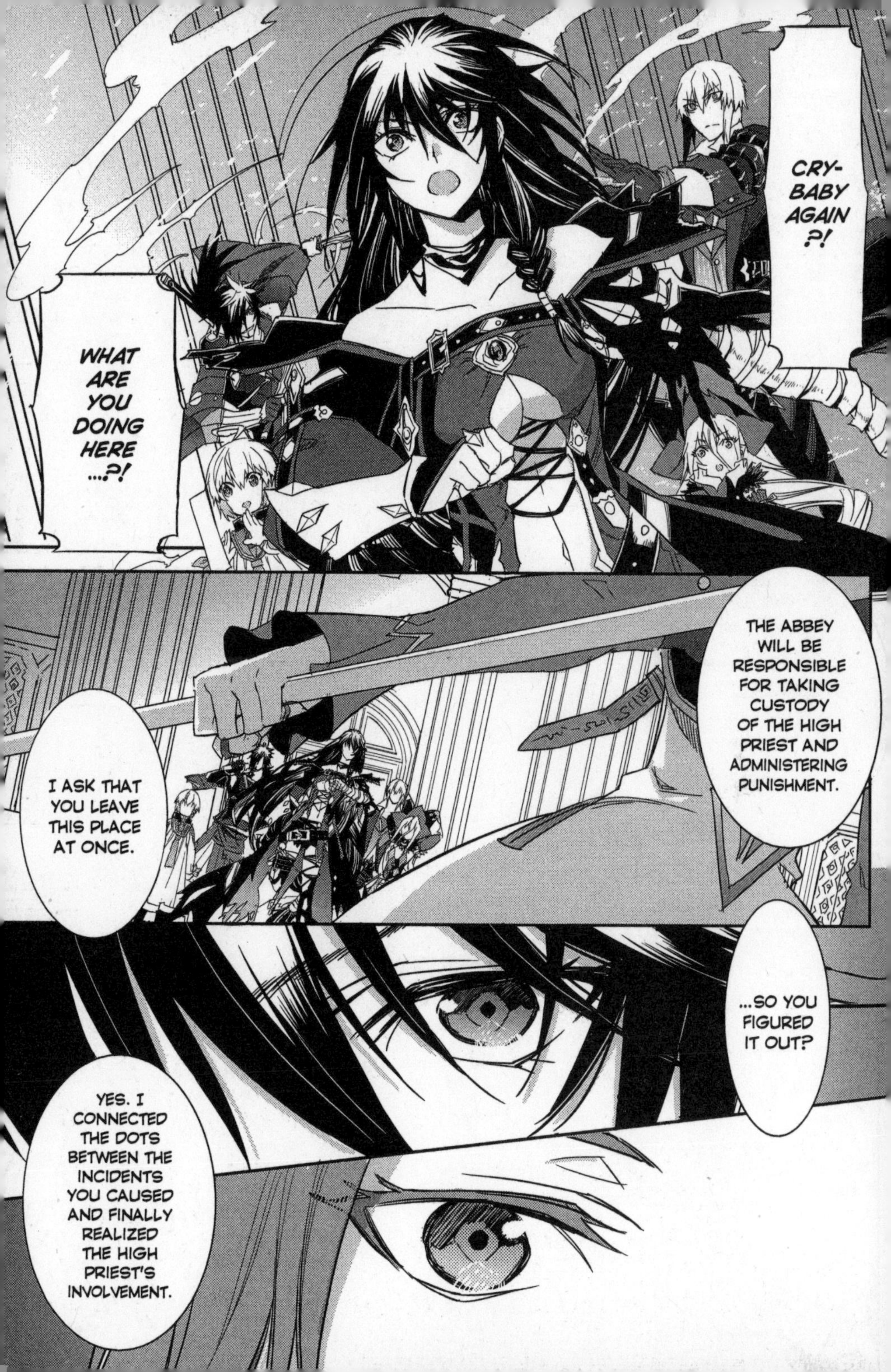
CRY-BABY AGAIN?!
WHAT ARE YOU DOING HERE ...?!
THE ABBEY WILL BE RESPONSIBLE FOR TAKING CUSTODY OF THE HIGH PRIEST AND ADMINISTERING PUNISHMENT.
I ASK THAT YOU LEAVE THIS PLACE AT ONCE.
...SO YOU FIGURED IT OUT?
YES. I CONNECTED THE DOTS BETWEEN THE INCIDENTS YOU CAUSED AND FINALLY REALIZED THE HIGH PRIEST'S INVOLVEMENT.

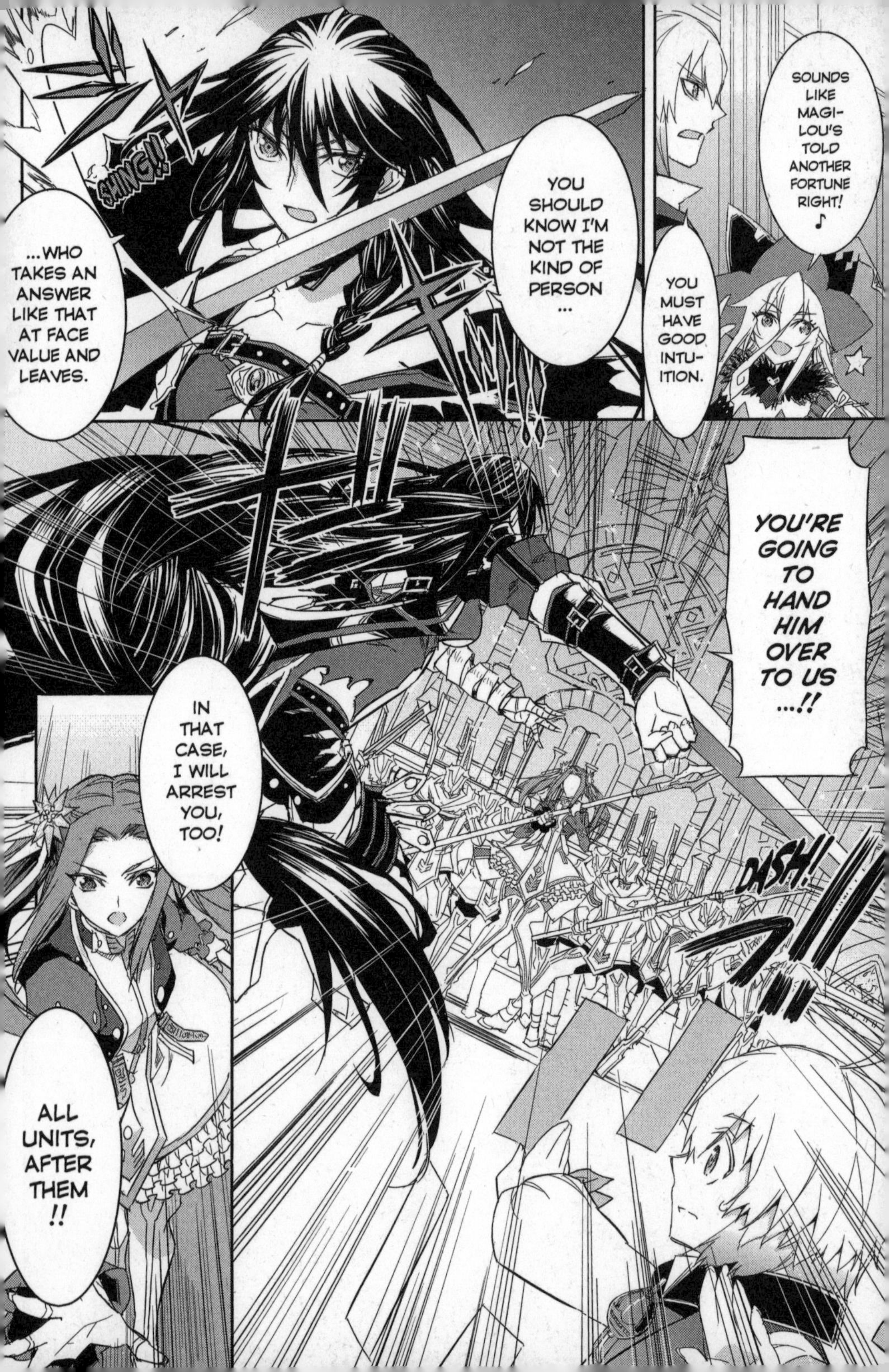
SOUNDS LIKE MAGILOU'S TOLD ANOTHER FORTUNE RIGHT! ♪
YOU MUST HAVE GOOD INTUITION.
SHING!!
YOU SHOULD KNOW I'M NOT THE KIND OF PERSON ...
...WHO TAKES AN ANSWER LIKE THAT AT FACE VALUE AND LEAVES.
YOU'RE GOING TO HAND HIM OVER TO US ...!!
IN THAT CASE, I WILL ARREST YOU, TOO!
DASH!!
ALL UNITS, AFTER THEM!!

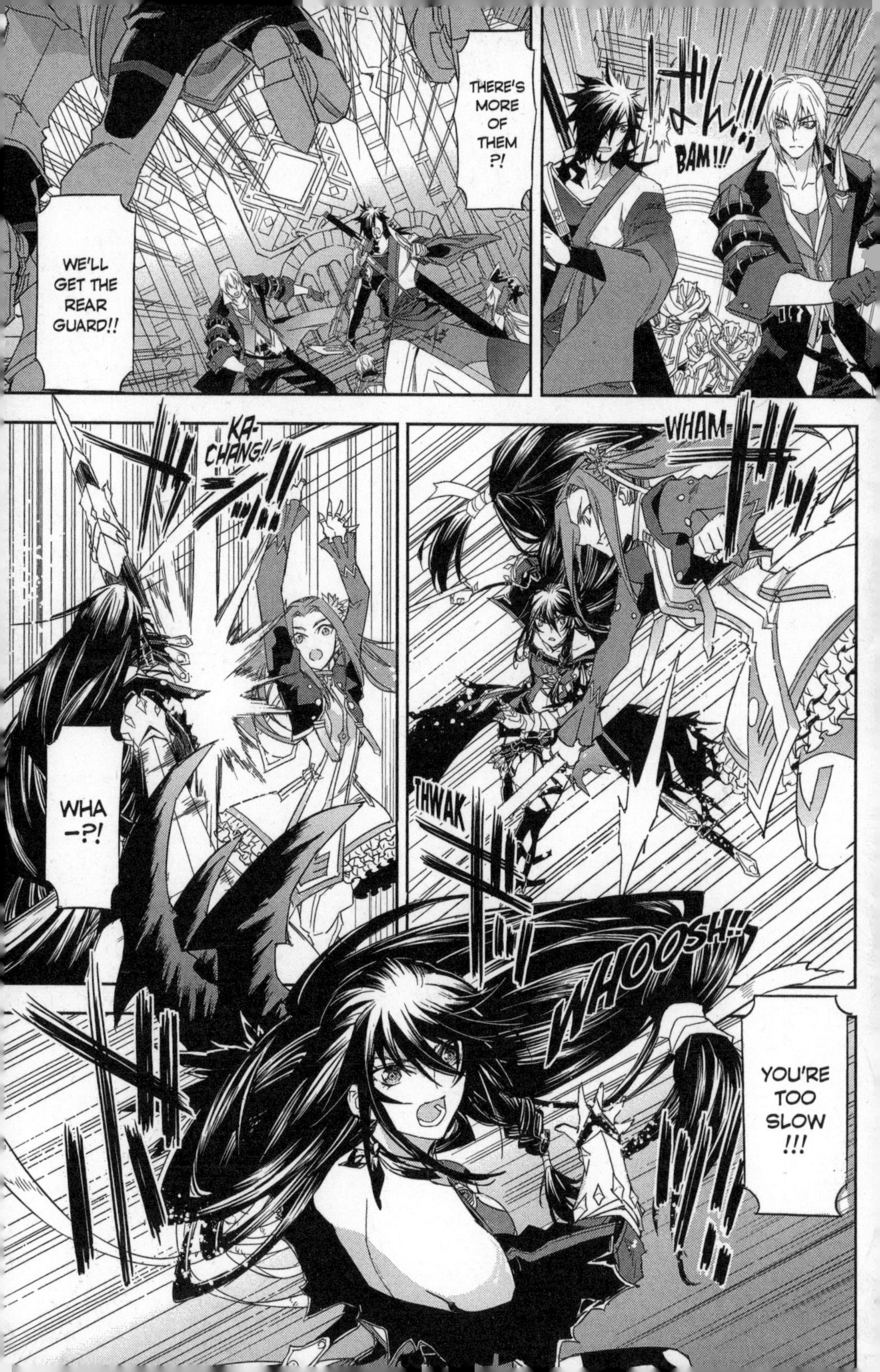
BAM!!!
THERE'S MORE OF THEM ?!
WE'LL GET THE REAR GUARD!!
WHAM
THWAK
KA-CHANG!!
WHA-?!
WHOOSH!!
YOU'RE TOO SLOW !!!

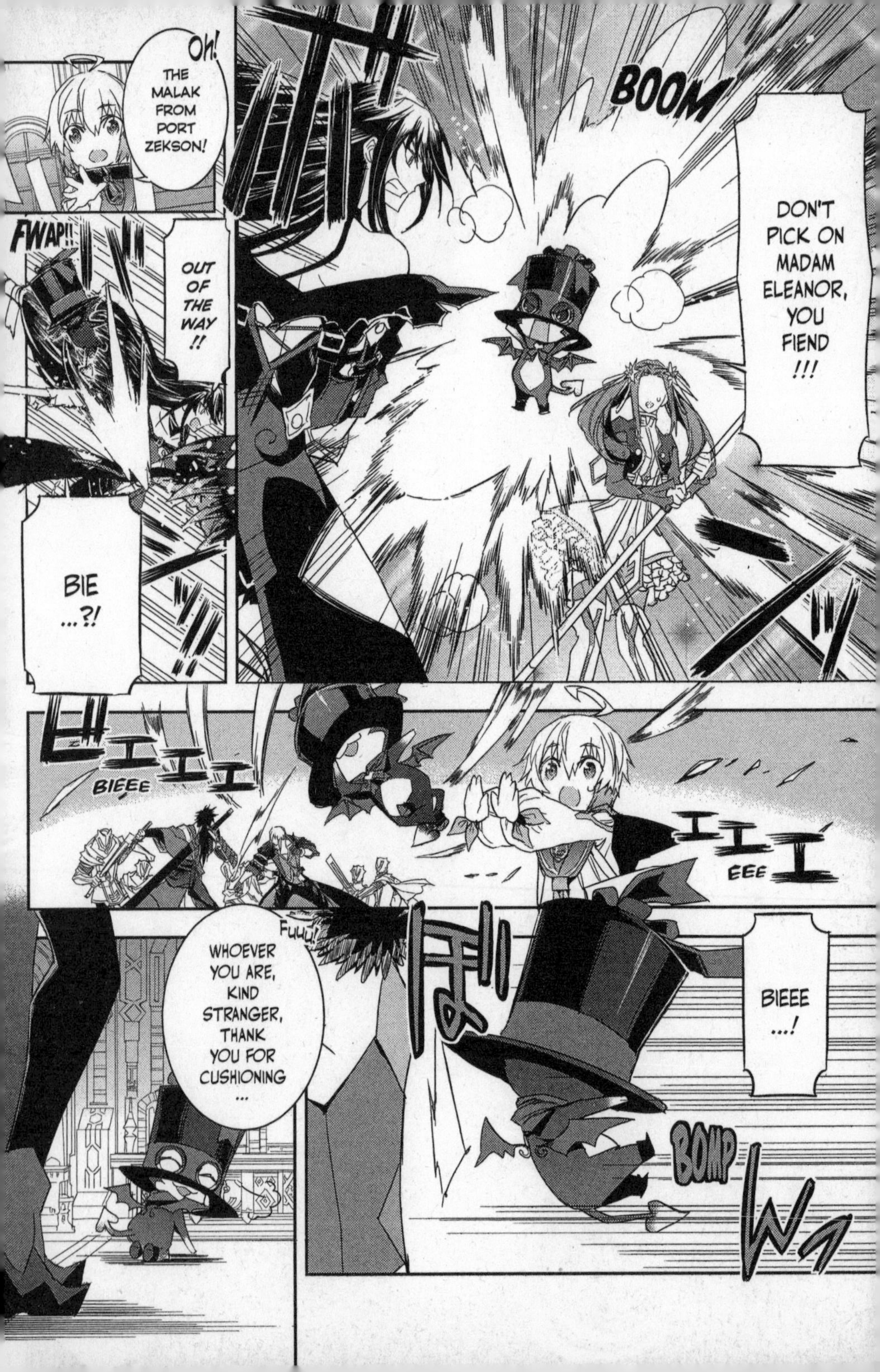
BOOM
DON'T PICK ON MADAM ELEANOR, YOU FIEND!!!
Oh! THE MALAK FROM PORT ZEKSON!
FWAP!!
OUT OF THE WAY!!
BIE...?!
EEE
BIEEE
BIEEE...!
BOMP
Fuuu!
WHOEVER YOU ARE, KIND STRANGER, THANK YOU FOR CUSHIONING...

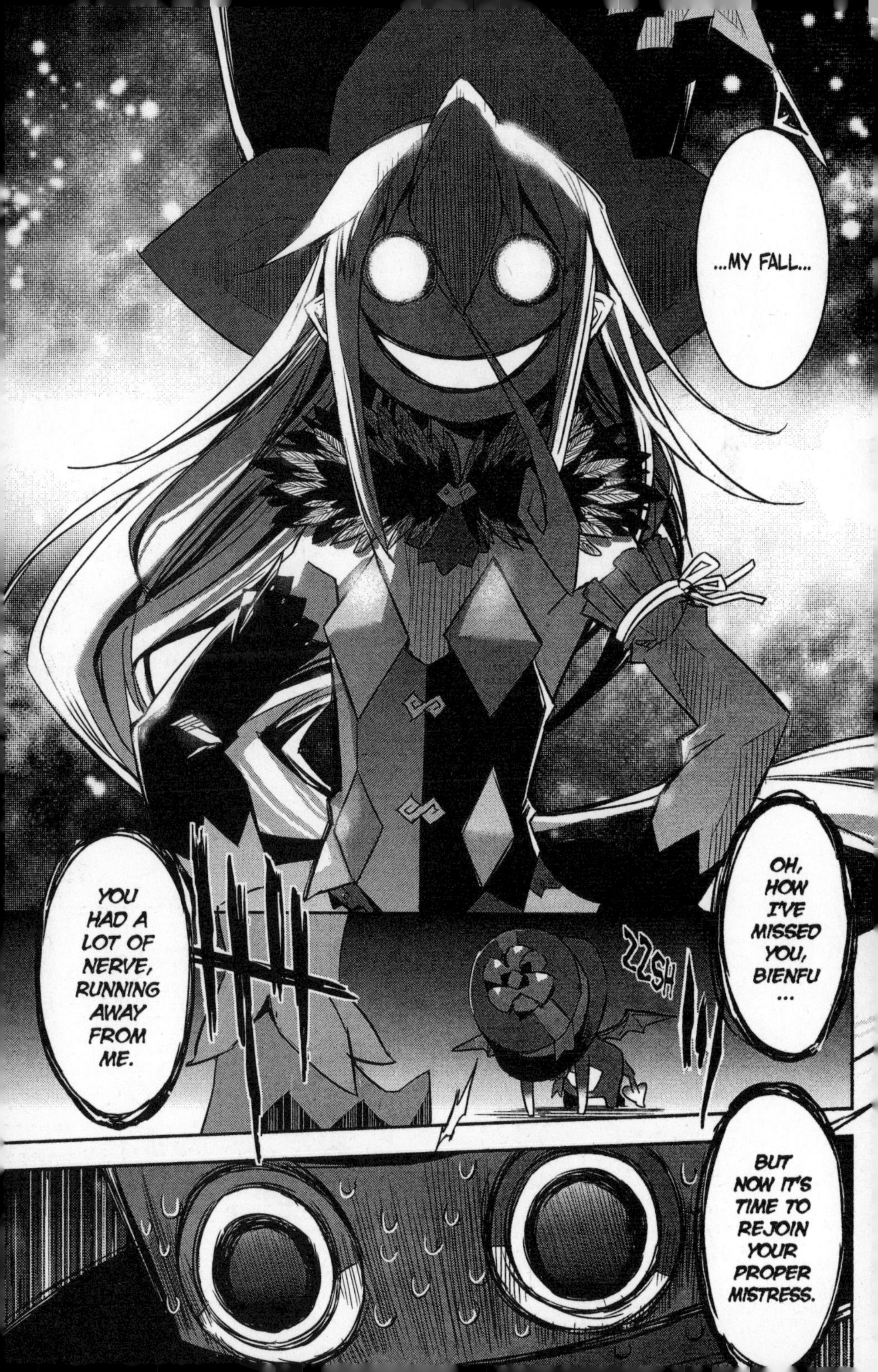
...MY FALL...
OH, HOW I'VE MISSED YOU, BIENFU...
ZZSH
YOU HAD A LOT OF NERVE, RUNNING AWAY FROM ME.
BUT NOW IT'S TIME TO REJOIN YOUR PROPER MISTRESS.

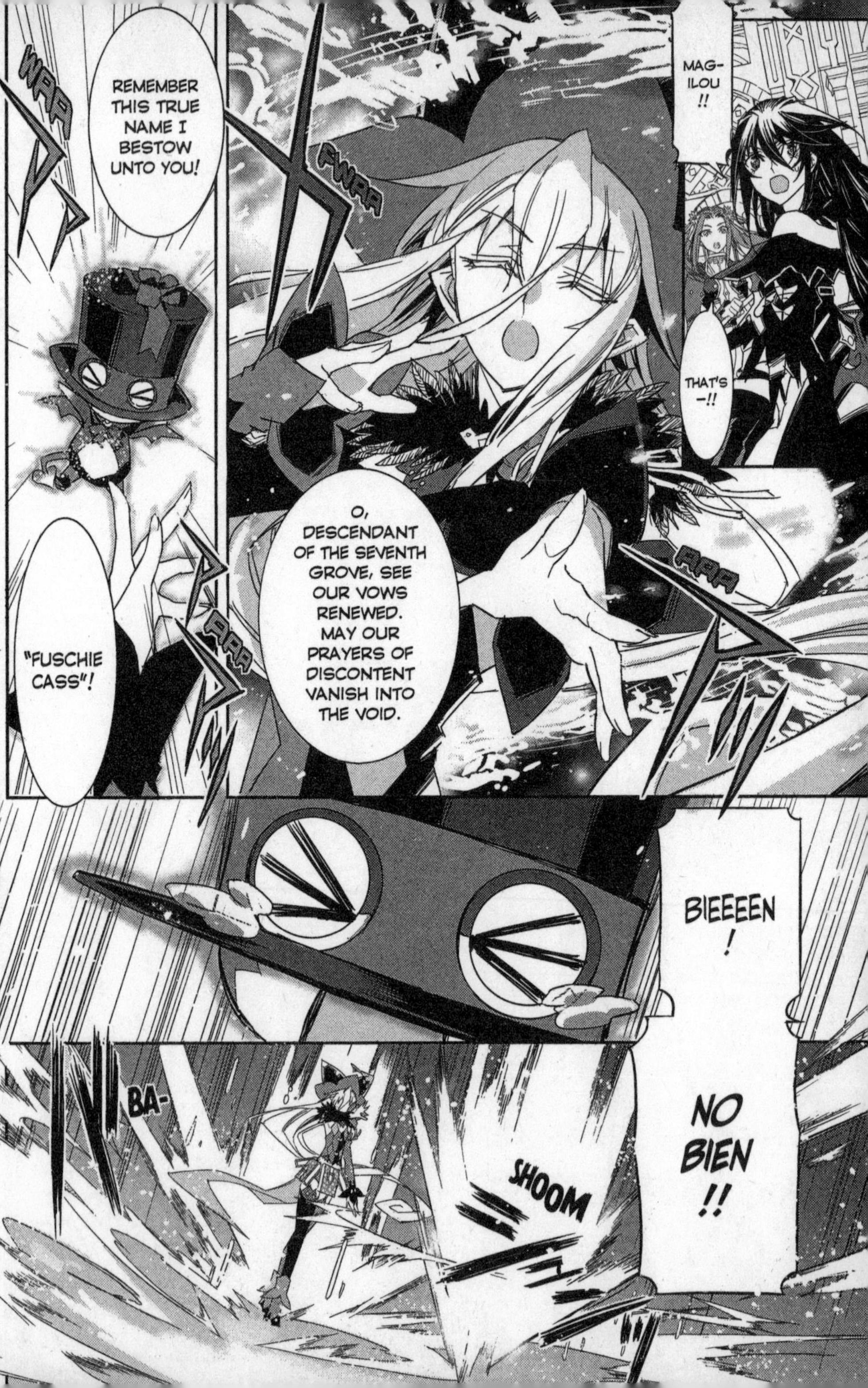
MAG-ILOU!!
THAT'S—!!
FWAA
O, DESCENDANT OF THE SEVENTH GROVE, SEE OUR VOWS RENEWED. MAY OUR PRAYERS OF DISCONTENT VANISH INTO THE VOID.
AAA
WAA
REMEMBER THIS TRUE NAME I BESTOW UNTO YOU!
"FUSCHIE CASS"!
PAAA
BIEEEEN!
NO BIEN!!
SHOOM
BA-

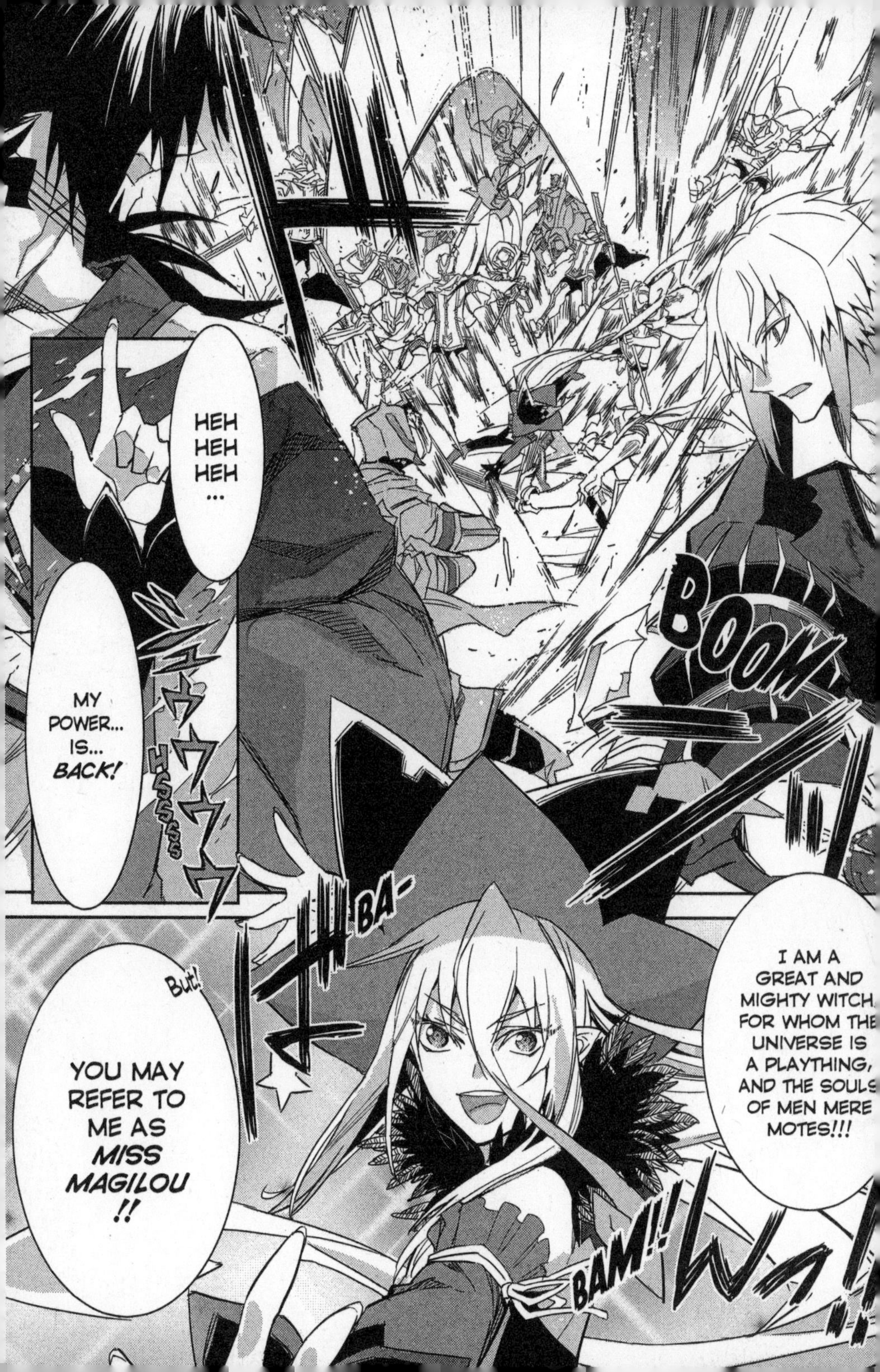
BOOM
HEH HEH HEH ...
MY POWER... IS... BACK!
HSSSSS
BA-
I AM A GREAT AND MIGHTY WITCH, FOR WHOM THE UNIVERSE IS A PLAYTHING, AND THE SOULS OF MEN MERE MOTES!!!
But!
YOU MAY REFER TO ME AS MISS MAGILOU !!
BAM!!

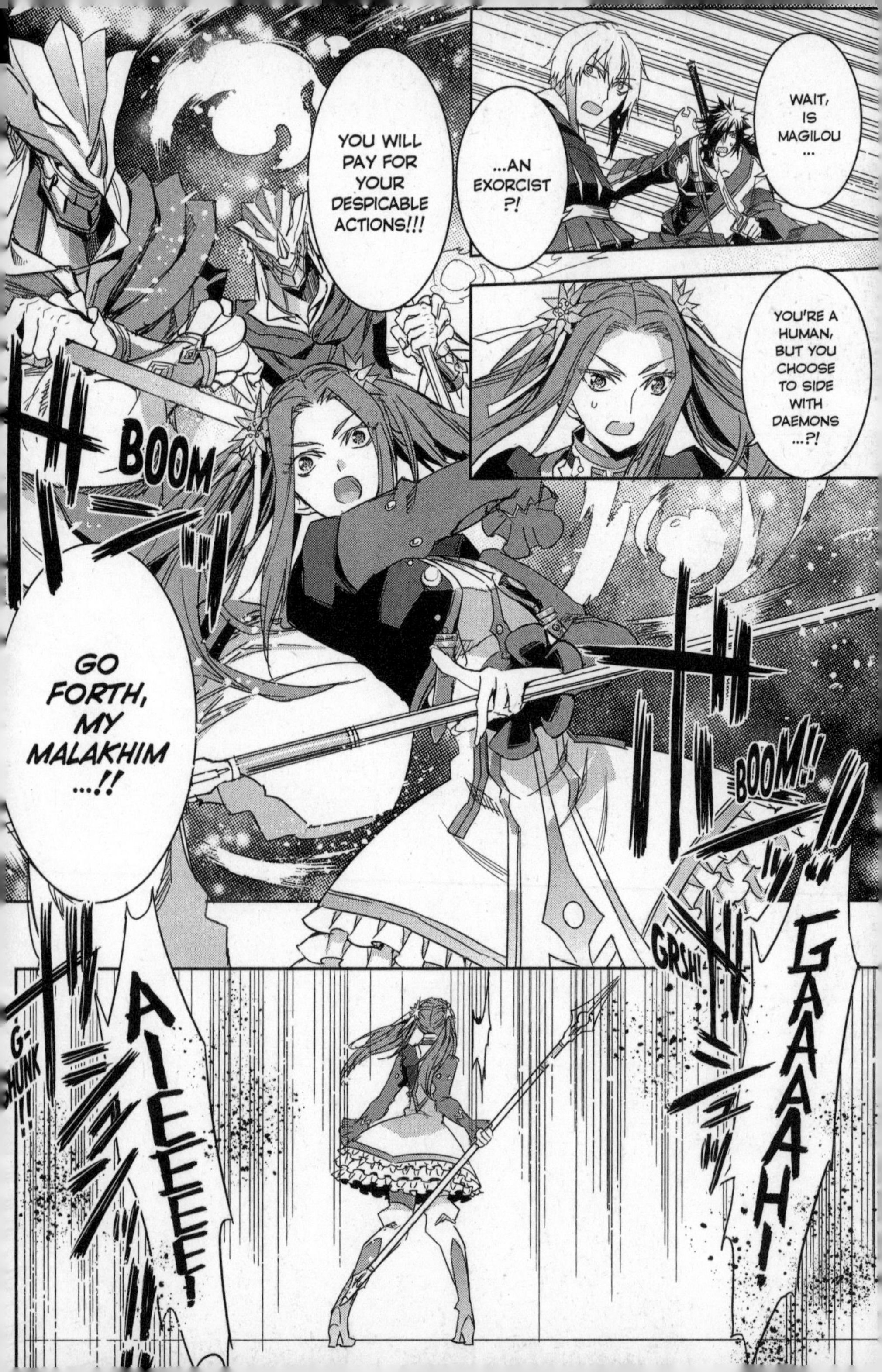
WAIT, IS MAGILOU ...
...AN EXORCIST ?!
YOU'RE A HUMAN, BUT YOU CHOOSE TO SIDE WITH DAEMONS ...?!
YOU WILL PAY FOR YOUR DESPICABLE ACTIONS!!!
BOOM
GO FORTH, MY MALAKHIM ...!!
BOOM!!
GRSH!
GAAAAH!
AIEEEEE
G-CHUNK!!

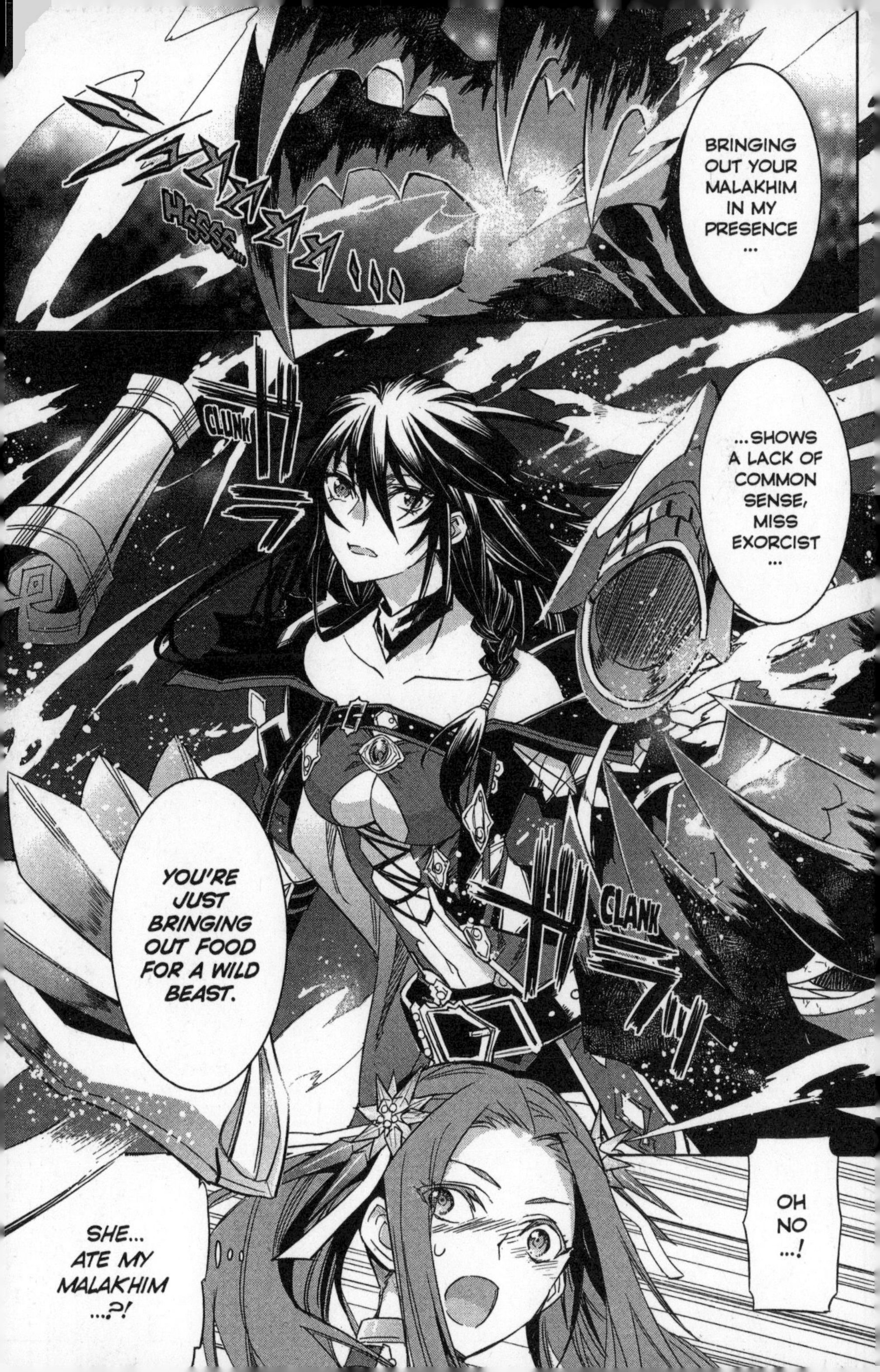
BRINGING OUT YOUR MALAKHIM IN MY PRESENCE ...
HSSSS...
...SHOWS A LACK OF COMMON SENSE, MISS EXORCIST ...
CLUNK
CLANK
YOU'RE JUST BRINGING OUT FOOD FOR A WILD BEAST.
OH NO ...!
SHE... ATE MY MALAKHIM ...?!

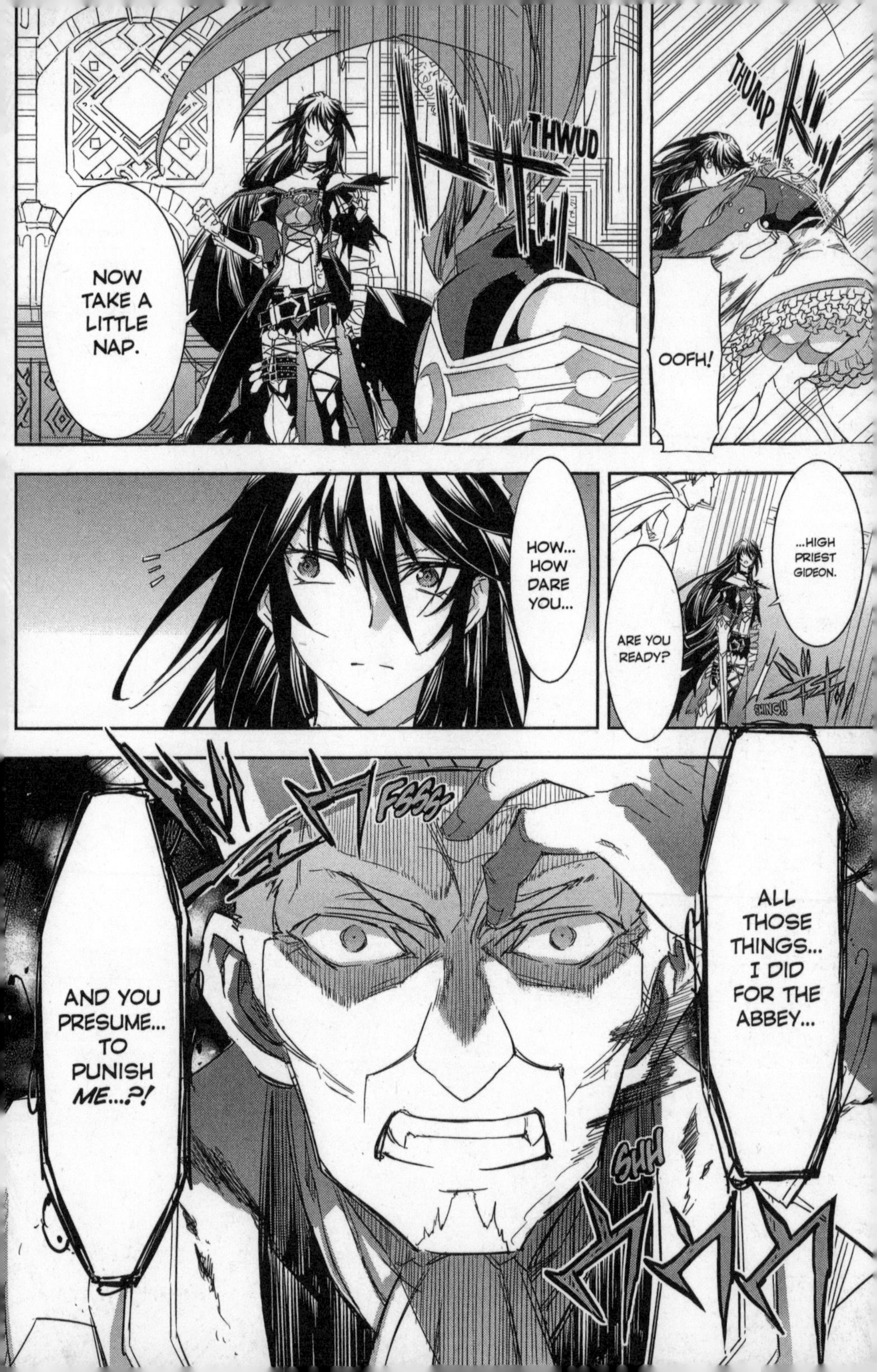
THUMP
OOFH!
THWUD
NOW TAKE A LITTLE NAP.
...HIGH PRIEST GIDEON.
ARE YOU READY?
SHING!!
HOW... HOW DARE YOU...
FSSS
ALL THOSE THINGS... I DID FOR THE ABBEY...
SUH
AND YOU PRESUME... TO PUNISH *ME*...?!

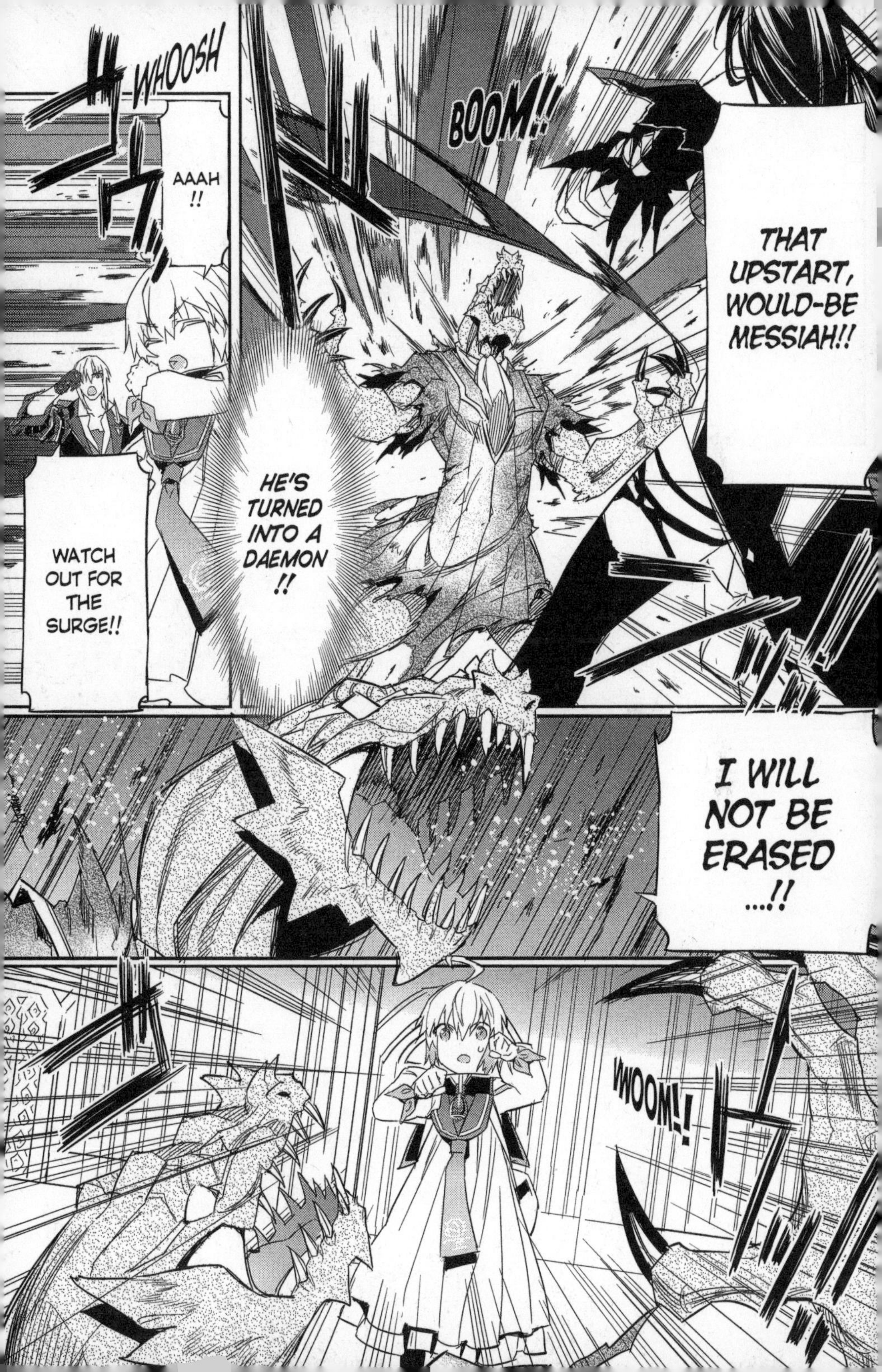
THAT UPSTART, WOULD-BE MESSIAH!!
BOOM!!
HE'S TURNED INTO A DAEMON!!
WHOOSH
AAAH!!
WATCH OUT FOR THE SURGE!!
I WILL NOT BE ERASED...!!
WOOM!!

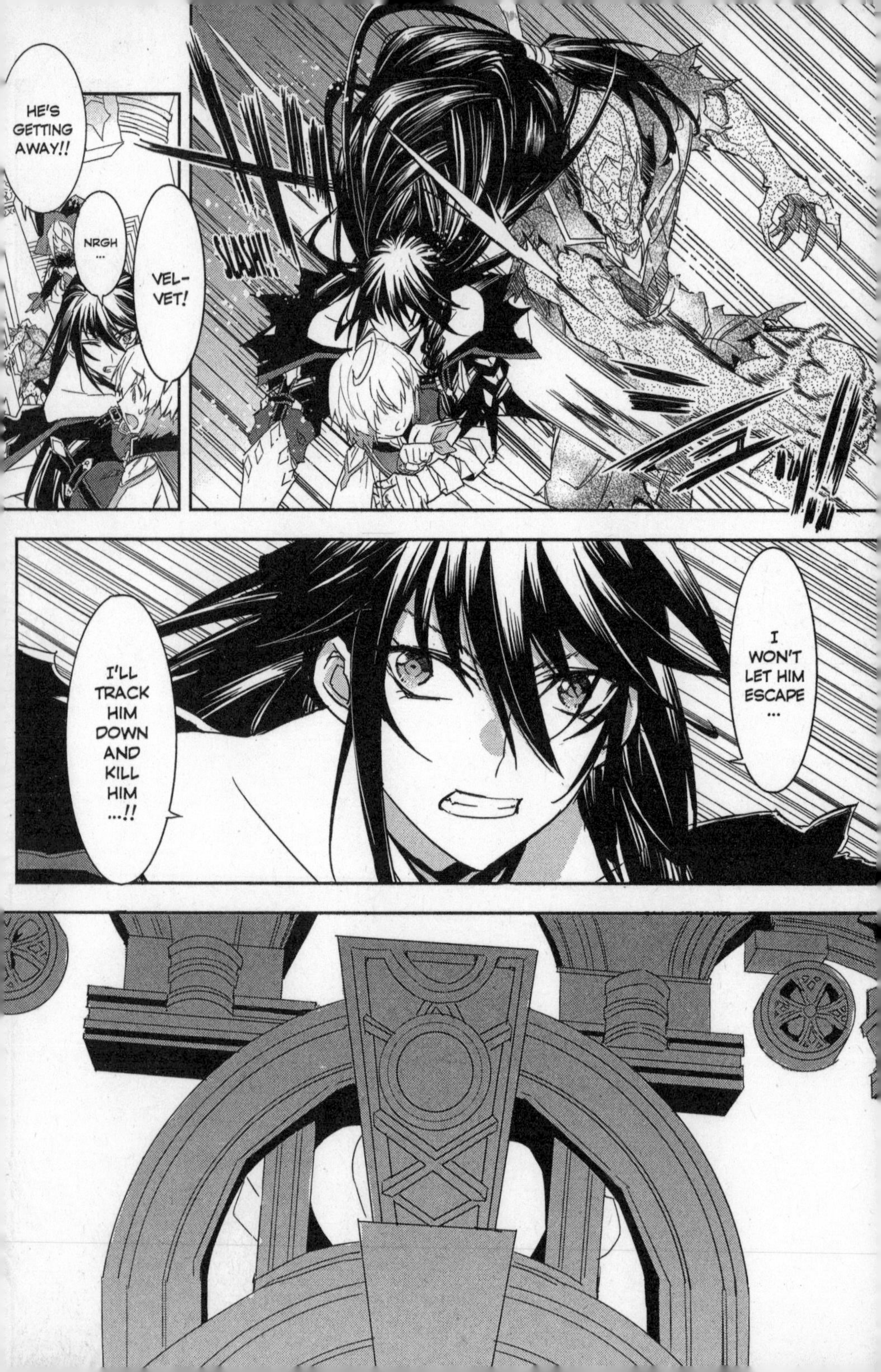
SLASH!!
HE'S GETTING AWAY!!
NRGH ...
VEL-VET!
I WON'T LET HIM ESCAPE ...
I'LL TRACK HIM DOWN AND KILL HIM ...!!

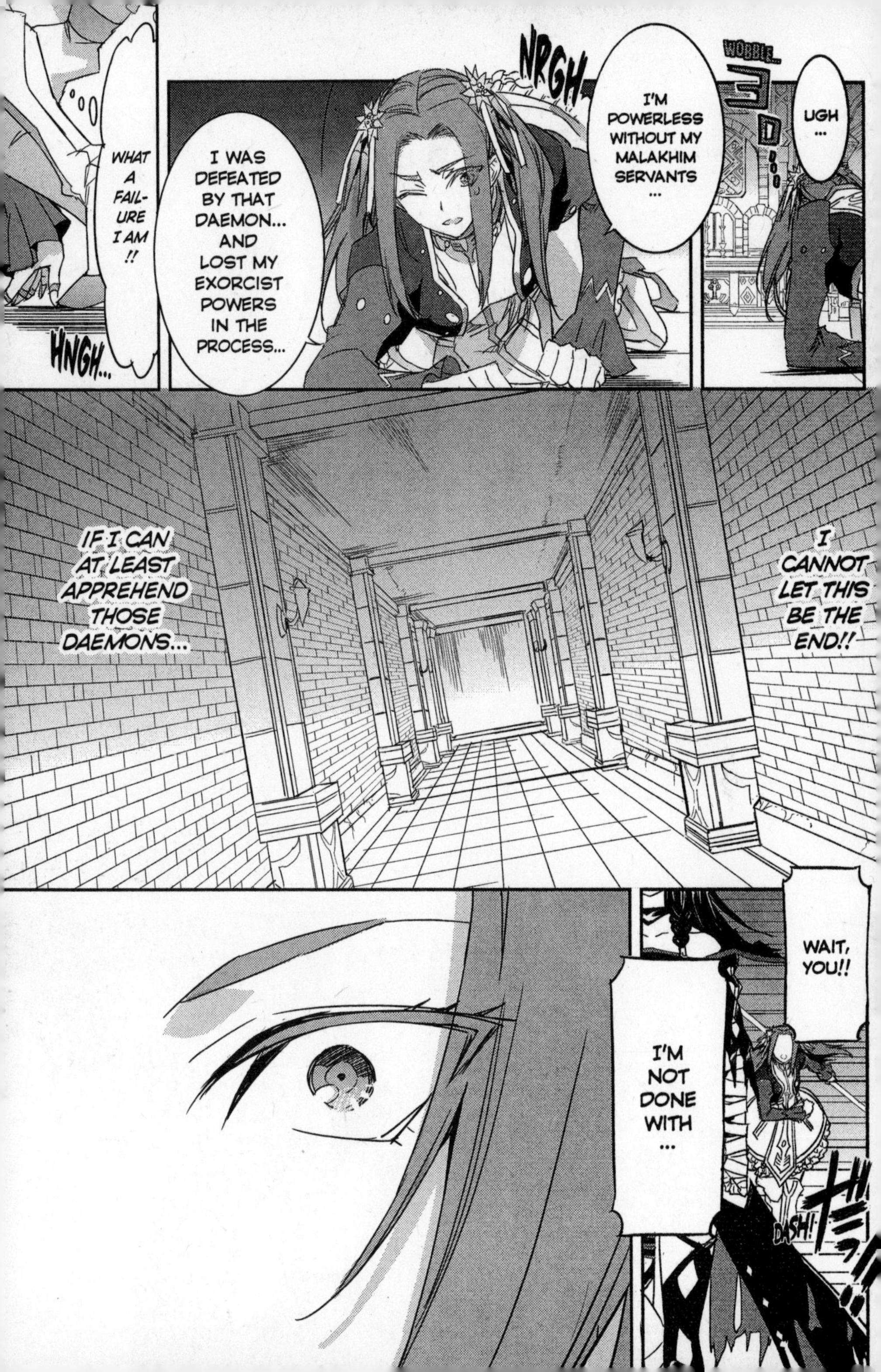
WOBBLE...
UGH ...
I'M POWERLESS WITHOUT MY MALAKHIM SERVANTS ...
NRGH
I WAS DEFEATED BY THAT DAEMON... AND LOST MY EXORCIST POWERS IN THE PROCESS...
WHAT A FAIL-URE I AM !!
HNGH...
I CANNOT LET THIS BE THE END!!
IF I CAN AT LEAST APPREHEND THOSE DAEMONS...
WAIT, YOU!!
I'M NOT DONE WITH ...
DASH!

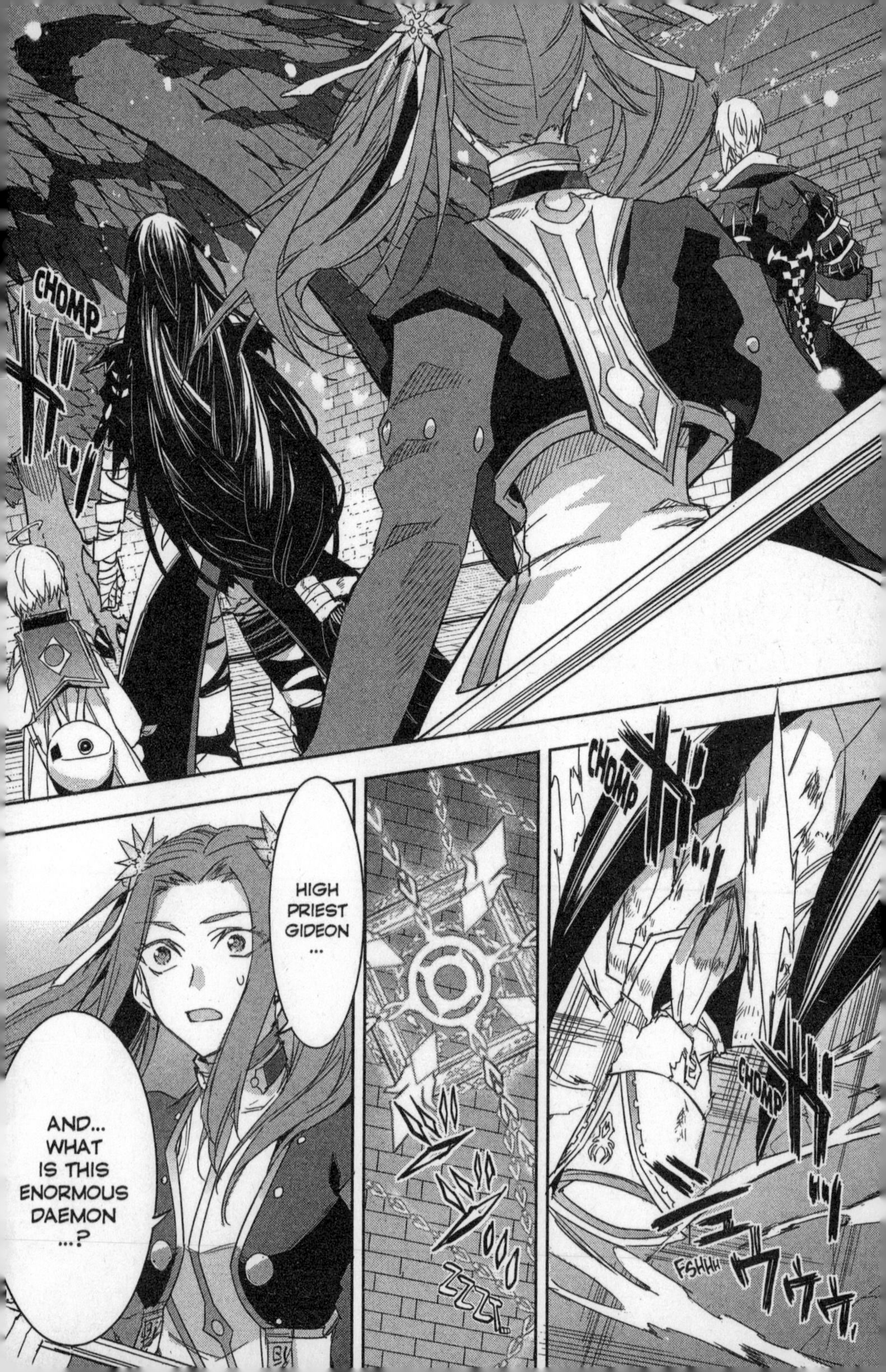
CHOMP
CHOMP
CHOMP
FSHHH
HIGH PRIEST GIDEON ...
AND... WHAT IS THIS ENORMOUS DAEMON ...?

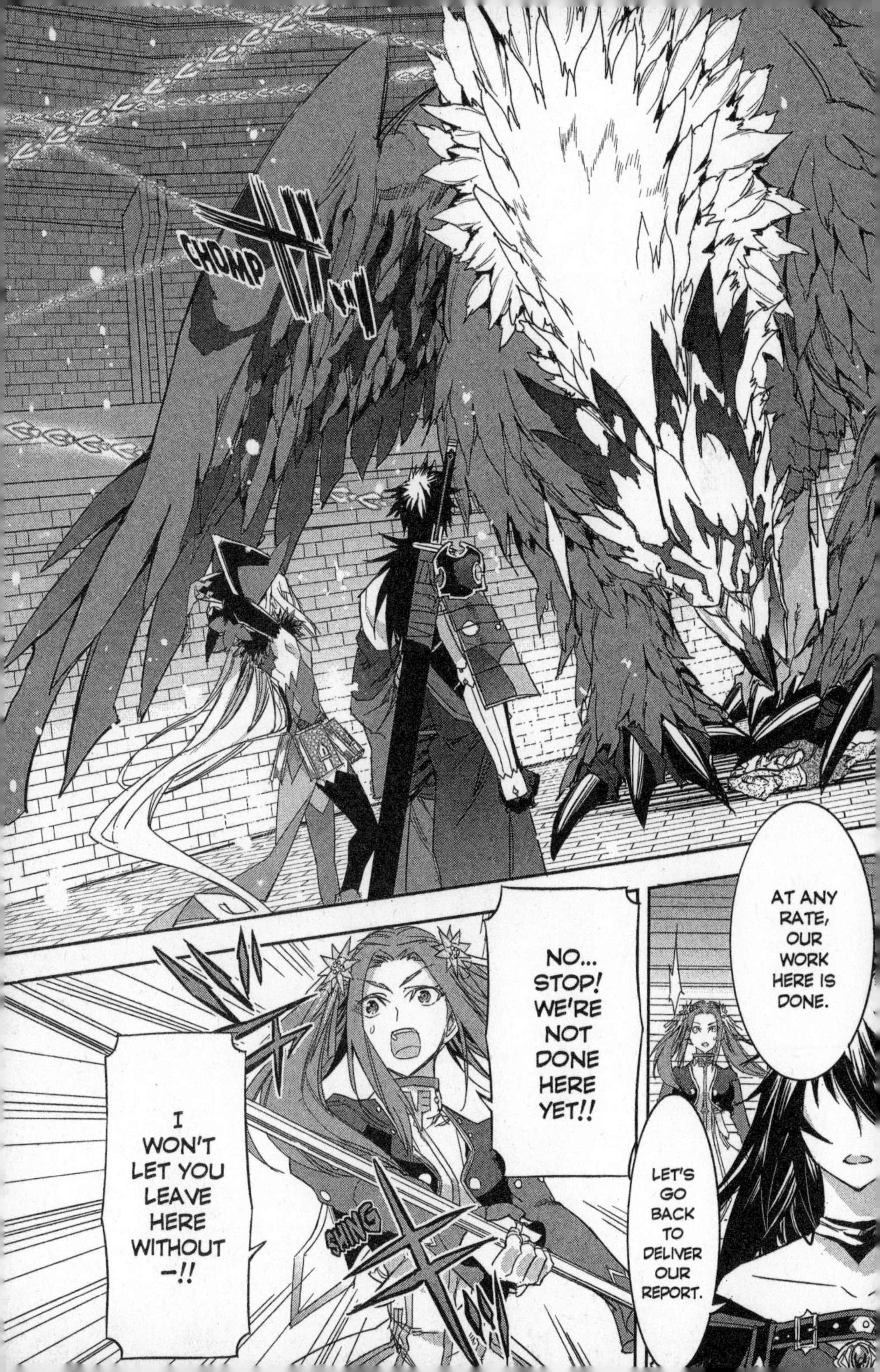
CHOMP
AT ANY RATE, OUR WORK HERE IS DONE.
LET'S GO BACK TO DELIVER OUR REPORT.
NO... STOP! WE'RE NOT DONE HERE YET!!
I WON'T LET YOU LEAVE HERE WITHOUT—!!
SHING

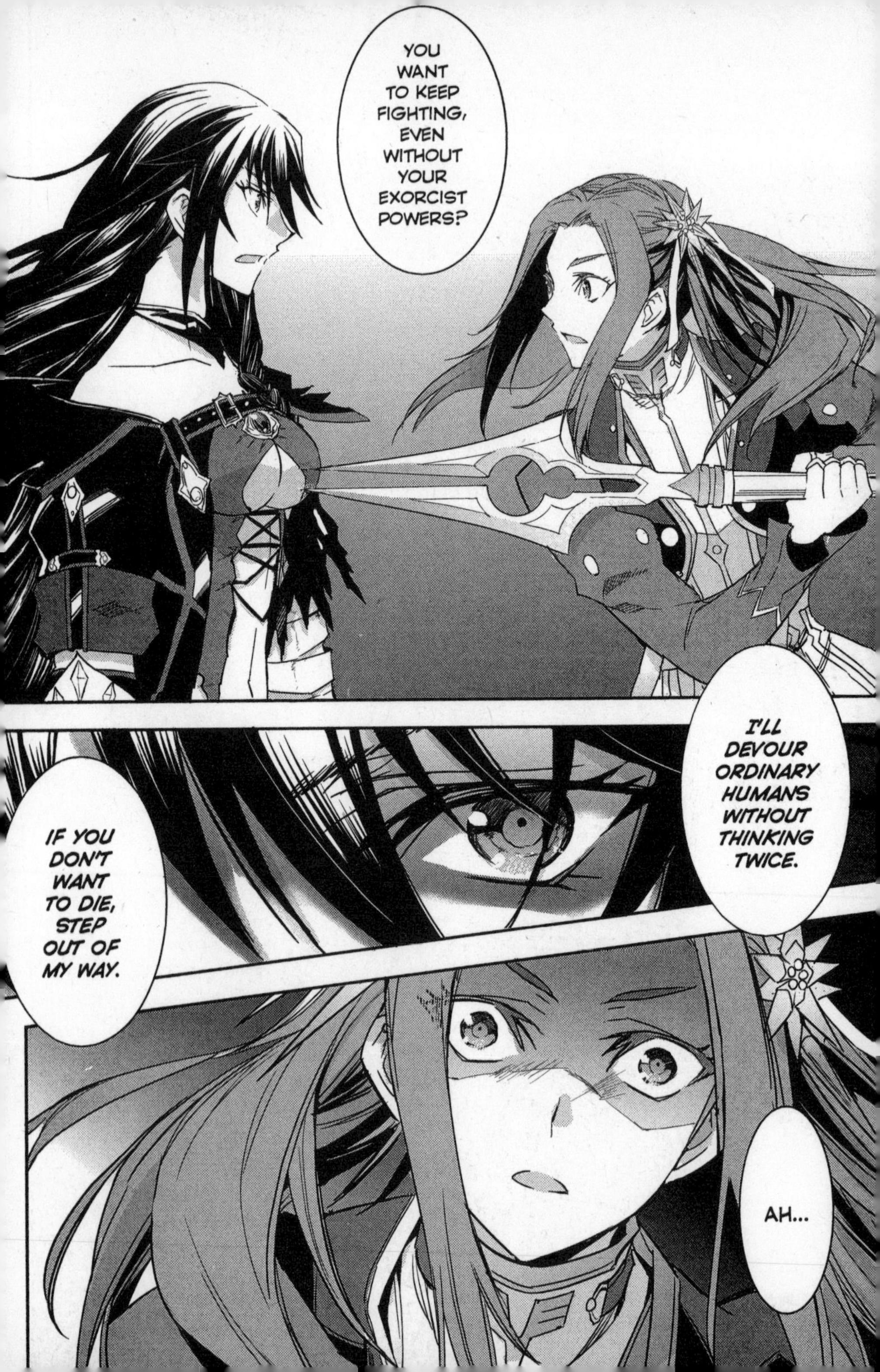
YOU WANT TO KEEP FIGHTING, EVEN WITHOUT YOUR EXORCIST POWERS?
I'LL DEVOUR ORDINARY HUMANS WITHOUT THINKING TWICE.
IF YOU DON'T WANT TO DIE, STEP OUT OF MY WAY.
AH...

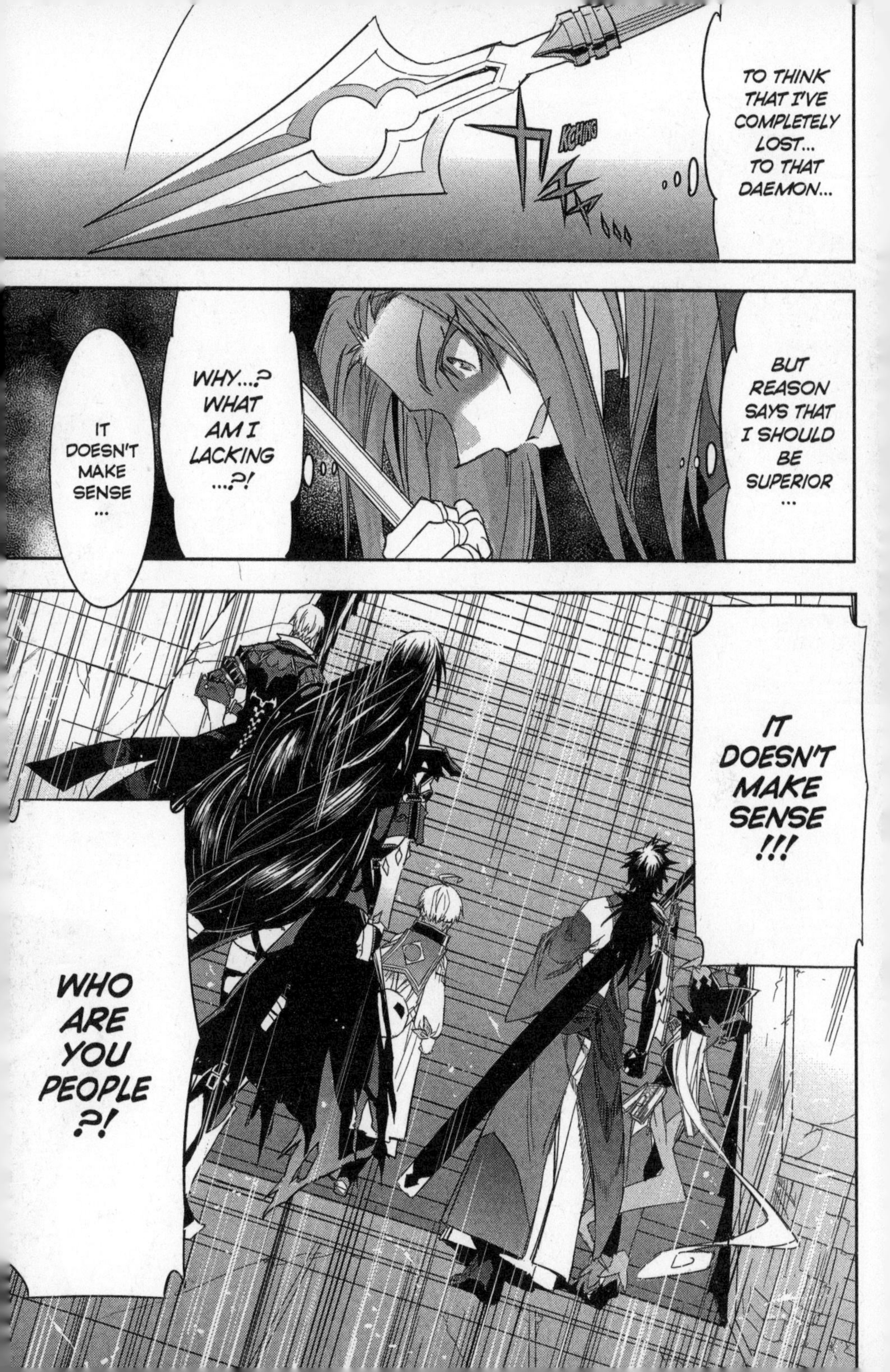
TO THINK THAT I'VE COMPLETELY LOST... TO THAT DAEMON...
KCHING
BUT REASON SAYS THAT I SHOULD BE SUPERIOR ...
WHY...? WHAT AM I LACKING ...?!
IT DOESN'T MAKE SENSE ...
IT DOESN'T MAKE SENSE !!!
WHO ARE YOU PEOPLE ?!

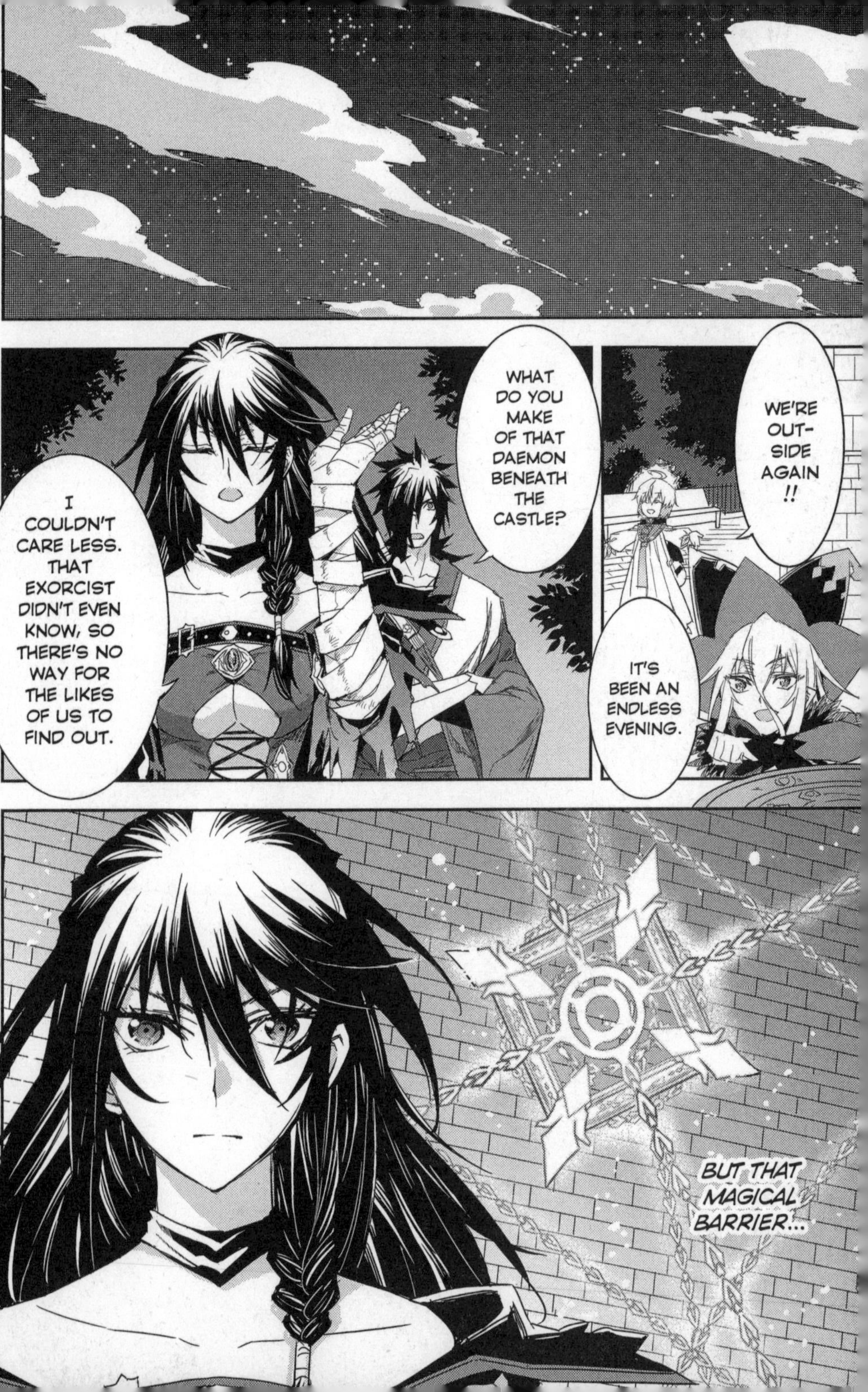
WE'RE OUT-SIDE AGAIN!!
IT'S BEEN AN ENDLESS EVENING.
WHAT DO YOU MAKE OF THAT DAEMON BENEATH THE CASTLE?
I COULDN'T CARE LESS. THAT EXORCIST DIDN'T EVEN KNOW, SO THERE'S NO WAY FOR THE LIKES OF US TO FIND OUT.
BUT THAT MAGICAL BARRIER...

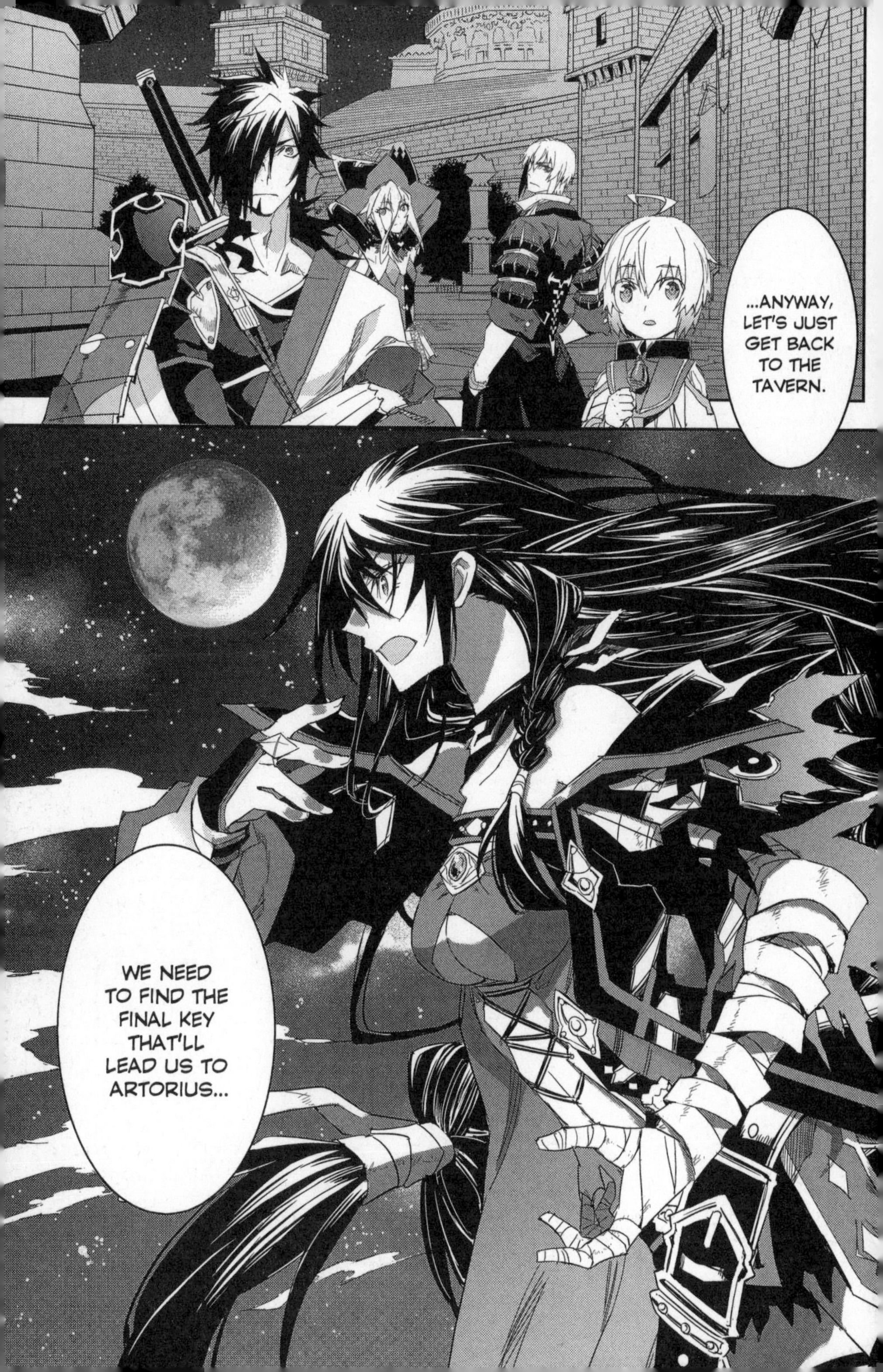
...ANYWAY, LET'S JUST GET BACK TO THE TAVERN.
WE NEED TO FIND THE FINAL KEY THAT'LL LEAD US TO ARTORIUS...

Magikazam

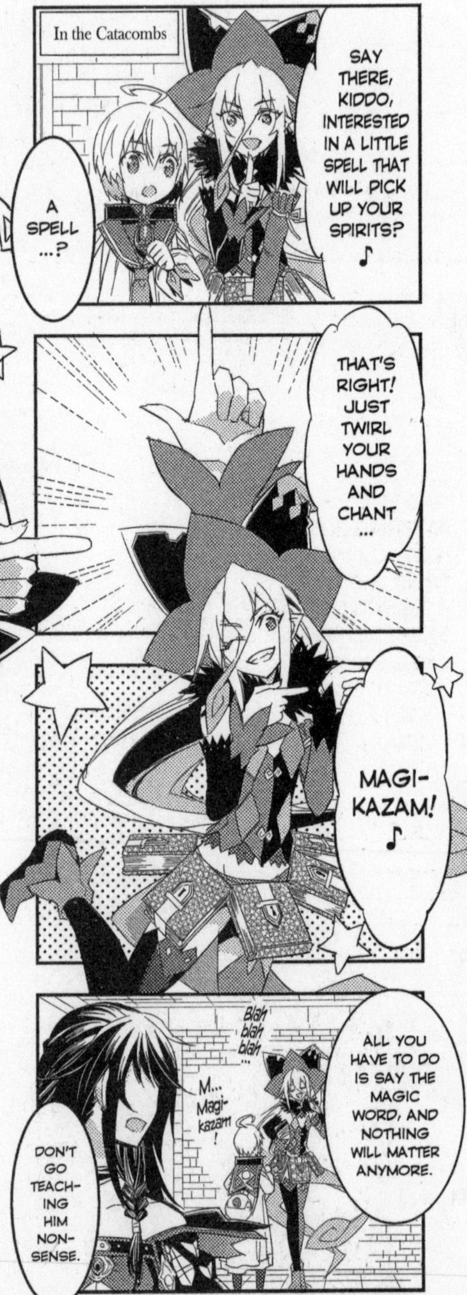
In the Catacombs
SAY THERE, KIDDO, INTERESTED IN A LITTLE SPELL THAT WILL PICK UP YOUR SPIRITS? ♪
A SPELL ...?
THAT'S RIGHT! JUST TWIRL YOUR HANDS AND CHANT ...
MAGI-KAZAM! ♪
ALL YOU HAVE TO DO IS SAY THE MAGIC WORD, AND NOTHING WILL MATTER ANYMORE.
Blah blah blah ...
M... Magi-kazam!
DON'T GO TEACH-ING HIM NON-SENSE.

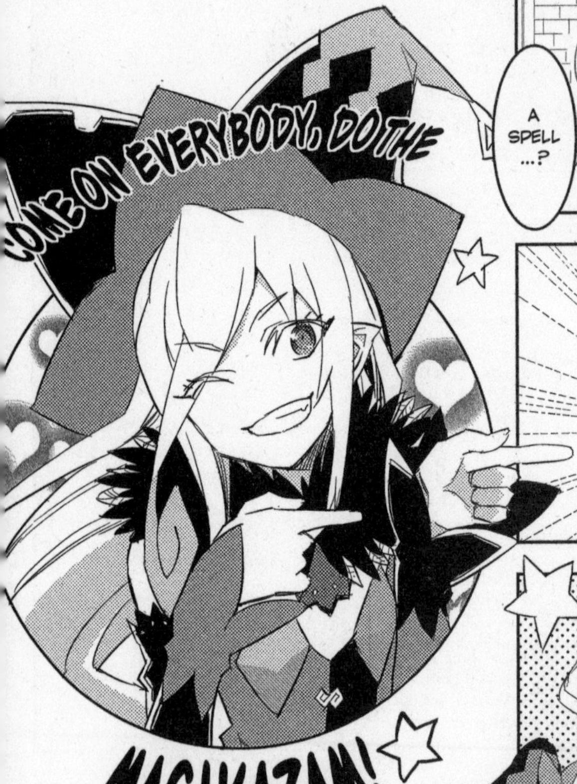
COME ON EVERYBODY, DO THE
MAGIKAZAM!

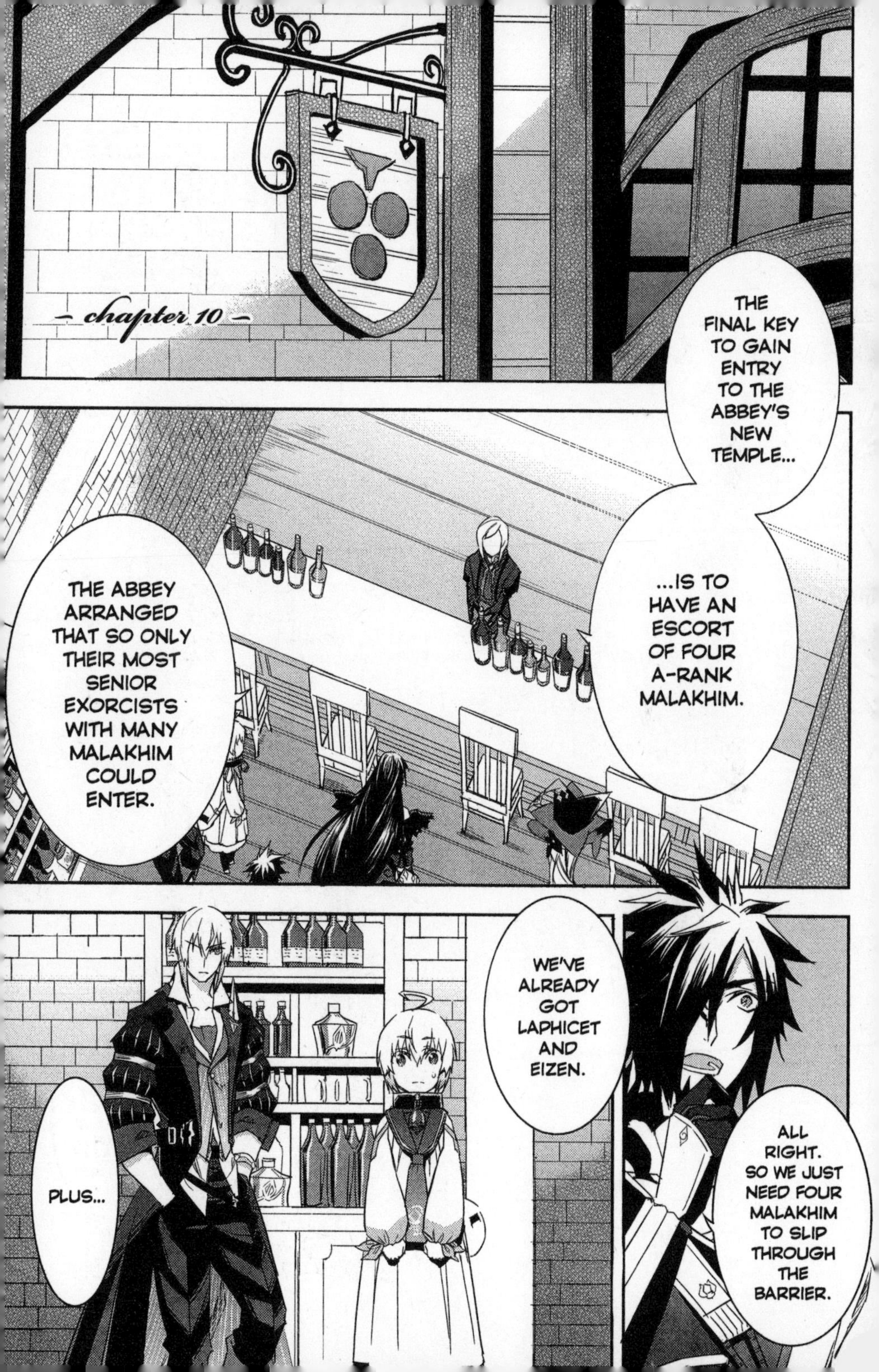

— chapter 10 —
THE FINAL KEY TO GAIN ENTRY TO THE ABBEY'S NEW TEMPLE...
...IS TO HAVE AN ESCORT OF FOUR A-RANK MALAKHIM.
THE ABBEY ARRANGED THAT SO ONLY THEIR MOST SENIOR EXORCISTS WITH MANY MALAKHIM COULD ENTER.
ALL RIGHT. SO WE JUST NEED FOUR MALAKHIM TO SLIP THROUGH THE BARRIER.
WE'VE ALREADY GOT LAPHICET AND EIZEN.
PLUS...

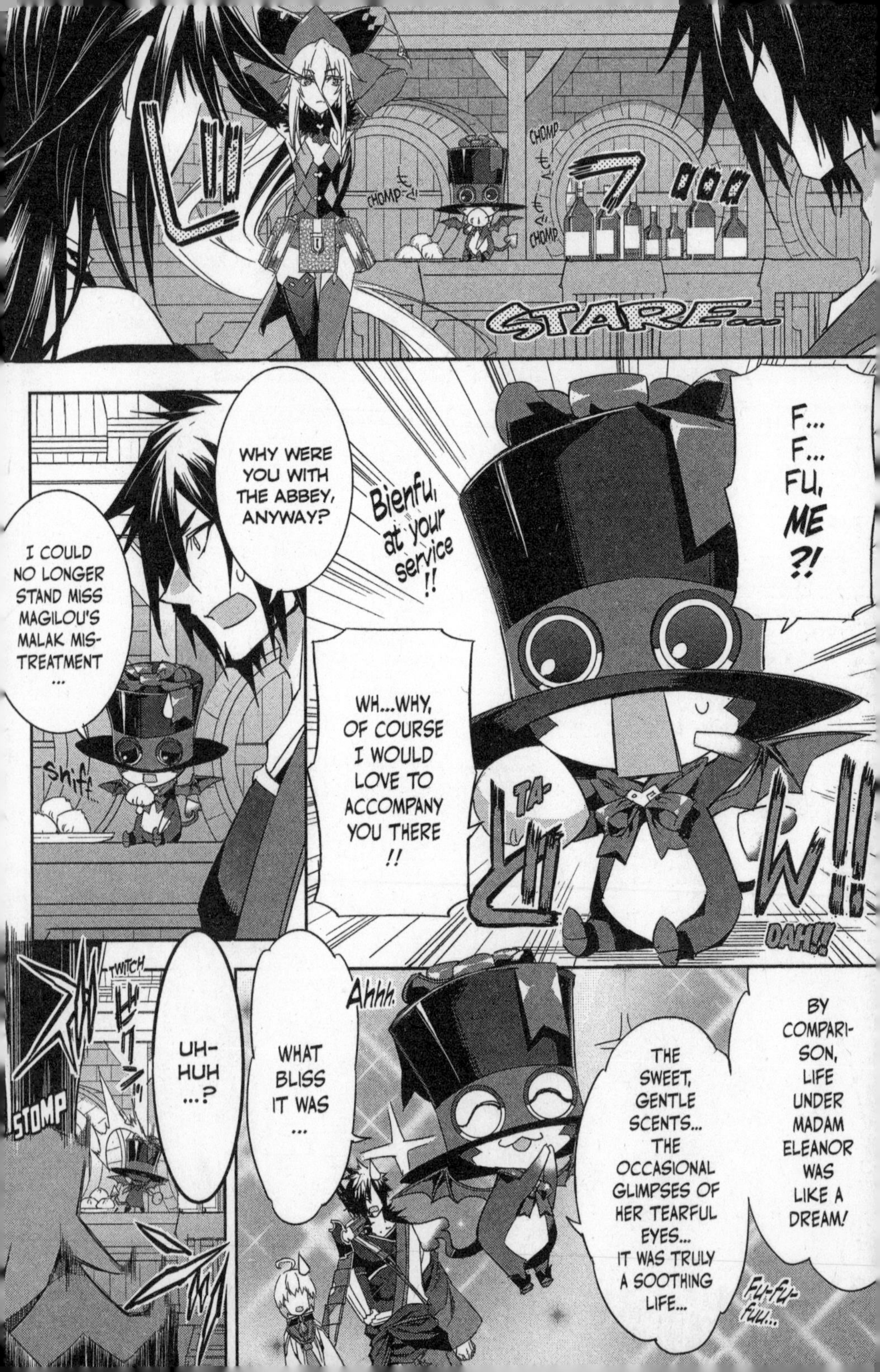
CHOMP
CHOMP
CHOMP
STARE...
F... F... FU, ME?!
Bienfu, at your service!!
WH...WHY, OF COURSE I WOULD LOVE TO ACCOMPANY YOU THERE!!
TA-
OAH!!
WHY WERE YOU WITH THE ABBEY, ANYWAY?
I COULD NO LONGER STAND MISS MAGILOU'S MALAK MIS-TREATMENT...
Sniff
BY COMPARI-SON, LIFE UNDER MADAM ELEANOR WAS LIKE A DREAM!
THE SWEET, GENTLE SCENTS... THE OCCASIONAL GLIMPSES OF HER TEARFUL EYES... IT WAS TRULY A SOOTHING LIFE...
Fu-fu-fuu...
Ahhh.
WHAT BLISS IT WAS...
UH-HUH...?
TWITCH
STOMP

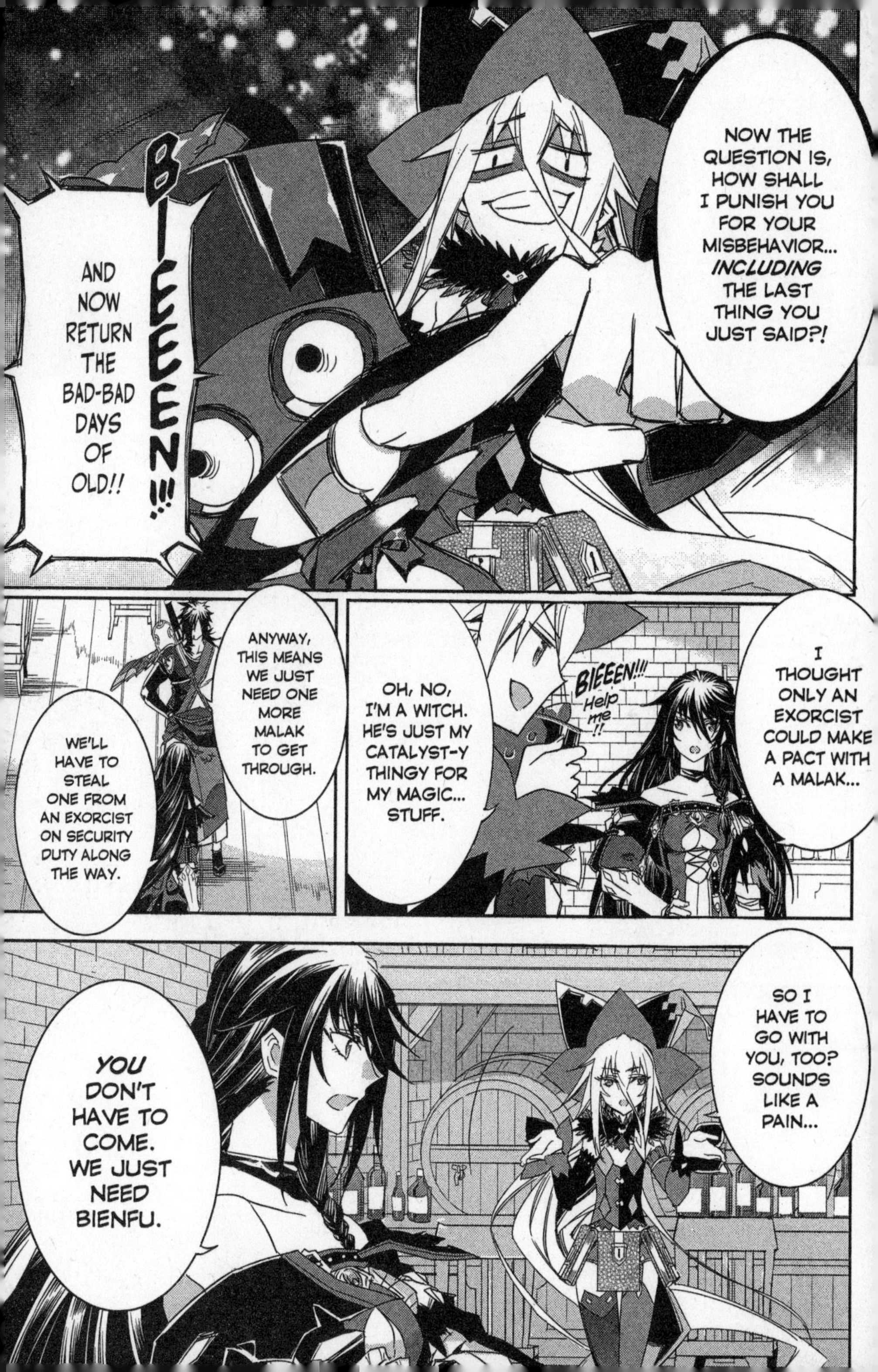
NOW THE QUESTION IS, HOW SHALL I PUNISH YOU FOR YOUR MISBEHAVIOR... *INCLUDING* THE LAST THING YOU JUST SAID?!
BIEEEEN!!!
AND NOW RETURN THE BAD-BAD DAYS OF OLD!!
I THOUGHT ONLY AN EXORCIST COULD MAKE A PACT WITH A MALAK...
BIEEEN!!! Help me!!
OH, NO, I'M A WITCH. HE'S JUST MY CATALYST-Y THINGY FOR MY MAGIC... STUFF.
ANYWAY, THIS MEANS WE JUST NEED ONE MORE MALAK TO GET THROUGH.
WE'LL HAVE TO STEAL ONE FROM AN EXORCIST ON SECURITY DUTY ALONG THE WAY.
SO I HAVE TO GO WITH YOU, TOO? SOUNDS LIKE A PAIN...
YOU DON'T HAVE TO COME. WE JUST NEED BIENFU.

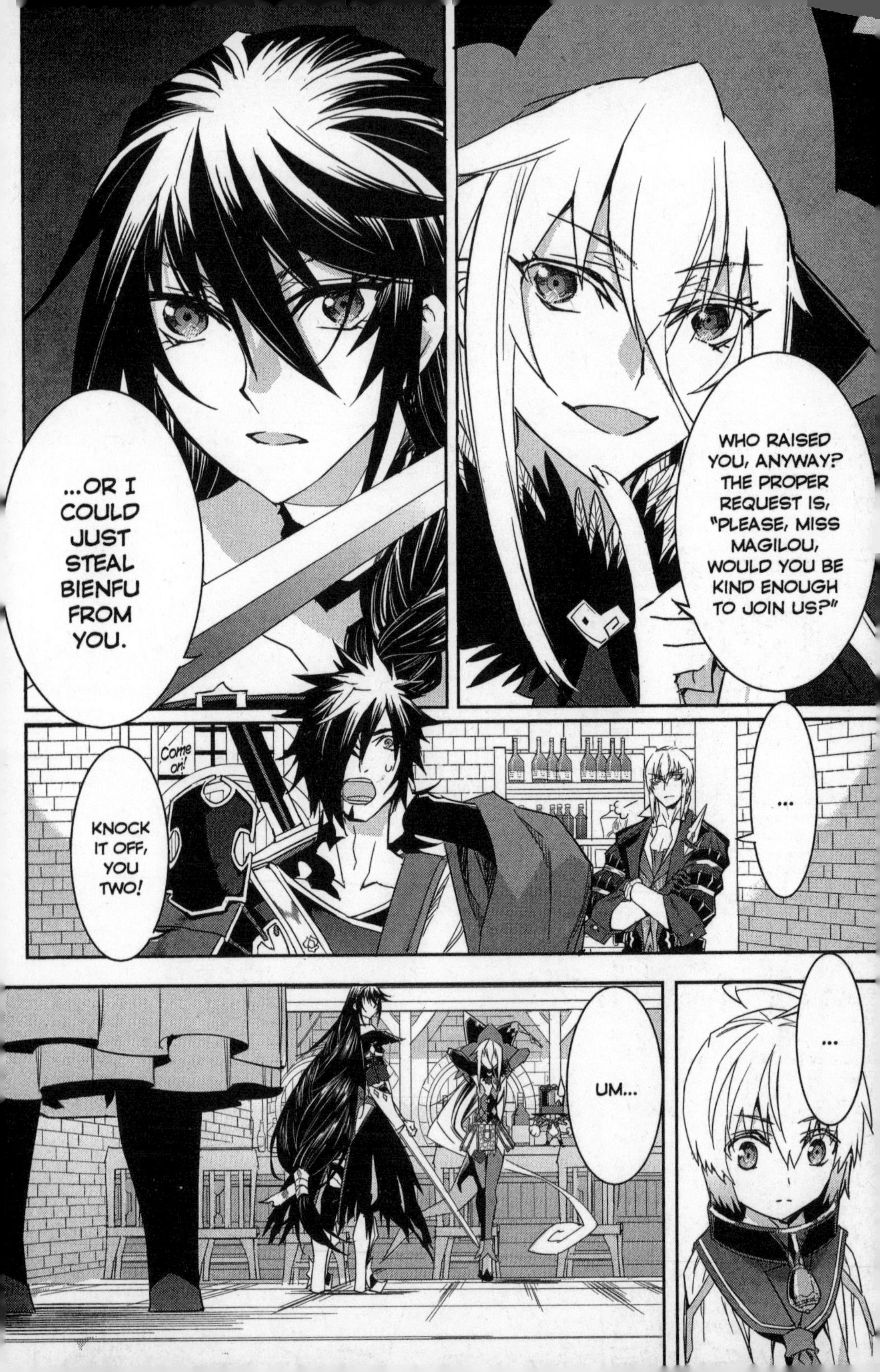
WHO RAISED YOU, ANYWAY? THE PROPER REQUEST IS, "PLEASE, MISS MAGILOU, WOULD YOU BE KIND ENOUGH TO JOIN US?"
...OR I COULD JUST STEAL BIENFU FROM YOU.
...
Come on!
KNOCK IT OFF, YOU TWO!
...
UM...

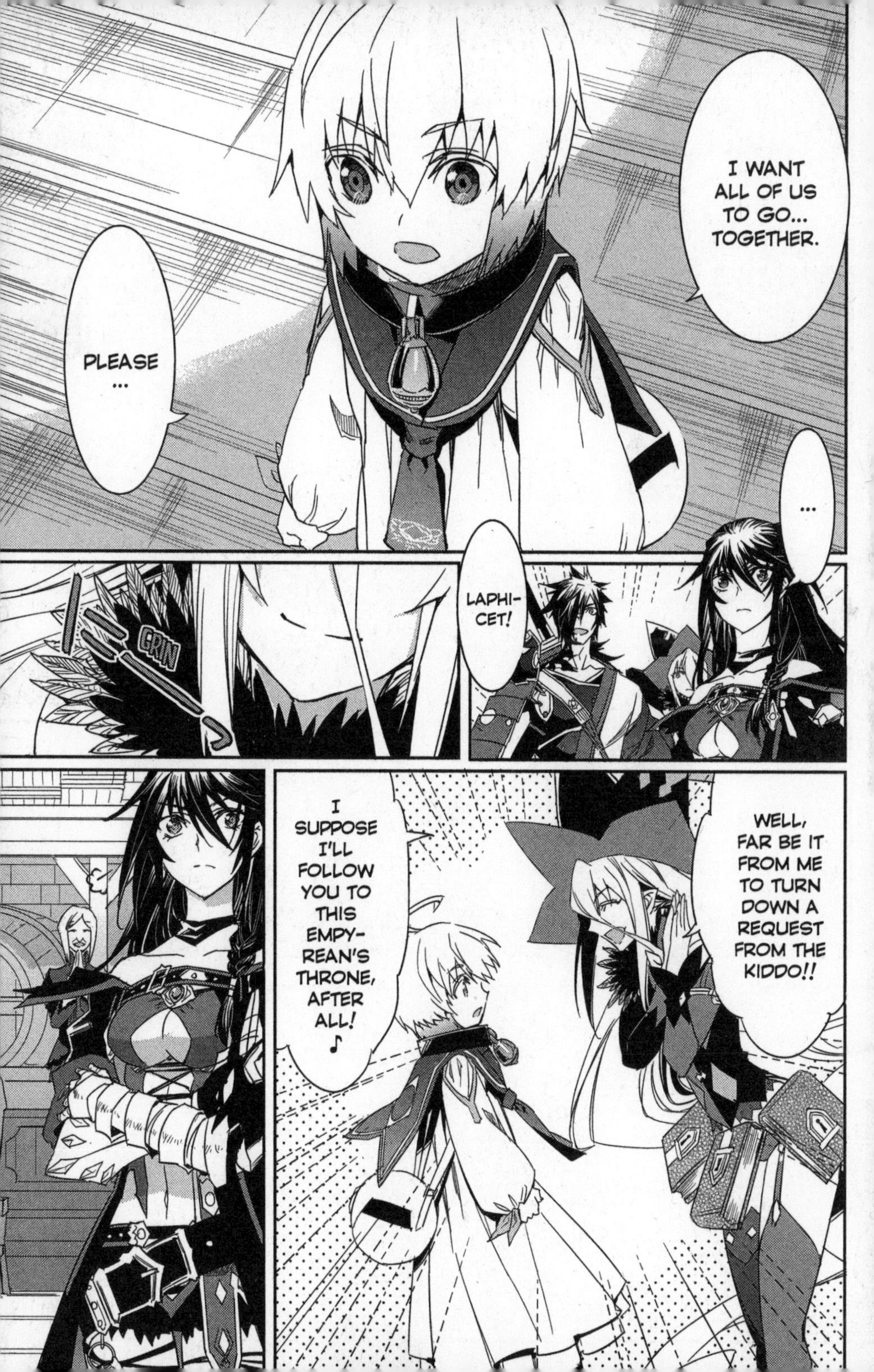
I WANT ALL OF US TO GO... TOGETHER.
PLEASE ...
...
LAPHI-CET!
GRIN
WELL, FAR BE IT FROM ME TO TURN DOWN A REQUEST FROM THE KIDDO!!
I SUPPOSE I'LL FOLLOW YOU TO THIS EMPYREAN'S THRONE, AFTER ALL! ♪

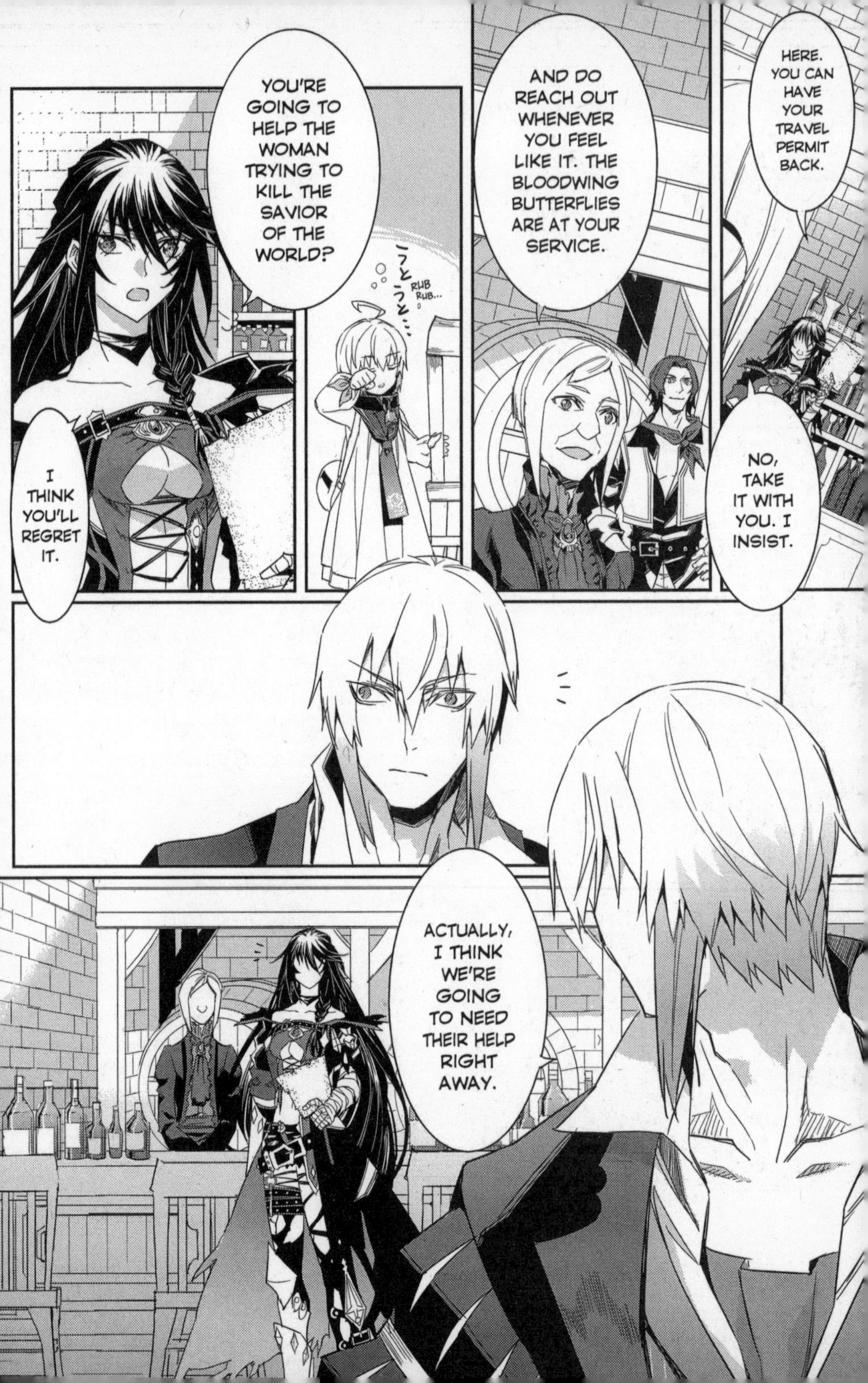
HERE. YOU CAN HAVE YOUR TRAVEL PERMIT BACK.
NO, TAKE IT WITH YOU. I INSIST.
AND DO REACH OUT WHENEVER YOU FEEL LIKE IT. THE BLOODWING BUTTERFLIES ARE AT YOUR SERVICE.
RUB RUB...
YOU'RE GOING TO HELP THE WOMAN TRYING TO KILL THE SAVIOR OF THE WORLD?
I THINK YOU'LL REGRET IT.
ACTUALLY, I THINK WE'RE GOING TO NEED THEIR HELP RIGHT AWAY.

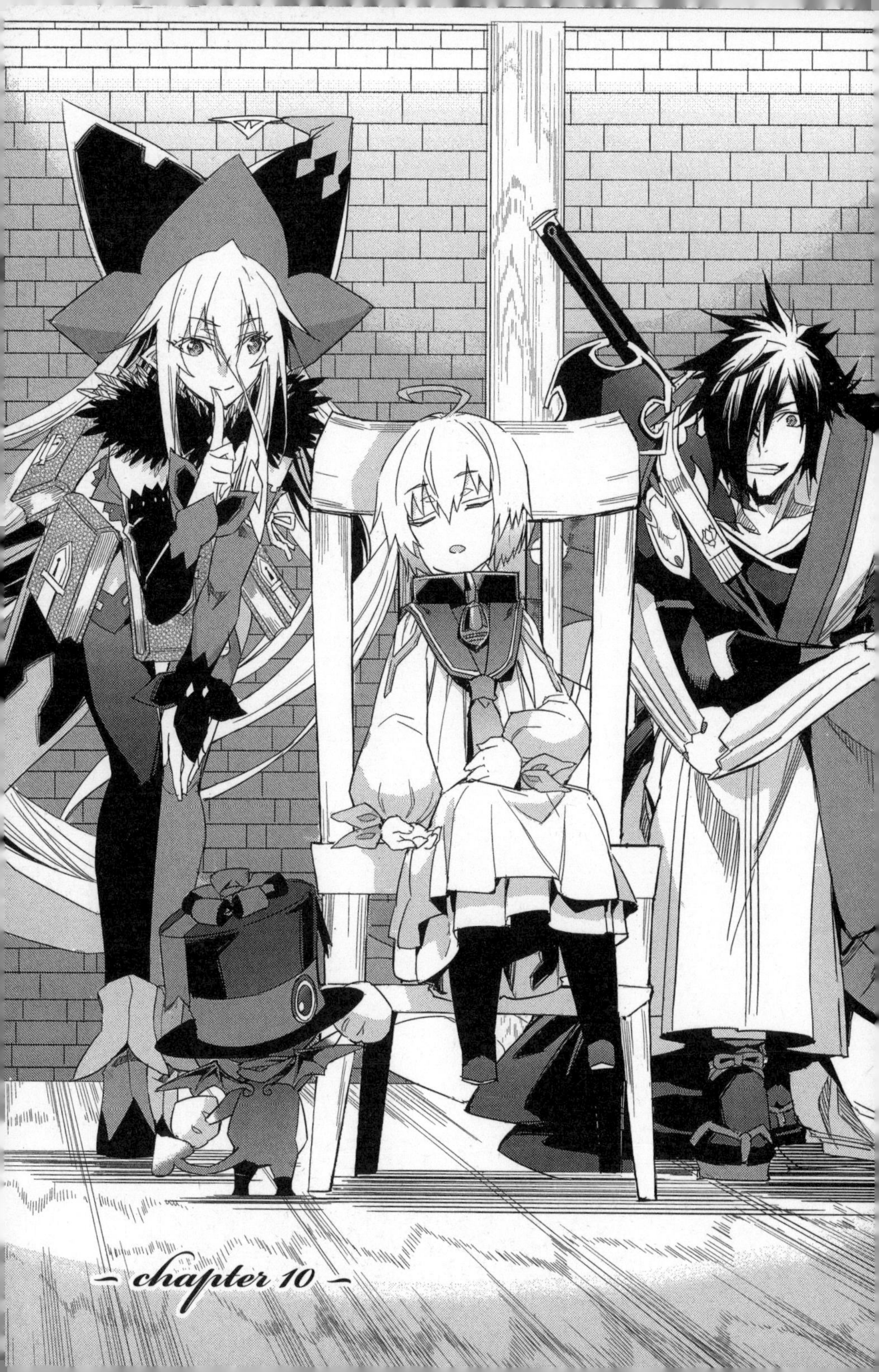
- chapter 10 -

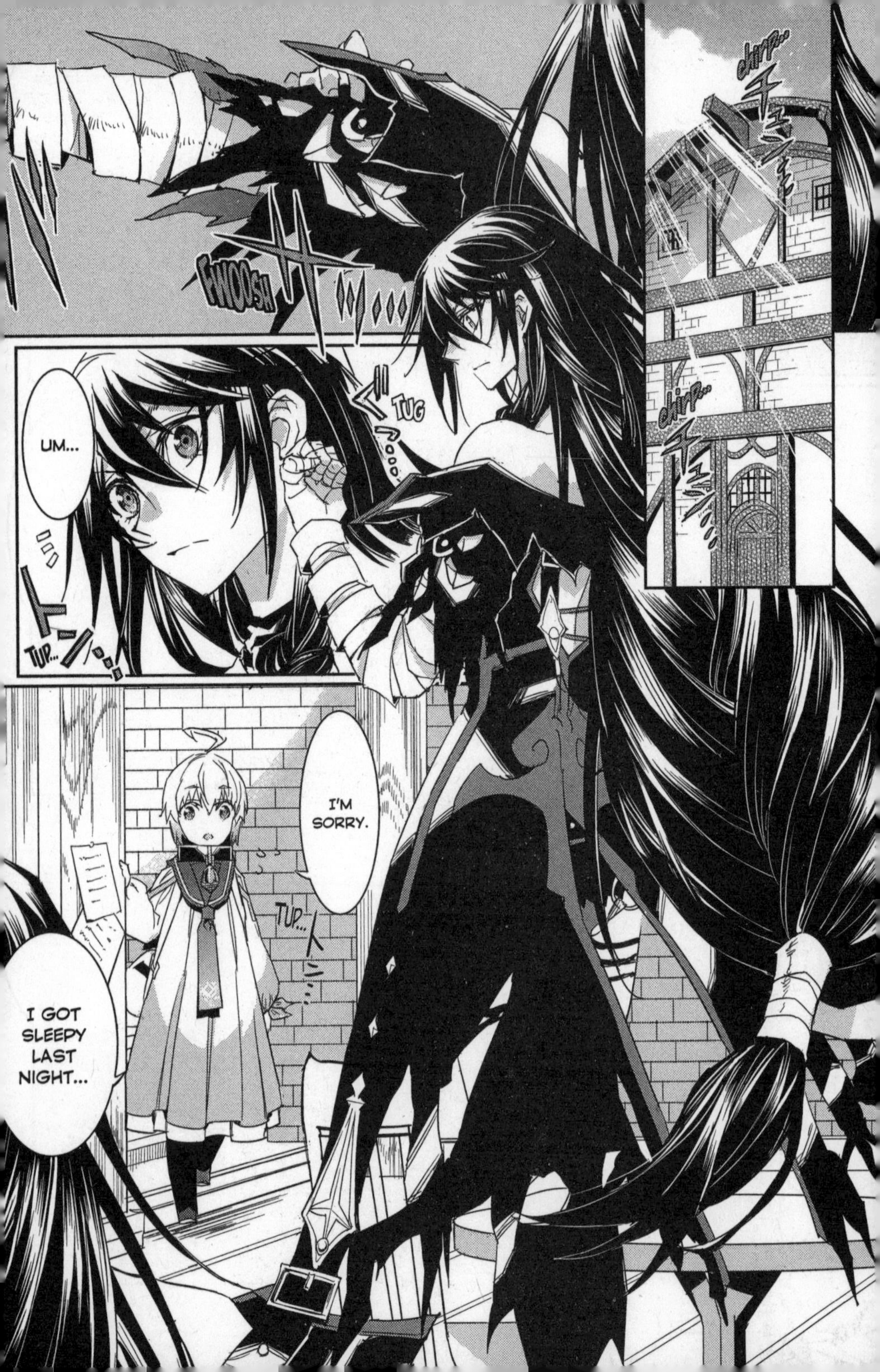
chirp...
chirp...
WHOOSH
TUG
UM...
TUP...
I'M SORRY.
TUP...
I GOT SLEEPY LAST NIGHT...

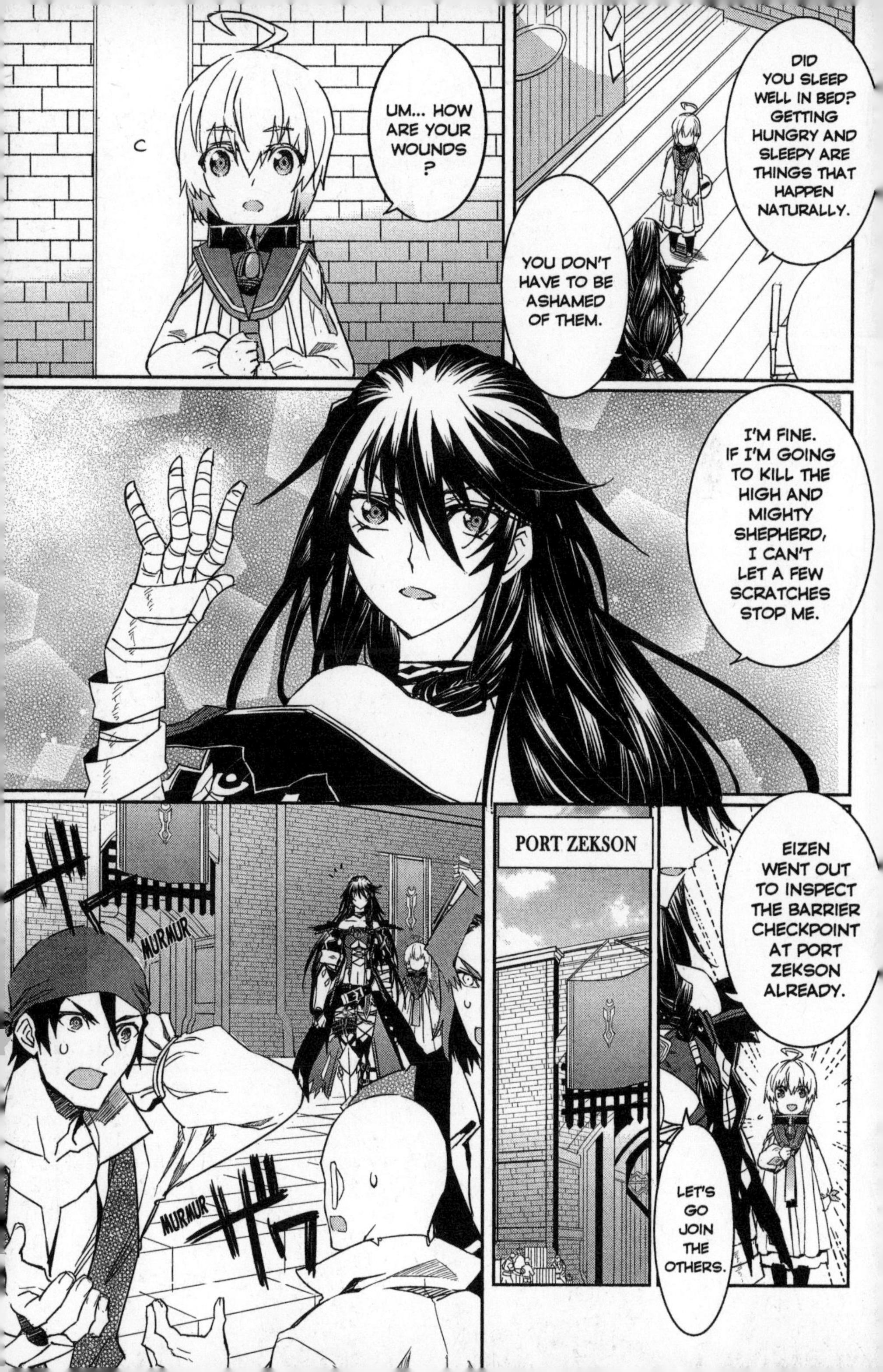
DID YOU SLEEP WELL IN BED? GETTING HUNGRY AND SLEEPY ARE THINGS THAT HAPPEN NATURALLY.
YOU DON'T HAVE TO BE ASHAMED OF THEM.
UM... HOW ARE YOUR WOUNDS?
I'M FINE. IF I'M GOING TO KILL THE HIGH AND MIGHTY SHEPHERD, I CAN'T LET A FEW SCRATCHES STOP ME.
PORT ZEKSON
EIZEN WENT OUT TO INSPECT THE BARRIER CHECKPOINT AT PORT ZEKSON ALREADY.
LET'S GO JOIN THE OTHERS.
MURMUR
MURMUR

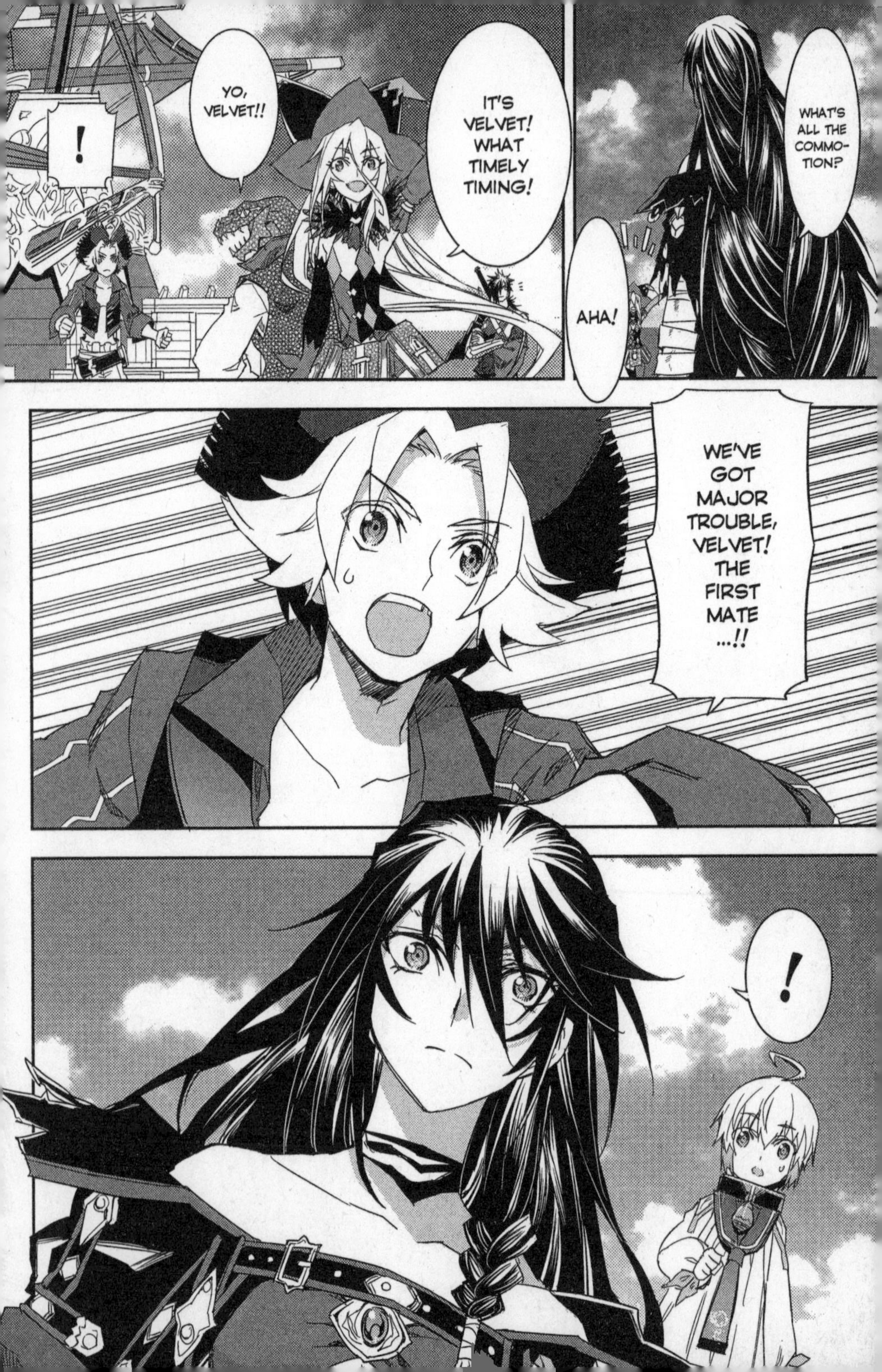
WHAT'S ALL THE COMMOTION?
AHA!
IT'S VELVET! WHAT TIMELY TIMING!
YO, VELVET!!
!
WE'VE GOT MAJOR TROUBLE, VELVET! THE FIRST MATE ...!!
!

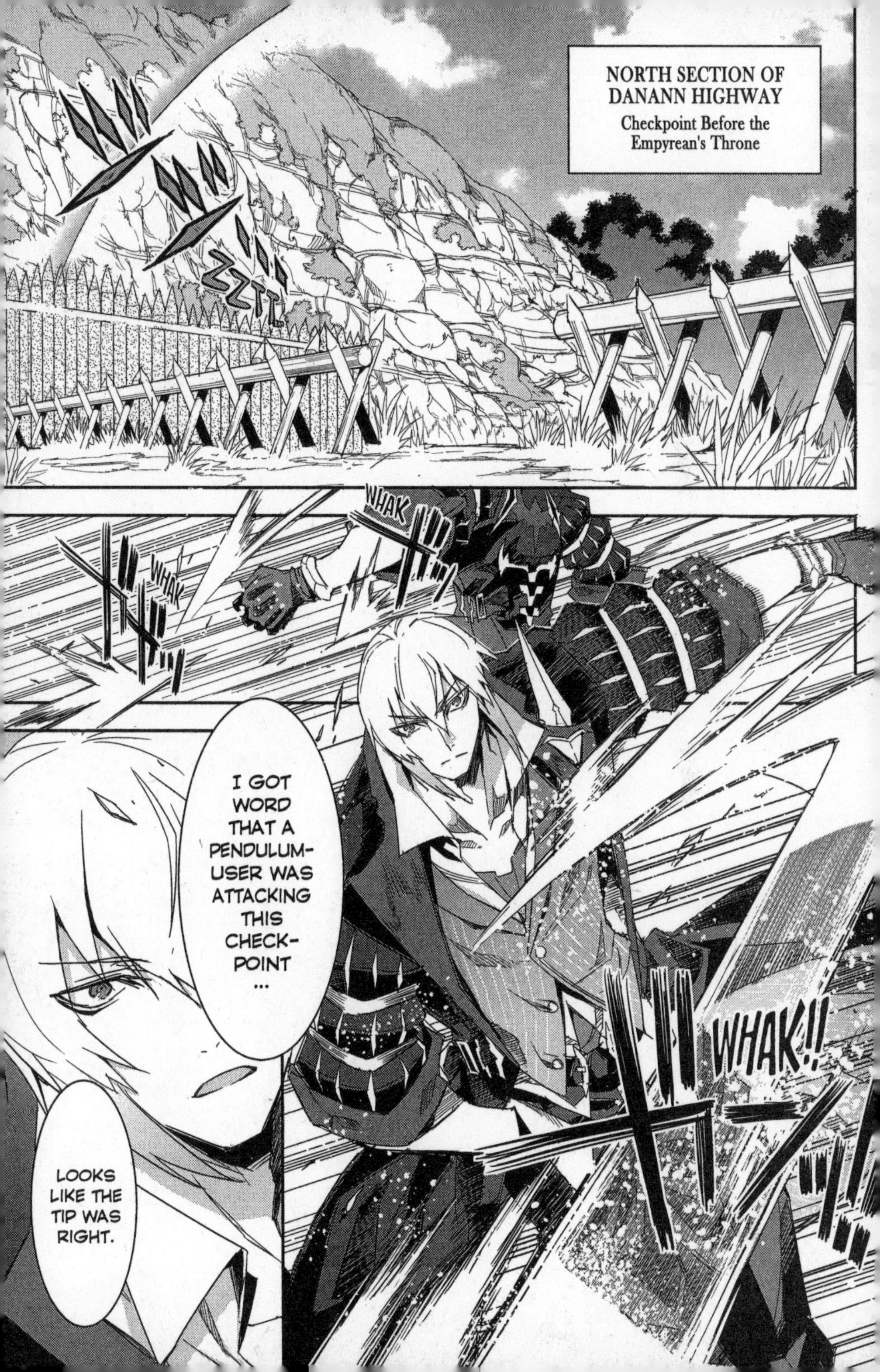
NORTH SECTION OF DANANN HIGHWAY
Checkpoint Before the Empyrean's Throne
ZZTT
WHAK
WHAK
WHAK!!
I GOT WORD THAT A PENDULUM-USER WAS ATTACKING THIS CHECK-POINT ...
LOOKS LIKE THE TIP WAS RIGHT.

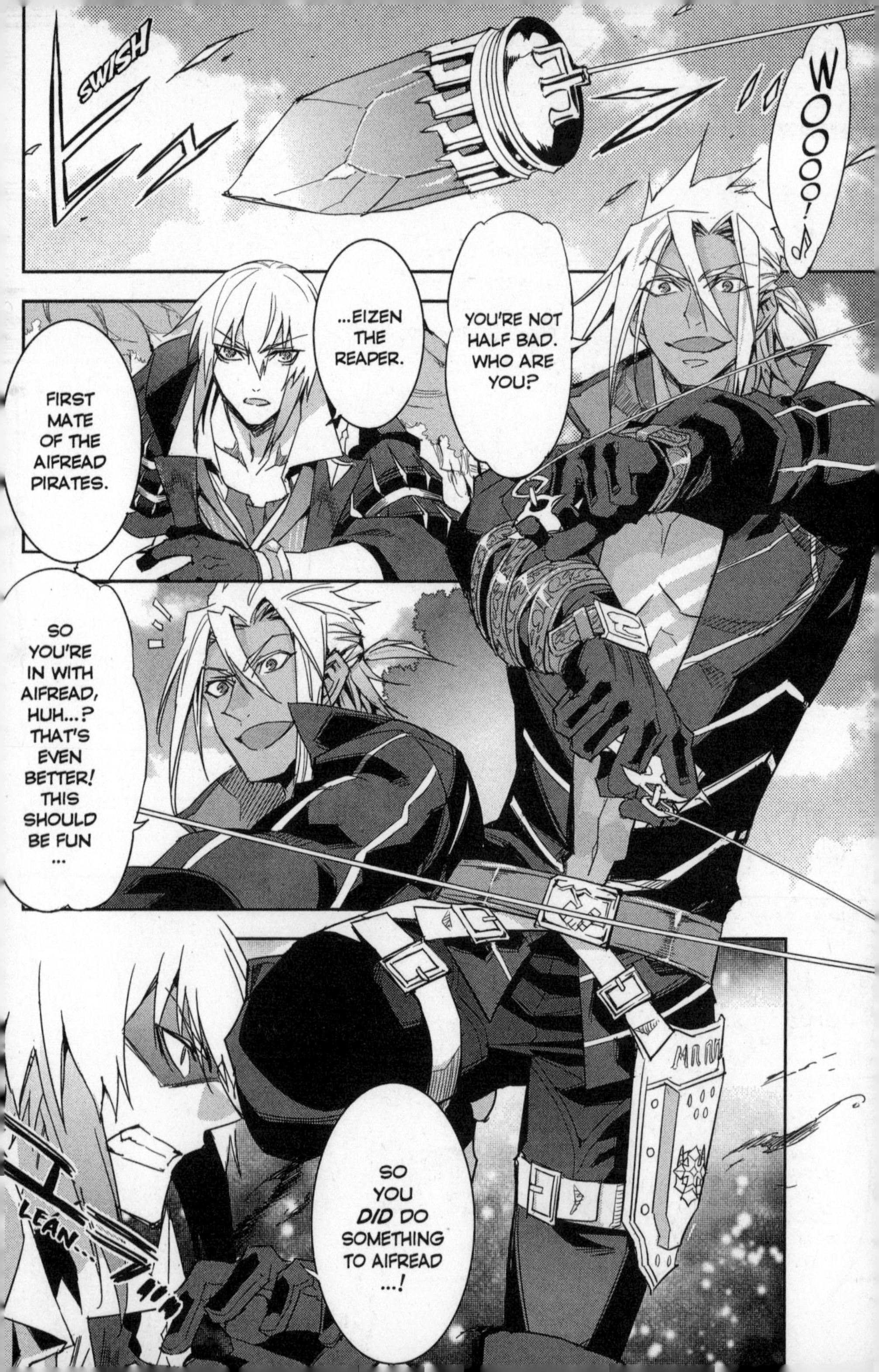
WOOOO!♪
SWISH
YOU'RE NOT HALF BAD. WHO ARE YOU?
...EIZEN THE REAPER.
FIRST MATE OF THE AIFREAD PIRATES.
SO YOU'RE IN WITH AIFREAD, HUH...? THAT'S EVEN BETTER! THIS SHOULD BE FUN ...
SO YOU *DID* DO SOMETHING TO AIFREAD ...!
LEAN...

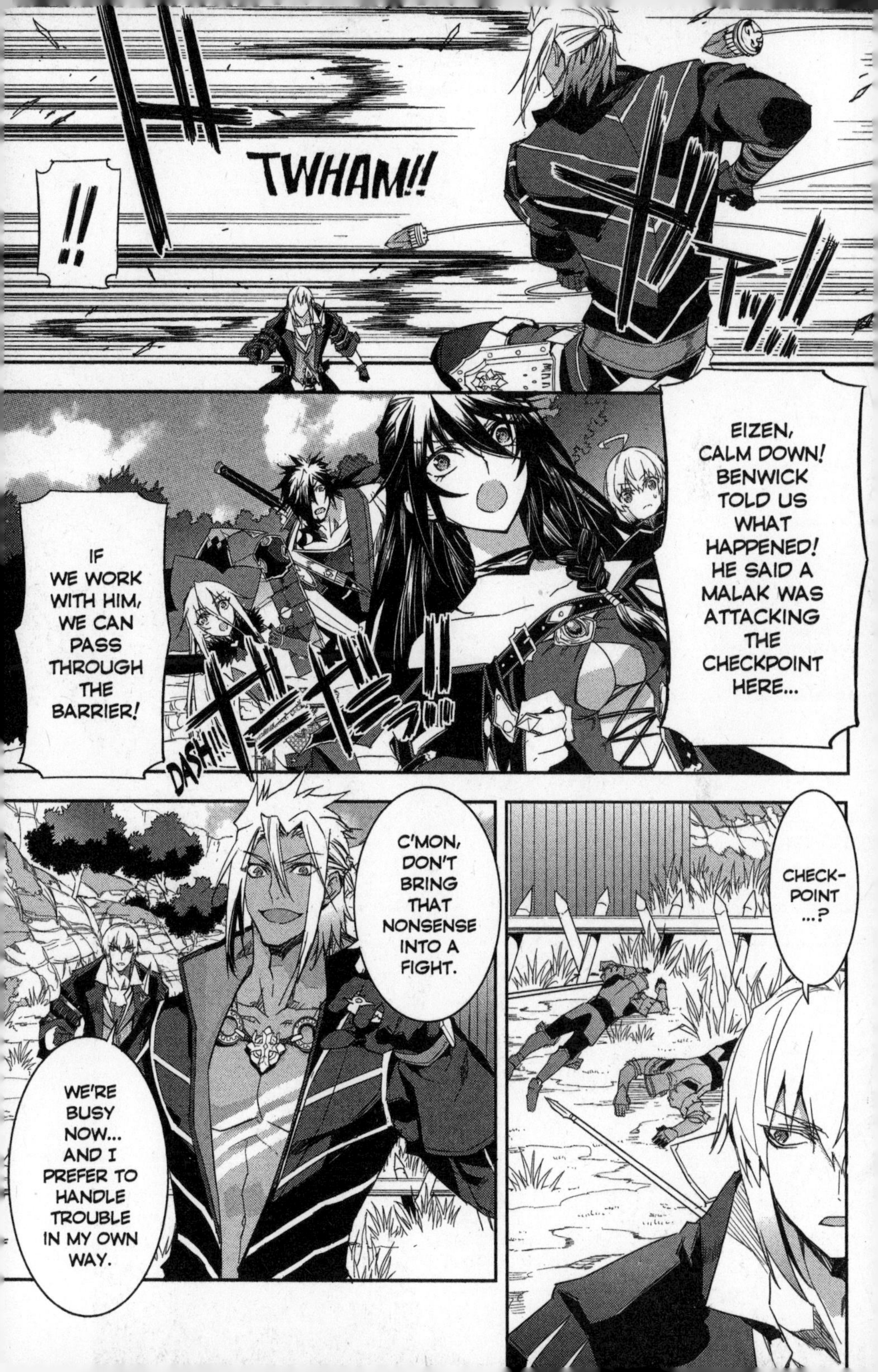
TWHAM!!
!!
EIZEN, CALM DOWN! BENWICK TOLD US WHAT HAPPENED! HE SAID A MALAK WAS ATTACKING THE CHECKPOINT HERE...
IF WE WORK WITH HIM, WE CAN PASS THROUGH THE BARRIER!
DASH!!
CHECK-POINT ...?
C'MON, DON'T BRING THAT NONSENSE INTO A FIGHT.
WE'RE BUSY NOW... AND I PREFER TO HANDLE TROUBLE IN MY OWN WAY.

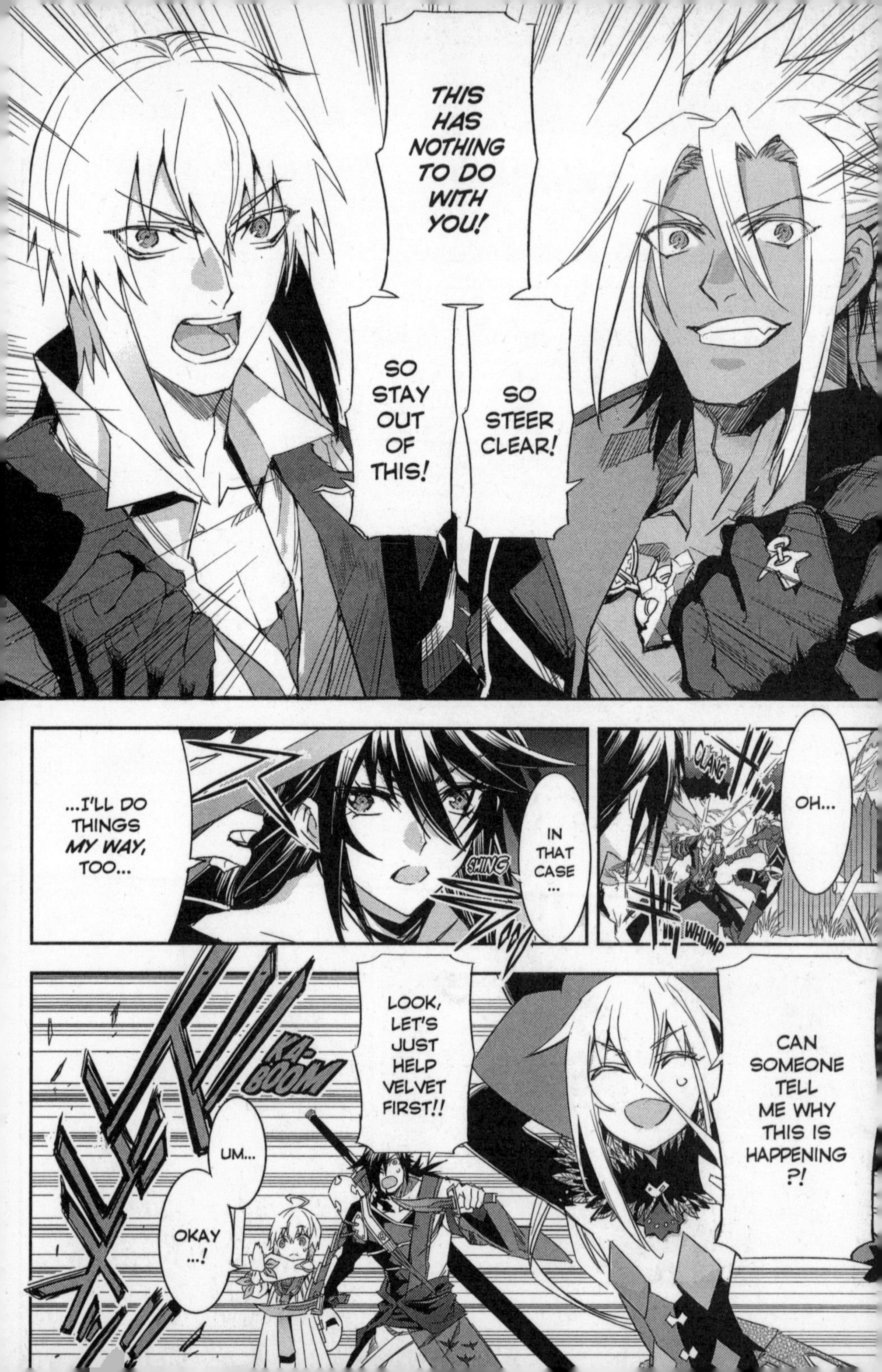
THIS HAS NOTHING TO DO WITH YOU!
SO STEER CLEAR!
SO STAY OUT OF THIS!
OH...
CLANG
WHUMP
IN THAT CASE ...
SHING
...I'LL DO THINGS *MY WAY,* TOO...
CAN SOMEONE TELL ME WHY THIS IS HAPPENING ?!
LOOK, LET'S JUST HELP VELVET FIRST!!
KA-BOOM
UM...
OKAY ...!

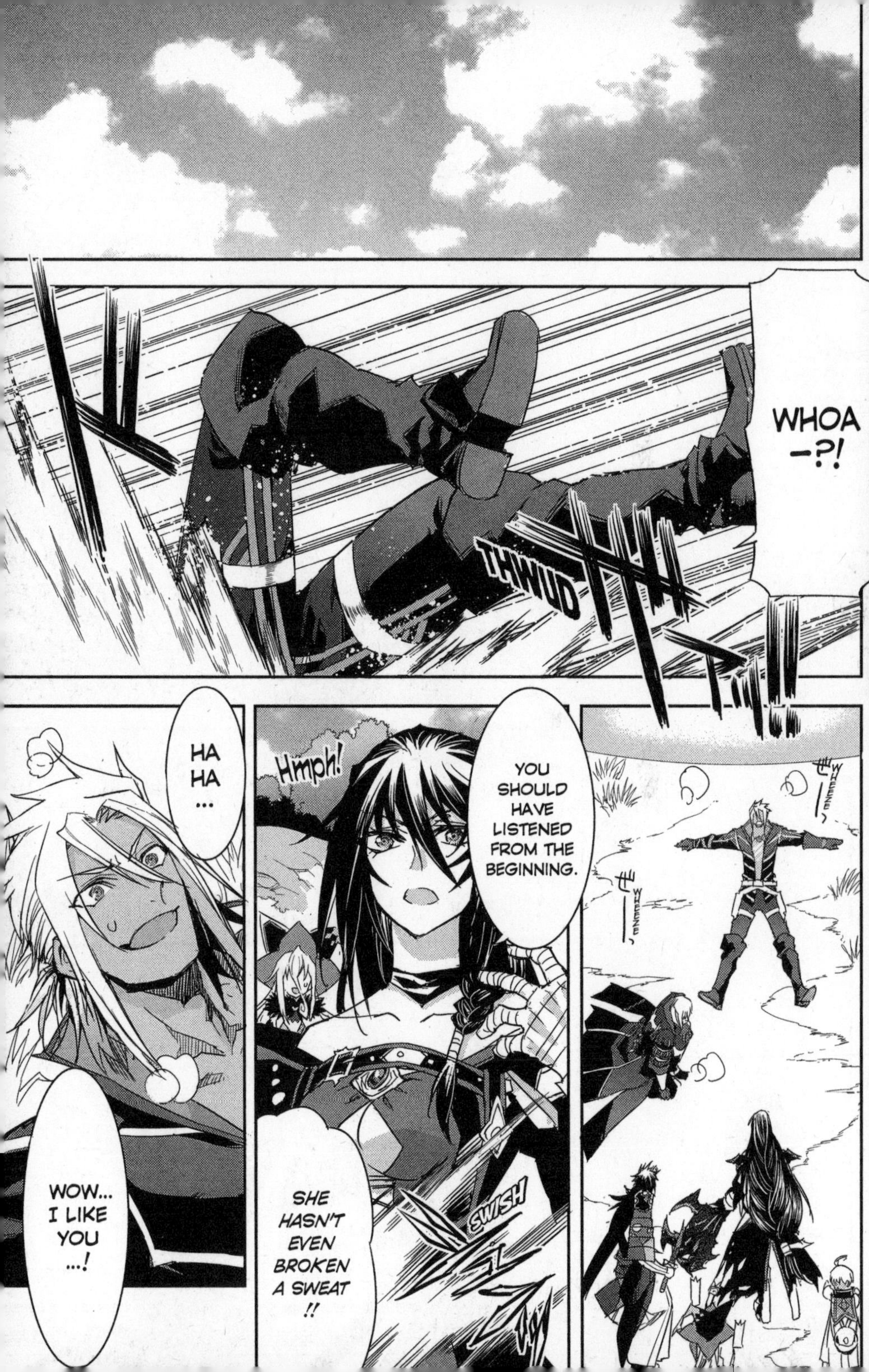
WHOA—?!
THWUD
WHEEZE
WHEEZE
YOU SHOULD HAVE LISTENED FROM THE BEGINNING.
Hmph!
SWISH
SHE HASN'T EVEN BROKEN A SWEAT!!
HA HA...
WOW... I LIKE YOU...!

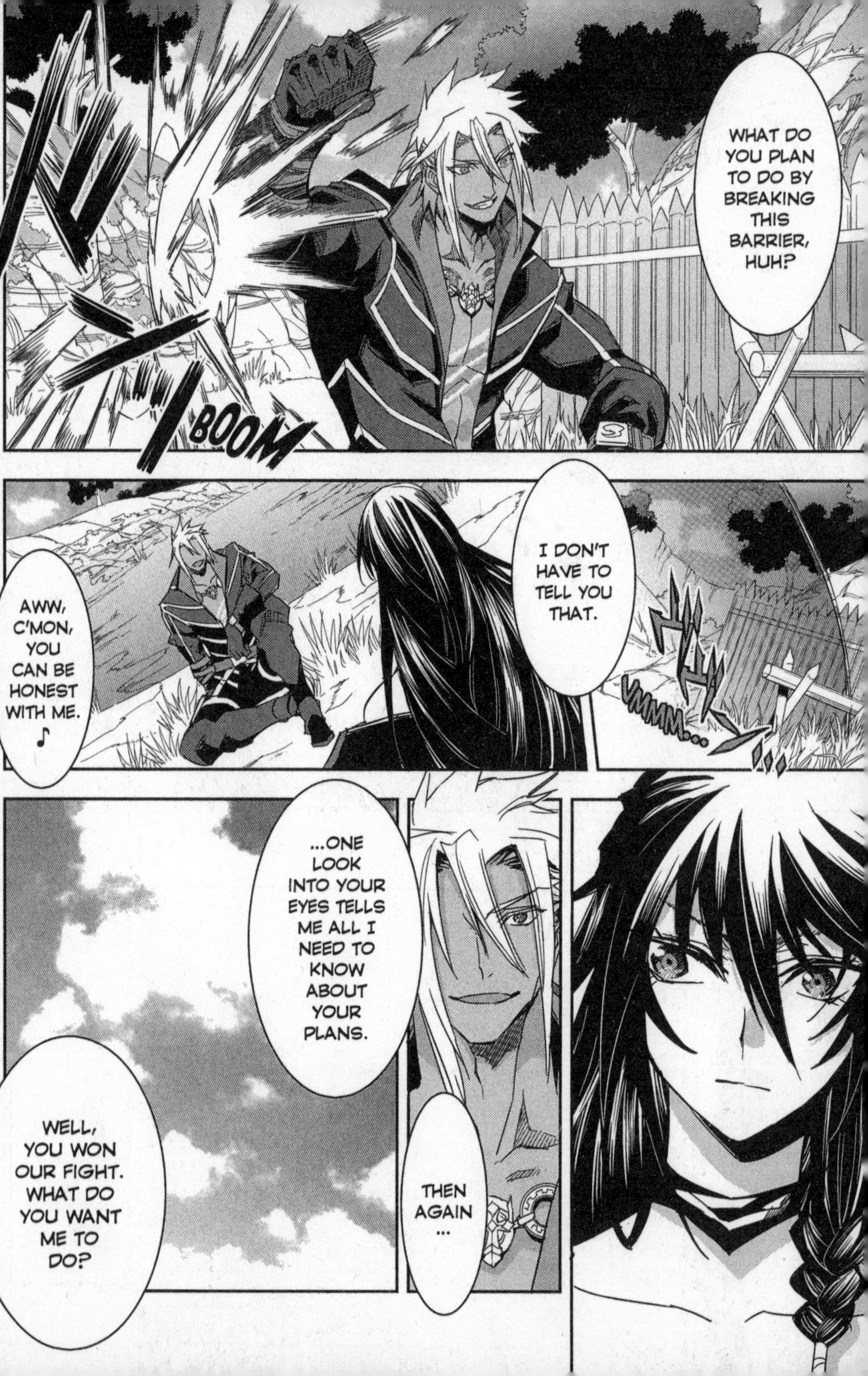
WHAT DO YOU PLAN TO DO BY BREAKING THIS BARRIER, HUH?
BOOM
I DON'T HAVE TO TELL YOU THAT.
VMMM...
AWW, C'MON, YOU CAN BE HONEST WITH ME. ♪
THEN AGAIN ...
...ONE LOOK INTO YOUR EYES TELLS ME ALL I NEED TO KNOW ABOUT YOUR PLANS.
WELL, YOU WON OUR FIGHT. WHAT DO YOU WANT ME TO DO?

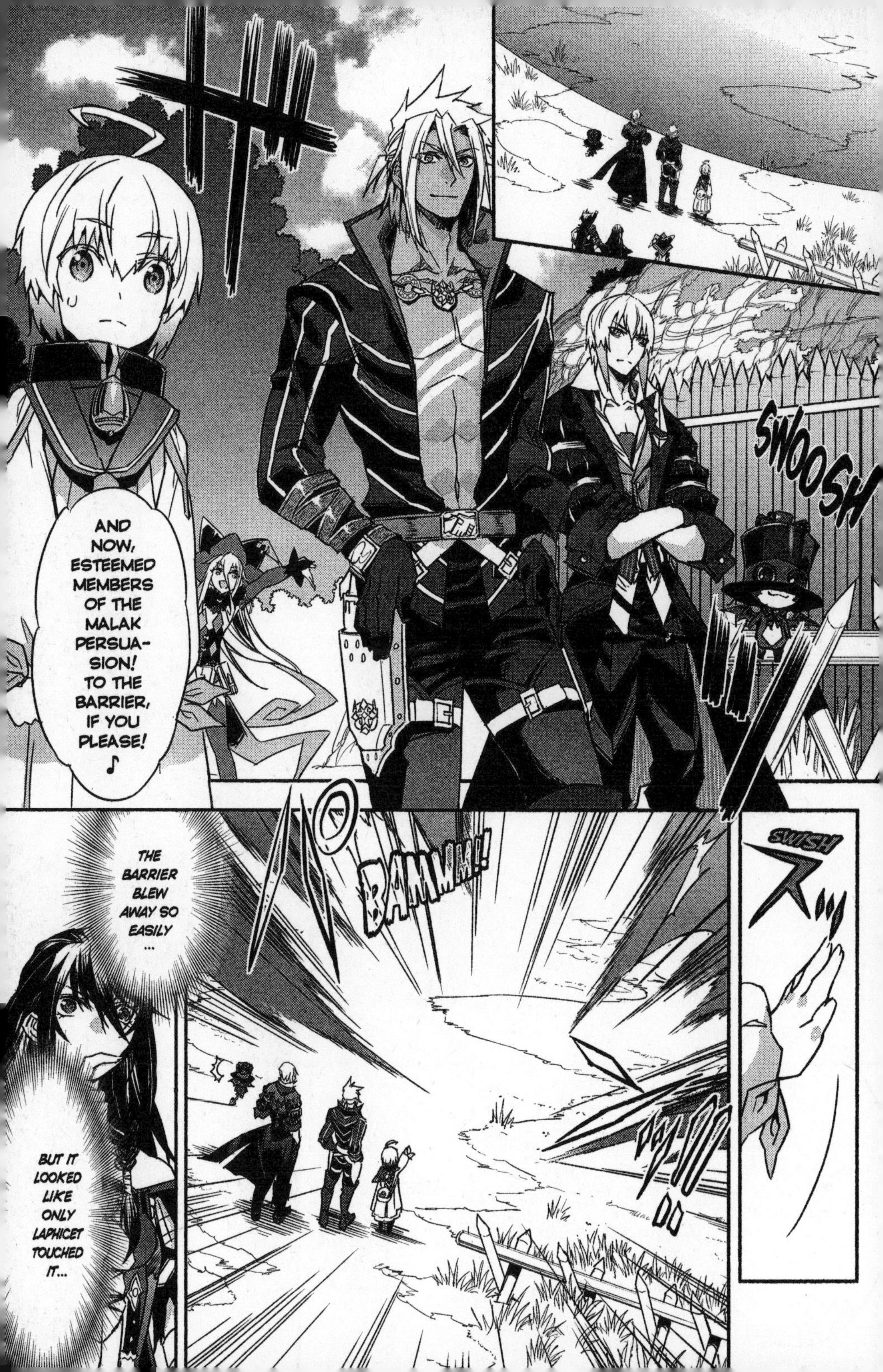
SWOOSH
AND NOW, ESTEEMED MEMBERS OF THE MALAK PERSUASION! TO THE BARRIER, IF YOU PLEASE! ♪
SWISH
BAMMM!!
THE BARRIER BLEW AWAY SO EASILY ...
BUT IT LOOKED LIKE ONLY LAPHICET TOUCHED IT...

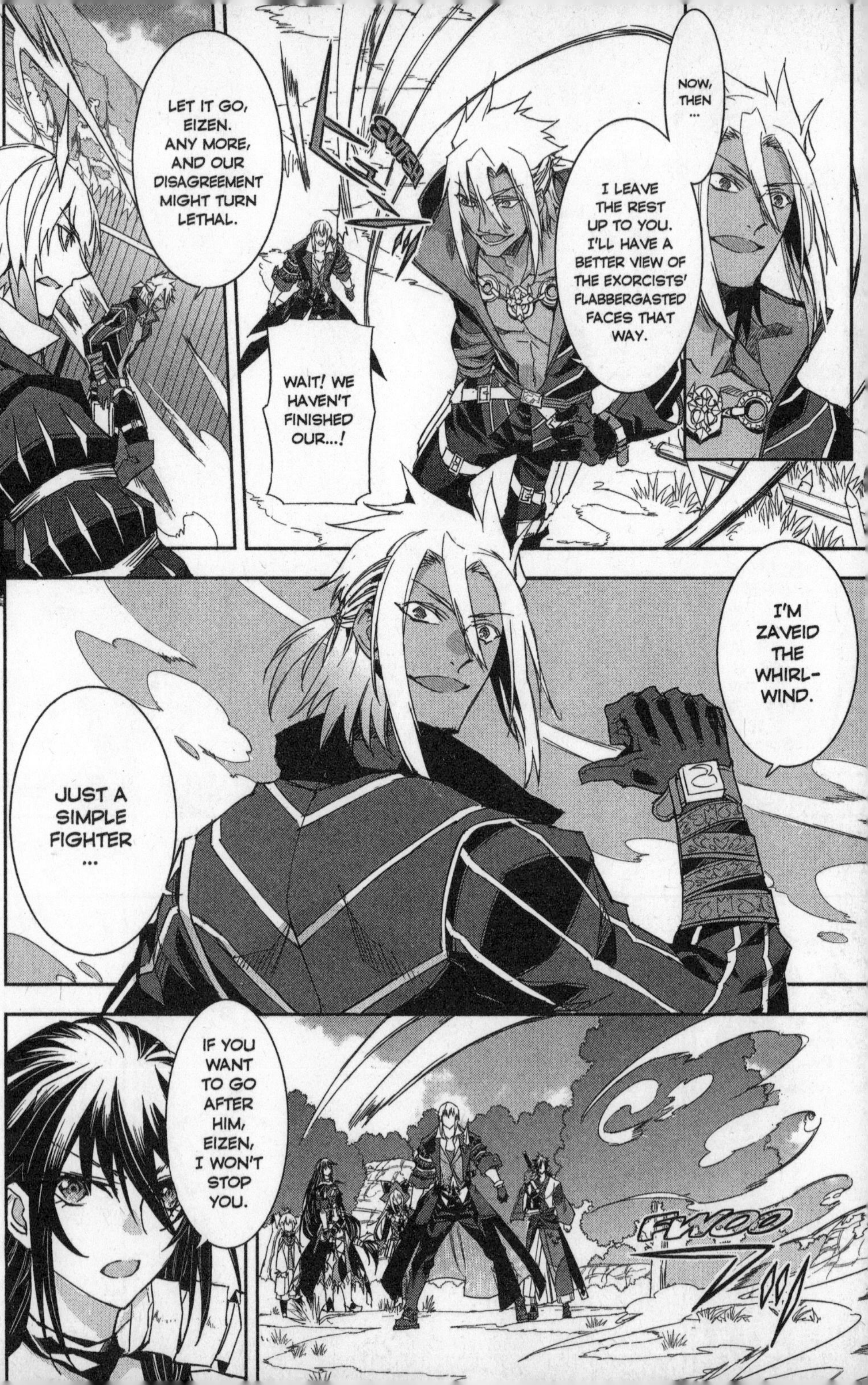
NOW, THEN ...
I LEAVE THE REST UP TO YOU. I'LL HAVE A BETTER VIEW OF THE EXORCISTS' FLABBERGASTED FACES THAT WAY.
SWISH
WAIT! WE HAVEN'T FINISHED OUR...!
LET IT GO, EIZEN. ANY MORE, AND OUR DISAGREEMENT MIGHT TURN LETHAL.
I'M ZAVEID THE WHIRL-WIND.
JUST A SIMPLE FIGHTER ...
FWOOO
IF YOU WANT TO GO AFTER HIM, EIZEN, I WON'T STOP YOU.

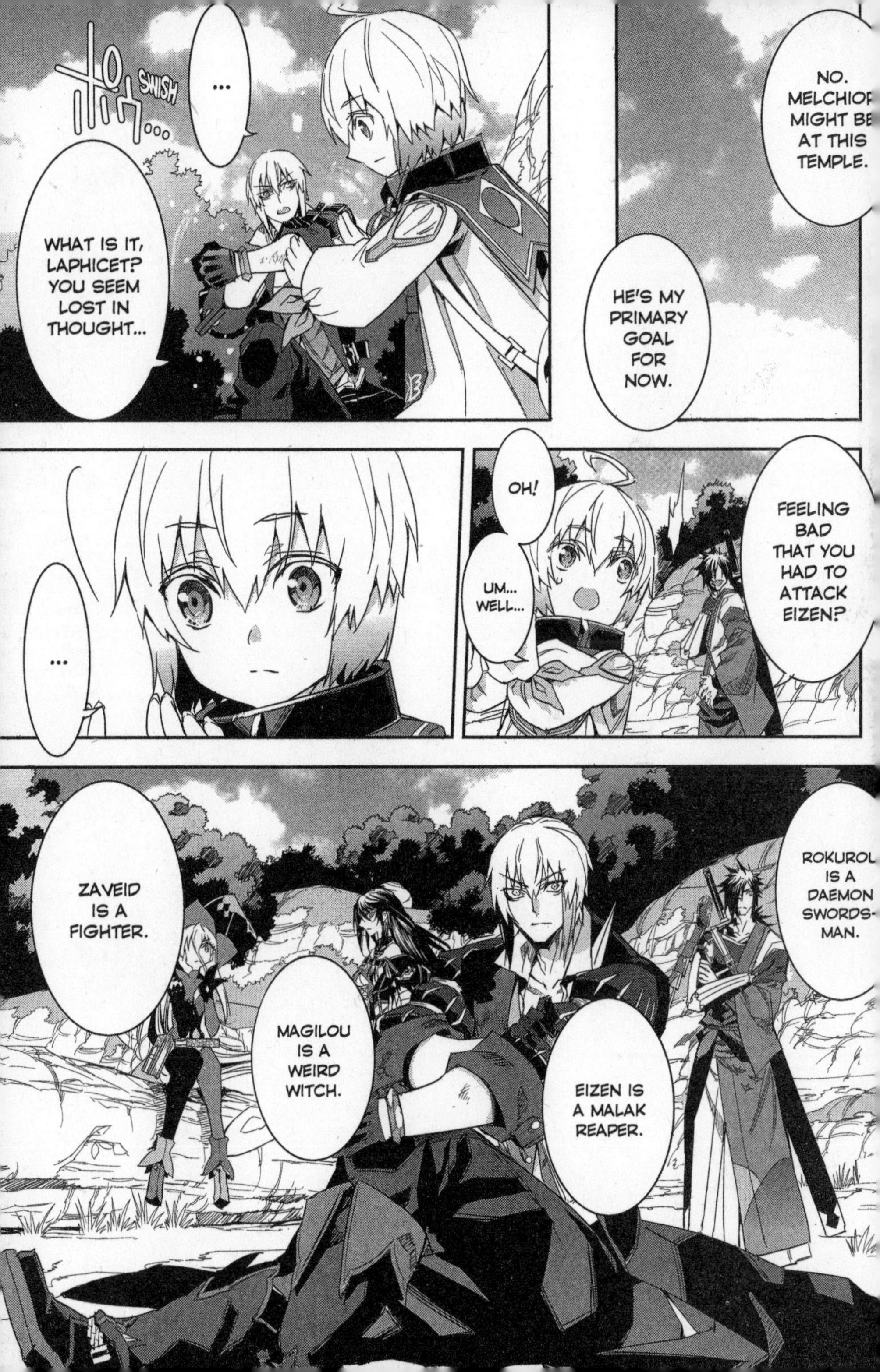

NO. MELCHIOR MIGHT BE AT THIS TEMPLE.
HE'S MY PRIMARY GOAL FOR NOW.
SWISH
...
WHAT IS IT, LAPHICET? YOU SEEM LOST IN THOUGHT...
FEELING BAD THAT YOU HAD TO ATTACK EIZEN?
OH!
UM... WELL...
...
ROKUROU IS A DAEMON SWORDS-MAN.
EIZEN IS A MALAK REAPER.
MAGILOU IS A WEIRD WITCH.
ZAVEID IS A FIGHTER.

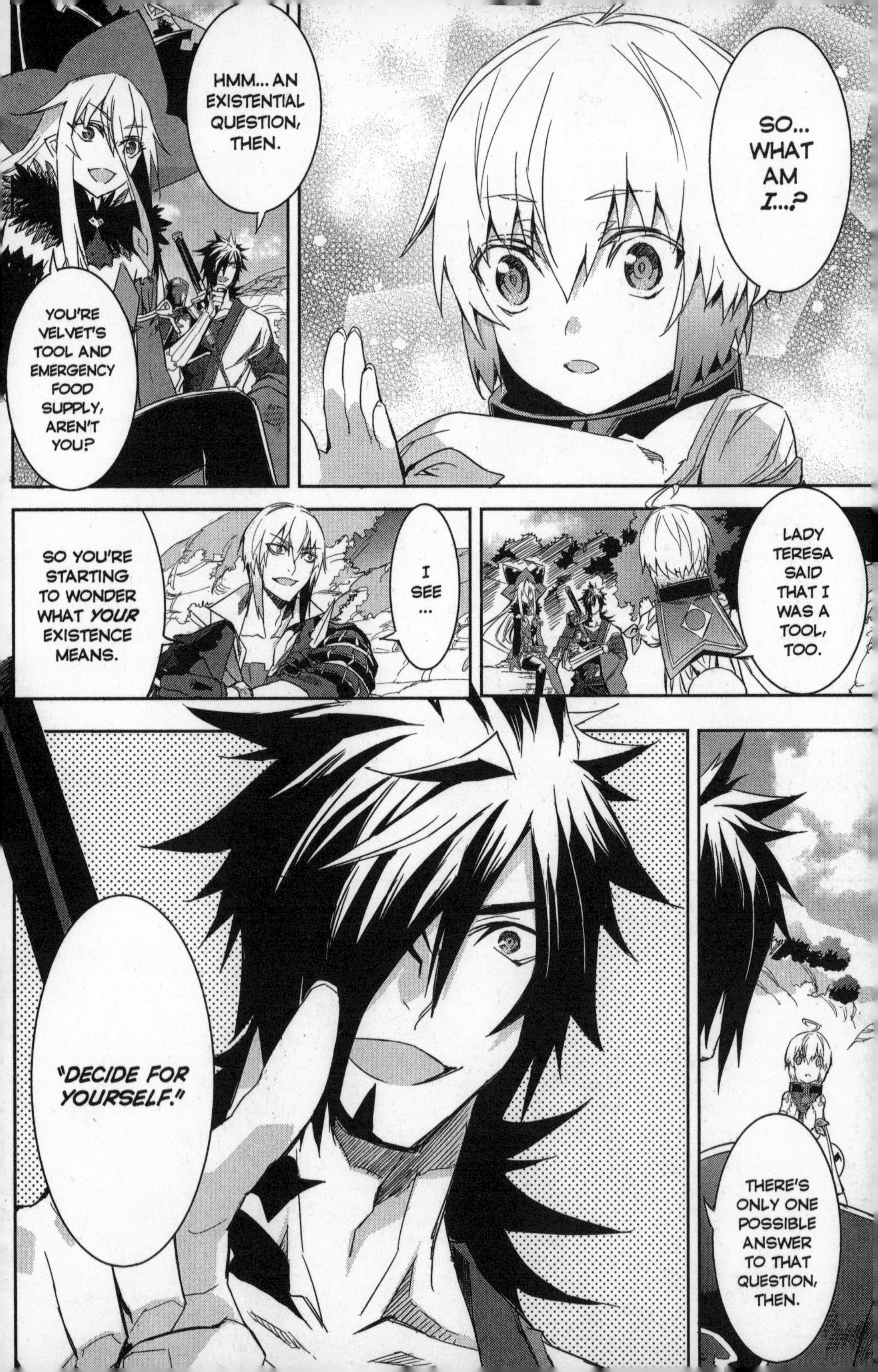
SO... WHAT AM I...?
HMM... AN EXISTENTIAL QUESTION, THEN.
YOU'RE VELVET'S TOOL AND EMERGENCY FOOD SUPPLY, AREN'T YOU?
LADY TERESA SAID THAT I WAS A TOOL, TOO.
I SEE...
SO YOU'RE STARTING TO WONDER WHAT YOUR EXISTENCE MEANS.
THERE'S ONLY ONE POSSIBLE ANSWER TO THAT QUESTION, THEN.
"DECIDE FOR YOURSELF."

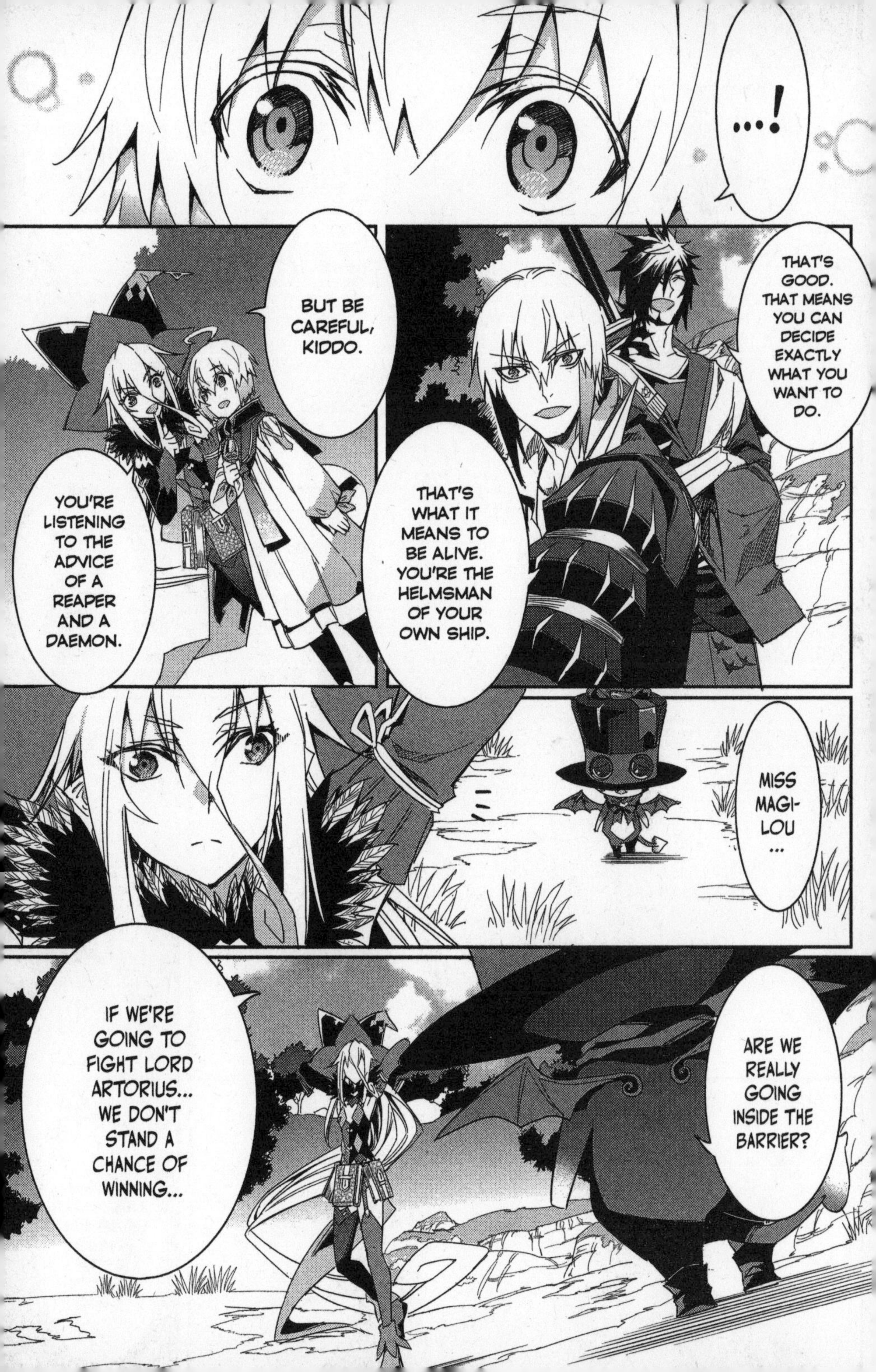
...!
THAT'S GOOD. THAT MEANS YOU CAN DECIDE EXACTLY WHAT YOU WANT TO DO.
THAT'S WHAT IT MEANS TO BE ALIVE. YOU'RE THE HELMSMAN OF YOUR OWN SHIP.
BUT BE CAREFUL, KIDDO.
YOU'RE LISTENING TO THE ADVICE OF A REAPER AND A DAEMON.
MISS MAGI-LOU ...
ARE WE REALLY GOING INSIDE THE BARRIER?
IF WE'RE GOING TO FIGHT LORD ARTORIUS... WE DON'T STAND A CHANCE OF WINNING...

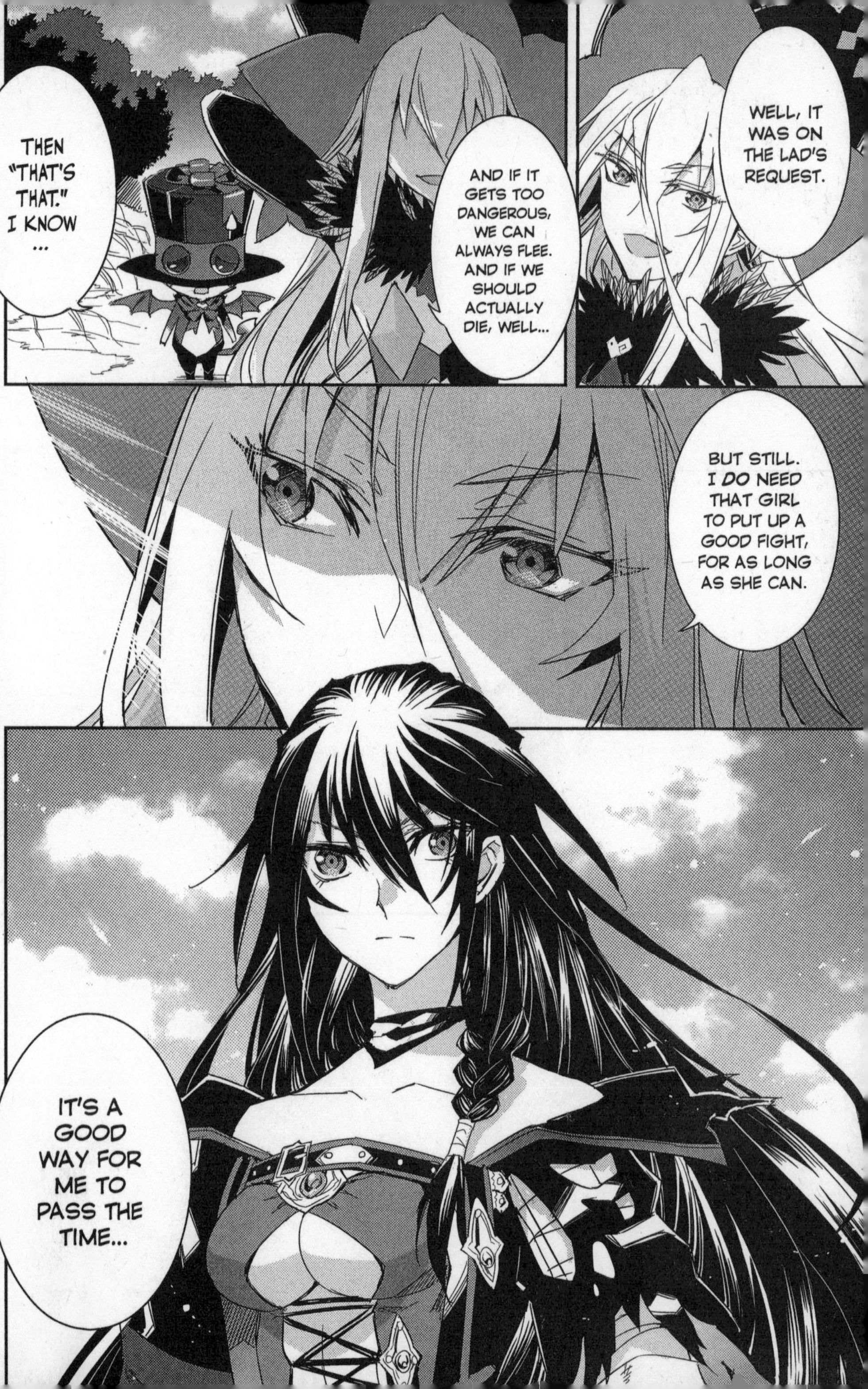
WELL, IT WAS ON THE LAD'S REQUEST.
AND IF IT GETS TOO DANGEROUS, WE CAN ALWAYS FLEE. AND IF WE SHOULD ACTUALLY DIE, WELL...
THEN "THAT'S THAT." I KNOW ...
BUT STILL. I *DO* NEED THAT GIRL TO PUT UP A GOOD FIGHT, FOR AS LONG AS SHE CAN.
IT'S A GOOD WAY FOR ME TO PASS THE TIME...

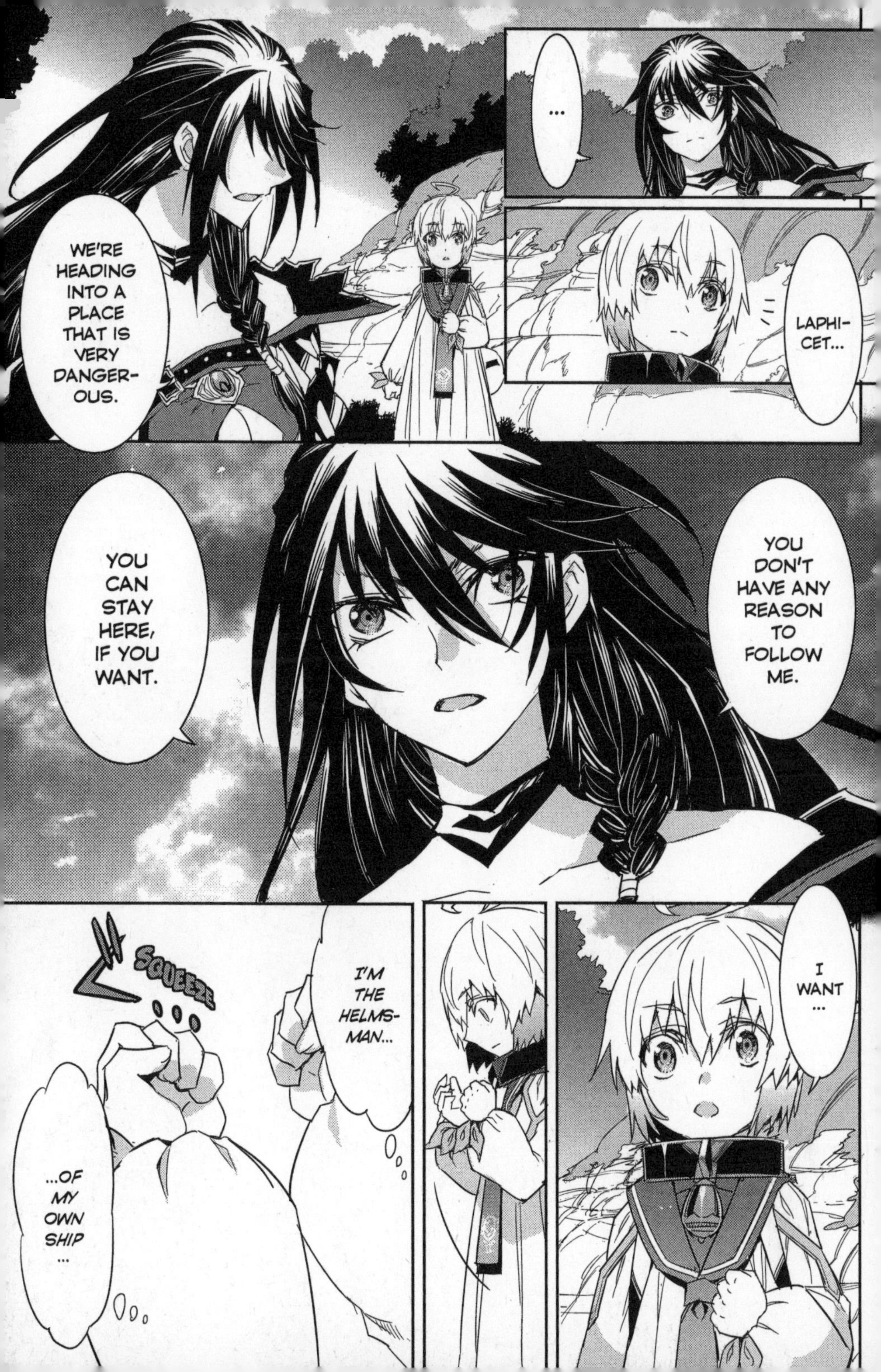
...
LAPHICET...
WE'RE HEADING INTO A PLACE THAT IS VERY DANGEROUS.
YOU DON'T HAVE ANY REASON TO FOLLOW ME.
YOU CAN STAY HERE, IF YOU WANT.
I WANT ...
I'M THE HELMSMAN...
SQUEEEZE
...OF MY OWN SHIP ...

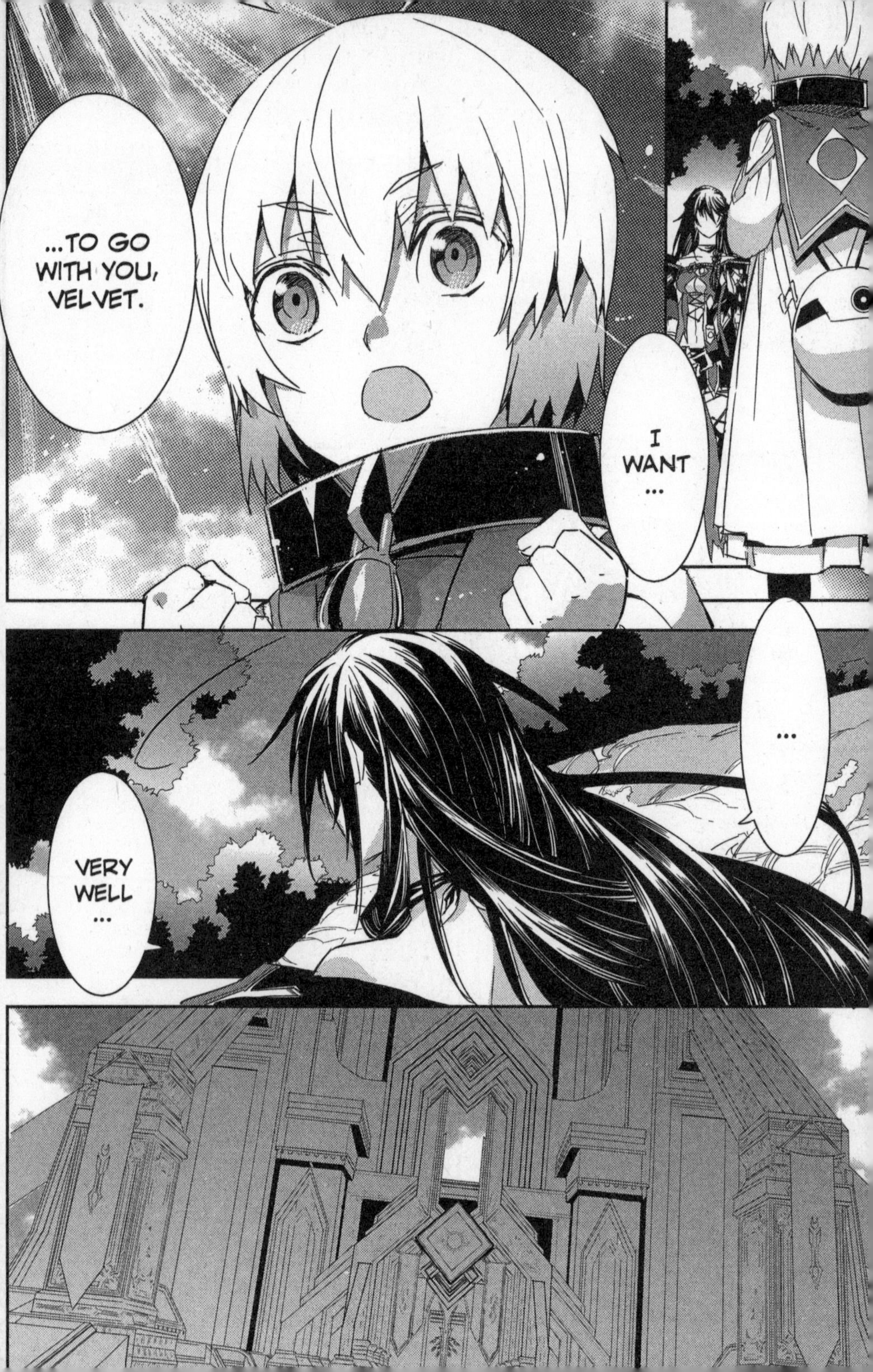
I WANT ...
...TO GO WITH YOU, VELVET.
...
VERY WELL ...

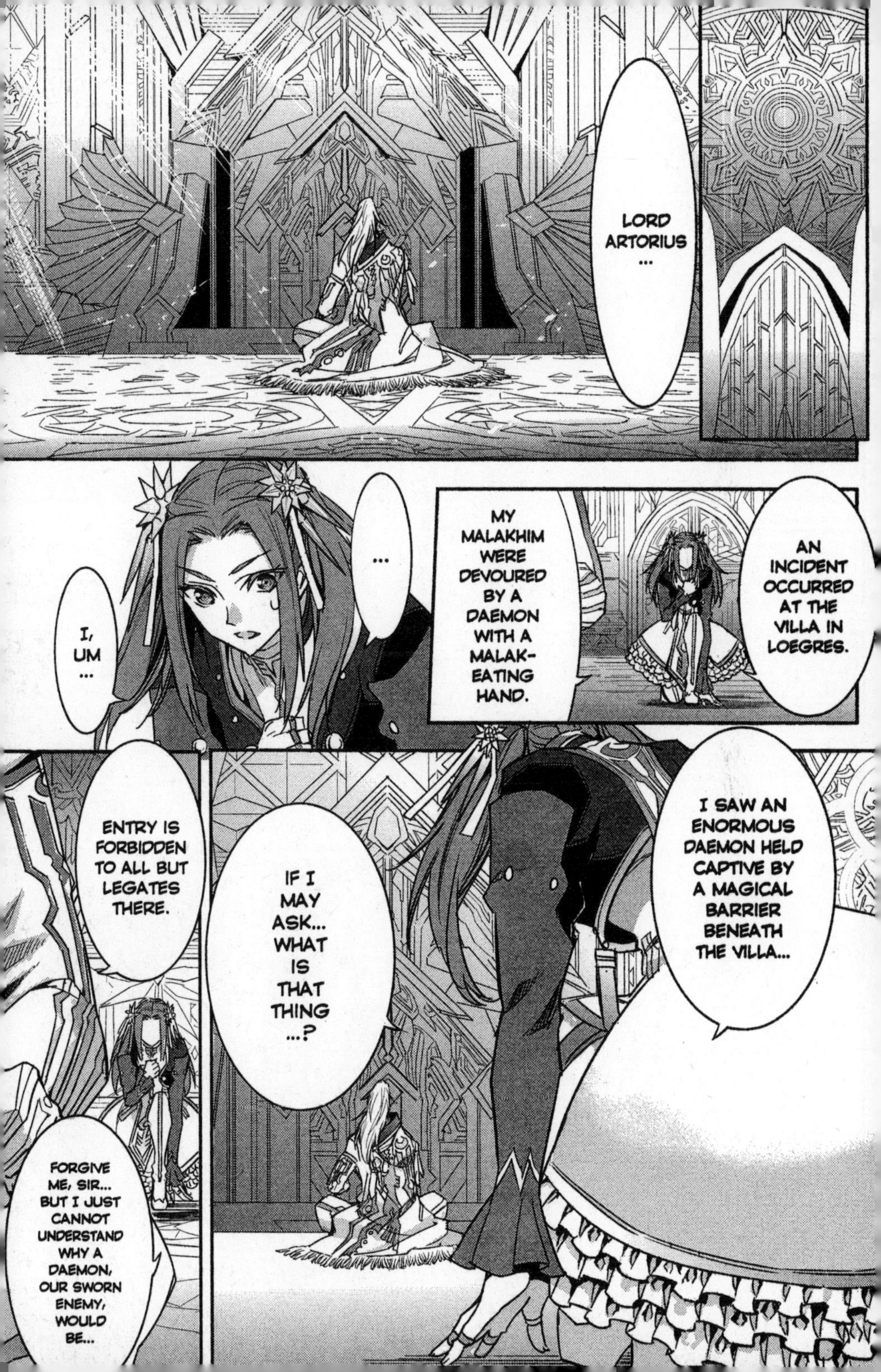
LORD ARTORIUS ...
AN INCIDENT OCCURRED AT THE VILLA IN LOEGRES.
MY MALAKHIM WERE DEVOURED BY A DAEMON WITH A MALAK-EATING HAND.
...
I, UM ...
I SAW AN ENORMOUS DAEMON HELD CAPTIVE BY A MAGICAL BARRIER BENEATH THE VILLA...
IF I MAY ASK... WHAT IS THAT THING ...?
ENTRY IS FORBIDDEN TO ALL BUT LEGATES THERE.
FORGIVE ME, SIR... BUT I JUST CANNOT UNDERSTAND WHY A DAEMON, OUR SWORN ENEMY, WOULD BE...

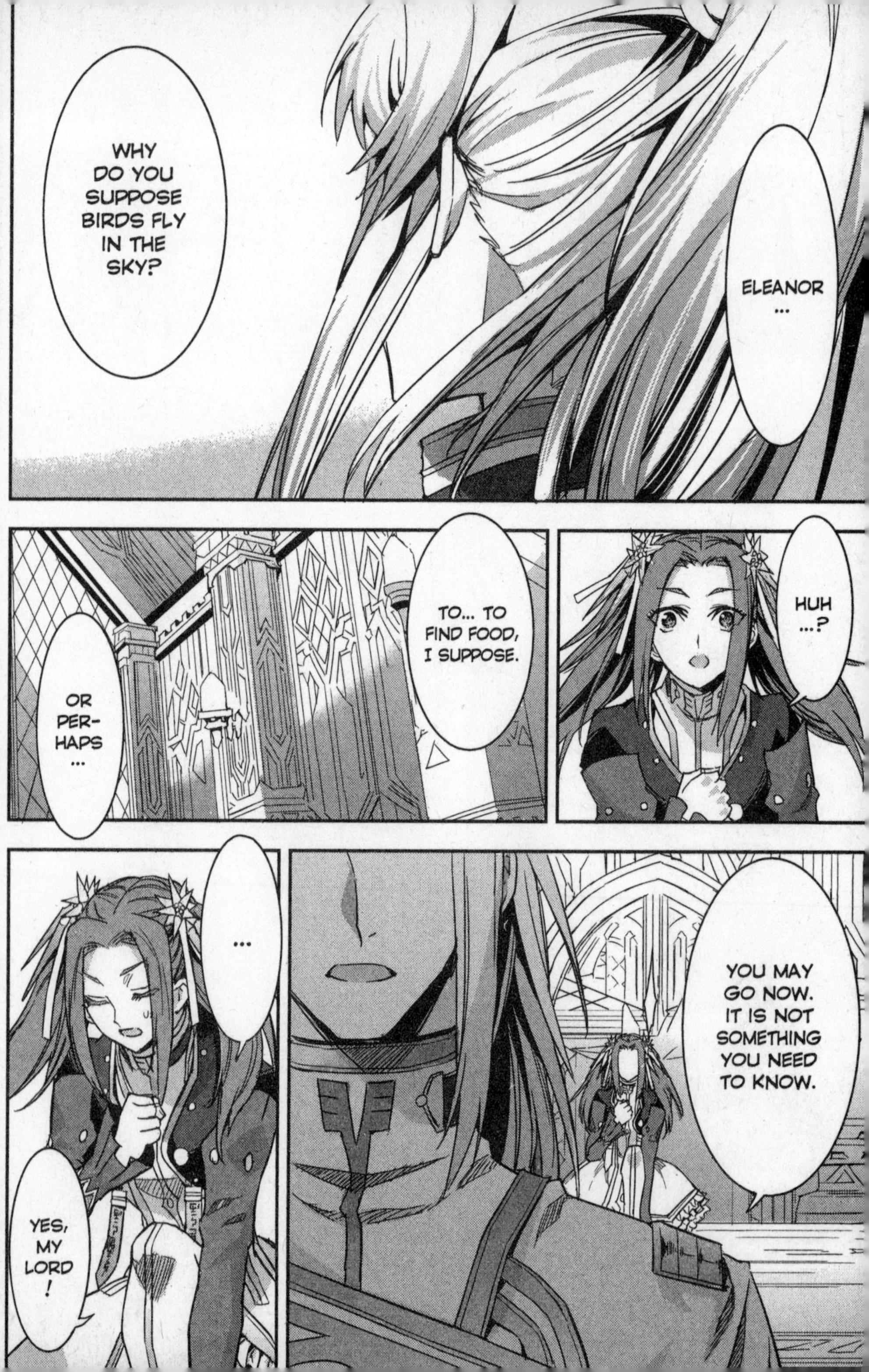
ELEANOR ...
WHY DO YOU SUPPOSE BIRDS FLY IN THE SKY?
HUH ...?
TO... TO FIND FOOD, I SUPPOSE.
OR PER-HAPS ...
YOU MAY GO NOW. IT IS NOT SOMETHING YOU NEED TO KNOW.
...
YES, MY LORD!

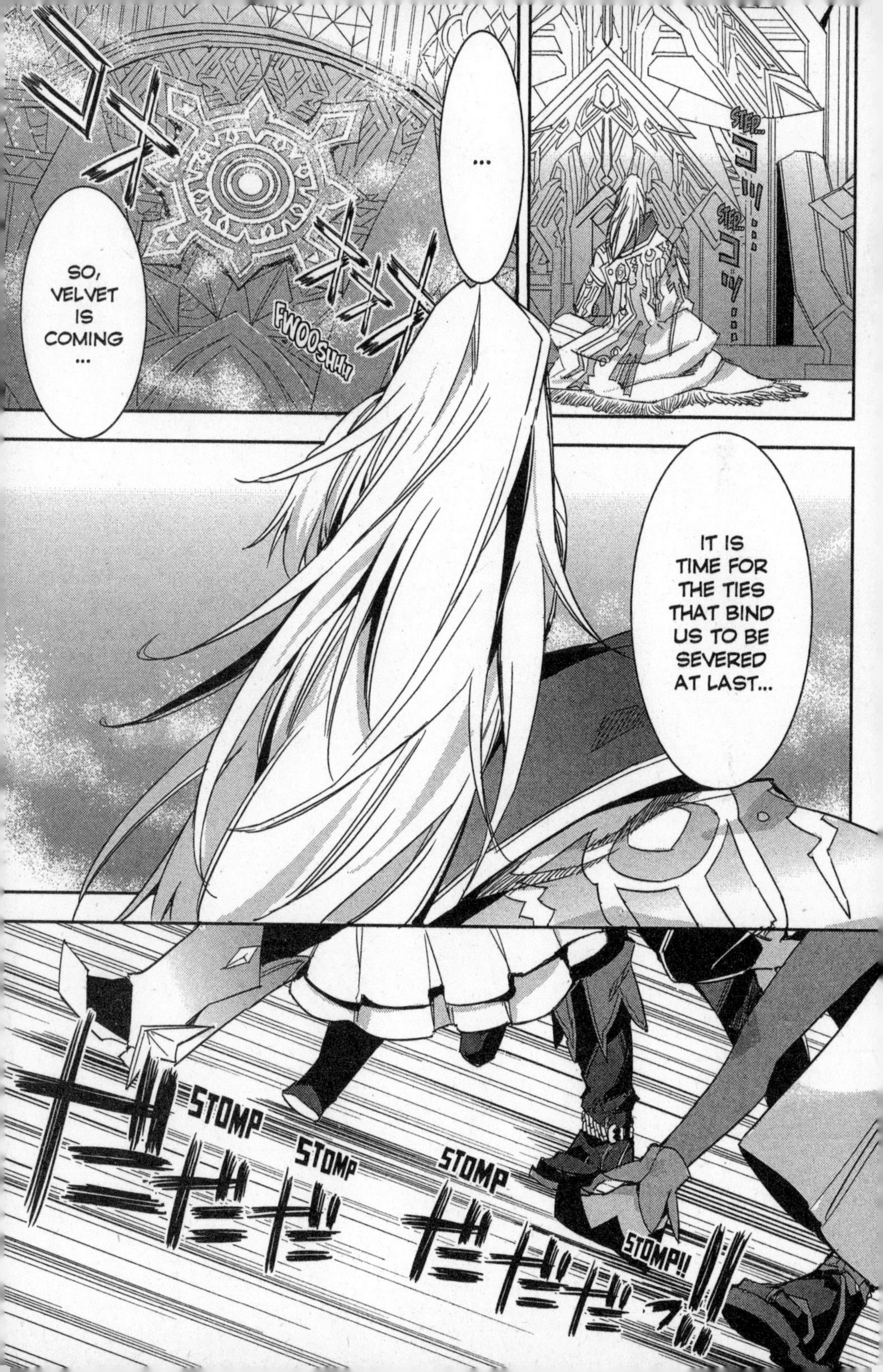
STEP...
STEP...
...
SO, VELVET IS COMING...
FWOOSHH
IT IS TIME FOR THE TIES THAT BIND US TO BE SEVERED AT LAST...
STOMP
STOMP
STOMP
STOMP!!

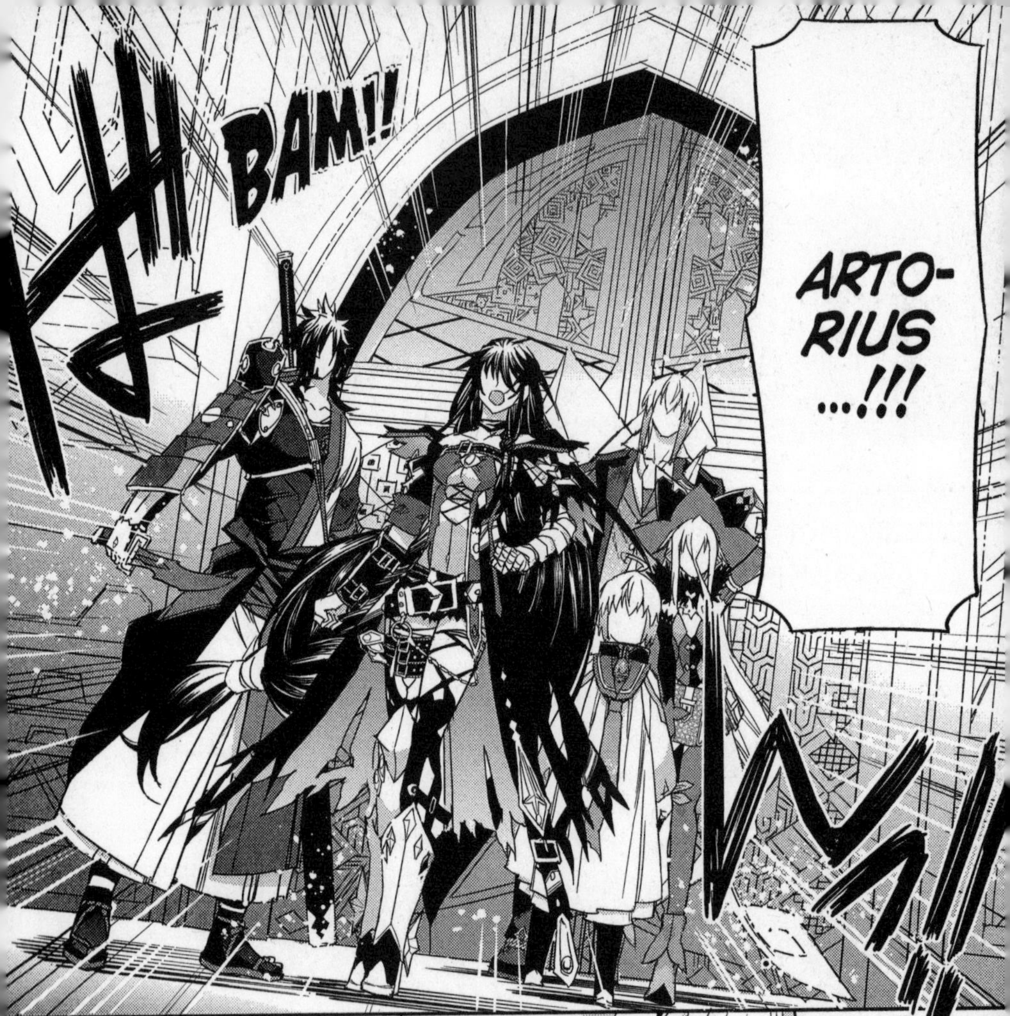
ARTO-
RIUS
...!!!
BAM!!
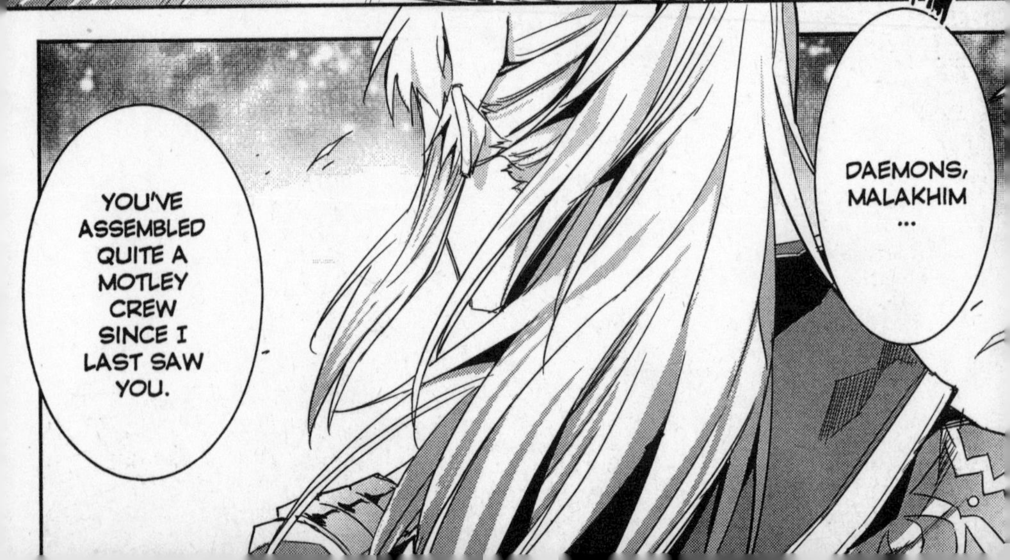
DAEMONS, MALAKHIM ...
YOU'VE ASSEMBLED QUITE A MOTLEY CREW SINCE I LAST SAW YOU.

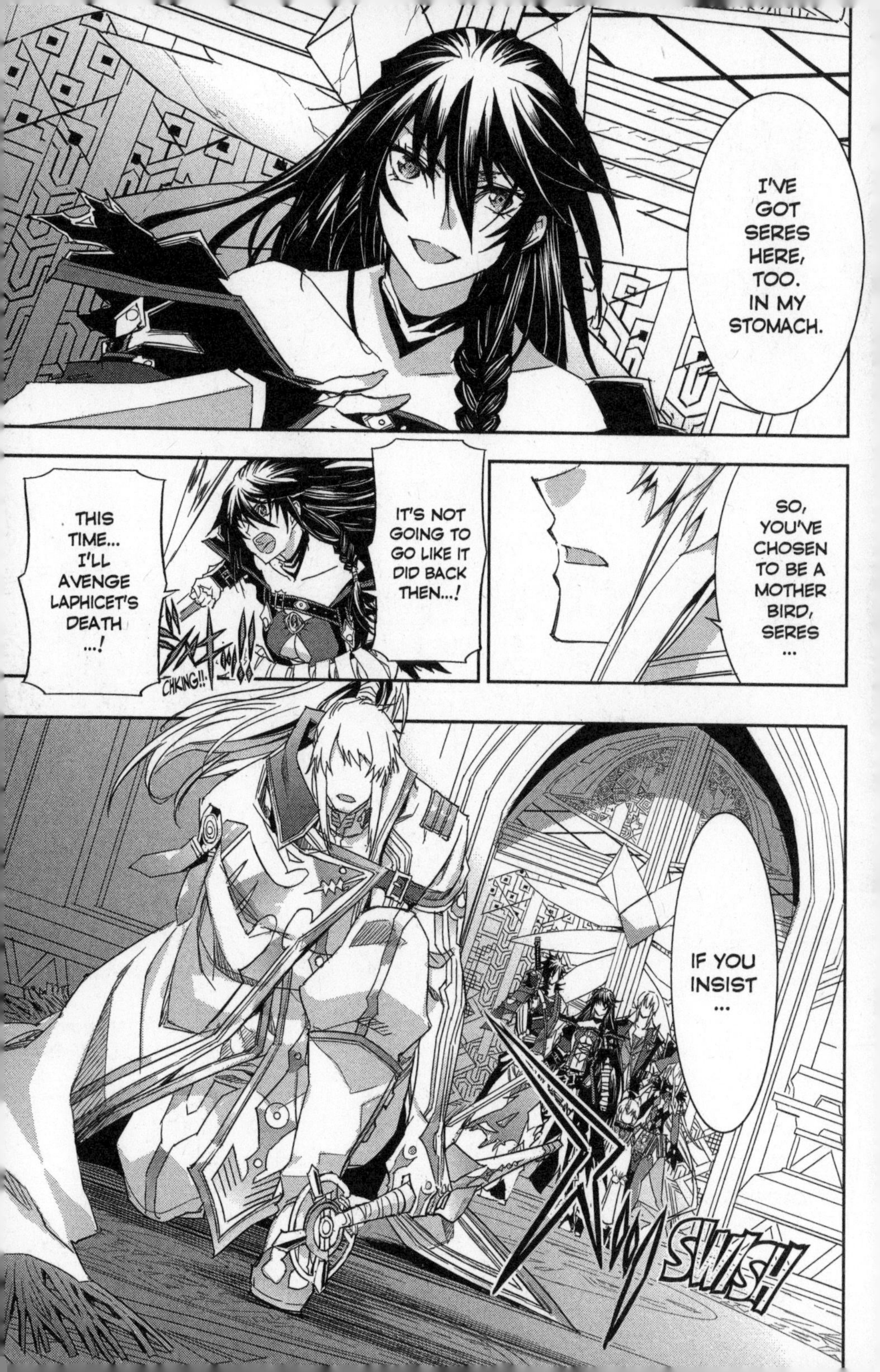
I'VE GOT SERES HERE, TOO. IN MY STOMACH.
SO, YOU'VE CHOSEN TO BE A MOTHER BIRD, SERES...
IT'S NOT GOING TO GO LIKE IT DID BACK THEN...!
THIS TIME... I'LL AVENGE LAPHICET'S DEATH...!
CHKING!!
IF YOU INSIST...
SWISH!

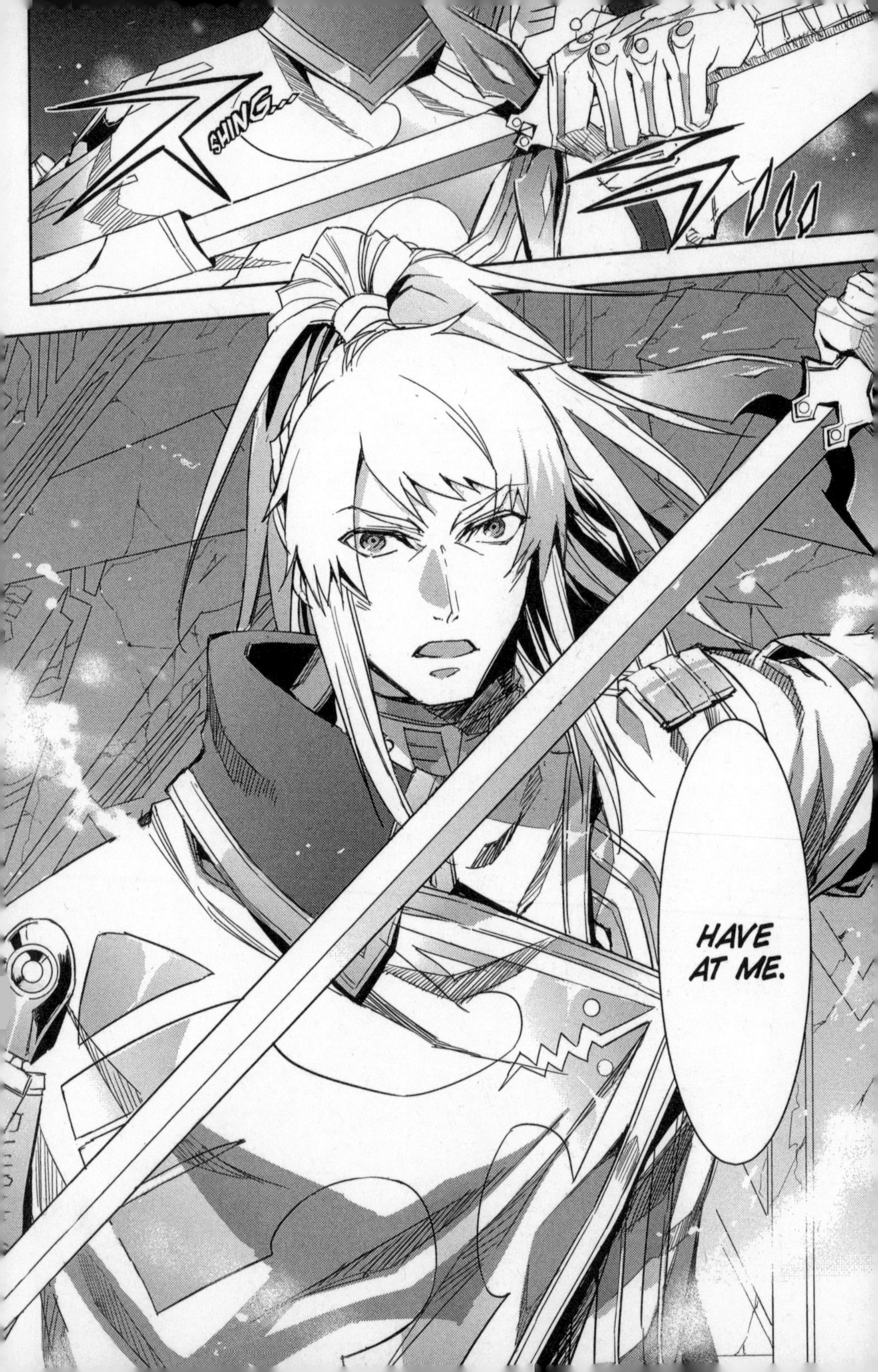
SHING...
HAVE AT ME.

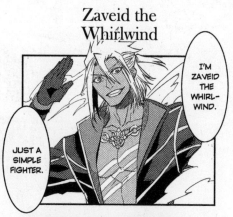

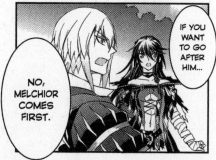

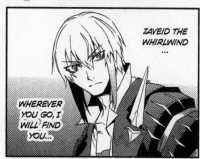

Zaveid the Whirlwind

I'M ZAVEID THE WHIRL-WIND.
JUST A SIMPLE FIGHTER.
IF YOU WANT TO GO AFTER HIM...
NO, MELCHIOR COMES FIRST.
ZAVEID THE WHIRLWIND ...
WHEREVER YOU GO, I WILL FIND YOU...
HEY, CUTIE, FEEL LIKE TAKING A DETOUR FOR SOME TEA?
Port Zekson
HEY, THAT'S THE PENDULUM-USER...!

He didn't go that far.

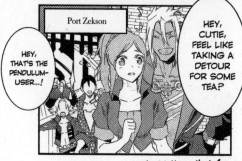

Tales of Berseria

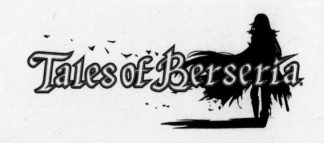

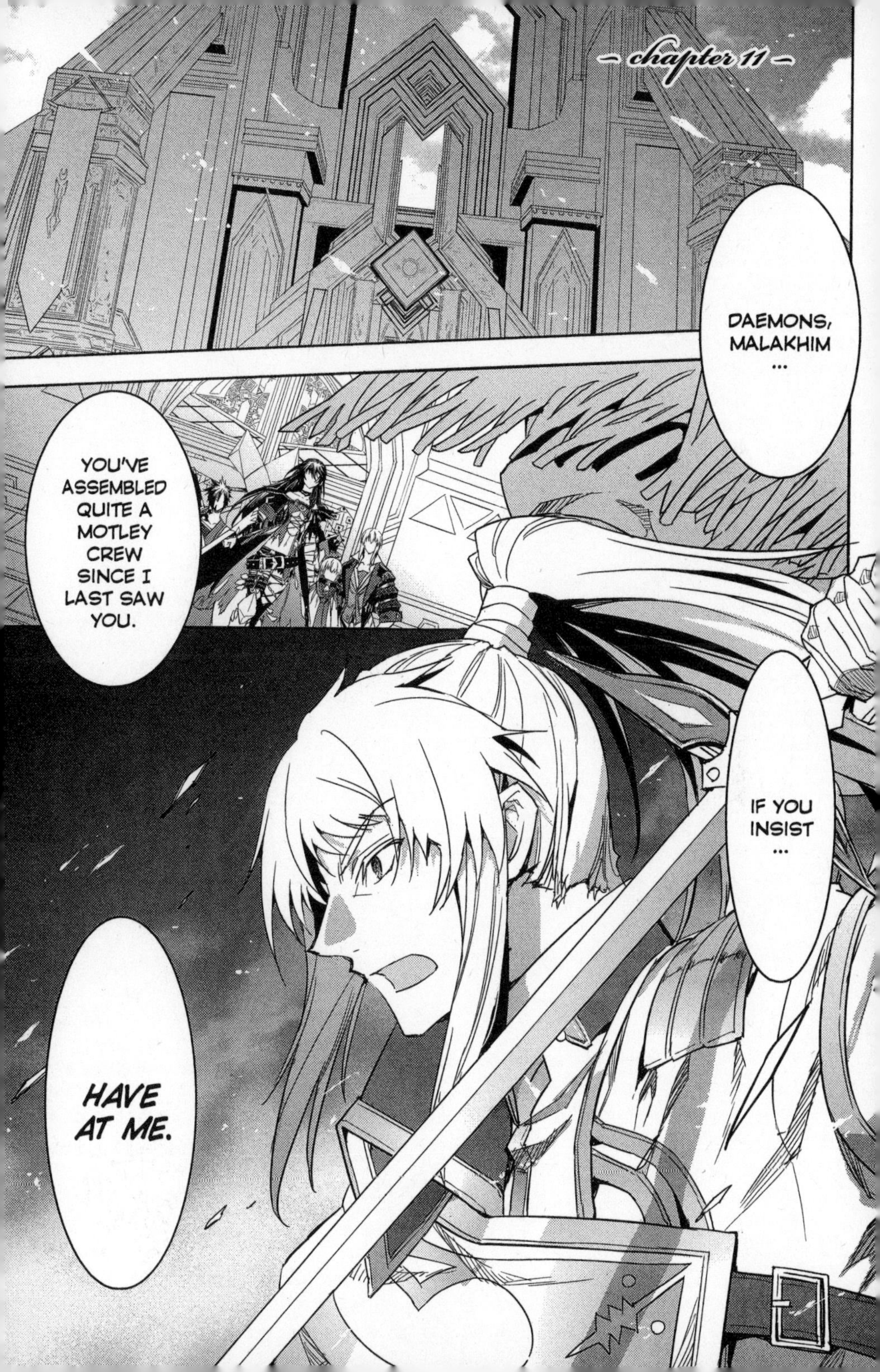

– chapter 11 –
DAEMONS, MALAKHIM ...
YOU'VE ASSEMBLED QUITE A MOTLEY CREW SINCE I LAST SAW YOU.
IF YOU INSIST ...
HAVE AT ME.

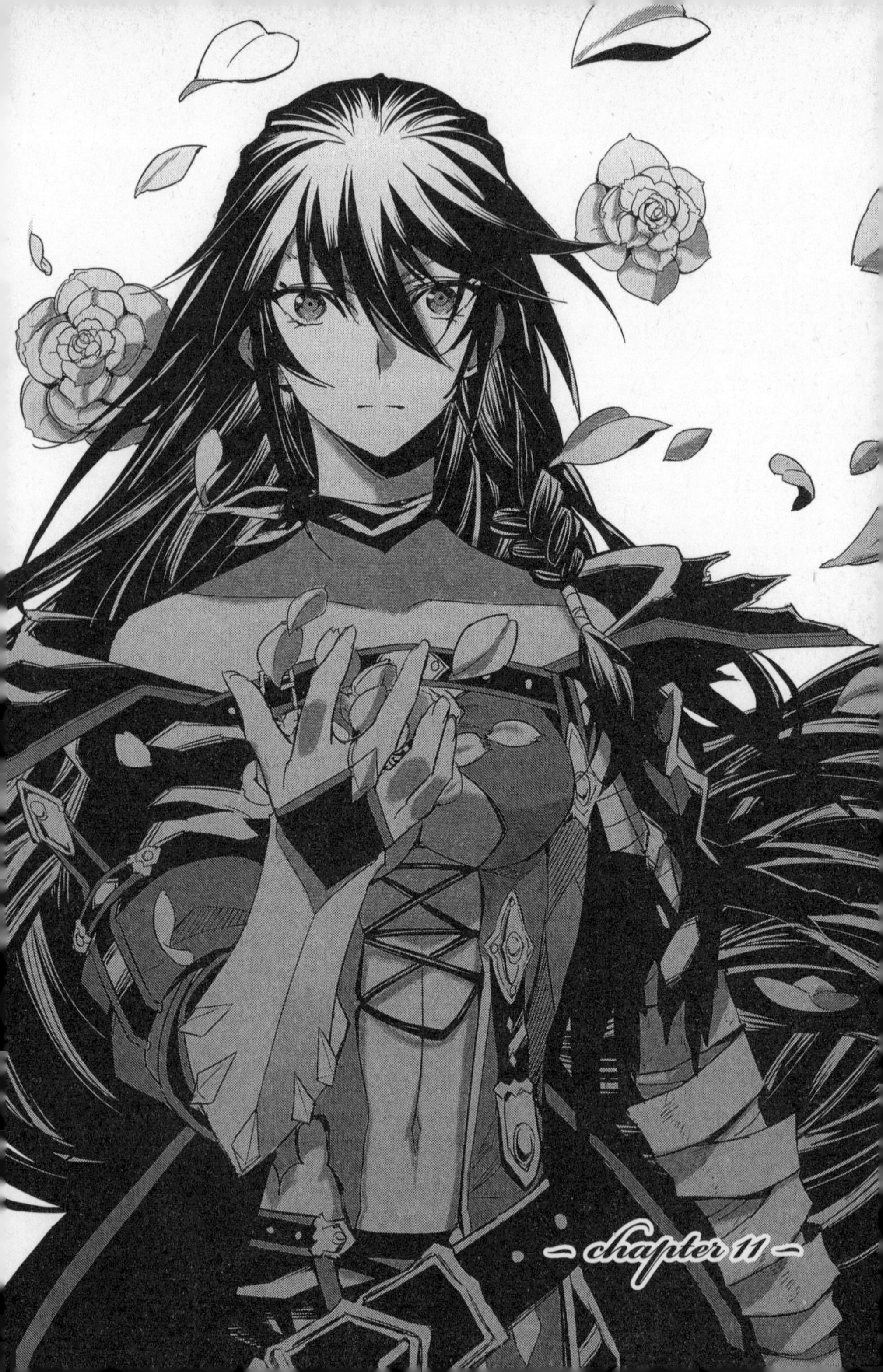
chapter 11

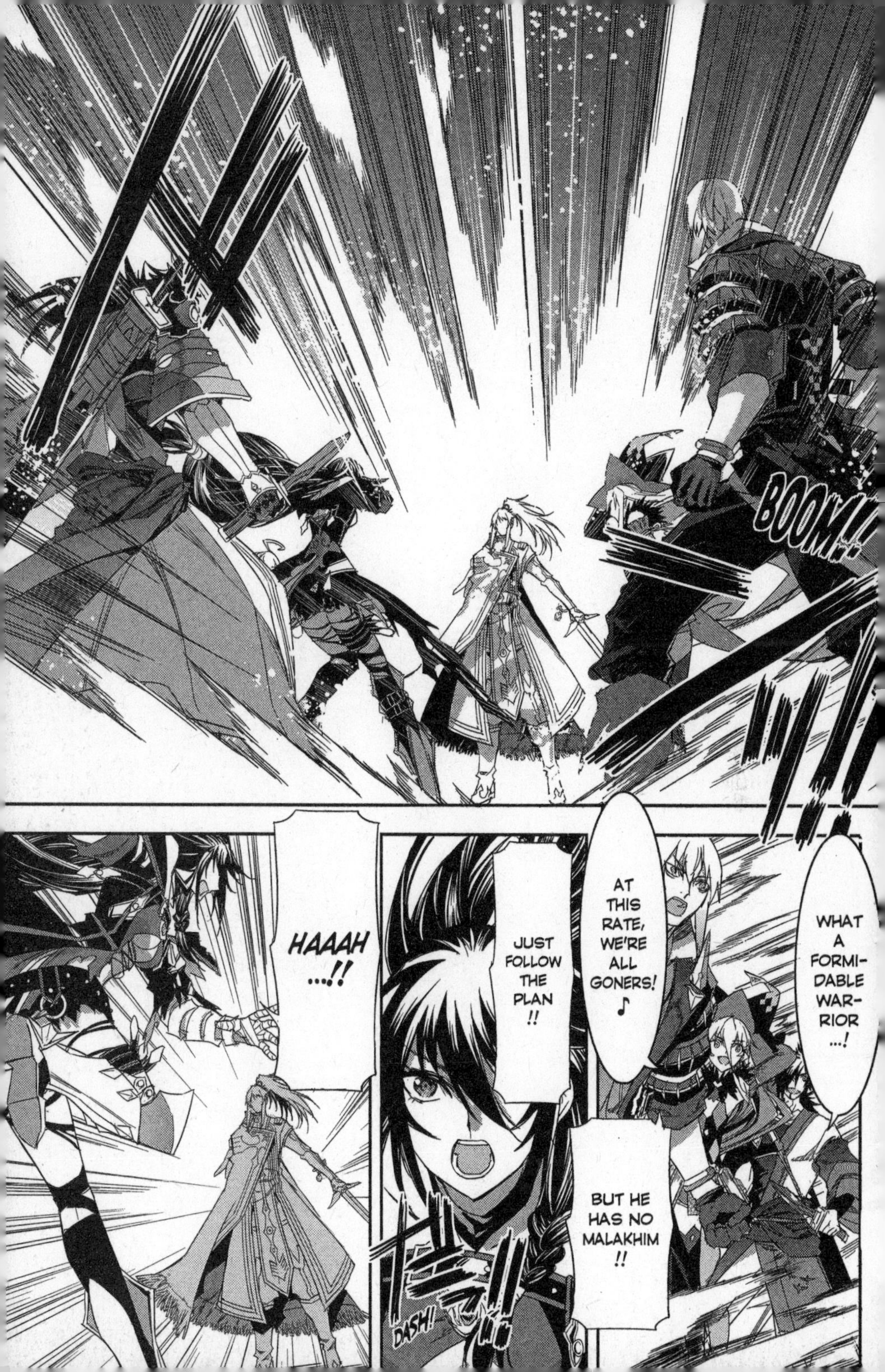
BOOM!!
WHAT A FORMIDABLE WARRIOR...!
AT THIS RATE, WE'RE ALL GONERS! ♪
JUST FOLLOW THE PLAN!!
BUT HE HAS NO MALAKHIM!!
DASH!
HAAAH...!!

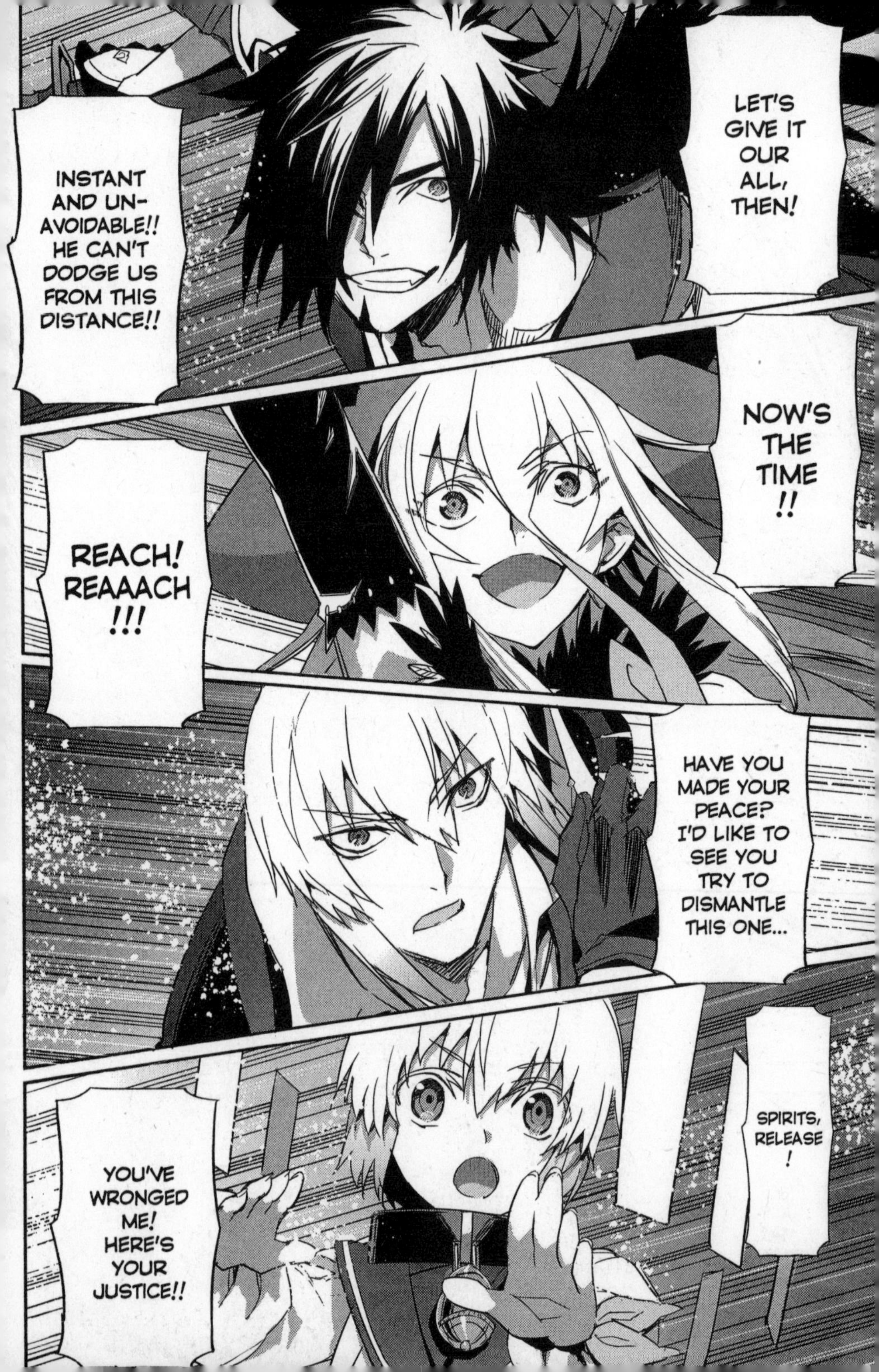
LET'S GIVE IT OUR ALL, THEN!
INSTANT AND UN-AVOIDABLE!! HE CAN'T DODGE US FROM THIS DISTANCE!!
NOW'S THE TIME!!
REACH! REAAACH!!!
HAVE YOU MADE YOUR PEACE? I'D LIKE TO SEE YOU TRY TO DISMANTLE THIS ONE...
SPIRITS, RELEASE!
YOU'VE WRONGED ME! HERE'S YOUR JUSTICE!!

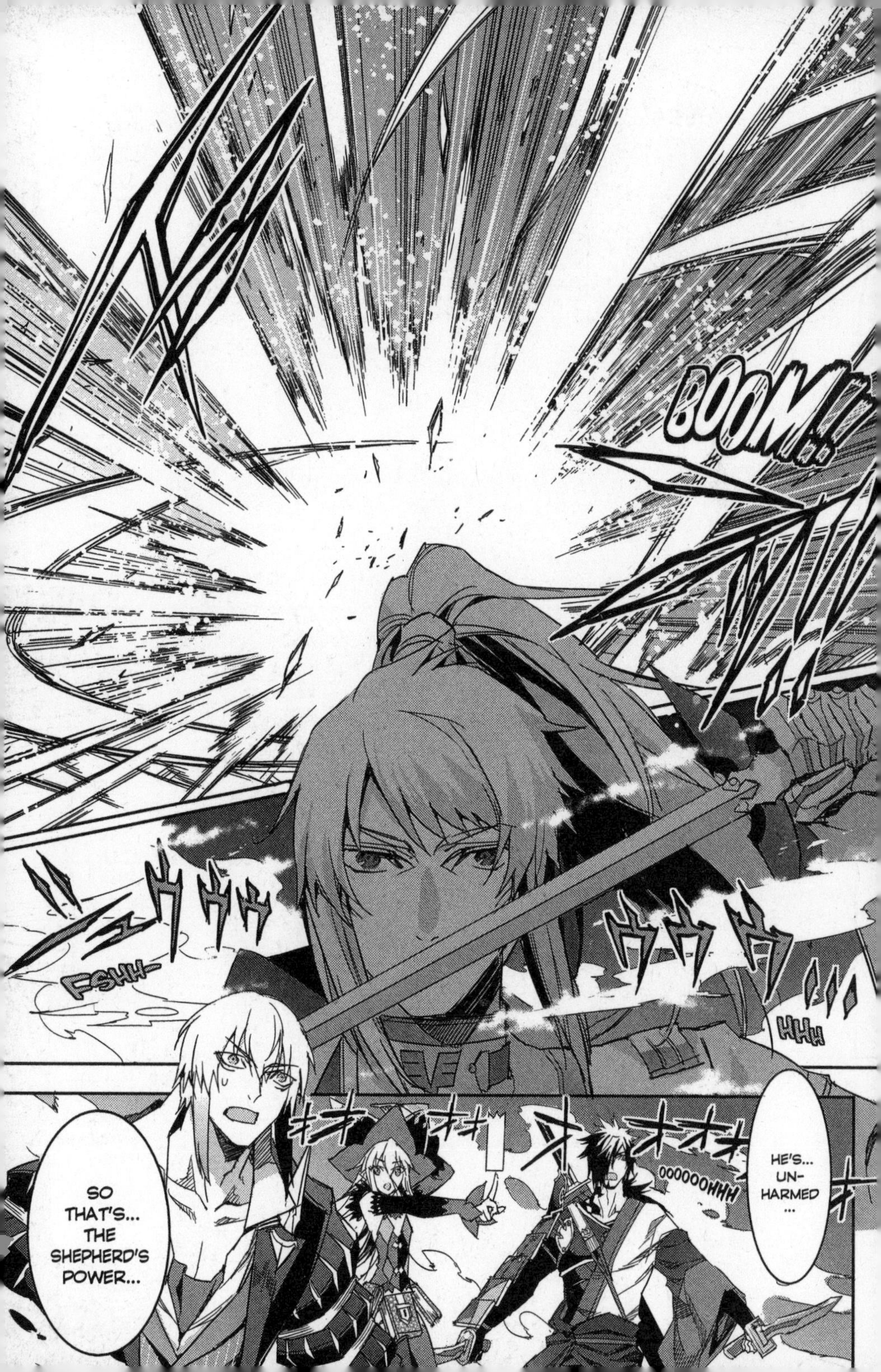
BOOM!!
HHH
FSHH-
HE'S... UN-HARMED...
OOOOOOHHH
SO THAT'S... THE SHEPHERD'S POWER...

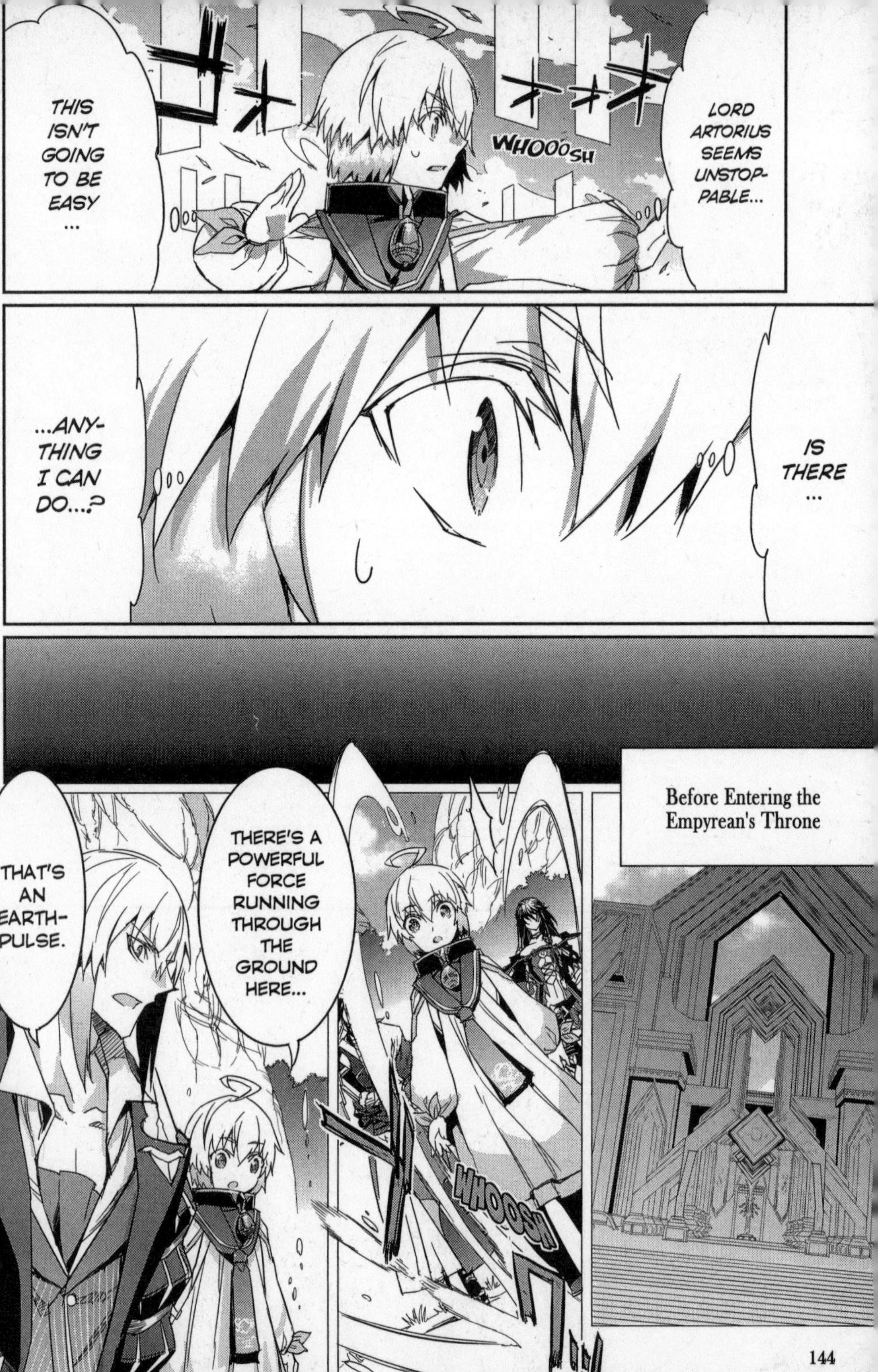
LORD ARTORIUS SEEMS UNSTOP-PABLE...
WHOOOSH
THIS ISN'T GOING TO BE EASY ...
IS THERE ...
...ANY-THING I CAN DO...?
Before Entering the Empyrean's Throne
WHOOSH
THERE'S A POWERFUL FORCE RUNNING THROUGH THE GROUND HERE...
THAT'S AN EARTH-PULSE.

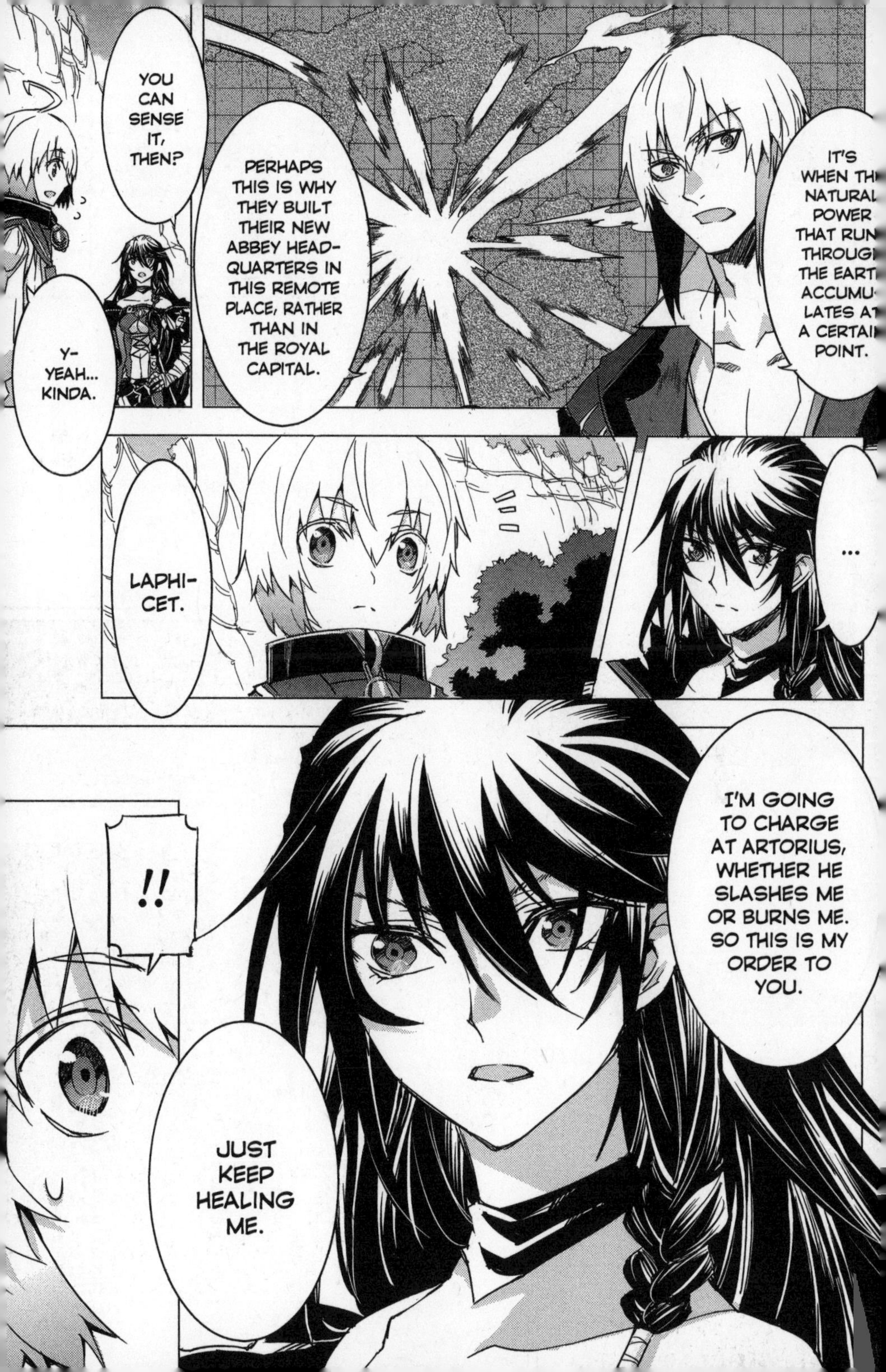
IT'S WHEN TH NATURAL POWER THAT RUN THROUG THE EART ACCUMU-LATES AT A CERTAI POINT.
PERHAPS THIS IS WHY THEY BUILT THEIR NEW ABBEY HEAD-QUARTERS IN THIS REMOTE PLACE, RATHER THAN IN THE ROYAL CAPITAL.
YOU CAN SENSE IT, THEN?
Y-YEAH... KINDA.
...
LAPHI-CET.
I'M GOING TO CHARGE AT ARTORIUS, WHETHER HE SLASHES ME OR BURNS ME. SO THIS IS MY ORDER TO YOU.
!!
JUST KEEP HEALING ME.

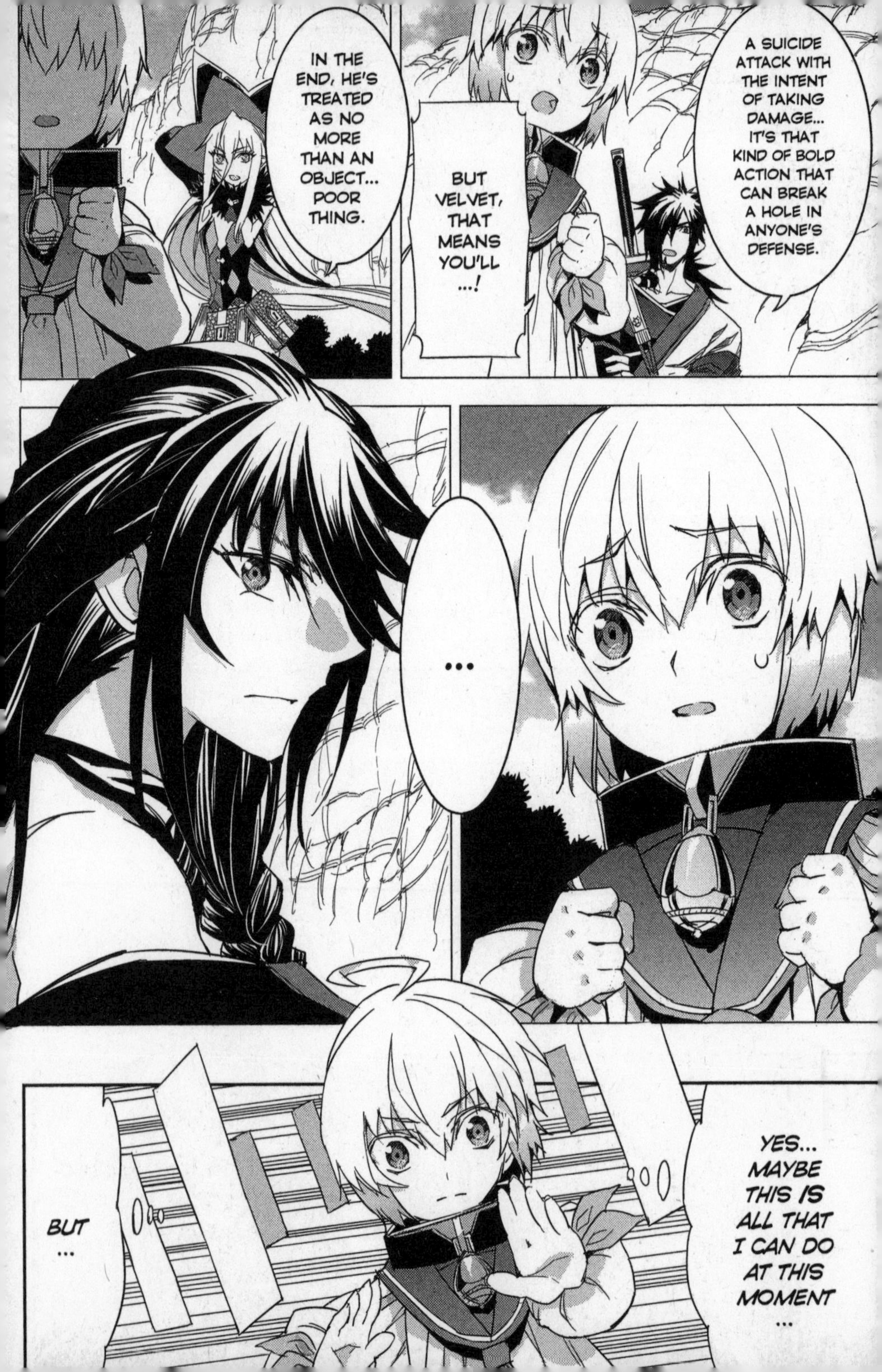
A SUICIDE ATTACK WITH THE INTENT OF TAKING DAMAGE... IT'S THAT KIND OF BOLD ACTION THAT CAN BREAK A HOLE IN ANYONE'S DEFENSE.
BUT VELVET, THAT MEANS YOU'LL ...!
IN THE END, HE'S TREATED AS NO MORE THAN AN OBJECT... POOR THING.
...
YES... MAYBE THIS IS ALL THAT I CAN DO AT THIS MOMENT ...
BUT ...

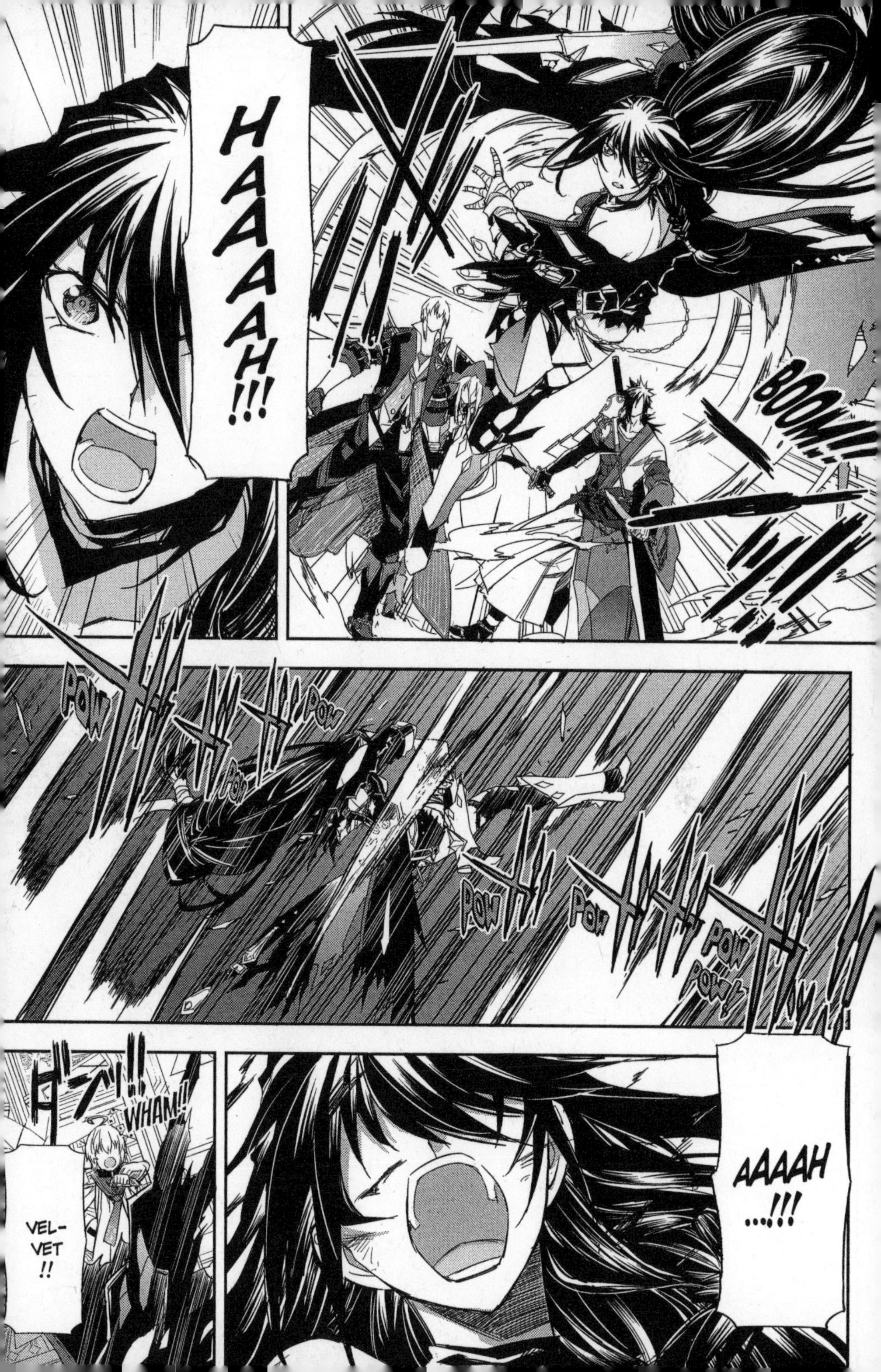
BOOM!!!
HAAAAAH!!!
POW
POW
POW
POW
POW
POW
POW
AAAAH
...!!!
WHAM!!
VEL-
VET
!!

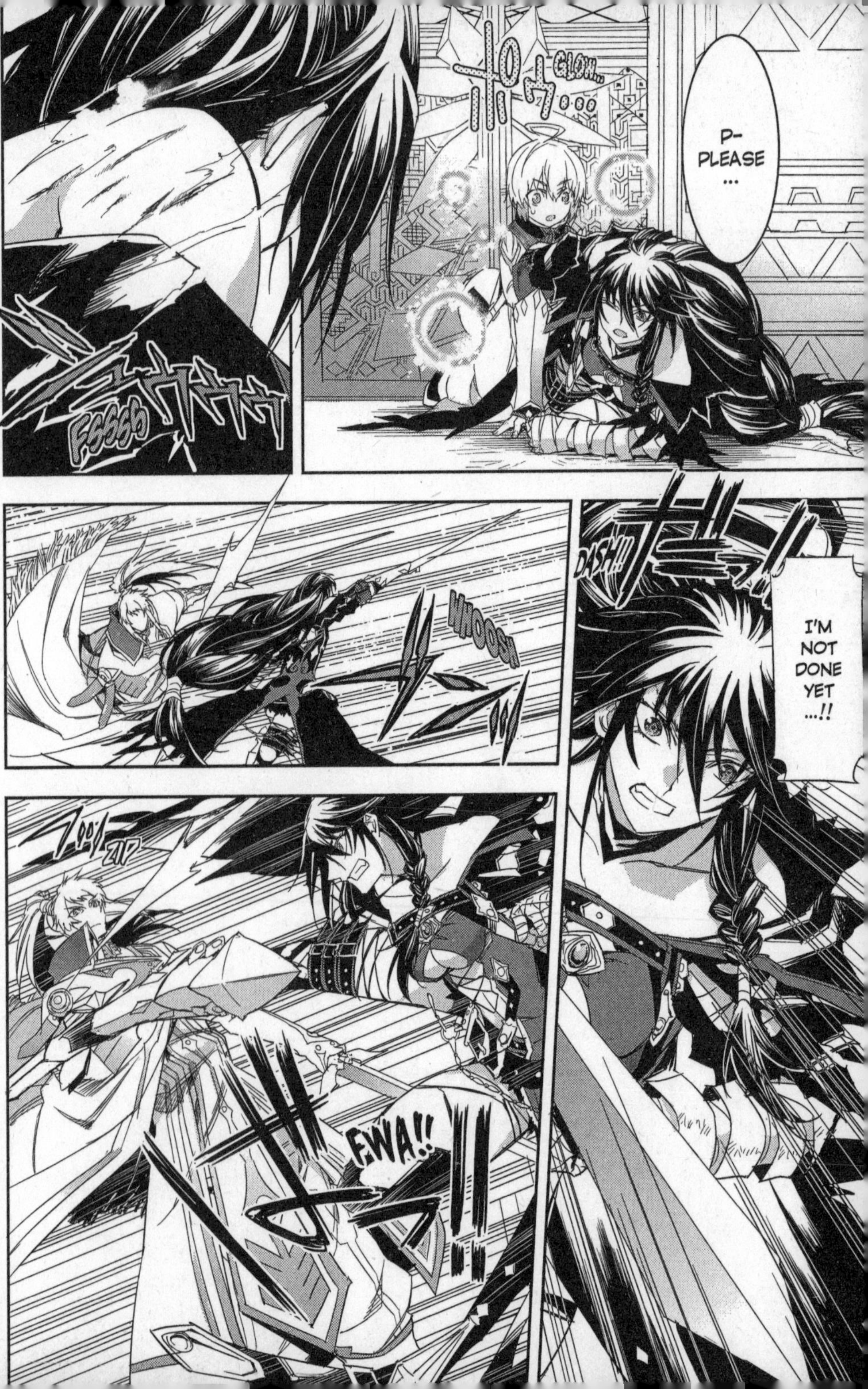
P-PLEASE ...
GLOW...
FSSSH
DASH!!
I'M NOT DONE YET ...!!
WHOOSH
ZIP
FWA!!

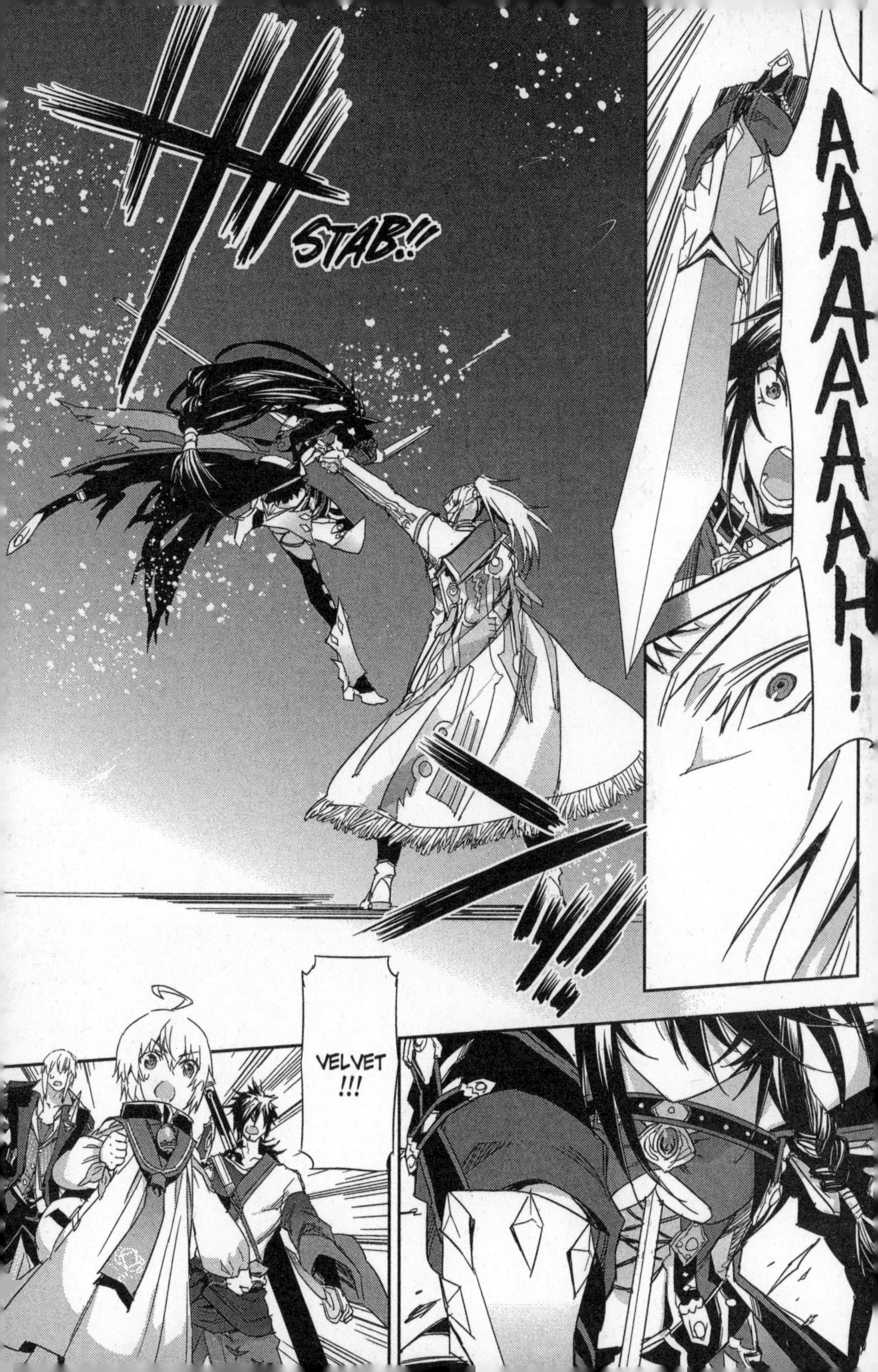
AAAAAAH!
STAB!!
VELVET !!!

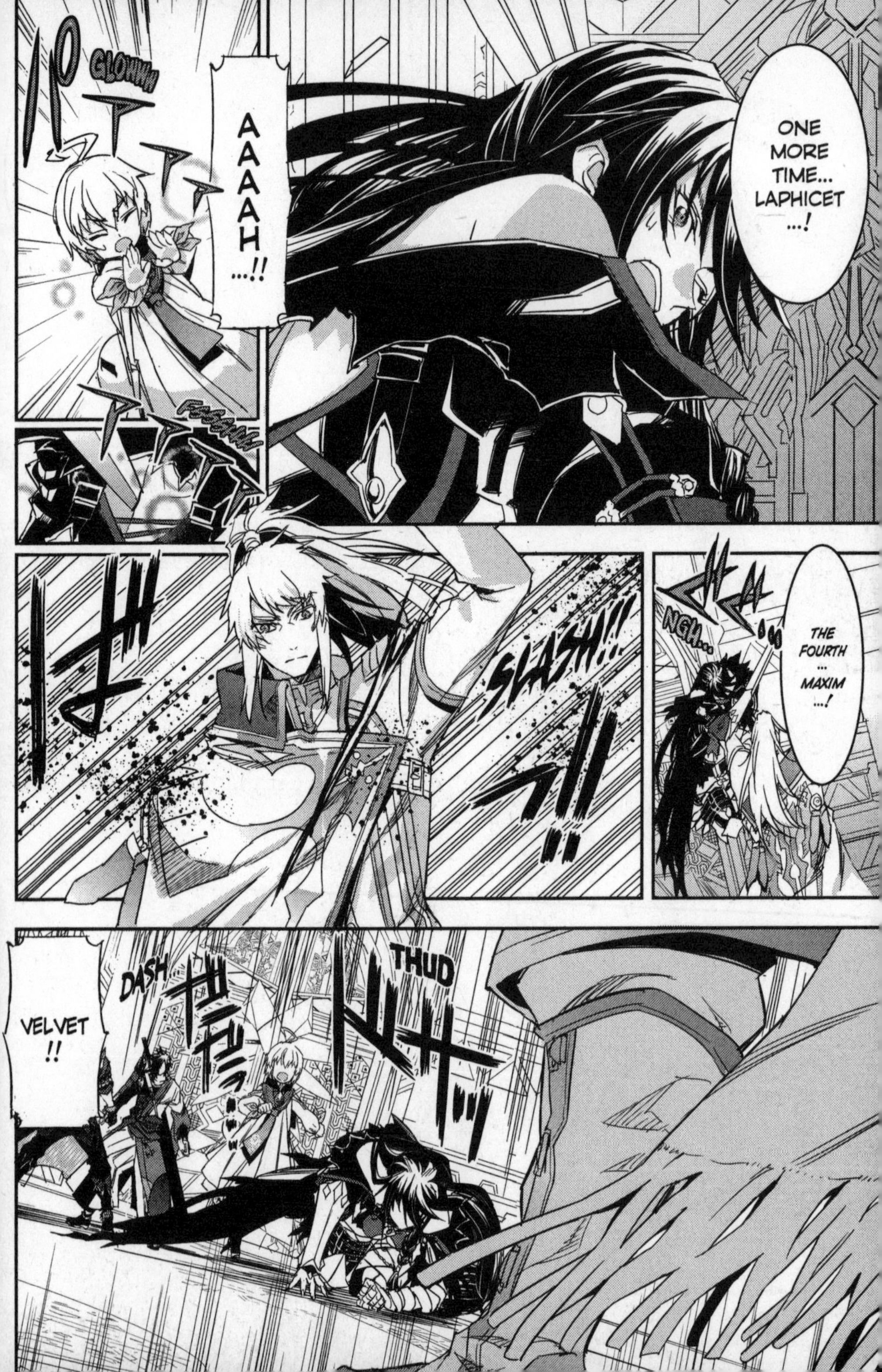
ONE MORE TIME... LAPHICET ...!
GLOWWW
AAAAH ...!!
NGH...
THE FOURTH ... MAXIM ...!
SLASH!!!
THUD
DASH
VELVET !!

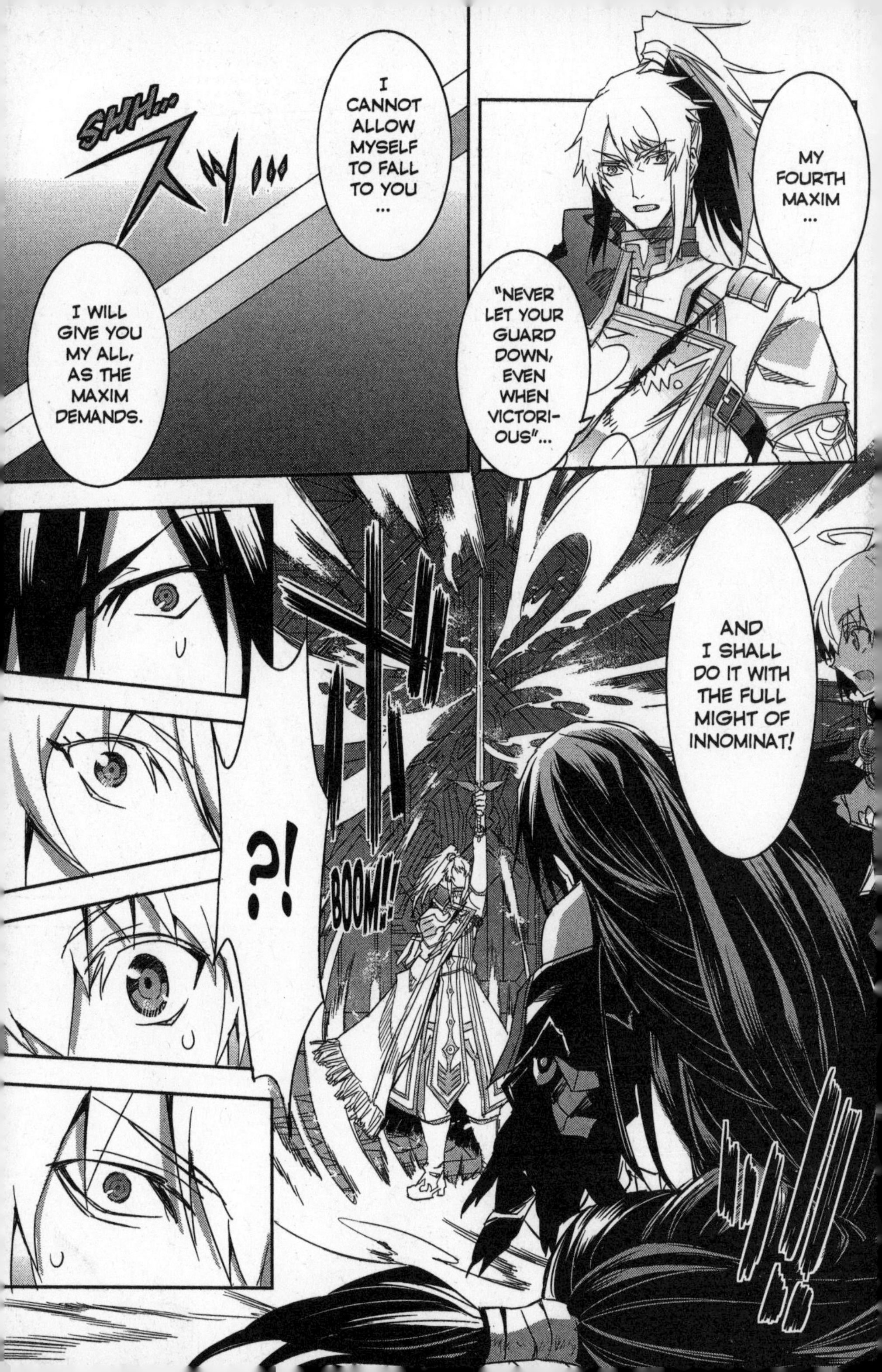
MY FOURTH MAXIM ...
"NEVER LET YOUR GUARD DOWN, EVEN WHEN VICTORI-OUS"...
I CANNOT ALLOW MYSELF TO FALL TO YOU ...
SHH...
I WILL GIVE YOU MY ALL, AS THE MAXIM DEMANDS.
AND I SHALL DO IT WITH THE FULL MIGHT OF INNOMINAT!
BOOM!!
?!

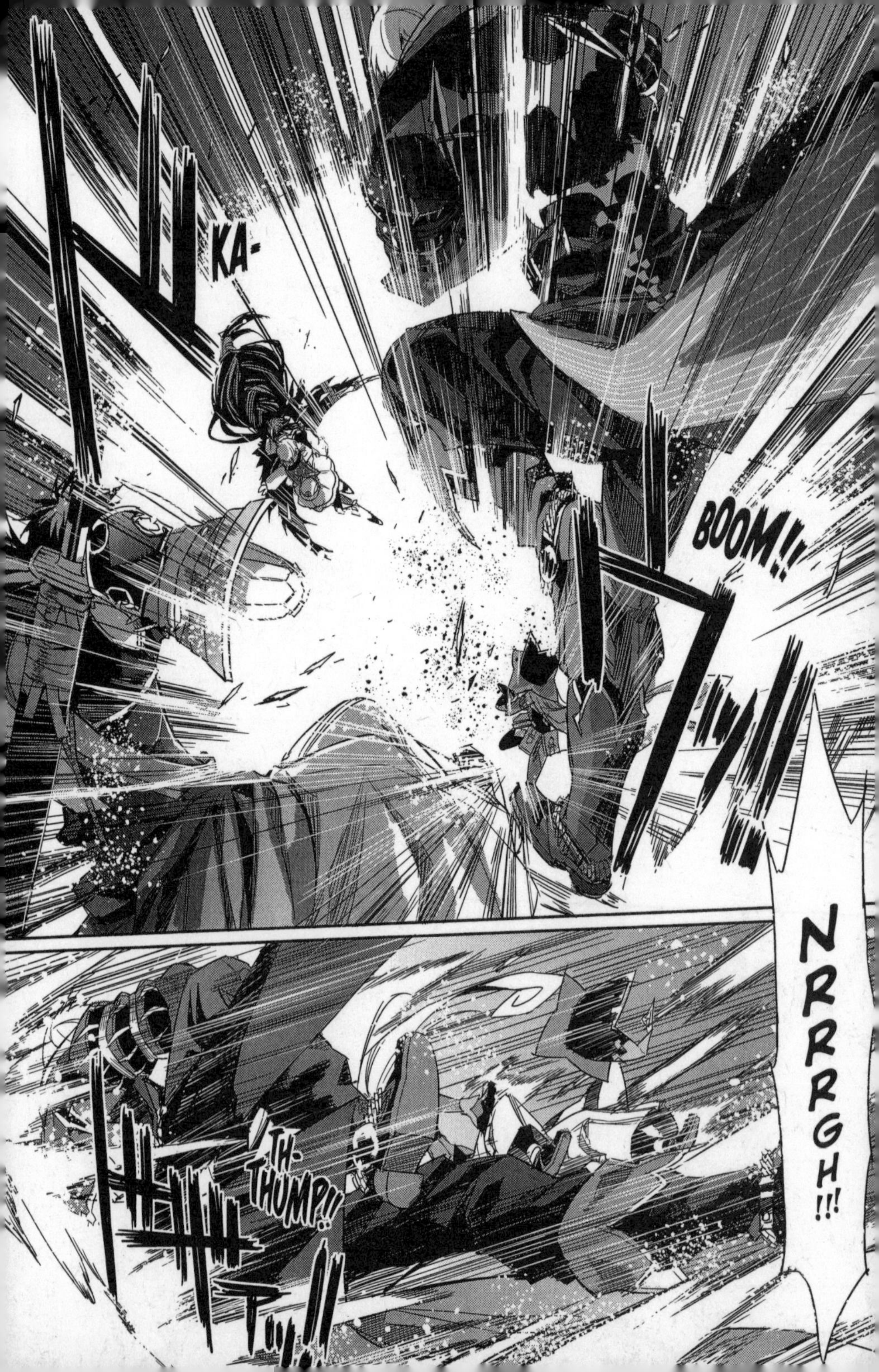
BOOM!!
KA-
NRRRGH!!!
TH-THUMP!!

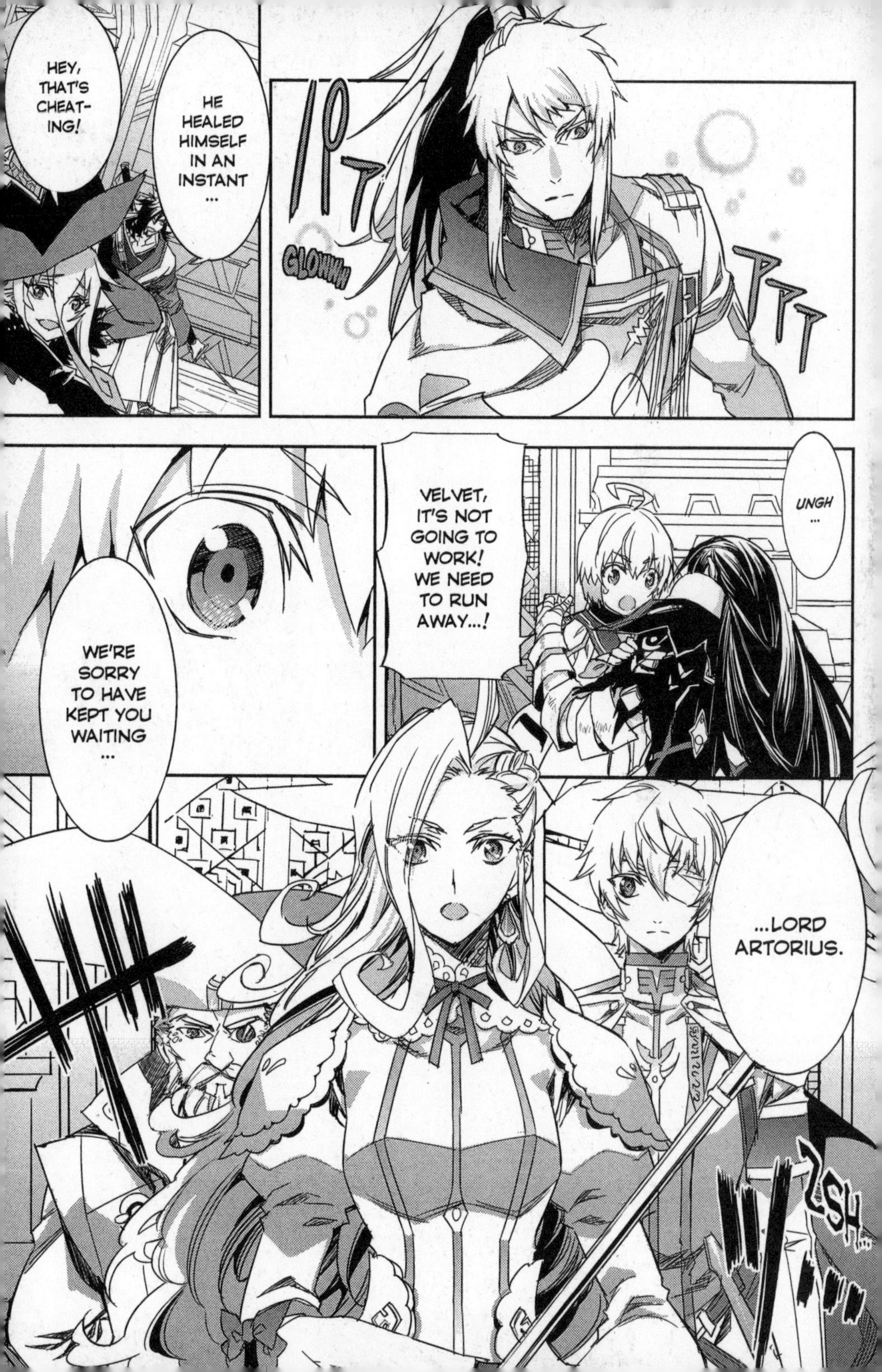
GLOWWW
HE HEALED HIMSELF IN AN INSTANT ...
HEY, THAT'S CHEAT-ING!
UNGH ...
VELVET, IT'S NOT GOING TO WORK! WE NEED TO RUN AWAY...!
WE'RE SORRY TO HAVE KEPT YOU WAITING ...
...LORD ARTORIUS.
ZSH...

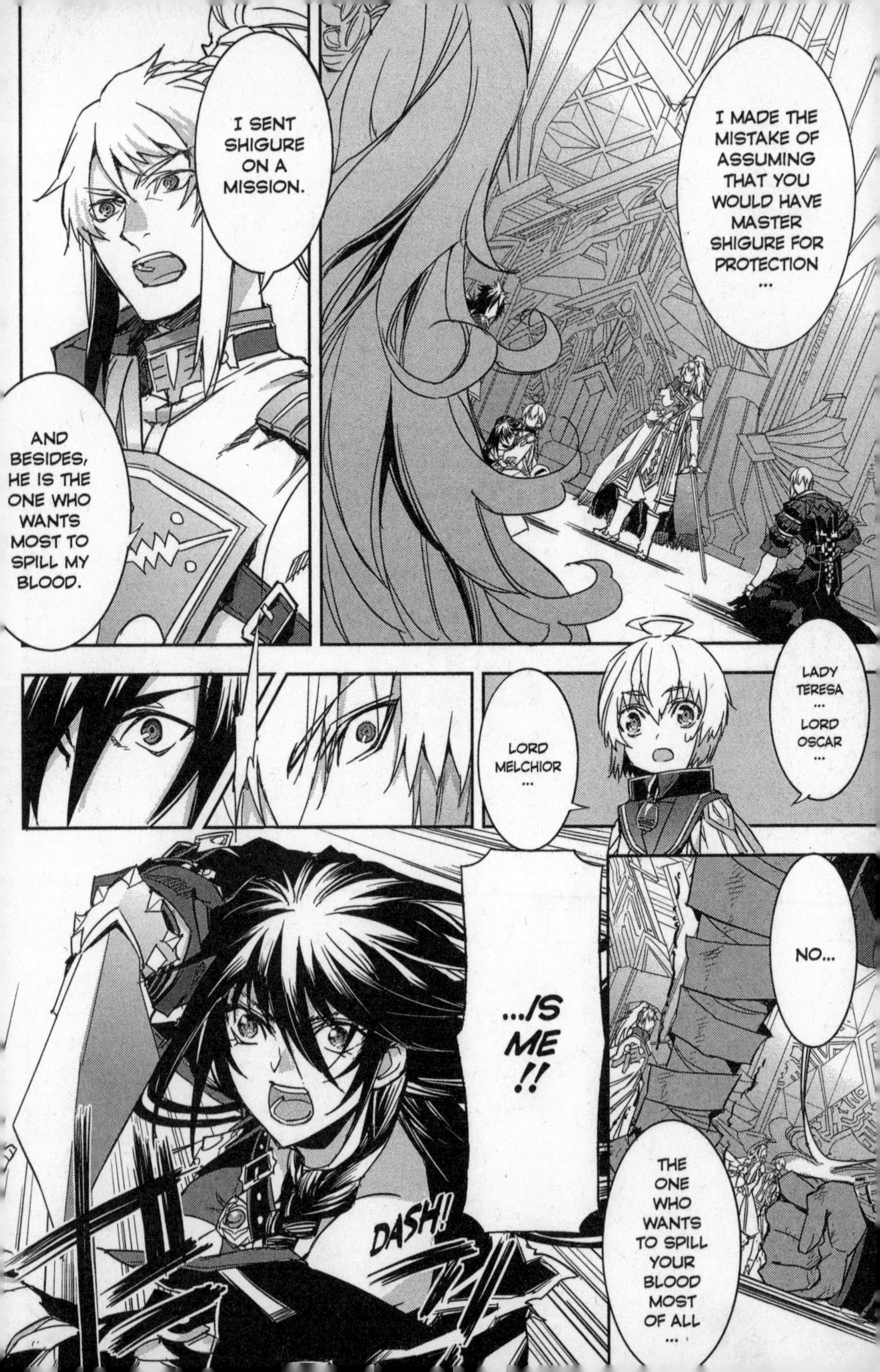
I MADE THE MISTAKE OF ASSUMING THAT YOU WOULD HAVE MASTER SHIGURE FOR PROTECTION ...
I SENT SHIGURE ON A MISSION.
AND BESIDES, HE IS THE ONE WHO WANTS MOST TO SPILL MY BLOOD.
LADY TERESA ... LORD OSCAR ...
LORD MELCHIOR ...
NO...
THE ONE WHO WANTS TO SPILL YOUR BLOOD MOST OF ALL ...
...IS ME!!
DASH!

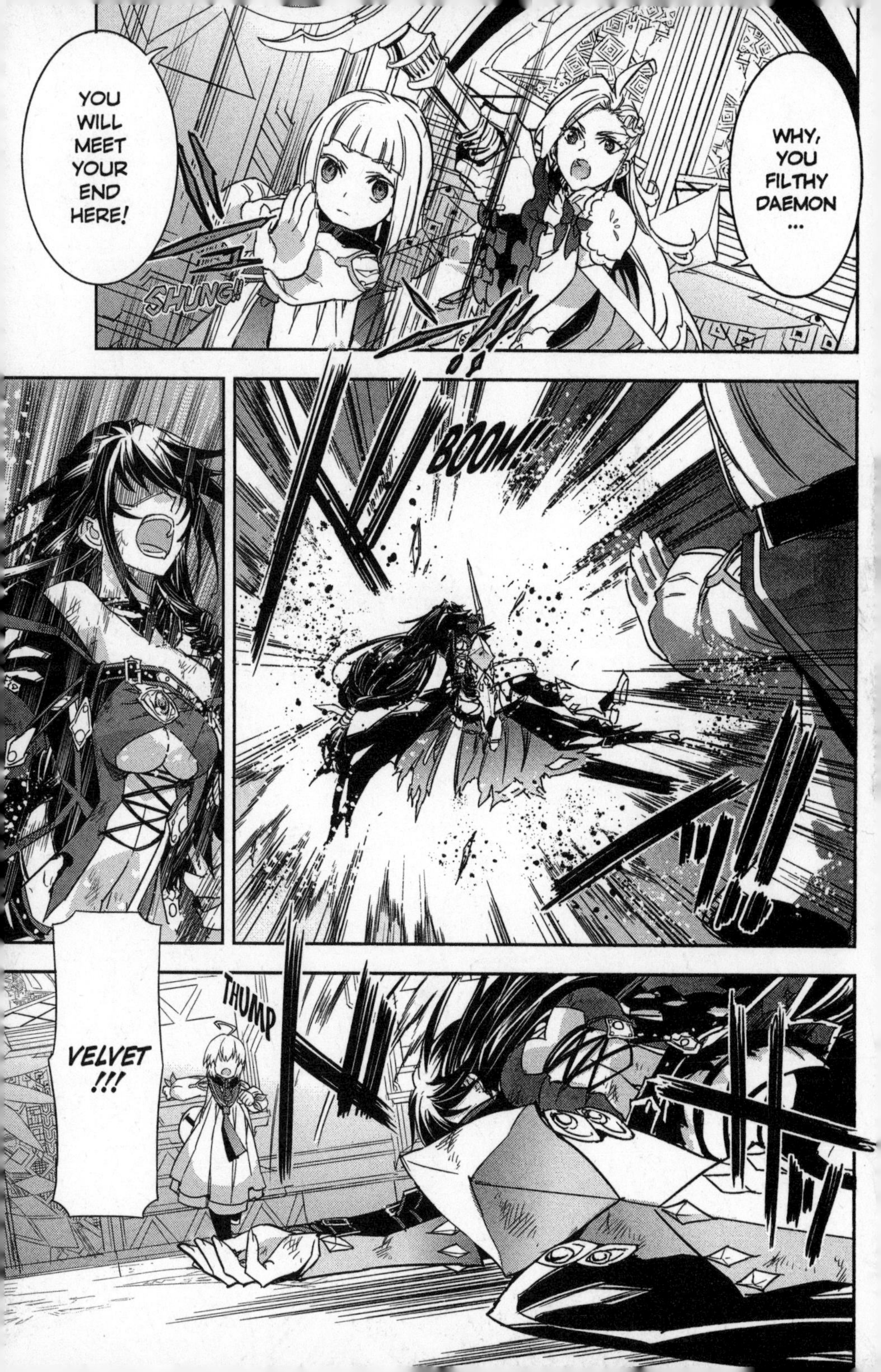
WHY, YOU FILTHY DAEMON ...
YOU WILL MEET YOUR END HERE!
SHUNG!!
BOOM!!
THUMP
VELVET !!!

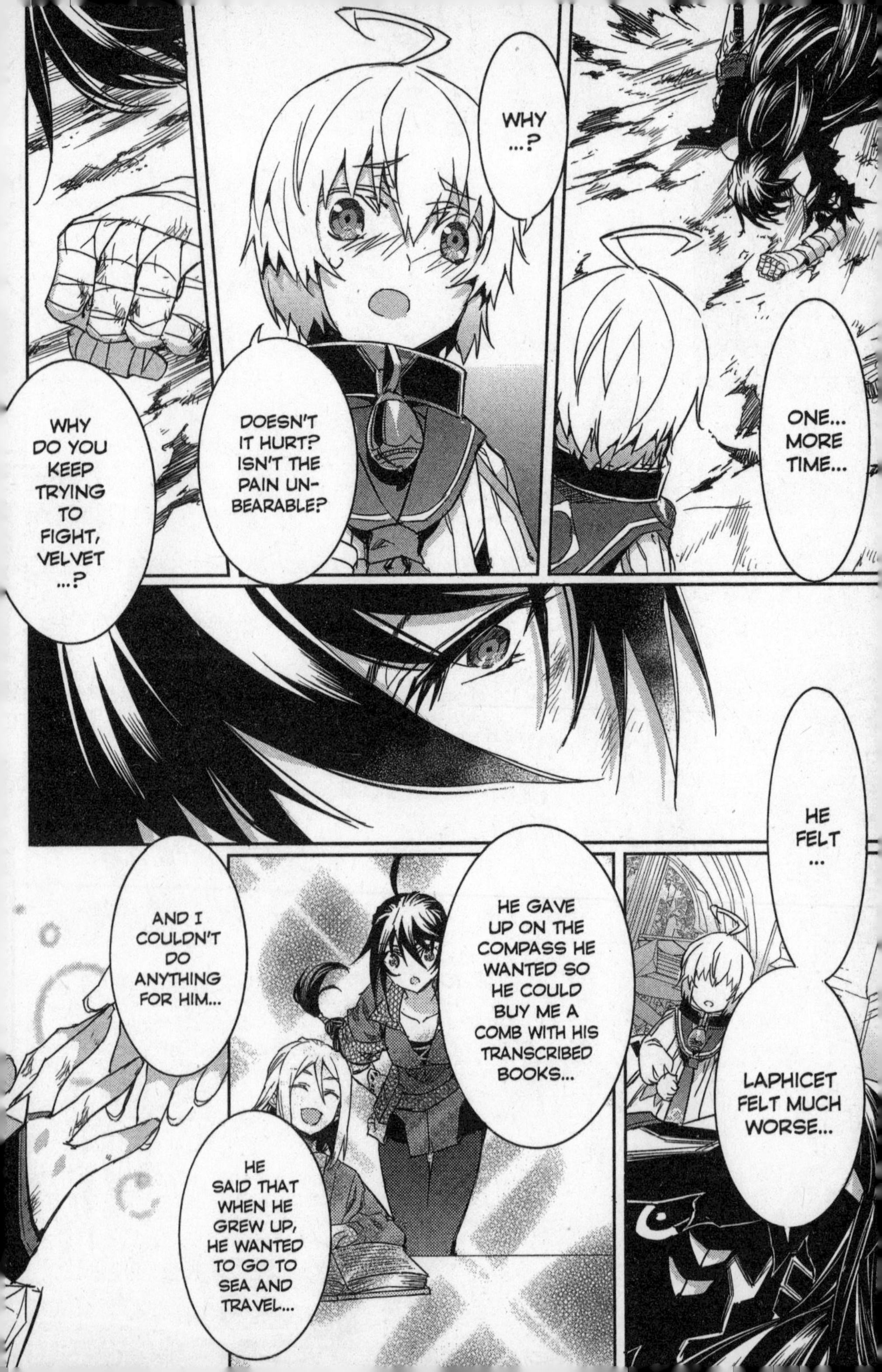
ONE... MORE TIME...
WHY ...?
DOESN'T IT HURT? ISN'T THE PAIN UN-BEARABLE?
WHY DO YOU KEEP TRYING TO FIGHT, VELVET ...?
HE FELT ...
LAPHICET FELT MUCH WORSE...
HE GAVE UP ON THE COMPASS HE WANTED SO HE COULD BUY ME A COMB WITH HIS TRANSCRIBED BOOKS...
HE SAID THAT WHEN HE GREW UP, HE WANTED TO GO TO SEA AND TRAVEL...
AND I COULDN'T DO ANYTHING FOR HIM...

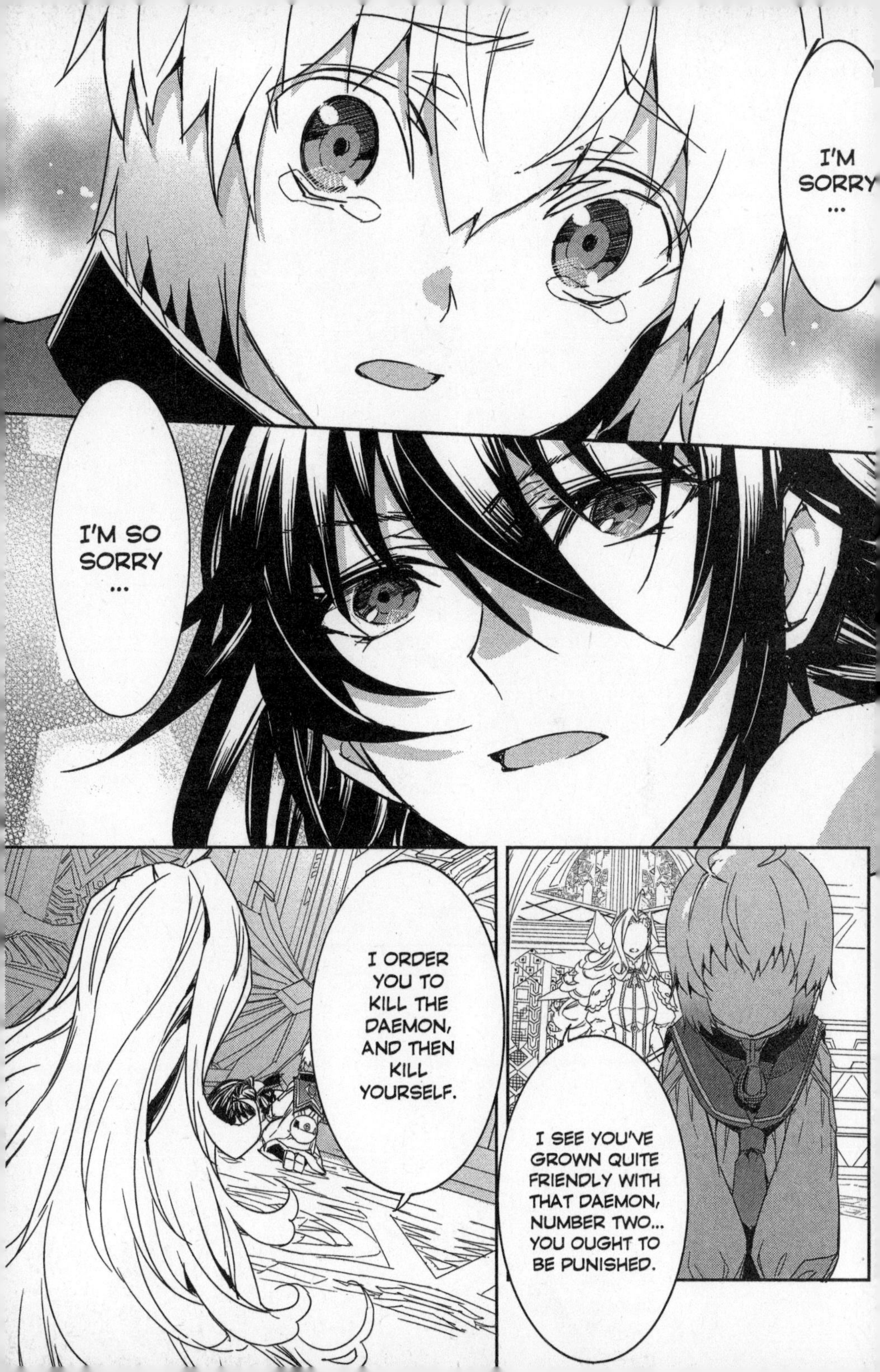
I'M SORRY ...
I'M SO SORRY ...
I SEE YOU'VE GROWN QUITE FRIENDLY WITH THAT DAEMON, NUMBER TWO... YOU OUGHT TO BE PUNISHED.
I ORDER YOU TO KILL THE DAEMON, AND THEN KILL YOURSELF.

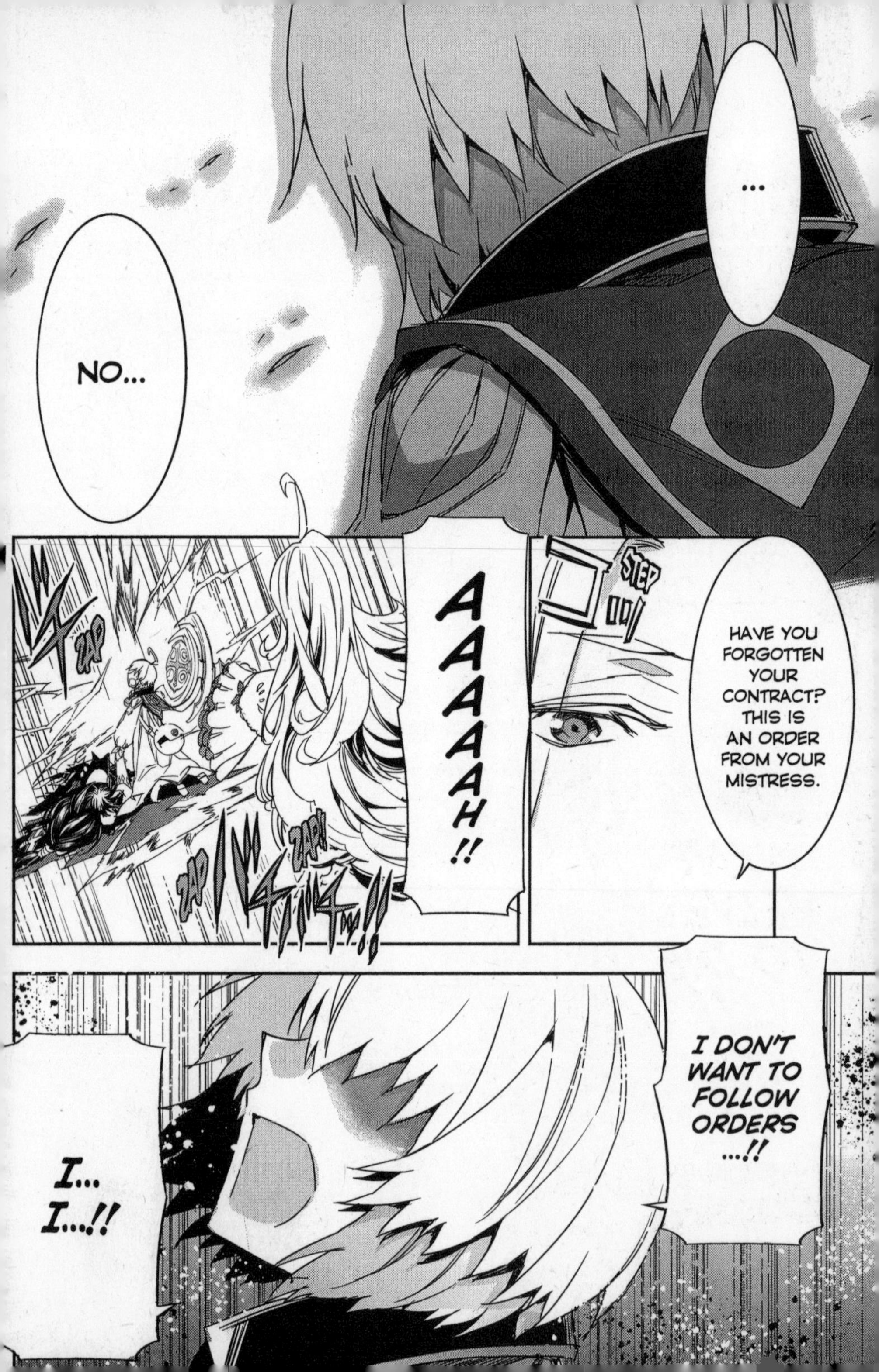
...
NO...
HAVE YOU FORGOTTEN YOUR CONTRACT? THIS IS AN ORDER FROM YOUR MISTRESS.
STEP
AAAAAAH!!
ZAP
ZAP!
ZAP
I DON'T WANT TO FOLLOW ORDERS ...!!
I... I...!!

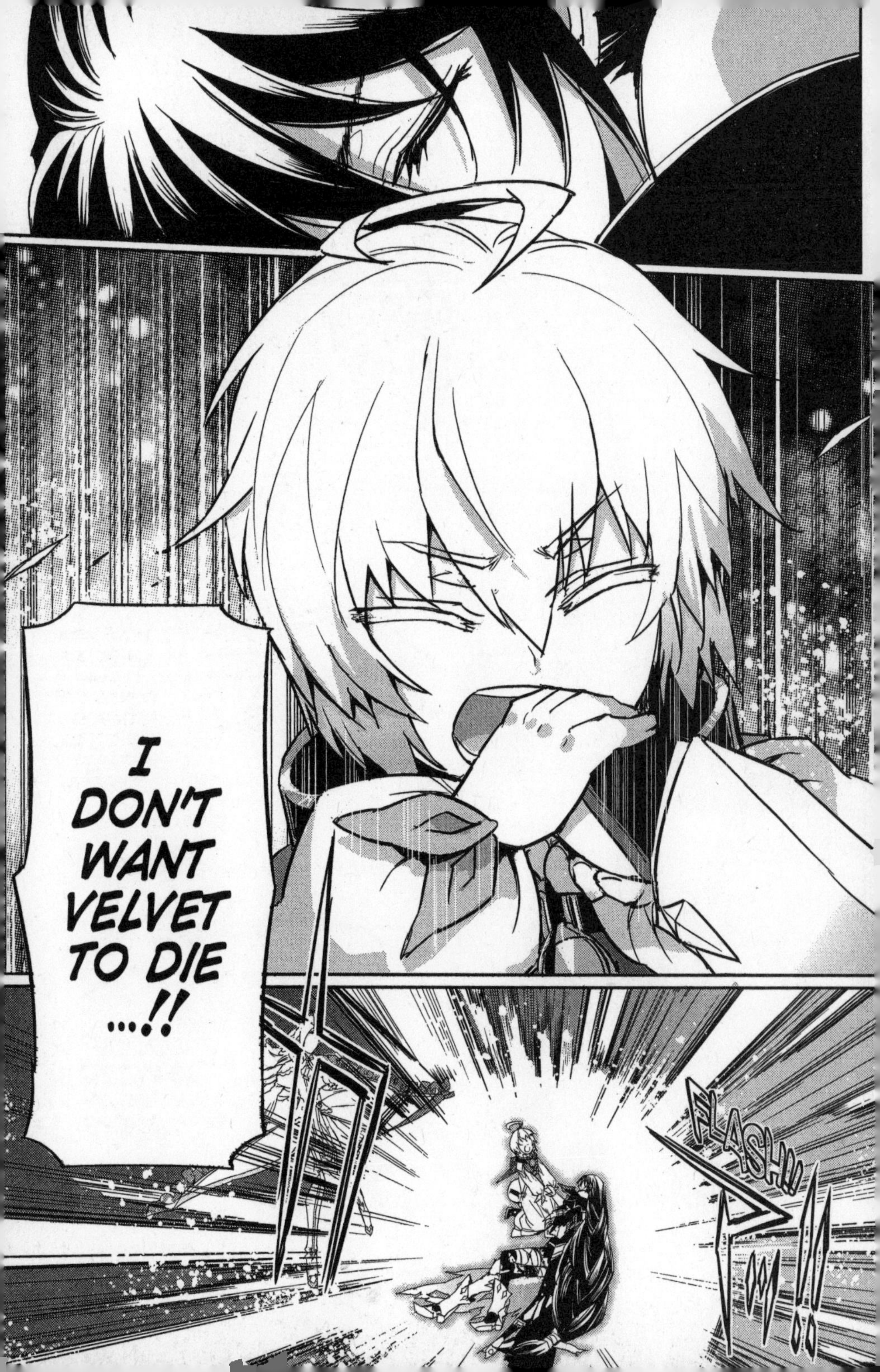
I DON'T WANT VELVET TO DIE ...!!
FLASH!!

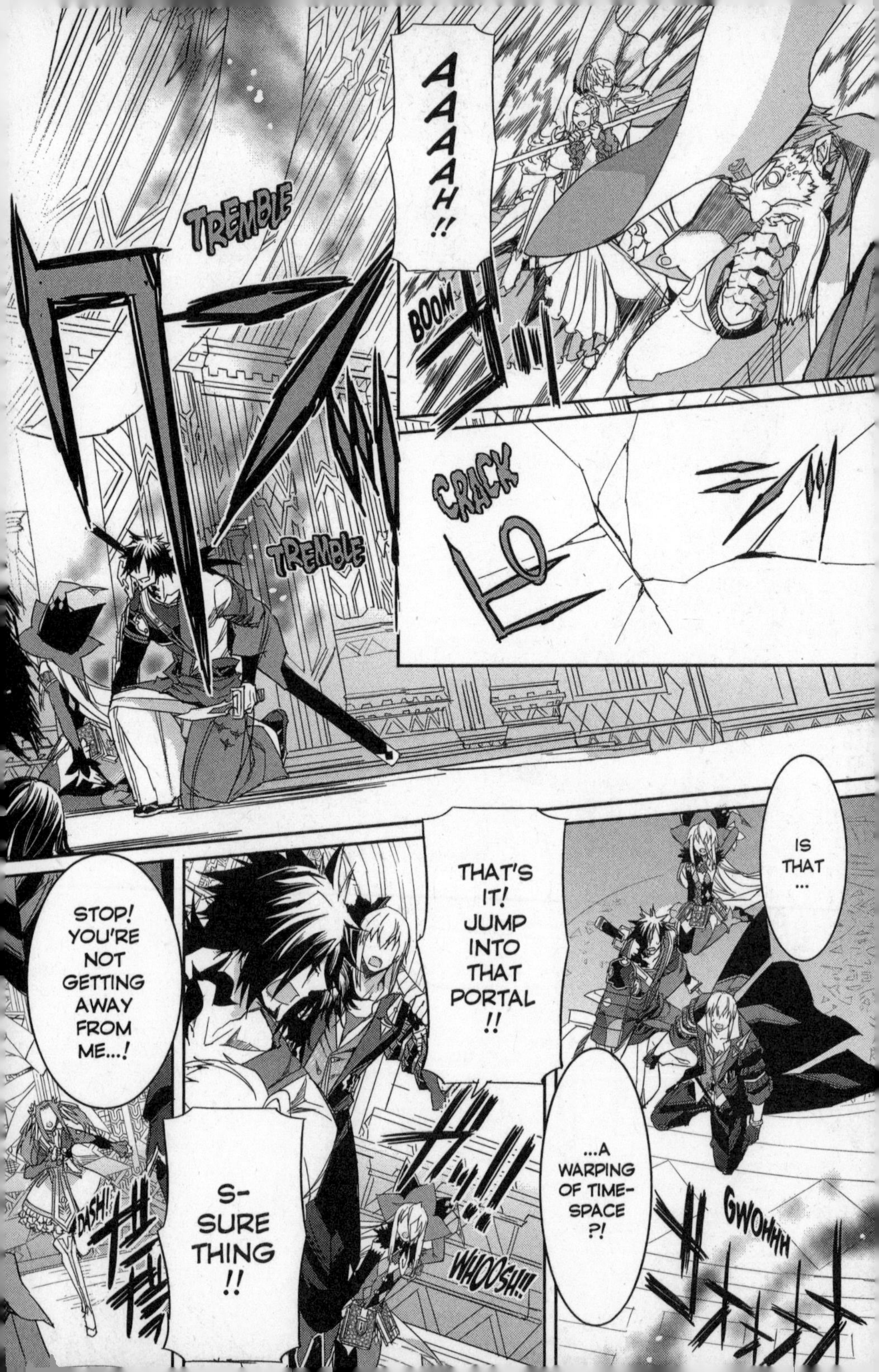
AAAAAH!!
BOOM
CRACK
TREMBLE
TREMBLE
IS THAT...
...A WARPING OF TIME-SPACE?!
GWOHHH
THAT'S IT! JUMP INTO THAT PORTAL!!
S-SURE THING!!
WHOOSH!!
STOP! YOU'RE NOT GETTING AWAY FROM ME...!
DASH!

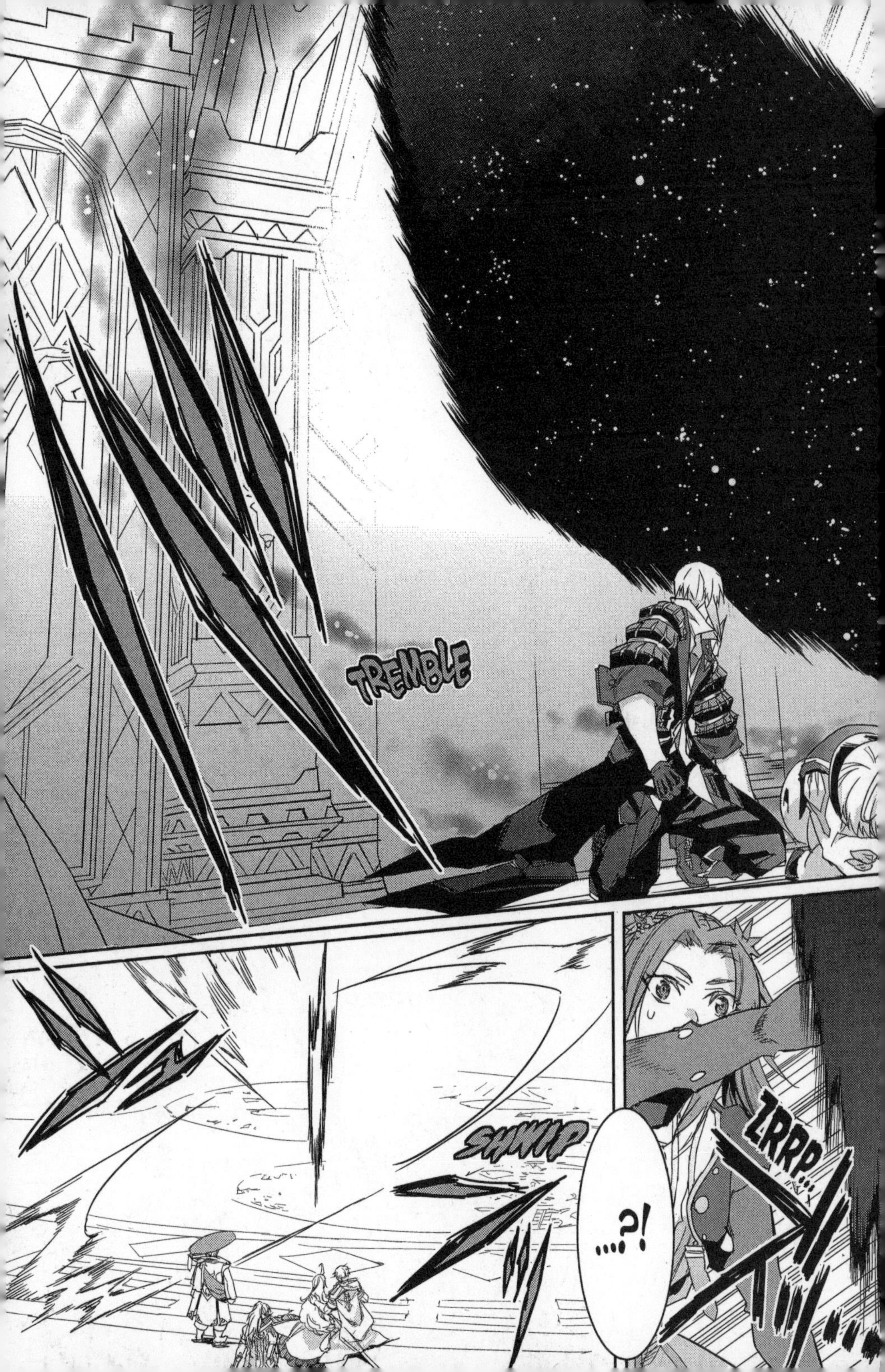
TREMBLE
ZRRP...
...?!
SHWIP

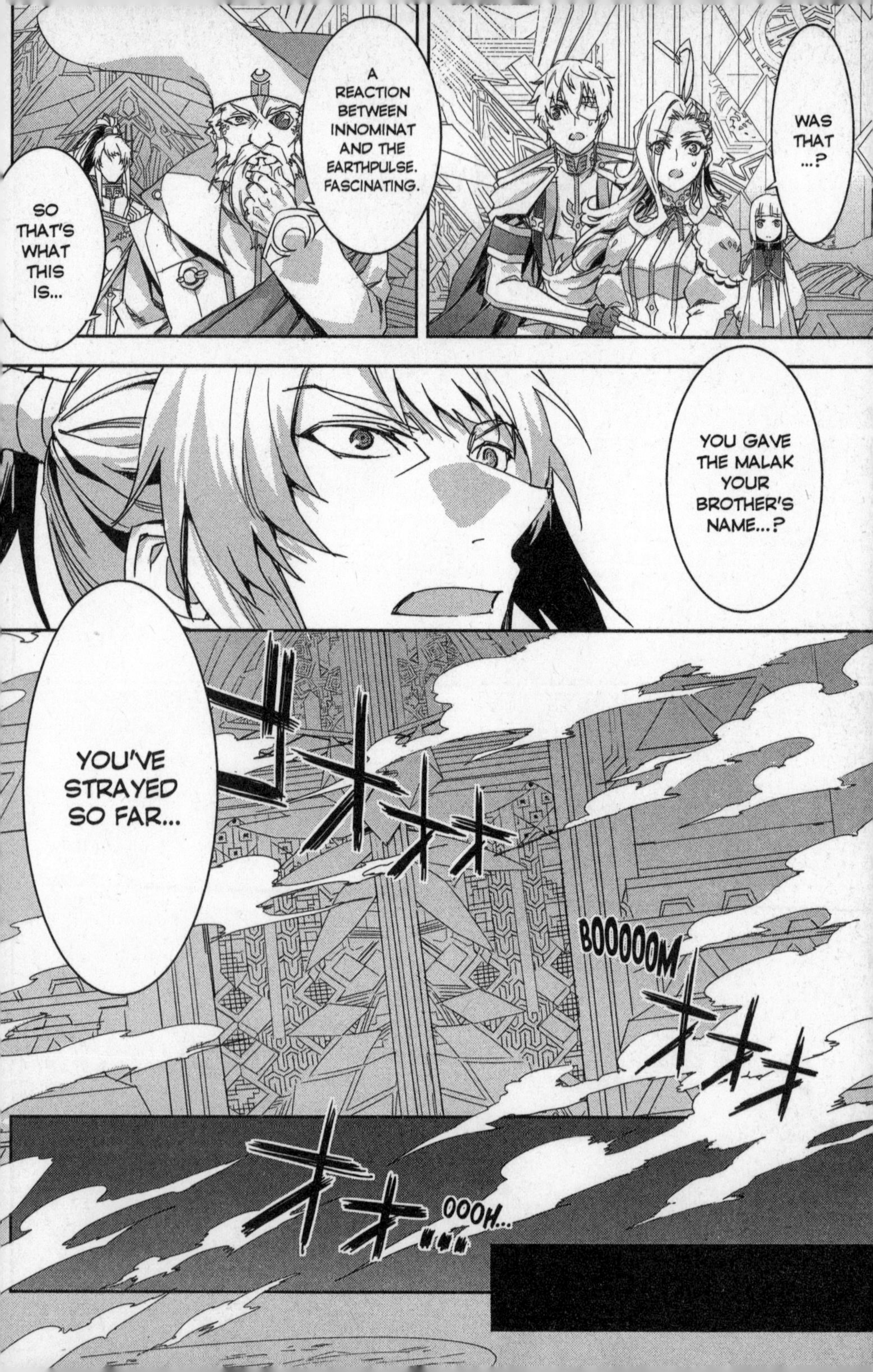
WAS THAT ...?
A REACTION BETWEEN INNOMINAT AND THE EARTHPULSE. FASCINATING.
SO THAT'S WHAT THIS IS...
YOU GAVE THE MALAK YOUR BROTHER'S NAME...?
YOU'VE STRAYED SO FAR...
BOOOOOM
OOOH...

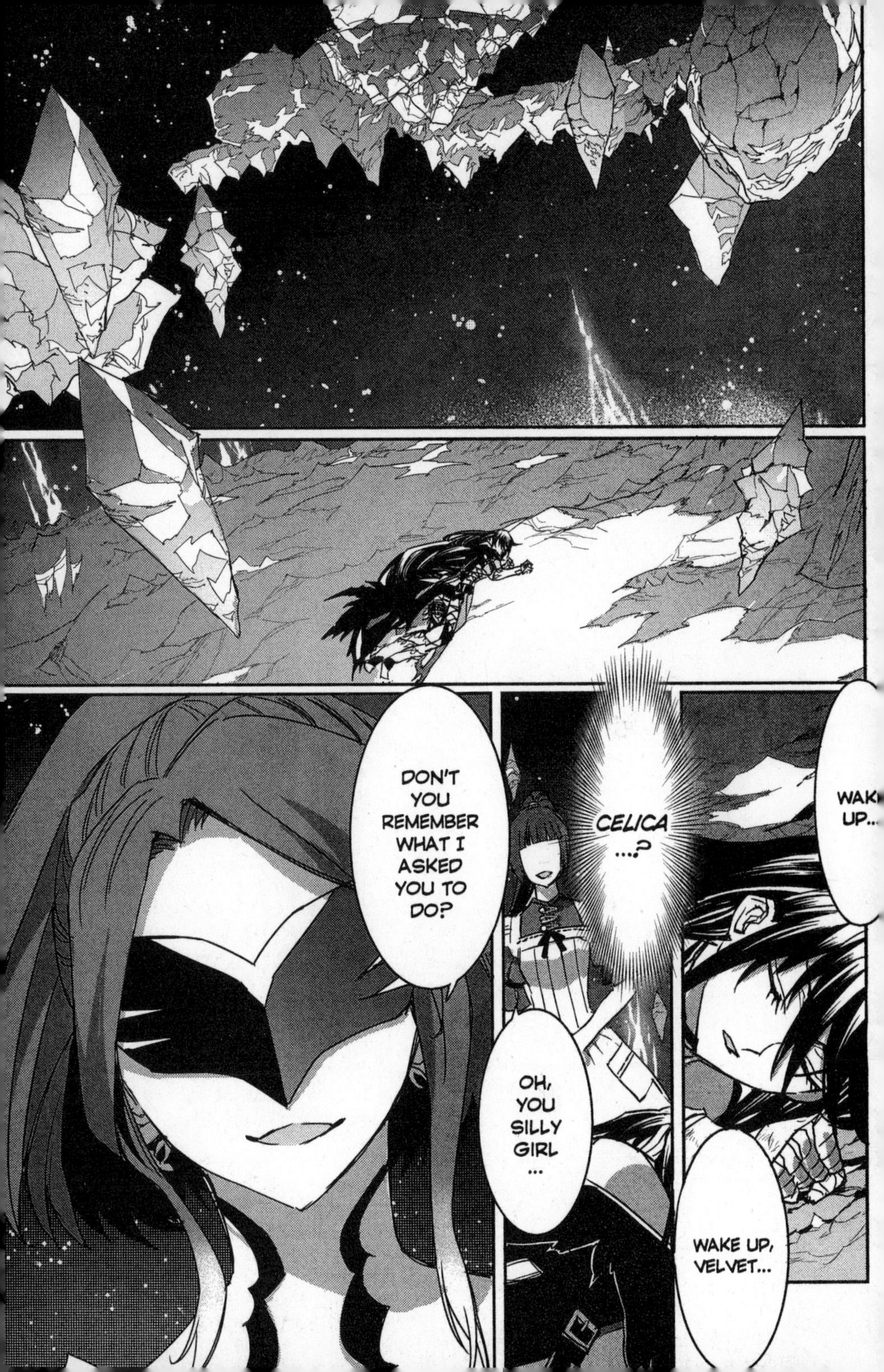
WAKE UP...
WAKE UP, VELVET...
CELICA ...?
OH, YOU SILLY GIRL ...
DON'T YOU REMEMBER WHAT I ASKED YOU TO DO?

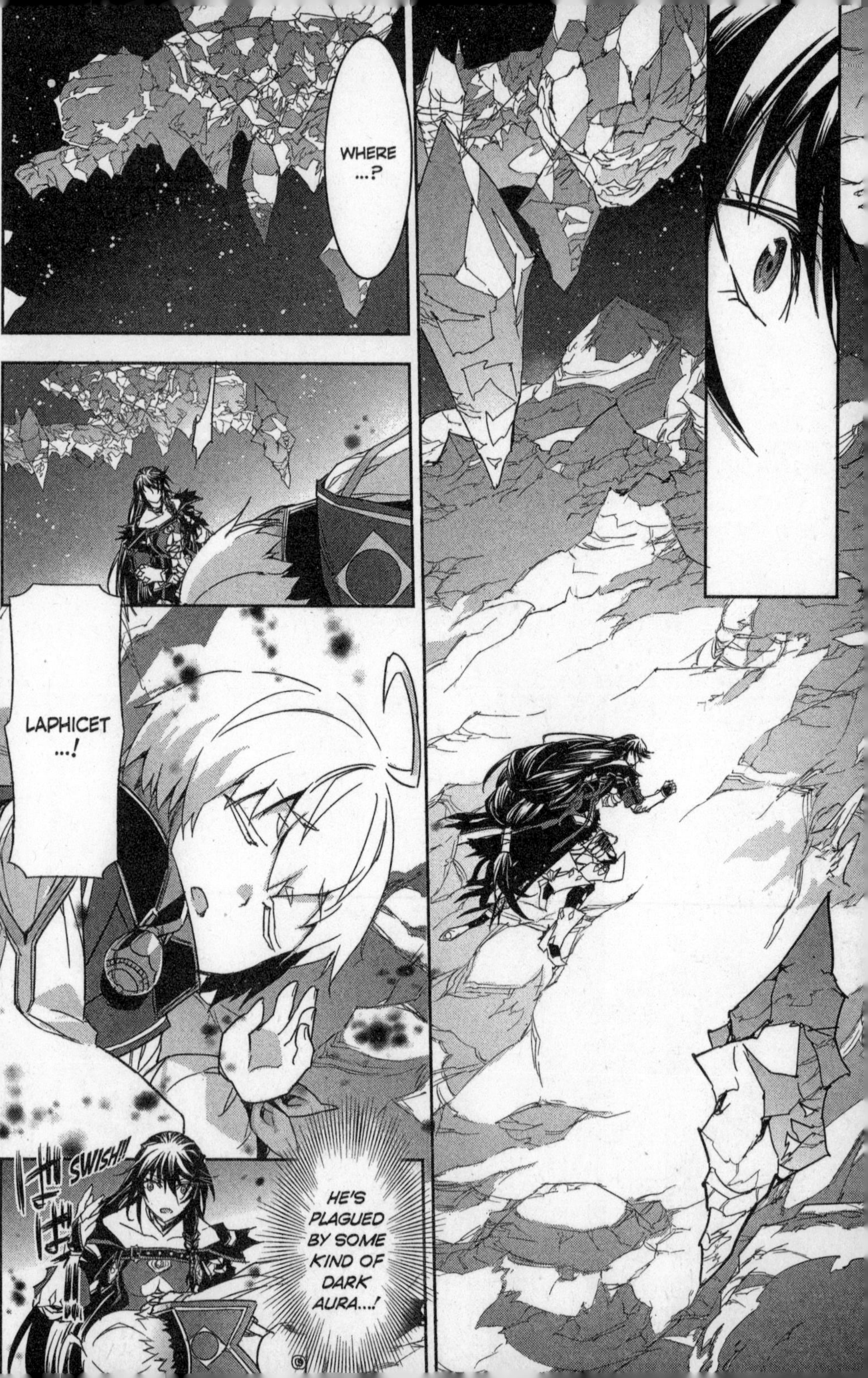
WHERE ...?
LAPHICET ...!
HE'S PLAGUED BY SOME KIND OF DARK AURA...!
SWISH!!

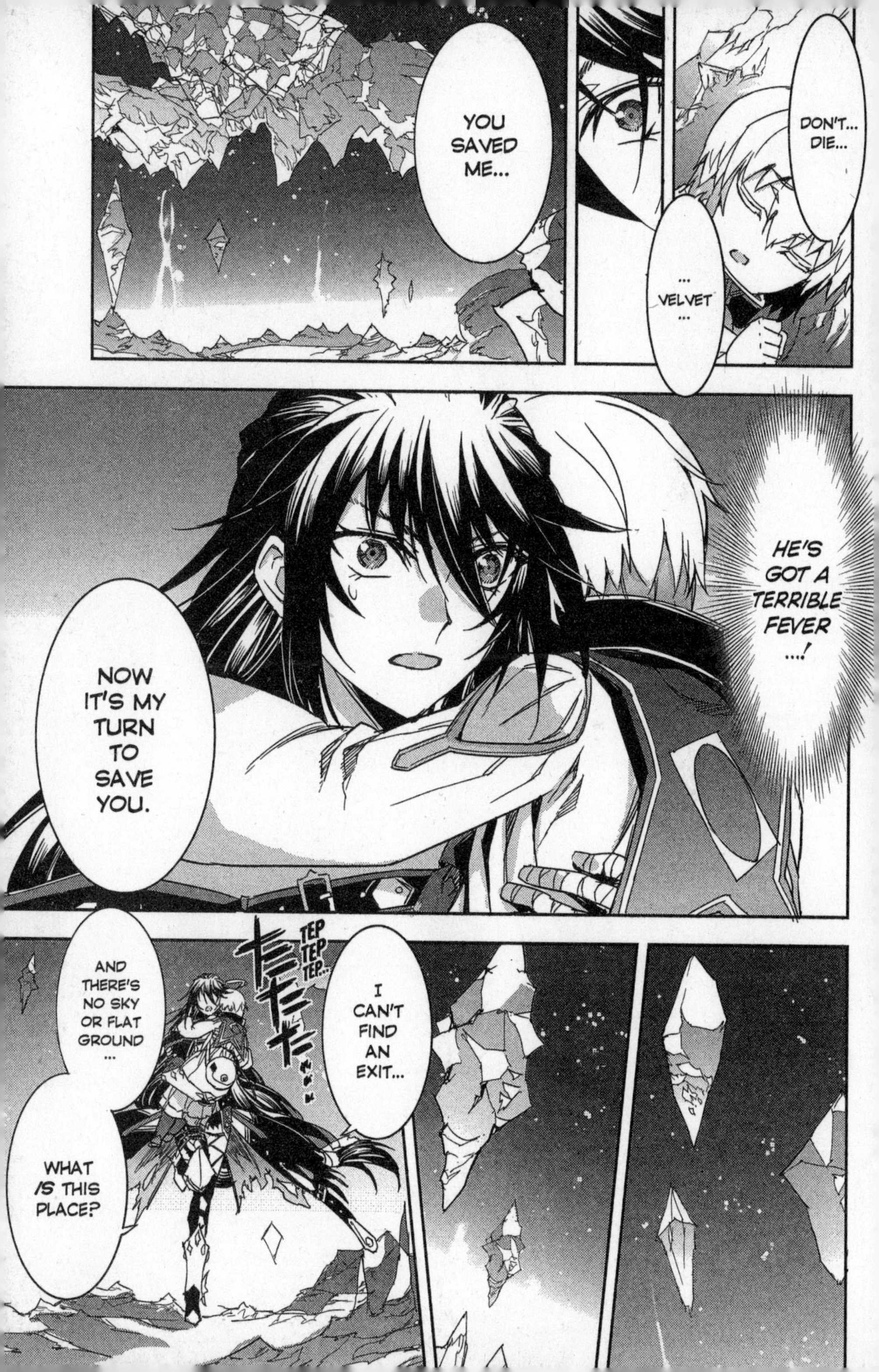
DON'T... DIE...
... VELVET ...
YOU SAVED ME...
HE'S GOT A TERRIBLE FEVER ...!
NOW IT'S MY TURN TO SAVE YOU.
TEP TEP TEP...
I CAN'T FIND AN EXIT...
AND THERE'S NO SKY OR FLAT GROUND ...
WHAT IS THIS PLACE?

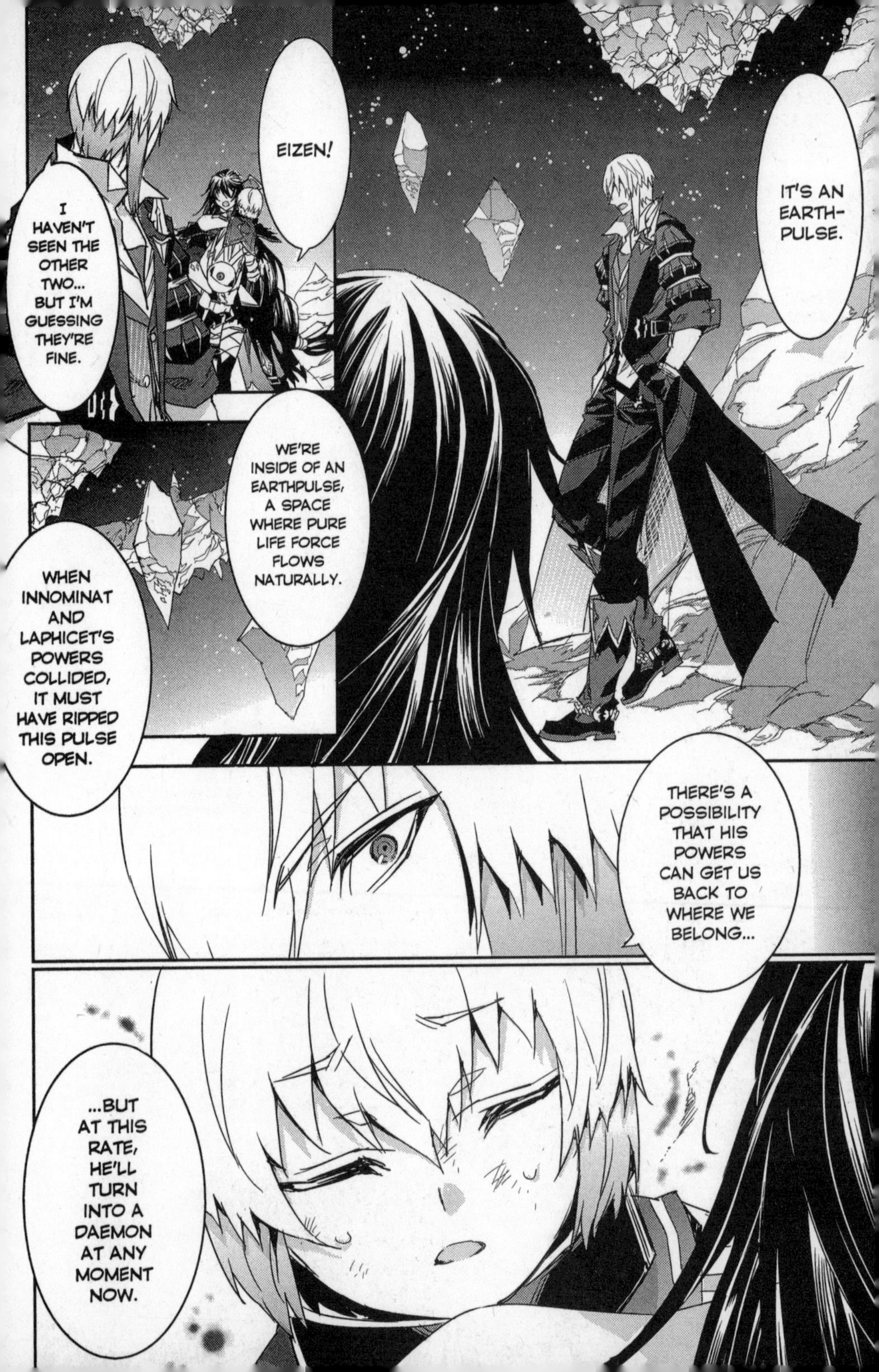
IT'S AN EARTH-PULSE.
WE'RE INSIDE OF AN EARTHPULSE, A SPACE WHERE PURE LIFE FORCE FLOWS NATURALLY.
EIZEN!
I HAVEN'T SEEN THE OTHER TWO... BUT I'M GUESSING THEY'RE FINE.
WHEN INNOMINAT AND LAPHICET'S POWERS COLLIDED, IT MUST HAVE RIPPED THIS PULSE OPEN.
THERE'S A POSSIBILITY THAT HIS POWERS CAN GET US BACK TO WHERE WE BELONG...
...BUT AT THIS RATE, HE'LL TURN INTO A DAEMON AT ANY MOMENT NOW.

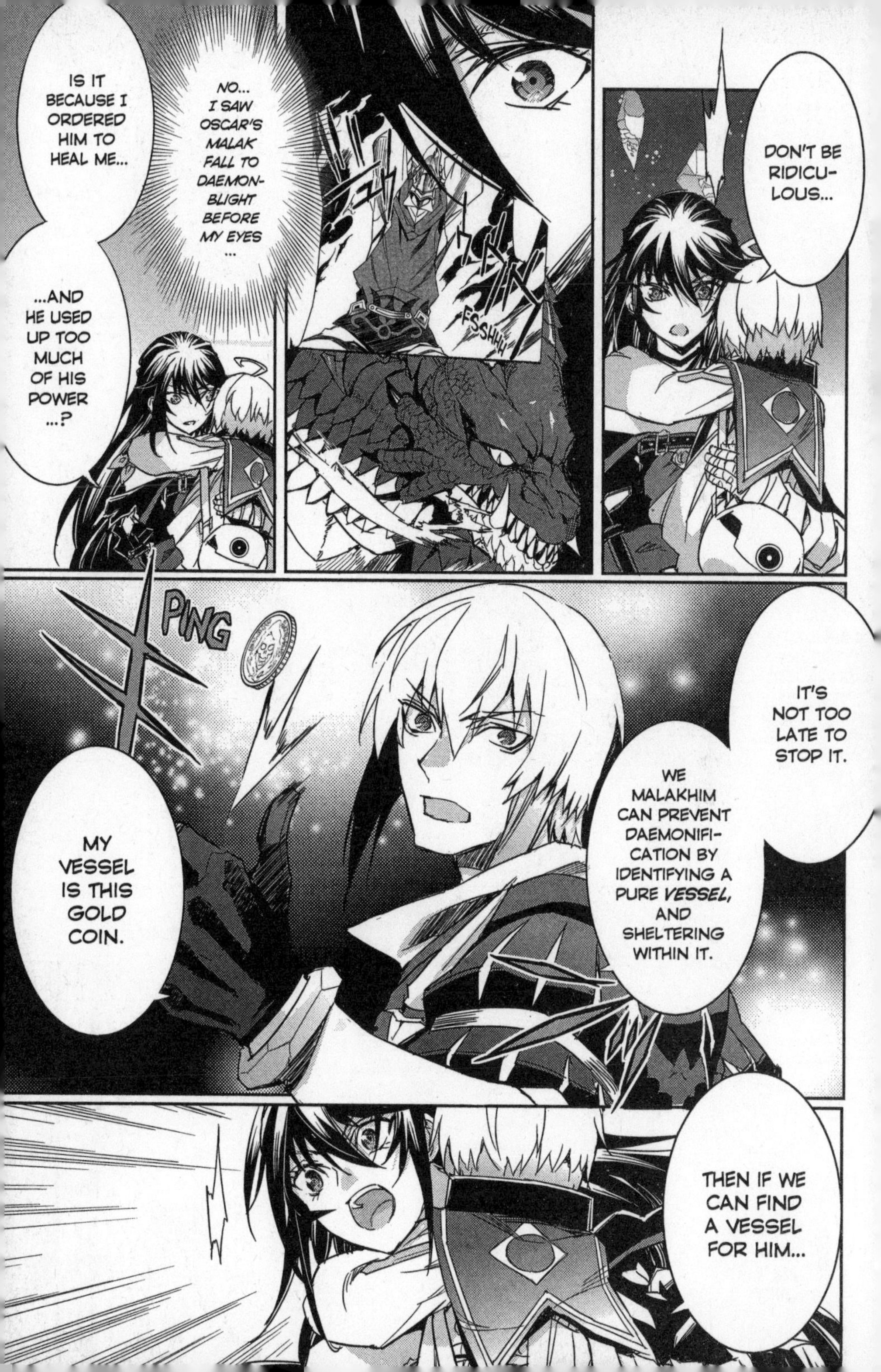
DON'T BE RIDICULOUS...
NO... I SAW OSCAR'S *MALAK* FALL TO DAEMONBLIGHT BEFORE MY EYES ...
FSSHHH
IS IT BECAUSE I ORDERED HIM TO HEAL ME...
...AND HE USED UP TOO MUCH OF HIS POWER ...?
IT'S NOT TOO LATE TO STOP IT.
WE MALAKHIM CAN PREVENT DAEMONIFICATION BY IDENTIFYING A PURE *VESSEL*, AND SHELTERING WITHIN IT.
PING
MY VESSEL IS THIS GOLD COIN.
THEN IF WE CAN FIND A VESSEL FOR HIM...

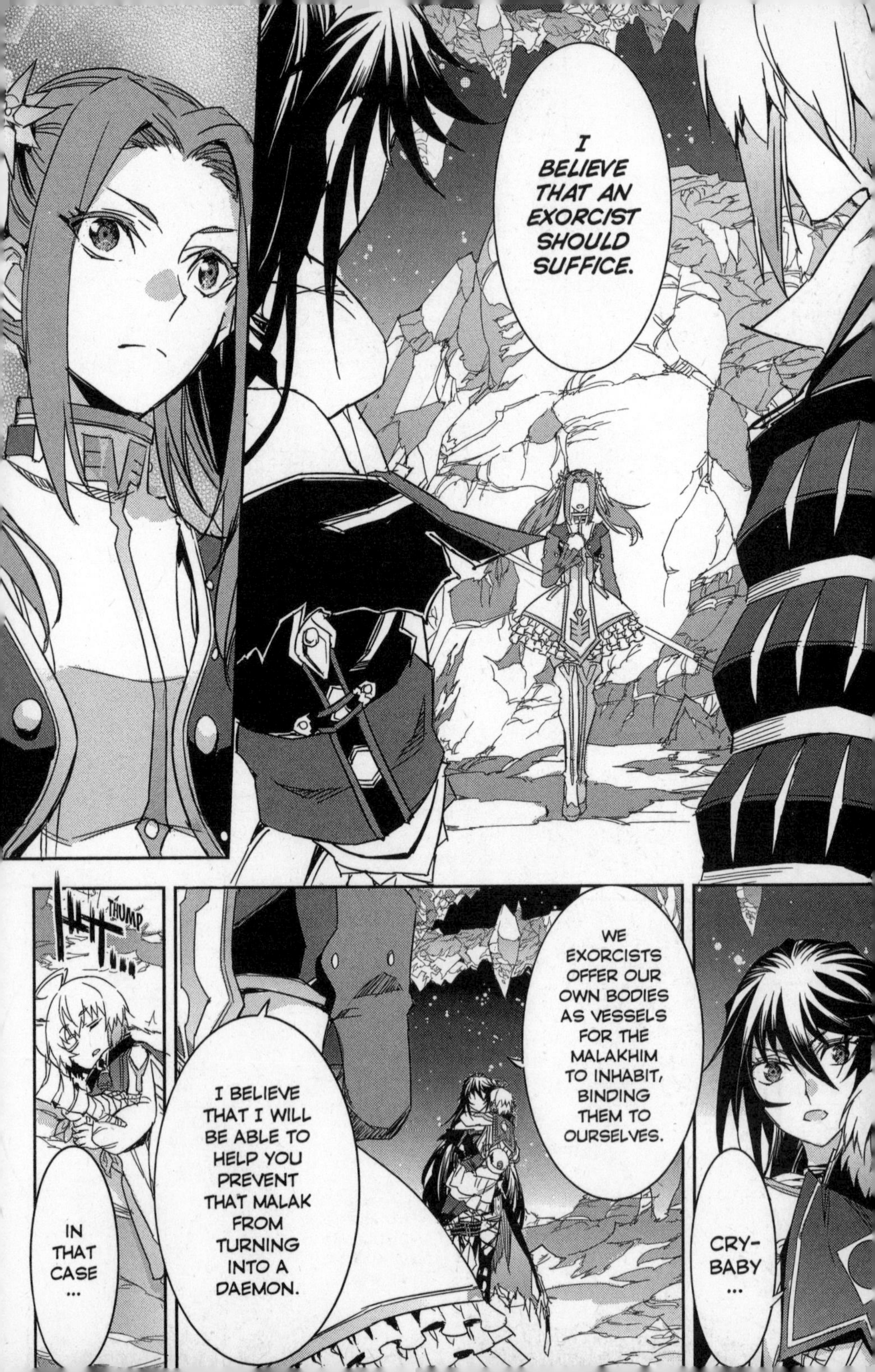
I BELIEVE THAT AN EXORCIST SHOULD SUFFICE.
CRY-BABY ...
WE EXORCISTS OFFER OUR OWN BODIES AS VESSELS FOR THE MALAKHIM TO INHABIT, BINDING THEM TO OURSELVES.
I BELIEVE THAT I WILL BE ABLE TO HELP YOU PREVENT THAT MALAK FROM TURNING INTO A DAEMON.
THUMP
IN THAT CASE ...

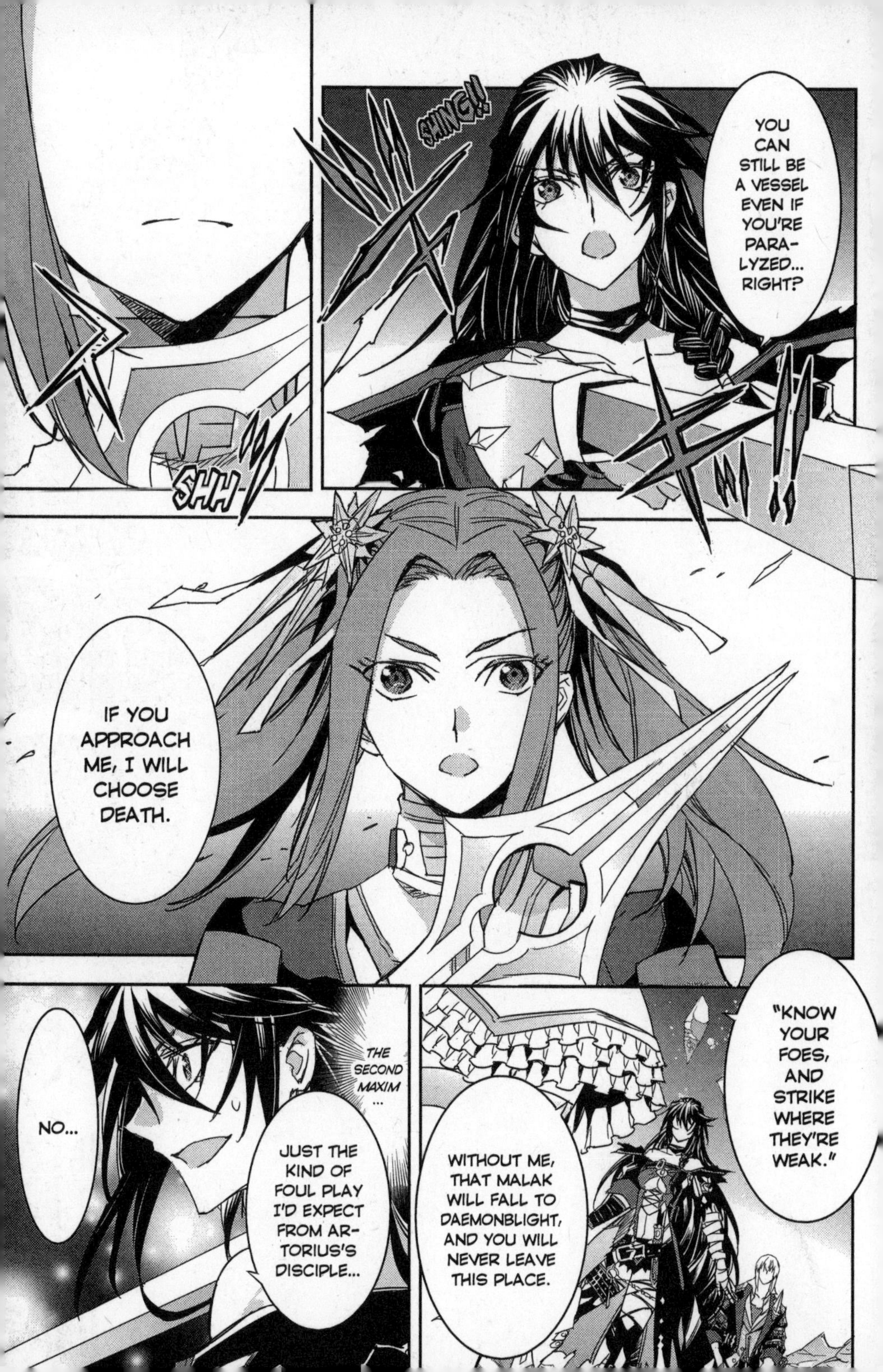
SHING!!
YOU CAN STILL BE A VESSEL EVEN IF YOU'RE PARA-LYZED... RIGHT?
SHH
IF YOU APPROACH ME, I WILL CHOOSE DEATH.
"KNOW YOUR FOES, AND STRIKE WHERE THEY'RE WEAK."
WITHOUT ME, THAT MALAK WILL FALL TO DAEMONBLIGHT, AND YOU WILL NEVER LEAVE THIS PLACE.
THE SECOND MAXIM...
JUST THE KIND OF FOUL PLAY I'D EXPECT FROM AR-TORIUS'S DISCIPLE...
NO...

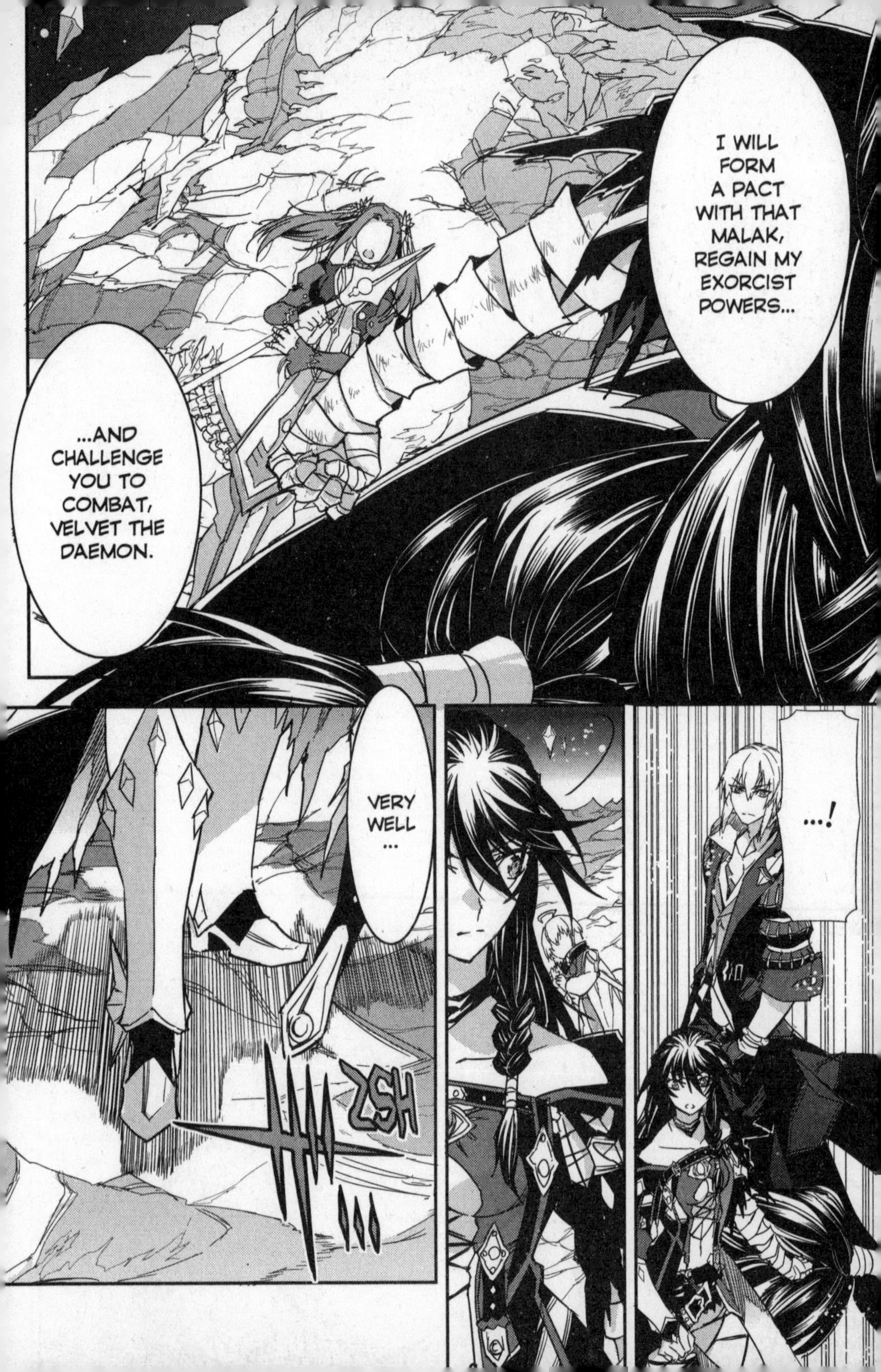
I WILL FORM A PACT WITH THAT MALAK, REGAIN MY EXORCIST POWERS...
...AND CHALLENGE YOU TO COMBAT, VELVET THE DAEMON.
...!
VERY WELL ...
ZSH

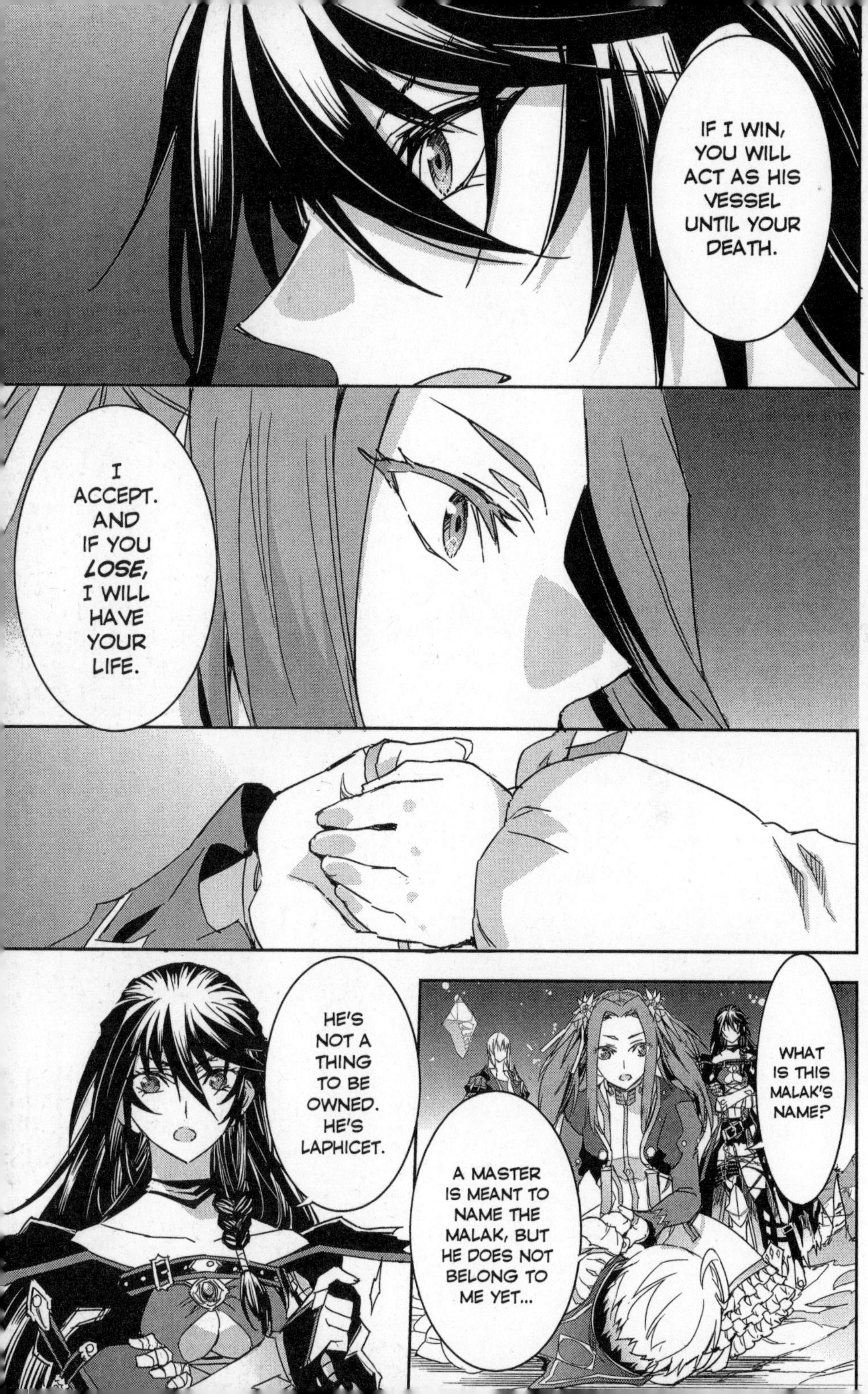
IF I WIN, YOU WILL ACT AS HIS VESSEL UNTIL YOUR DEATH.
I ACCEPT. AND IF YOU *LOSE,* I WILL HAVE YOUR LIFE.
WHAT IS THIS MALAK'S NAME?
A MASTER IS MEANT TO NAME THE MALAK, BUT HE DOES NOT BELONG TO ME YET...
HE'S NOT A THING TO BE OWNED. HE'S LAPHICET.

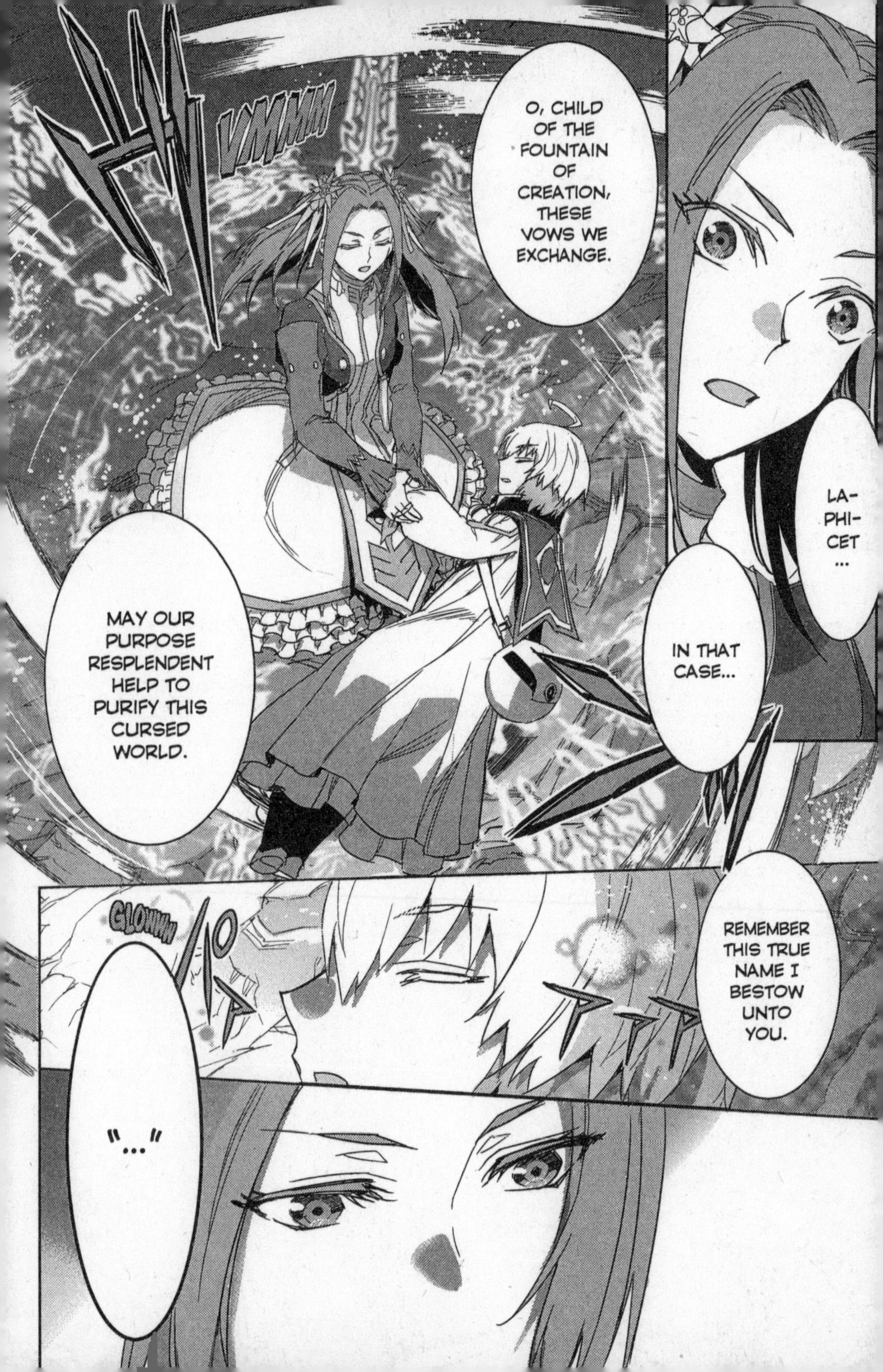
LA-PHI-CET...
IN THAT CASE...
VMMMM
O, CHILD OF THE FOUNTAIN OF CREATION, THESE VOWS WE EXCHANGE.
MAY OUR PURPOSE RESPLENDENT HELP TO PURIFY THIS CURSED WORLD.
REMEMBER THIS TRUE NAME I BESTOW UNTO YOU.
GLOWWW
"..."

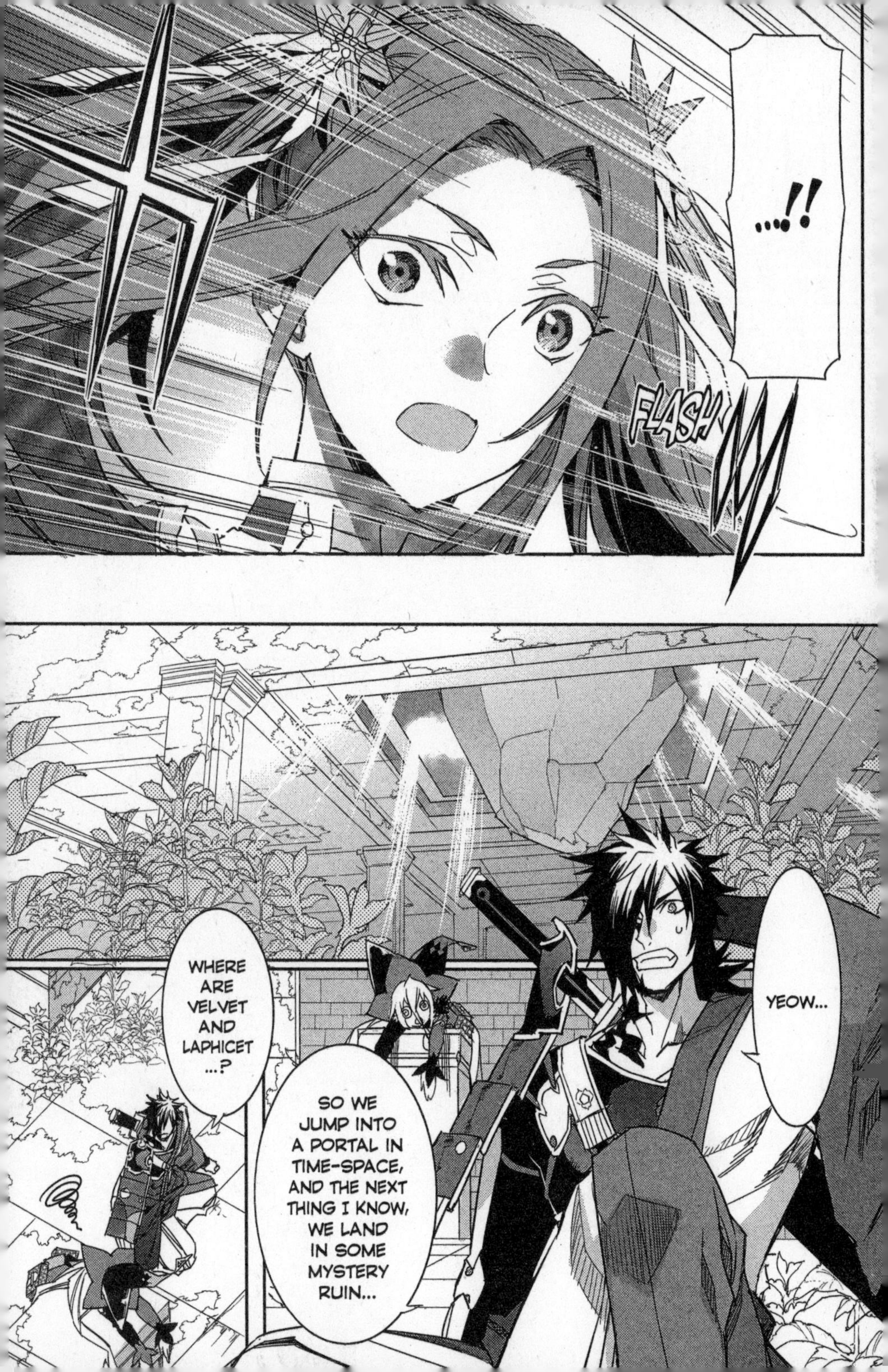
...!!
FLASH
YEOW...
SO WE JUMP INTO A PORTAL IN TIME-SPACE, AND THE NEXT THING I KNOW, WE LAND IN SOME MYSTERY RUIN...
WHERE ARE VELVET AND LAPHICET ...?

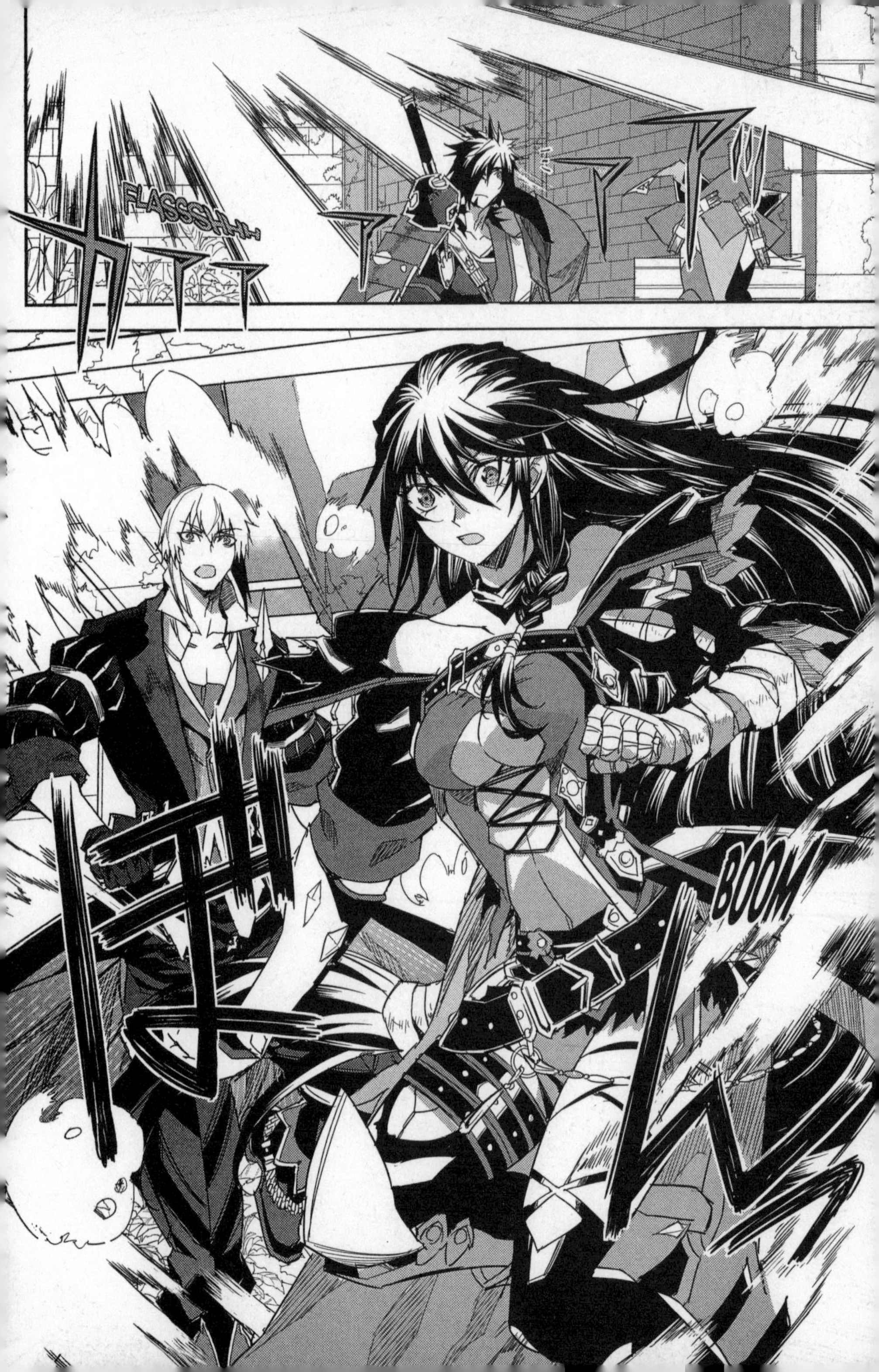
FLASSSHHHH
BOOM

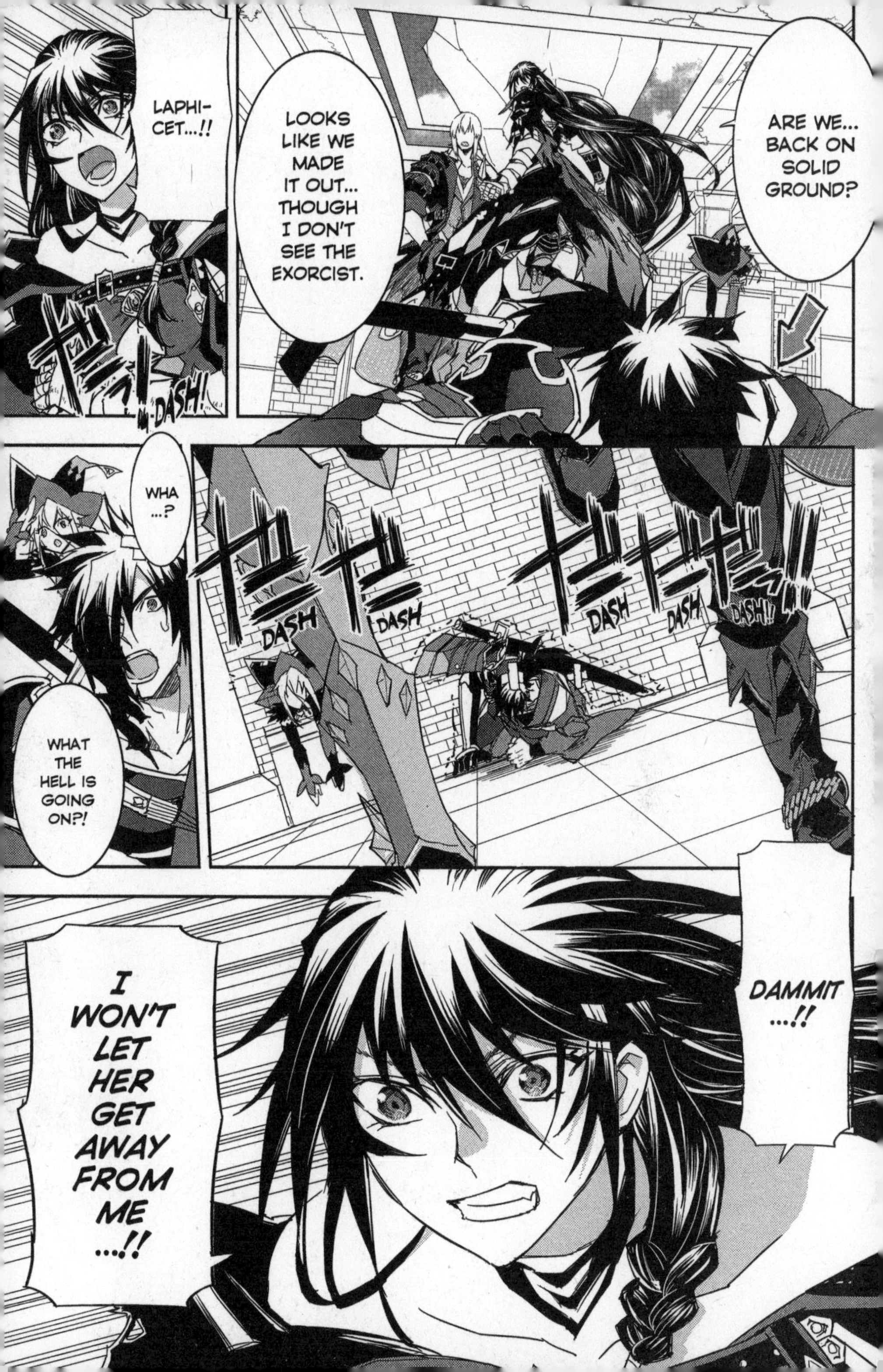
ARE WE... BACK ON SOLID GROUND?
LOOKS LIKE WE MADE IT OUT... THOUGH I DON'T SEE THE EXORCIST.
LAPHICET...!!
DASH!
DASH!!
DASH
DASH
DASH
DASH
WHA ...?
WHAT THE HELL IS GOING ON?!
DAMMIT ...!!
I WON'T LET HER GET AWAY FROM ME ...!!

Escaping the Earthpulse

DASH
DASH
DASH
DASH
DASH!!
WHAT THE HELL JUST HAPPENED ...?
FLASSSHhhh...
FLOP
FLASH
Stuff they dropped in the earthpulse
FLOP
YOU MAKE FOR A PRETTY GOOD CUSHION ...
WHAT... THE HELL... IT HURTS...

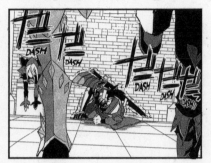

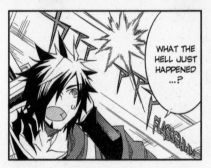

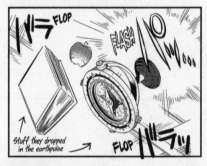

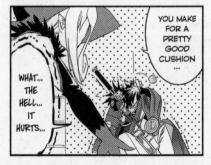

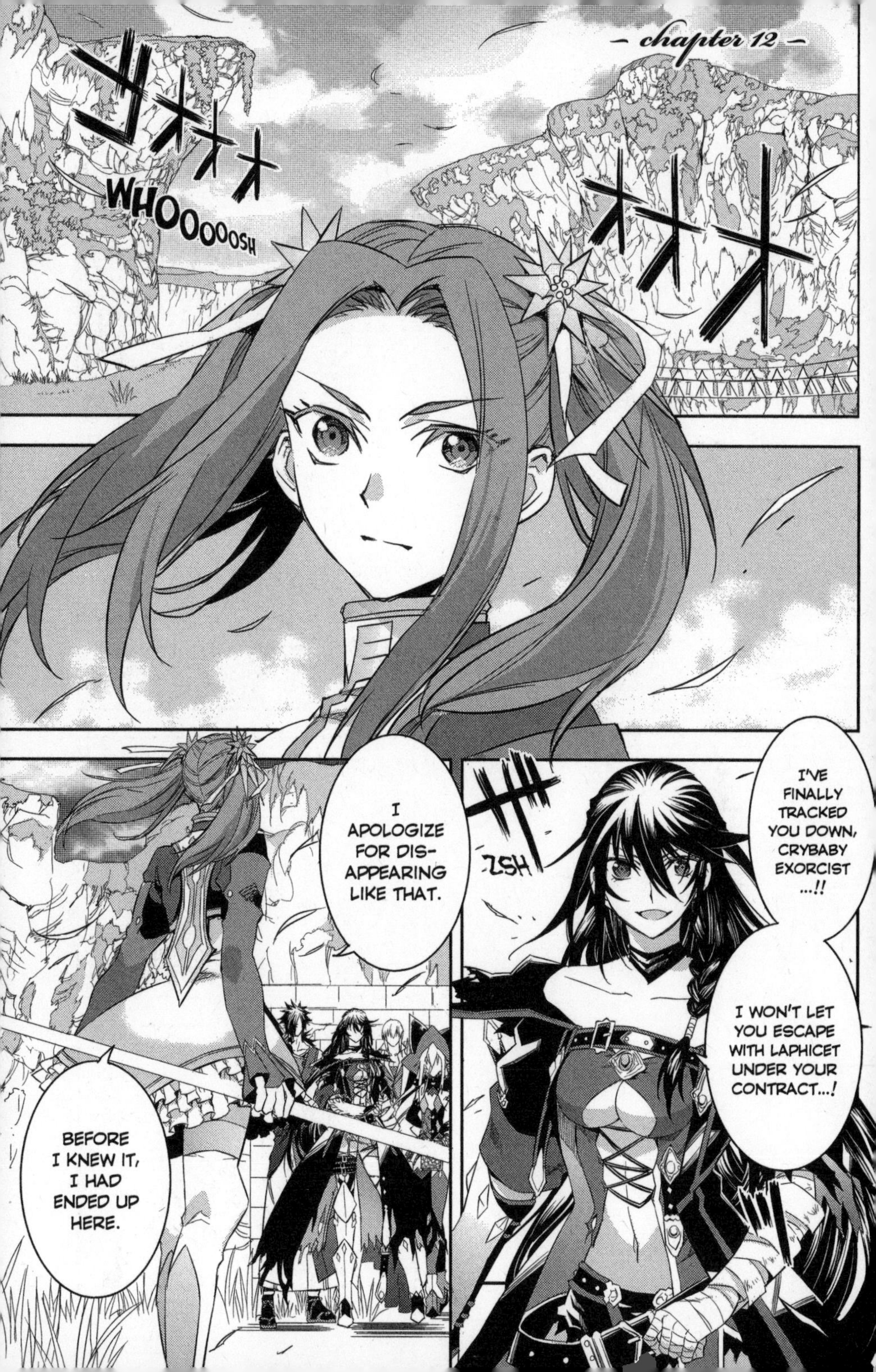
- chapter 12 -
WHOOOOOOSH
ZSH
I'VE FINALLY TRACKED YOU DOWN, CRYBABY EXORCIST ...!!
I WON'T LET YOU ESCAPE WITH LAPHICET UNDER YOUR CONTRACT...!
I APOLOGIZE FOR DIS-APPEARING LIKE THAT.
BEFORE I KNEW IT, I HAD ENDED UP HERE.

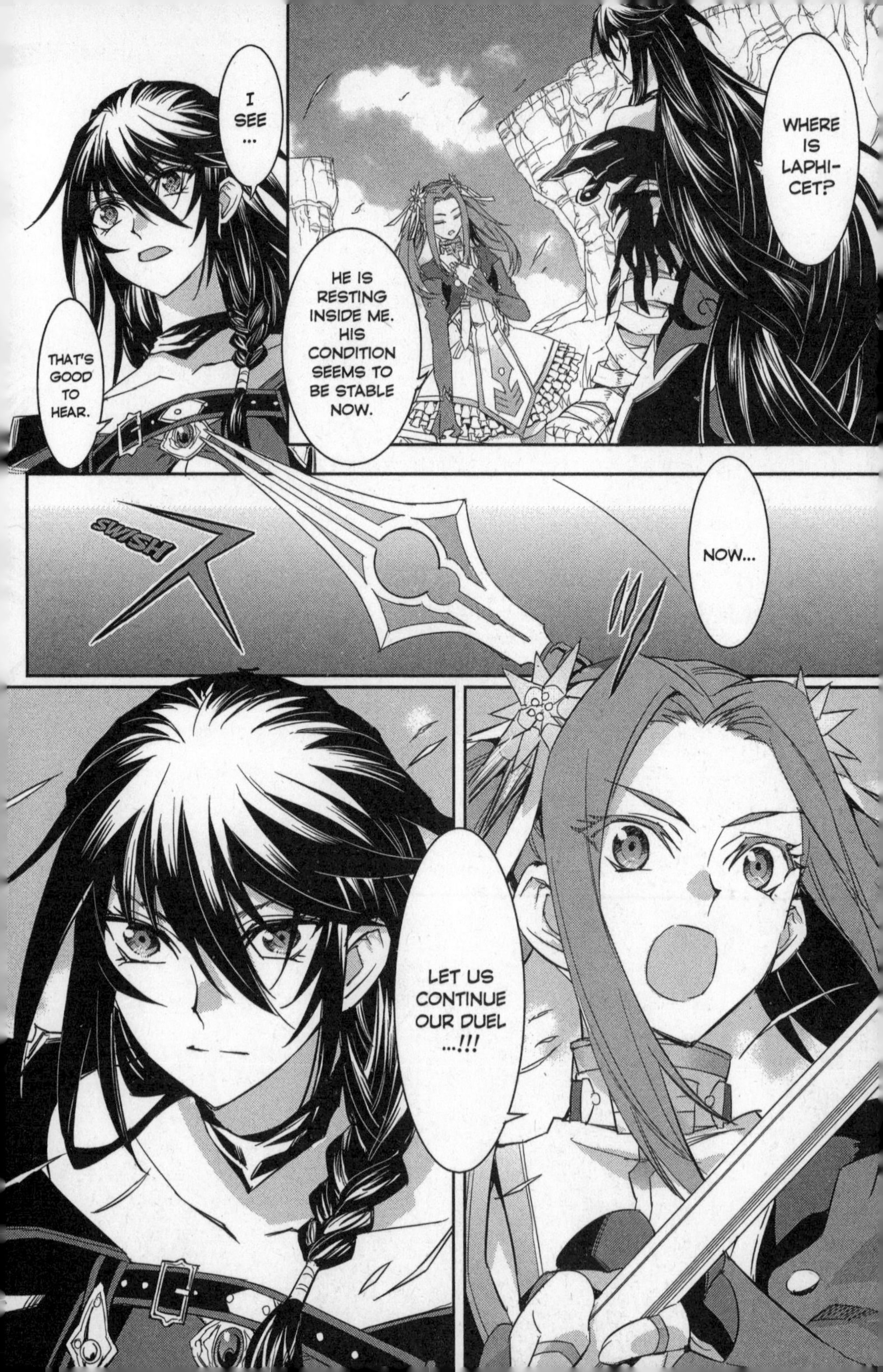
WHERE IS LAPHI-CET?
HE IS RESTING INSIDE ME. HIS CONDITION SEEMS TO BE STABLE NOW.
I SEE...
THAT'S GOOD TO HEAR.
NOW...
SWISH
LET US CONTINUE OUR DUEL...!!!

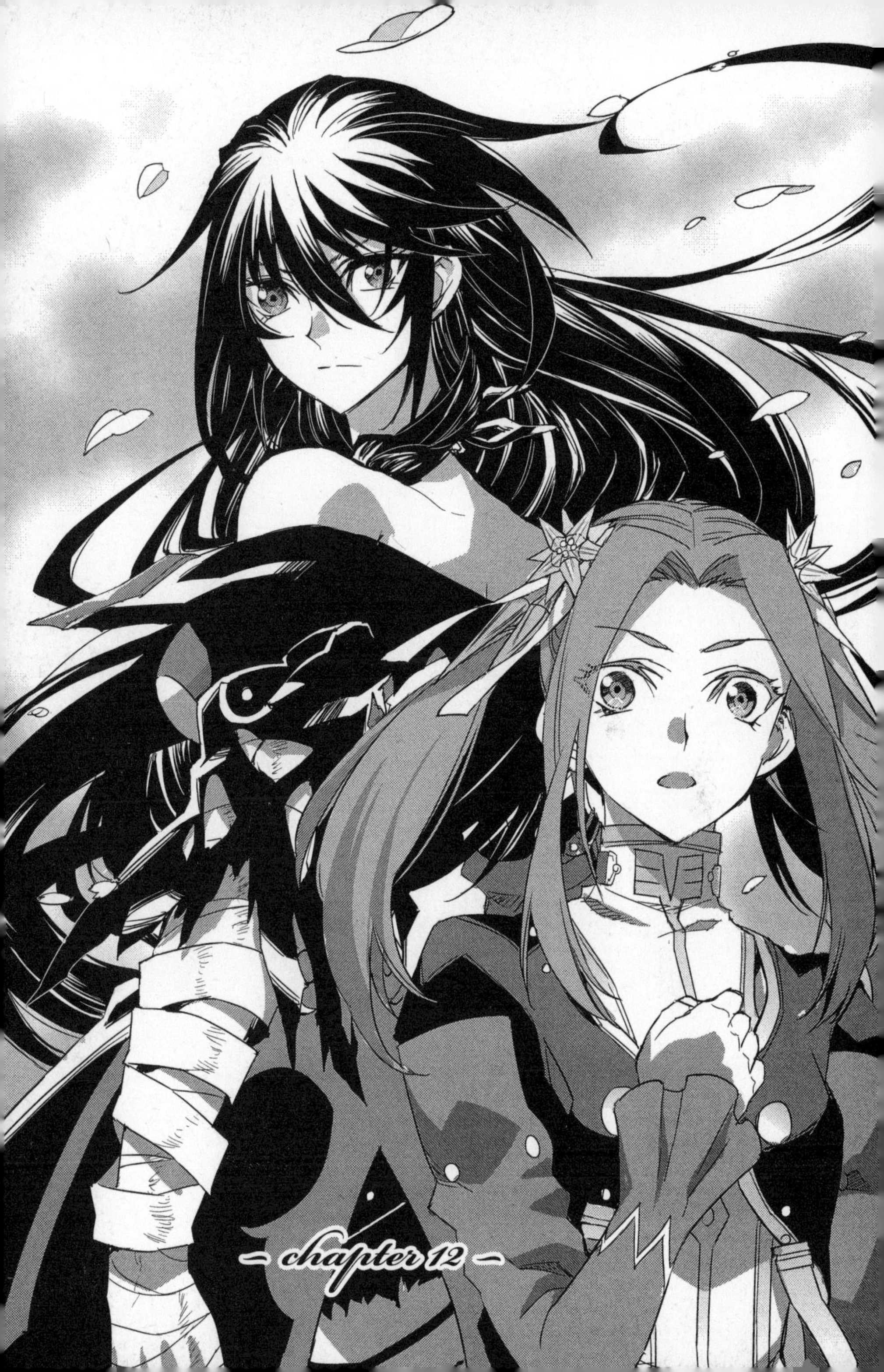
chapter 12

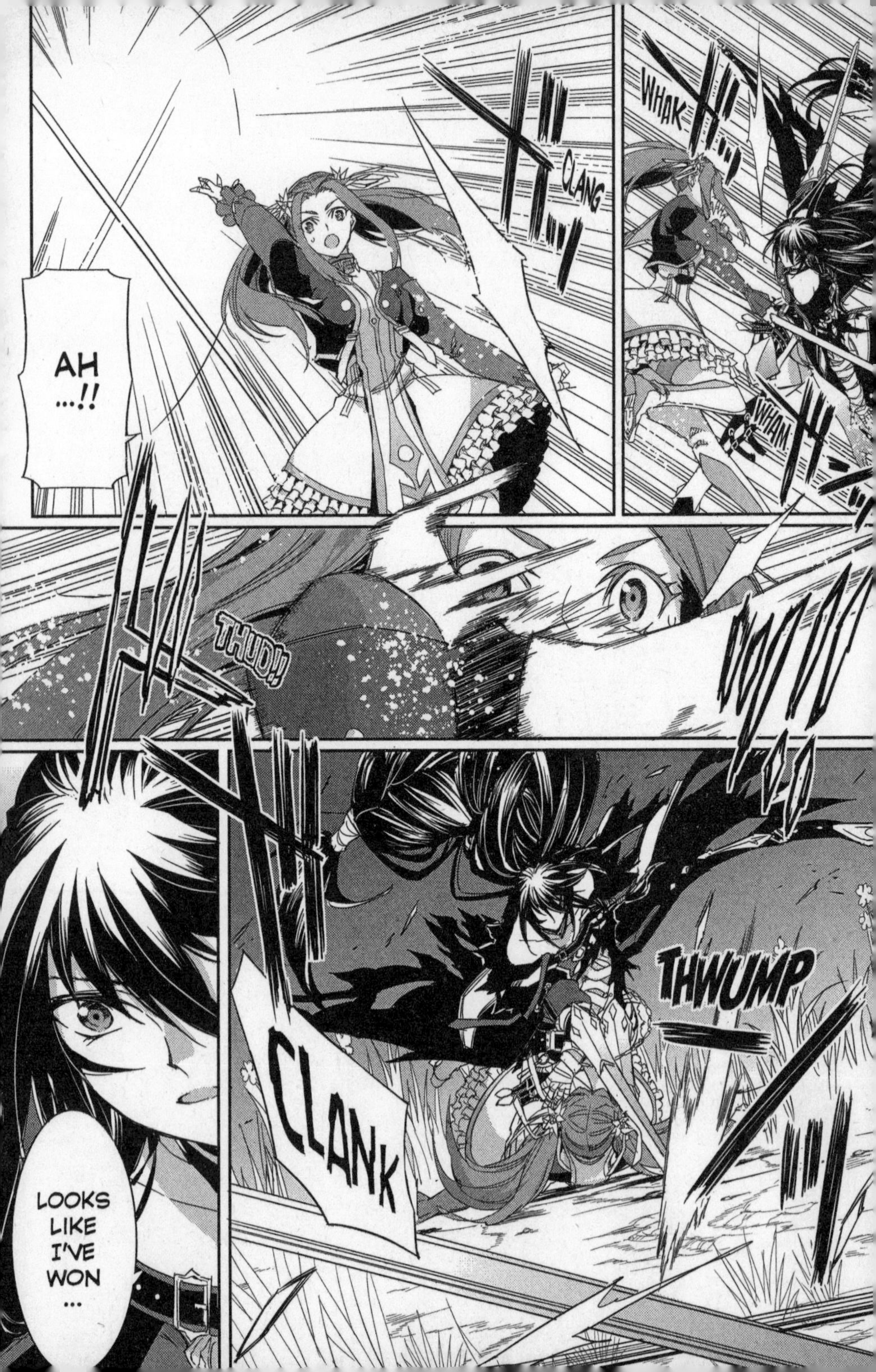
WHAK
WHAM
CLANG
AH ...!!
THUD!!
THWUMP
CLANK
LOOKS LIKE I'VE WON ...

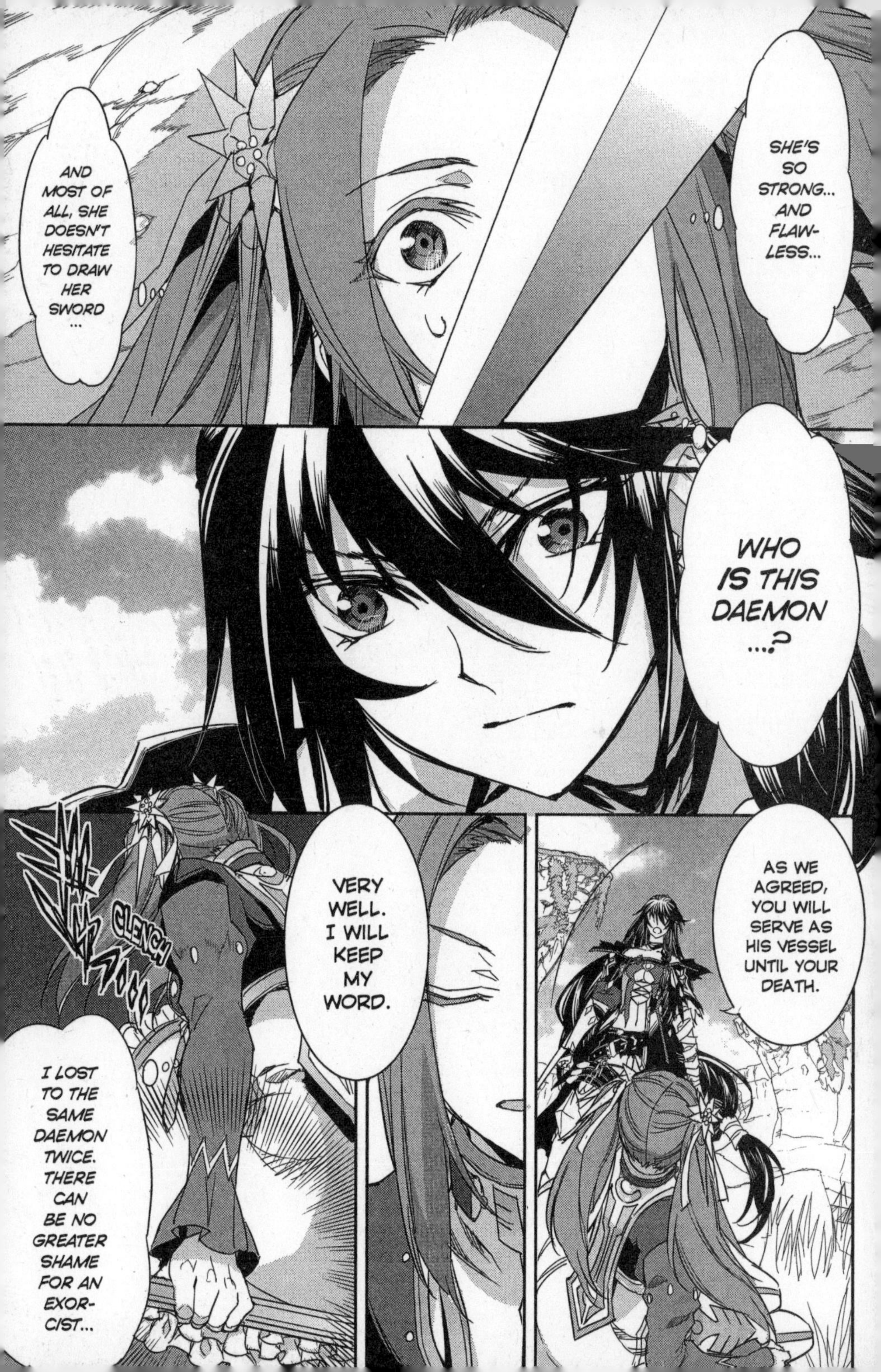
SHE'S SO STRONG... AND FLAWLESS...
AND MOST OF ALL, SHE DOESN'T HESITATE TO DRAW HER SWORD ...
WHO IS THIS DAEMON ...?
AS WE AGREED, YOU WILL SERVE AS HIS VESSEL UNTIL YOUR DEATH.
VERY WELL. I WILL KEEP MY WORD.
CLENCH
I LOST TO THE SAME DAEMON TWICE. THERE CAN BE NO GREATER SHAME FOR AN EXORCIST...

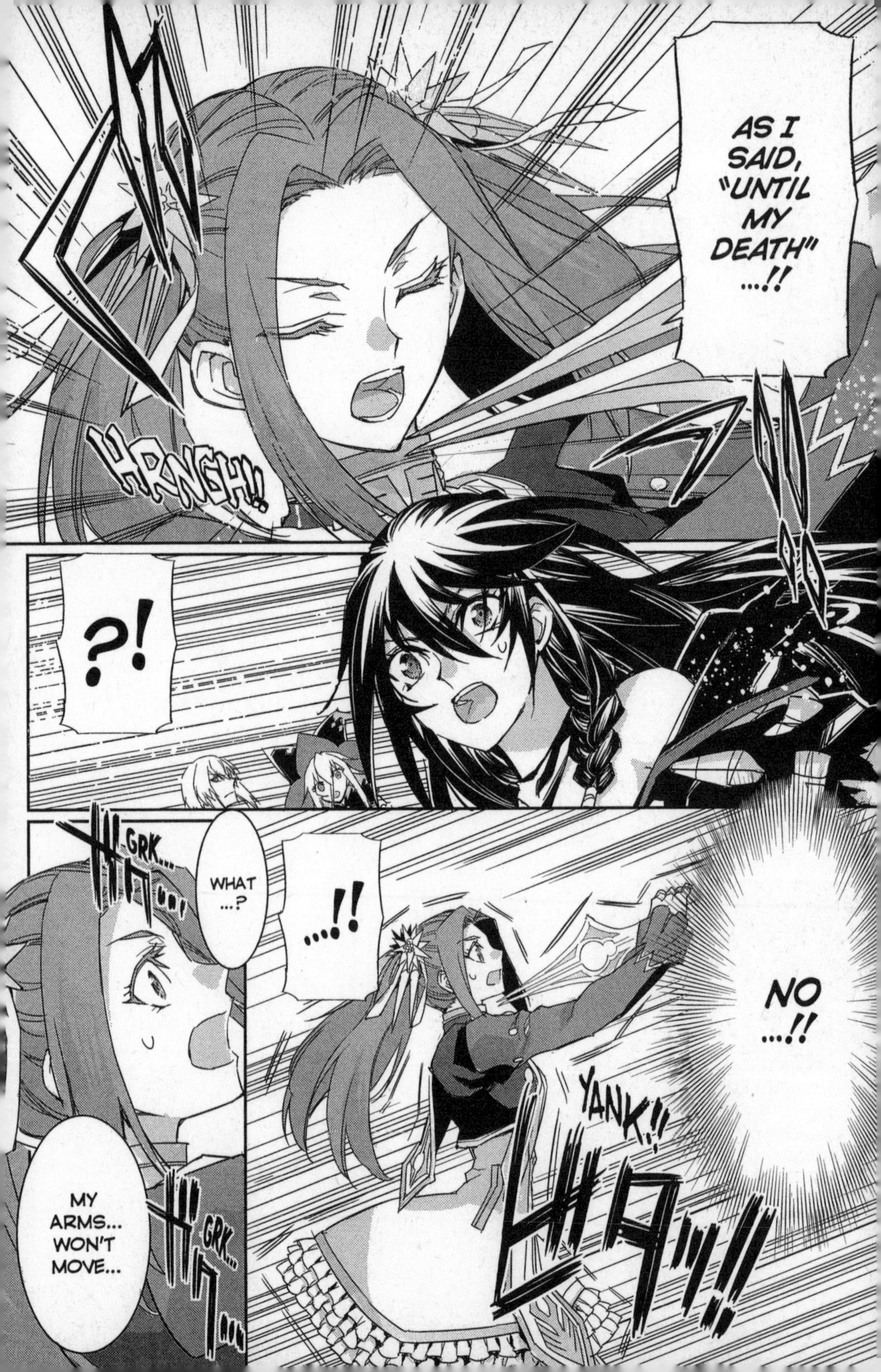
AS I SAID, "UNTIL MY DEATH" ...!!
HRNGH!!
?!
...!!
NO ...!!
YANK!!
GRK...
WHAT ...?
MY ARMS... WON'T MOVE...
GRK...

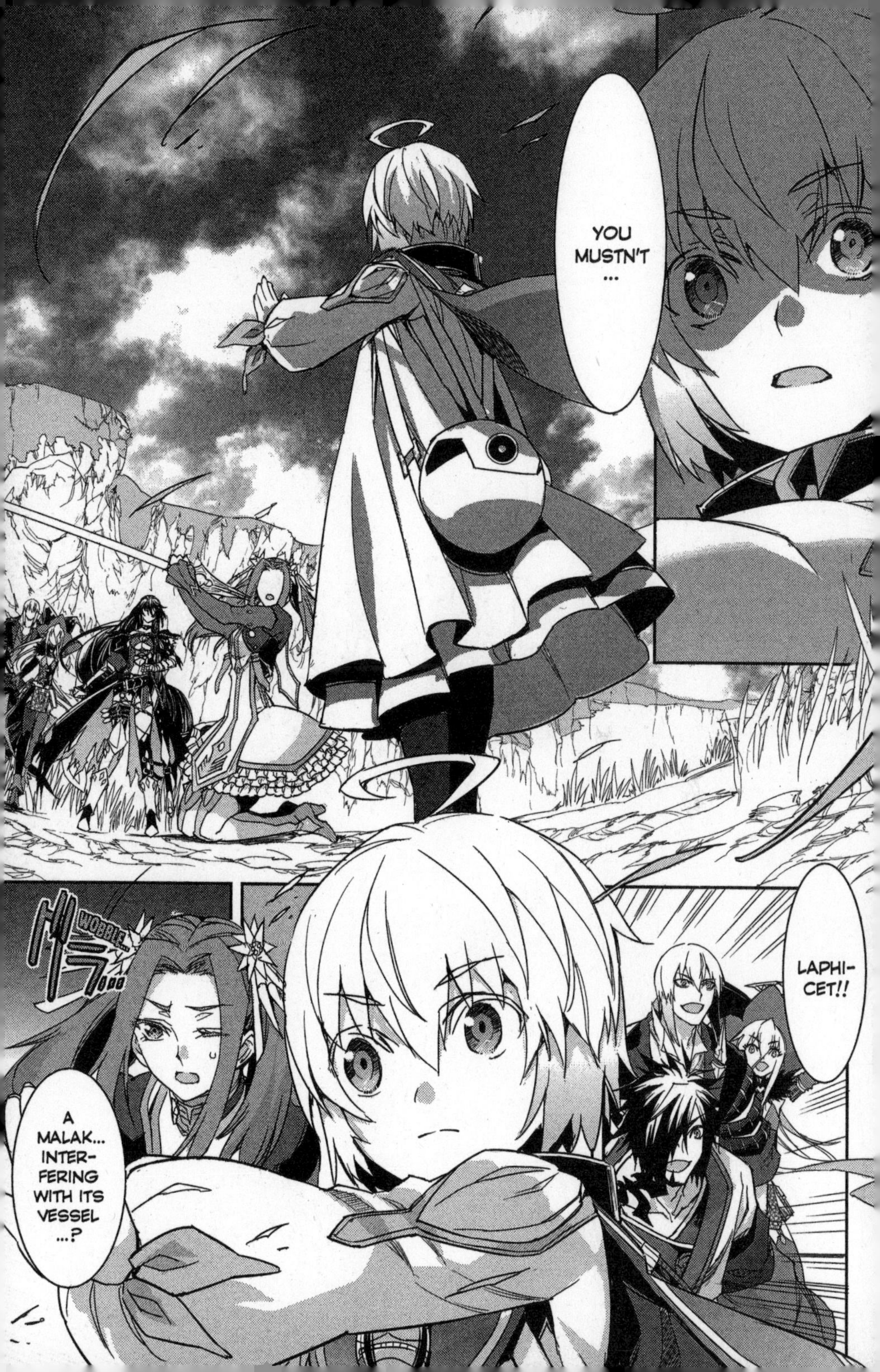
YOU MUSTN'T ...
LAPHI-CET!!
WOBBLE...
A MALAK... INTER-FERING WITH ITS VESSEL ...?

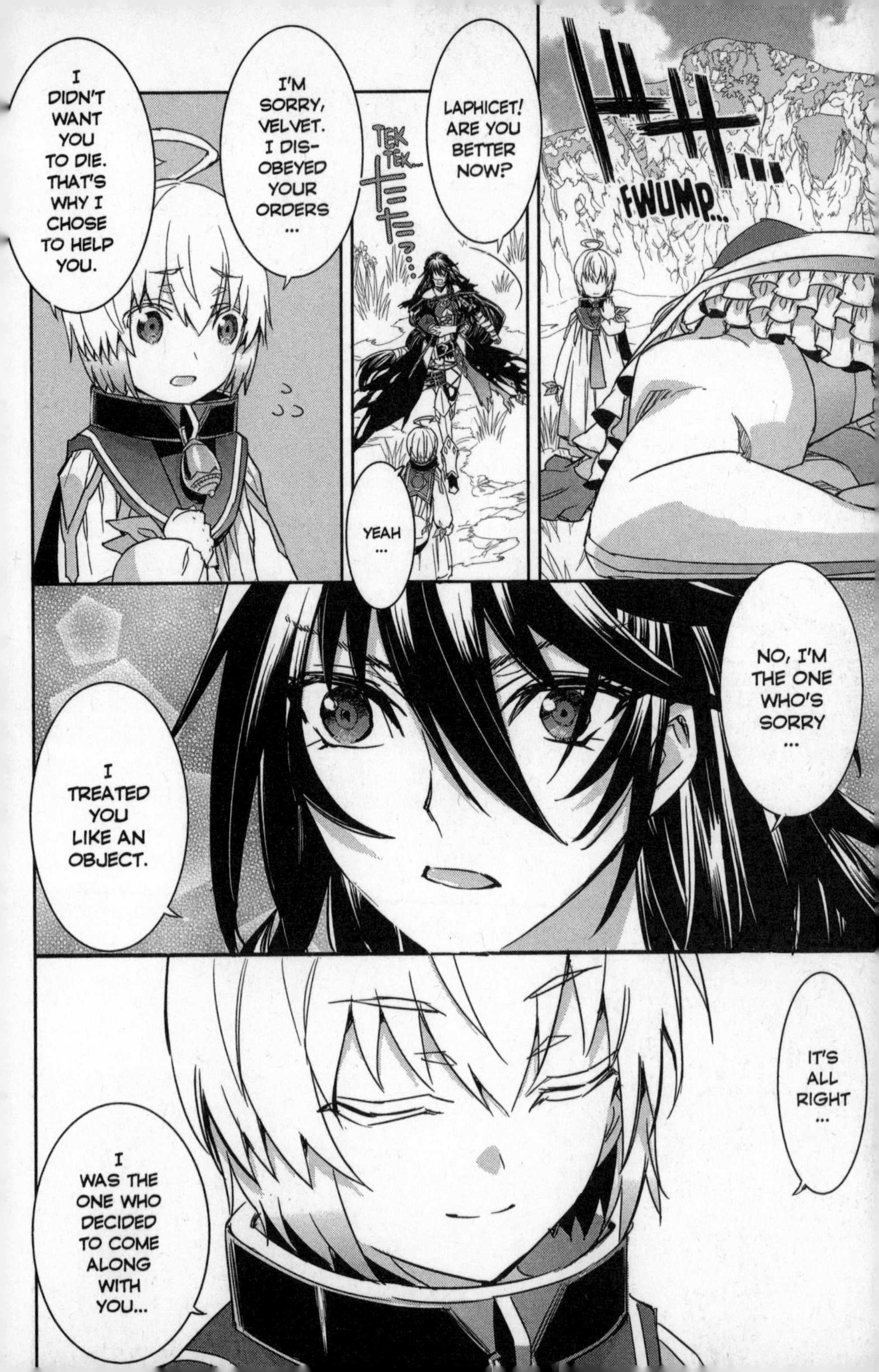
FWUMP...
LAPHICET! ARE YOU BETTER NOW?
TEK TEK...
YEAH ...
I'M SORRY, VELVET. I DIS-OBEYED YOUR ORDERS ...
I DIDN'T WANT YOU TO DIE. THAT'S WHY I CHOSE TO HELP YOU.
NO, I'M THE ONE WHO'S SORRY ...
I TREATED YOU LIKE AN OBJECT.
IT'S ALL RIGHT ...
I WAS THE ONE WHO DECIDED TO COME ALONG WITH YOU...

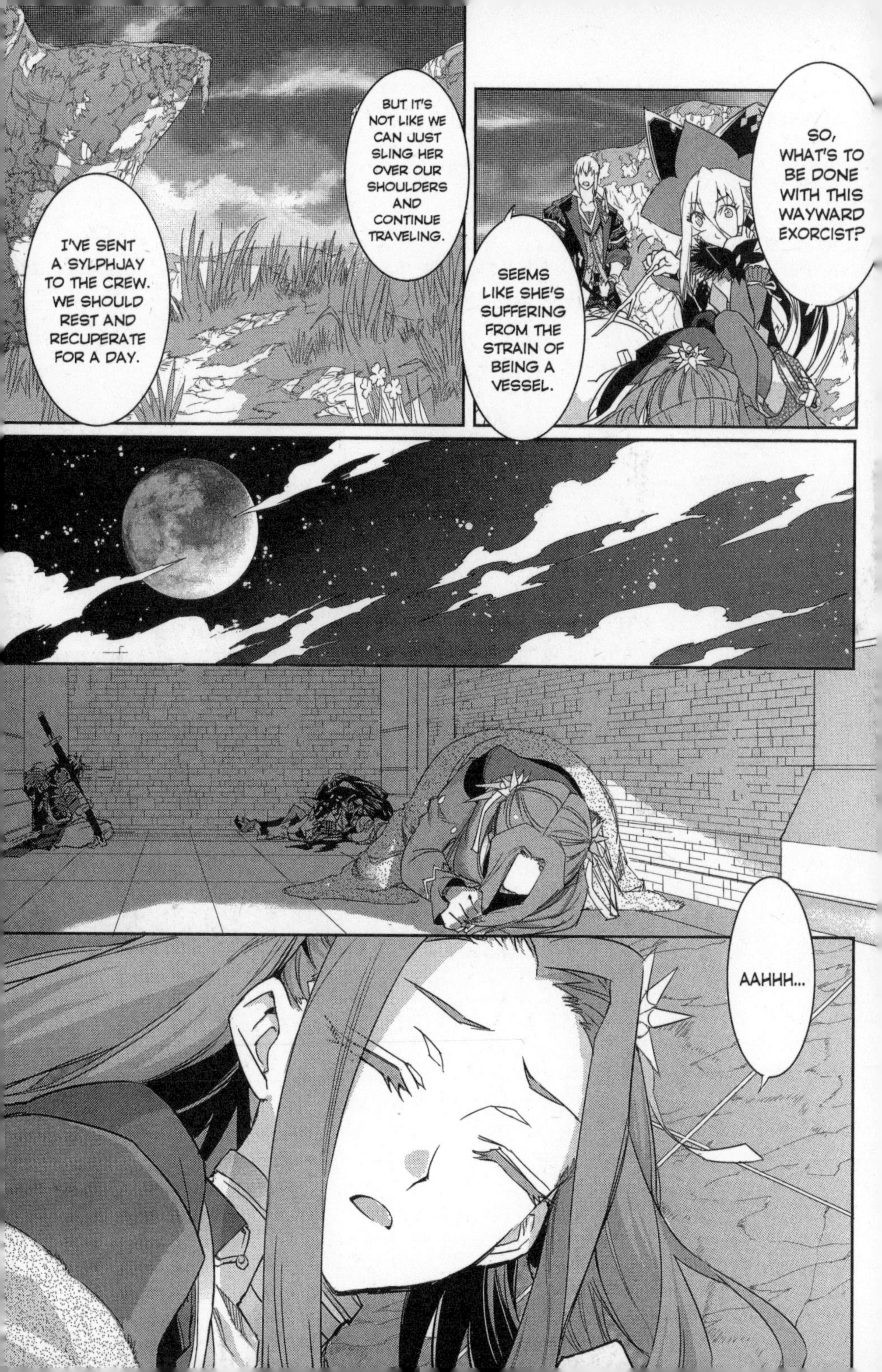
SO, WHAT'S TO BE DONE WITH THIS WAYWARD EXORCIST?
SEEMS LIKE SHE'S SUFFERING FROM THE STRAIN OF BEING A VESSEL.
BUT IT'S NOT LIKE WE CAN JUST SLING HER OVER OUR SHOULDERS AND CONTINUE TRAVELING.
I'VE SENT A SYLPHJAY TO THE CREW. WE SHOULD REST AND RECUPERATE FOR A DAY.
AAHHH...

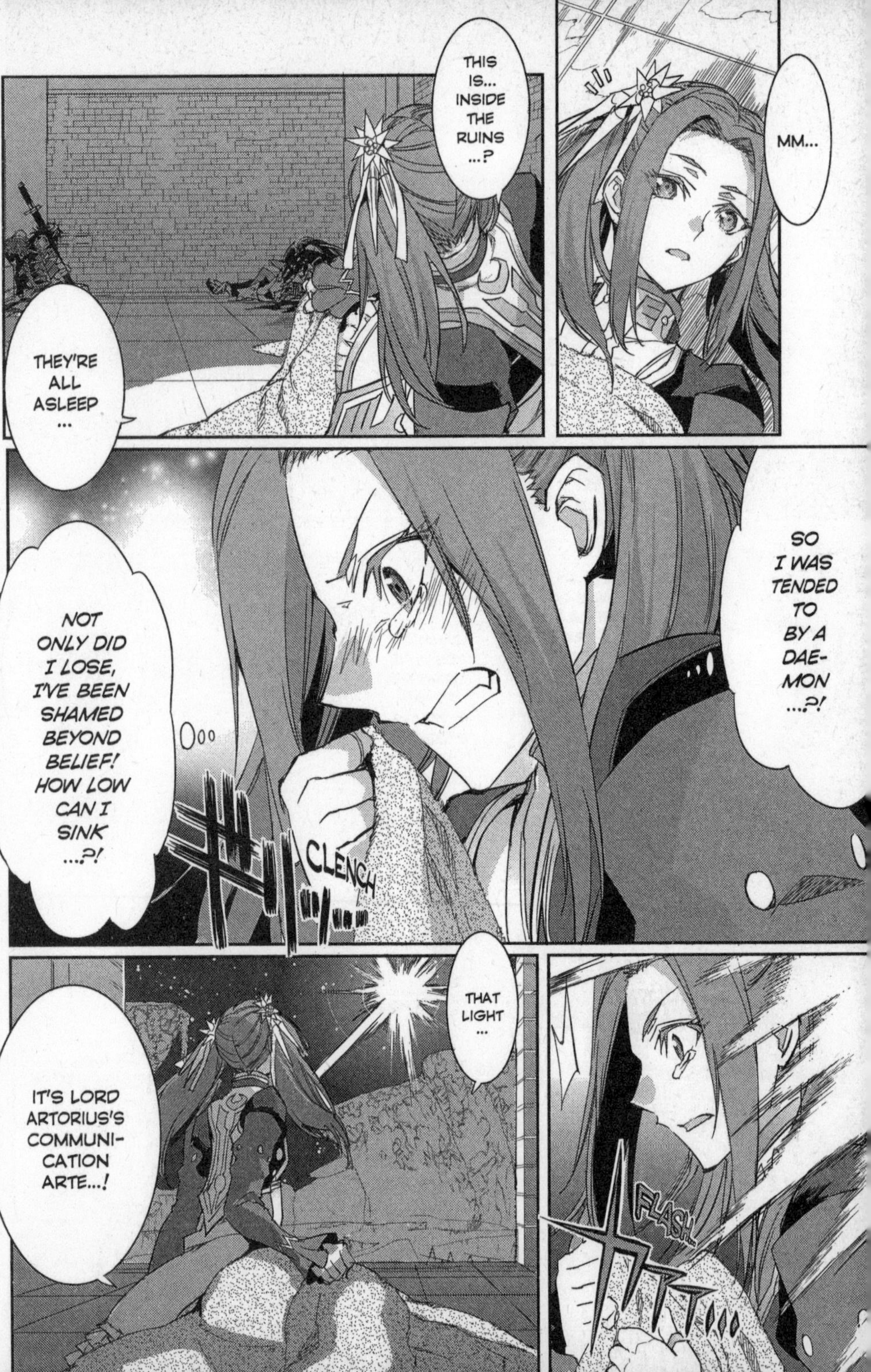
MM...
THIS IS... INSIDE THE RUINS ...?
THEY'RE ALL ASLEEP ...
SO I WAS TENDED TO BY A DAE-MON ...?!
NOT ONLY DID I LOSE, I'VE BEEN SHAMED BEYOND BELIEF! HOW LOW CAN I SINK ...?!
CLENCH
FLASH
THAT LIGHT ...
IT'S LORD ARTORIUS'S COMMUNI-CATION ARTE...!

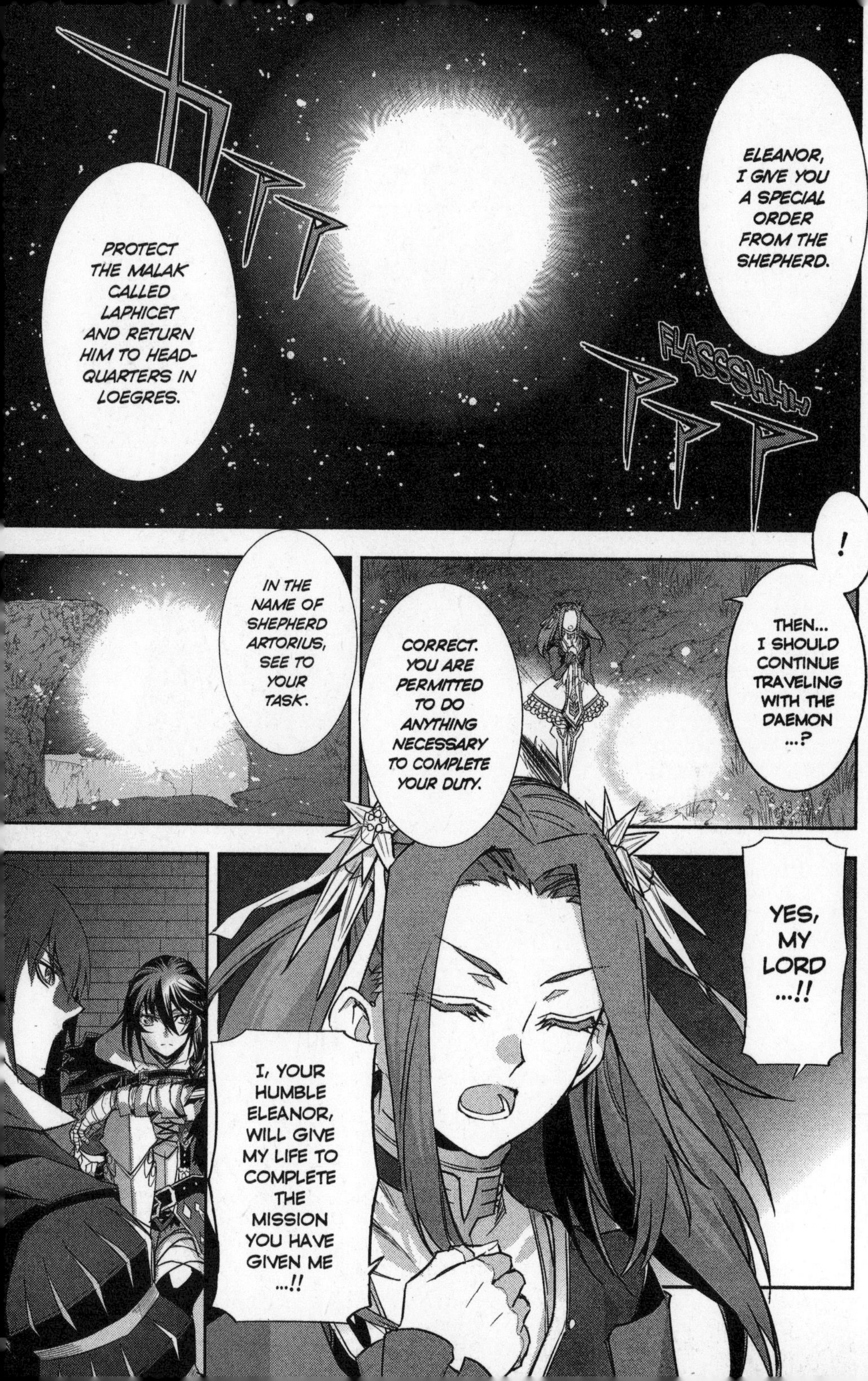
ELEANOR, I GIVE YOU A SPECIAL ORDER FROM THE SHEPHERD.
FLASSSHHHH
PROTECT THE MALAK CALLED LAPHICET AND RETURN HIM TO HEAD-QUARTERS IN LOEGRES.
!
THEN... I SHOULD CONTINUE TRAVELING WITH THE DAEMON ...?
CORRECT. YOU ARE PERMITTED TO DO ANYTHING NECESSARY TO COMPLETE YOUR DUTY.
IN THE NAME OF SHEPHERD ARTORIUS, SEE TO YOUR TASK.
YES, MY LORD ...!!
I, YOUR HUMBLE ELEANOR, WILL GIVE MY LIFE TO COMPLETE THE MISSION YOU HAVE GIVEN ME ...!!

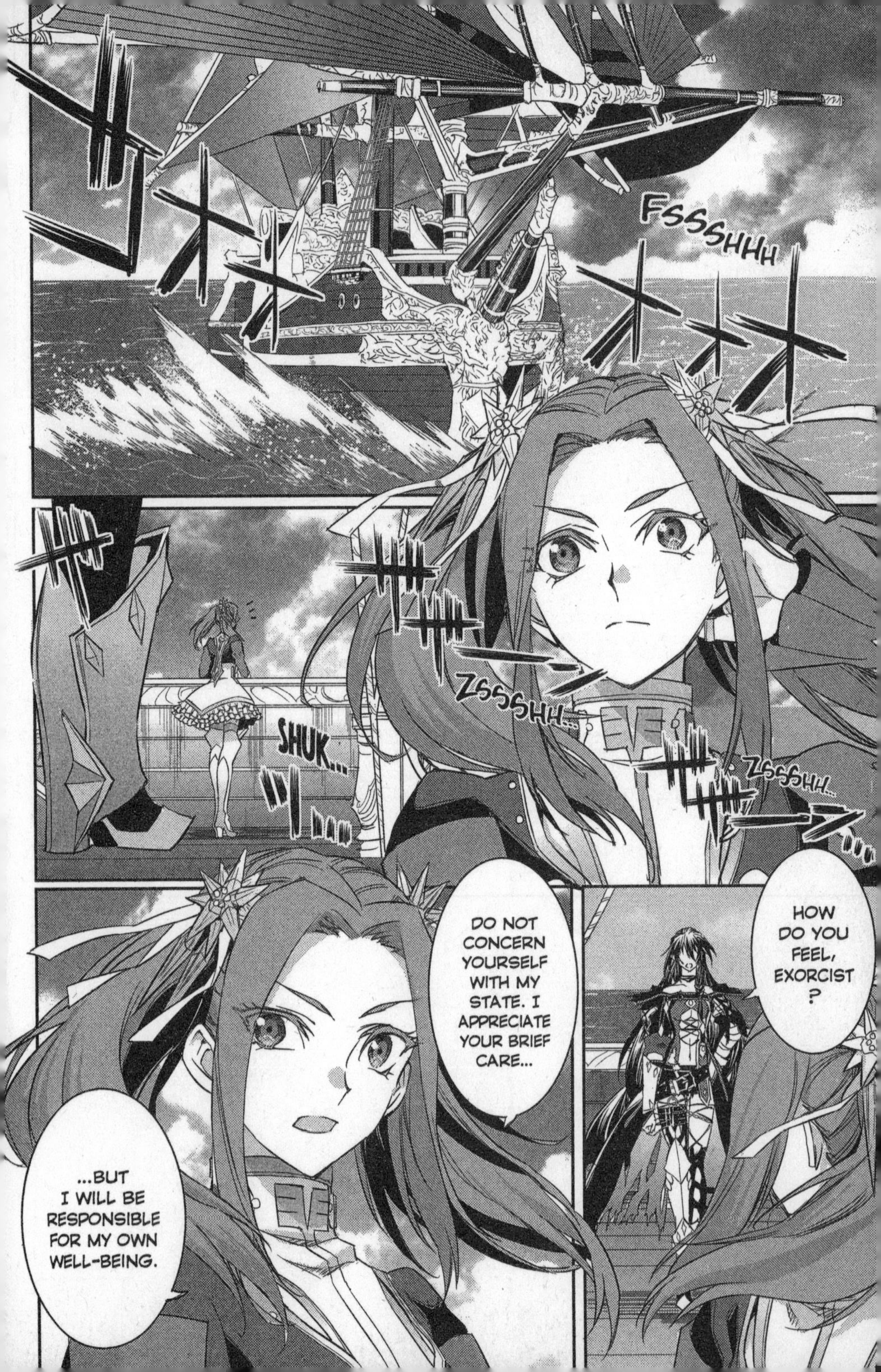
FSSSHHH
ZSSSHH...
ZSSSHH...
SHUK...
HOW DO YOU FEEL, EXORCIST?
DO NOT CONCERN YOURSELF WITH MY STATE. I APPRECIATE YOUR BRIEF CARE...
...BUT I WILL BE RESPONSIBLE FOR MY OWN WELL-BEING.

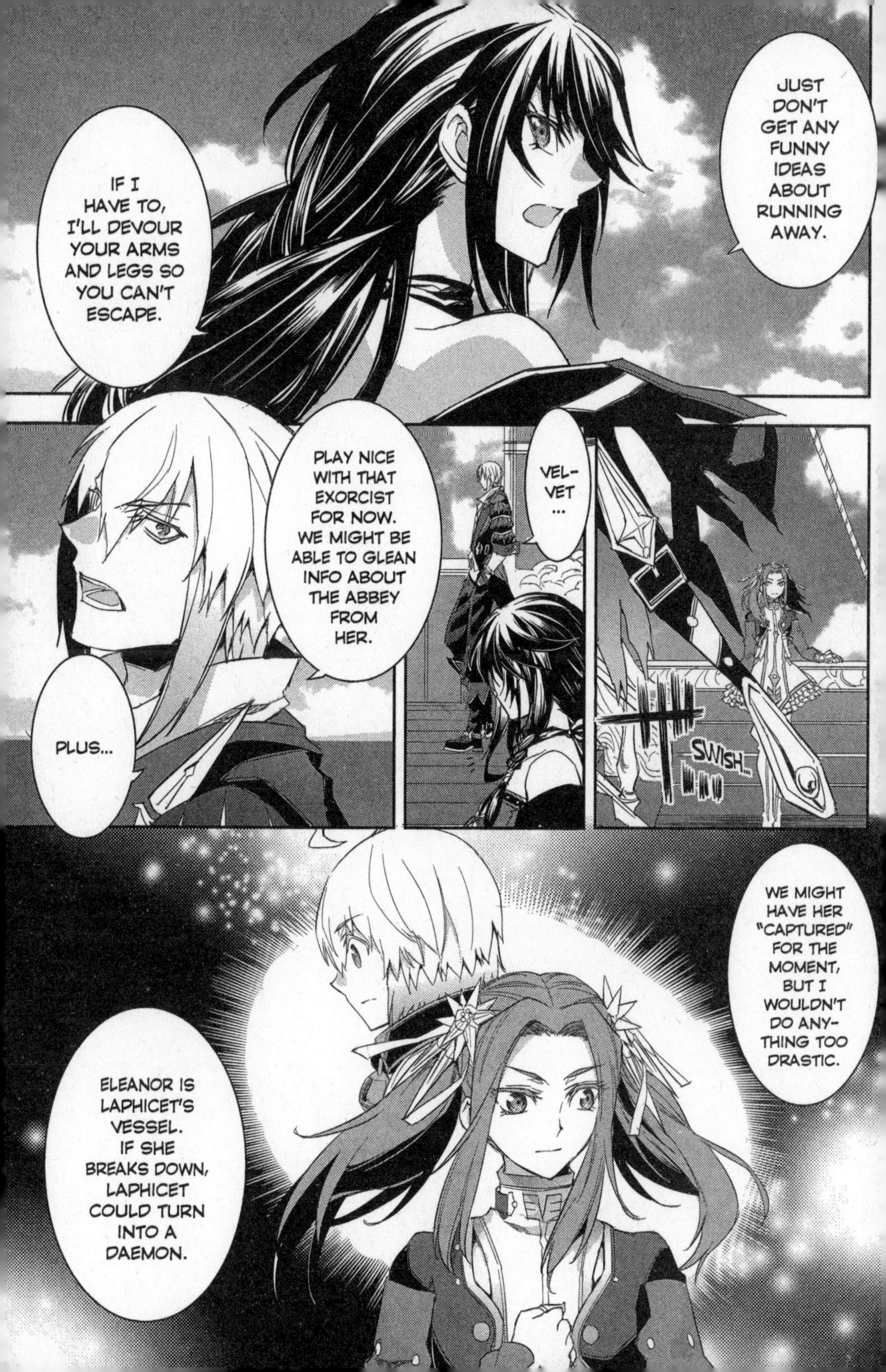
JUST DON'T GET ANY FUNNY IDEAS ABOUT RUNNING AWAY.
IF I HAVE TO, I'LL DEVOUR YOUR ARMS AND LEGS SO YOU CAN'T ESCAPE.
SWISH...
VEL-VET ...
PLAY NICE WITH THAT EXORCIST FOR NOW. WE MIGHT BE ABLE TO GLEAN INFO ABOUT THE ABBEY FROM HER.
PLUS...
WE MIGHT HAVE HER "CAPTURED" FOR THE MOMENT, BUT I WOULDN'T DO ANY-THING TOO DRASTIC.
ELEANOR IS LAPHICET'S VESSEL. IF SHE BREAKS DOWN, LAPHICET COULD TURN INTO A DAEMON.

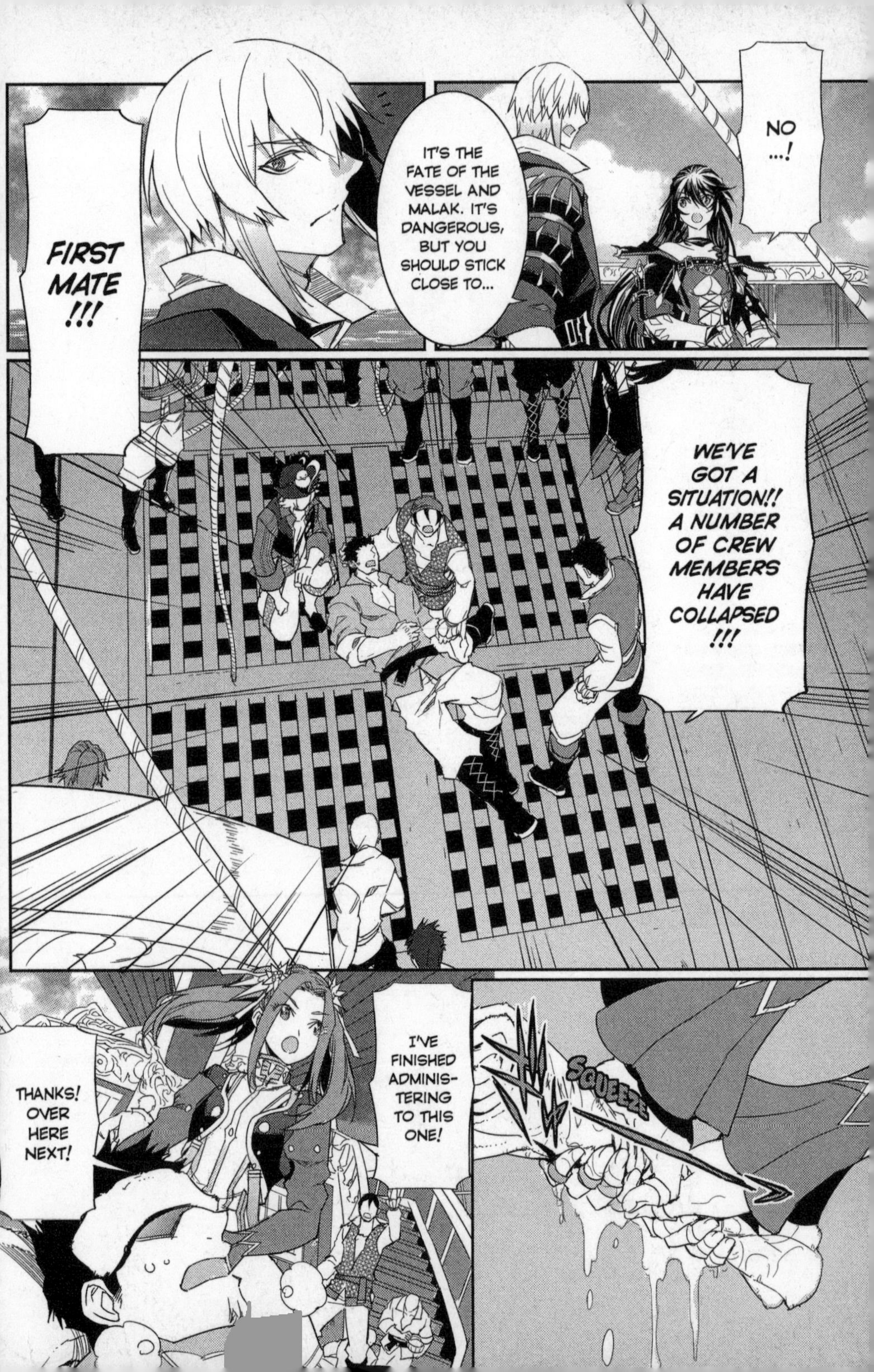
NO ...!
IT'S THE FATE OF THE VESSEL AND MALAK. IT'S DANGEROUS, BUT YOU SHOULD STICK CLOSE TO...
FIRST MATE !!!
WE'VE GOT A SITUATION!! A NUMBER OF CREW MEMBERS HAVE COLLAPSED !!!
SQUEEZE
I'VE FINISHED ADMINIS-TERING TO THIS ONE!
THANKS! OVER HERE NEXT!

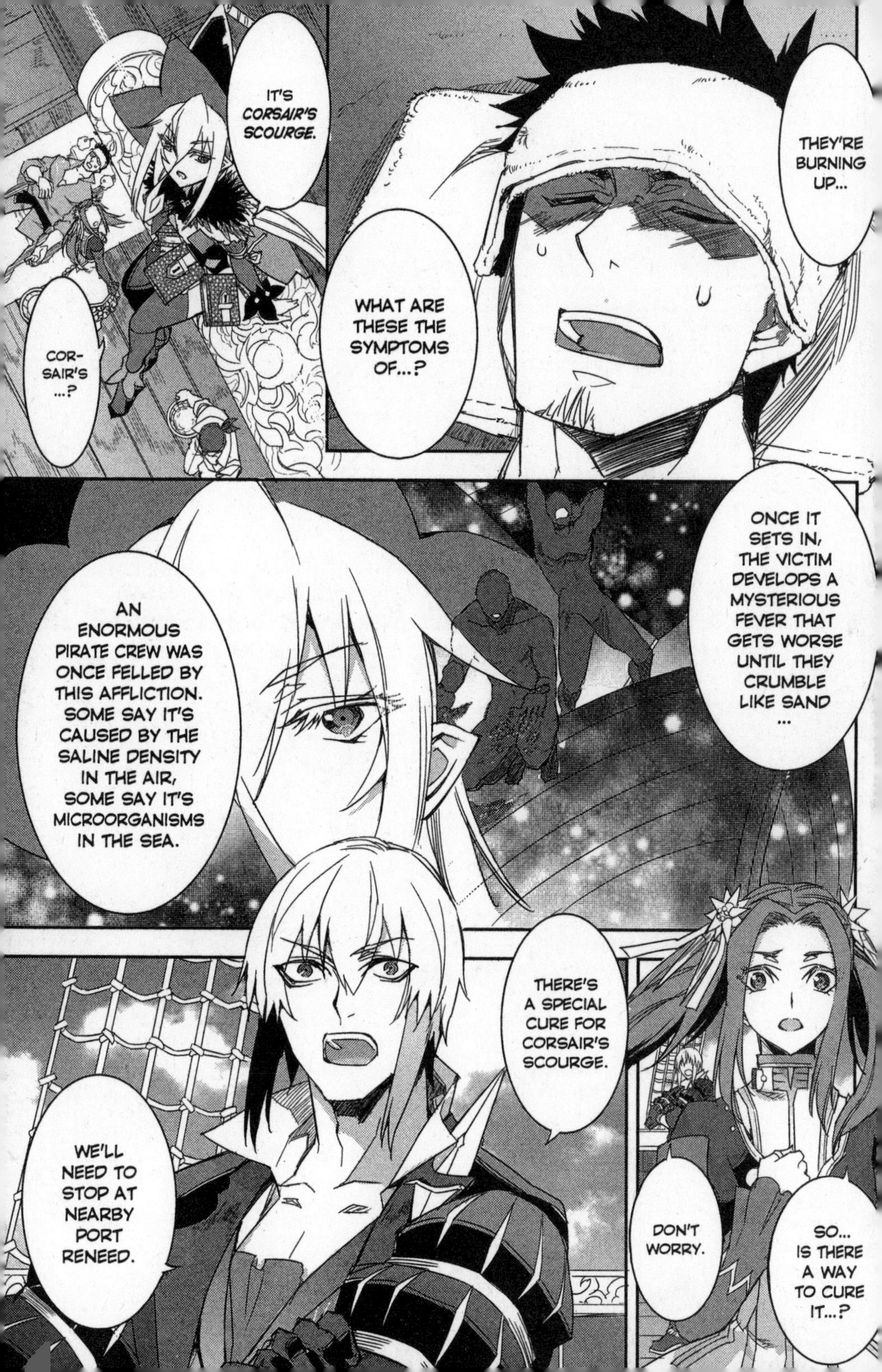
THEY'RE BURNING UP...
WHAT ARE THESE THE SYMPTOMS OF...?
IT'S CORSAIR'S SCOURGE.
COR-SAIR'S ...?
ONCE IT SETS IN, THE VICTIM DEVELOPS A MYSTERIOUS FEVER THAT GETS WORSE UNTIL THEY CRUMBLE LIKE SAND ...
AN ENORMOUS PIRATE CREW WAS ONCE FELLED BY THIS AFFLICTION. SOME SAY IT'S CAUSED BY THE SALINE DENSITY IN THE AIR, SOME SAY IT'S MICROORGANISMS IN THE SEA.
SO... IS THERE A WAY TO CURE IT...?
DON'T WORRY.
THERE'S A SPECIAL CURE FOR CORSAIR'S SCOURGE.
WE'LL NEED TO STOP AT NEARBY PORT RENEED.

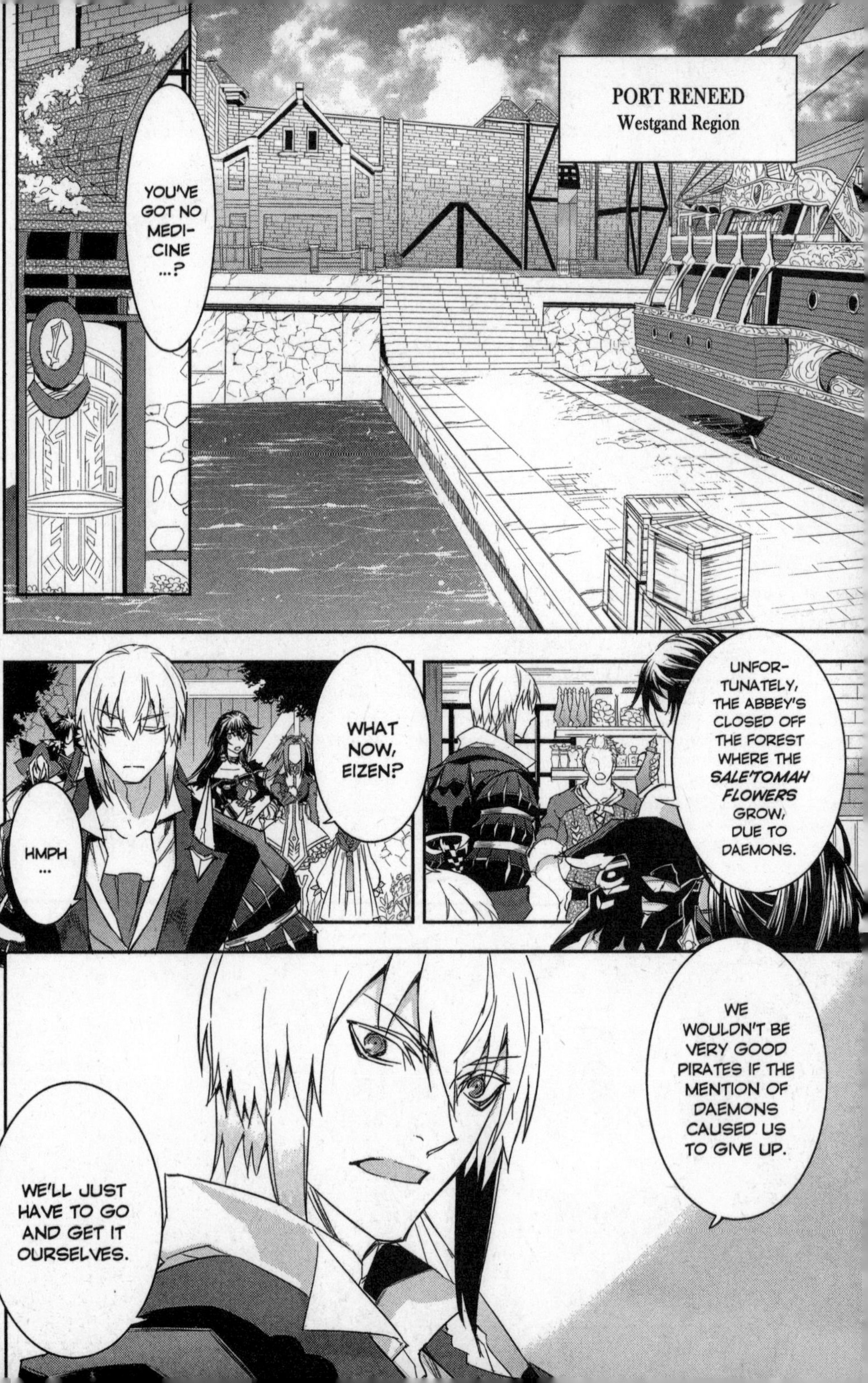
PORT RENEED
Westgand Region
YOU'VE GOT NO MEDI-CINE ...?
UNFOR-TUNATELY, THE ABBEY'S CLOSED OFF THE FOREST WHERE THE *SALE'TOMAH FLOWERS* GROW, DUE TO DAEMONS.
WHAT NOW, EIZEN?
HMPH ...
WE WOULDN'T BE VERY GOOD PIRATES IF THE MENTION OF DAEMONS CAUSED US TO GIVE UP.
WE'LL JUST HAVE TO GO AND GET IT OURSELVES.

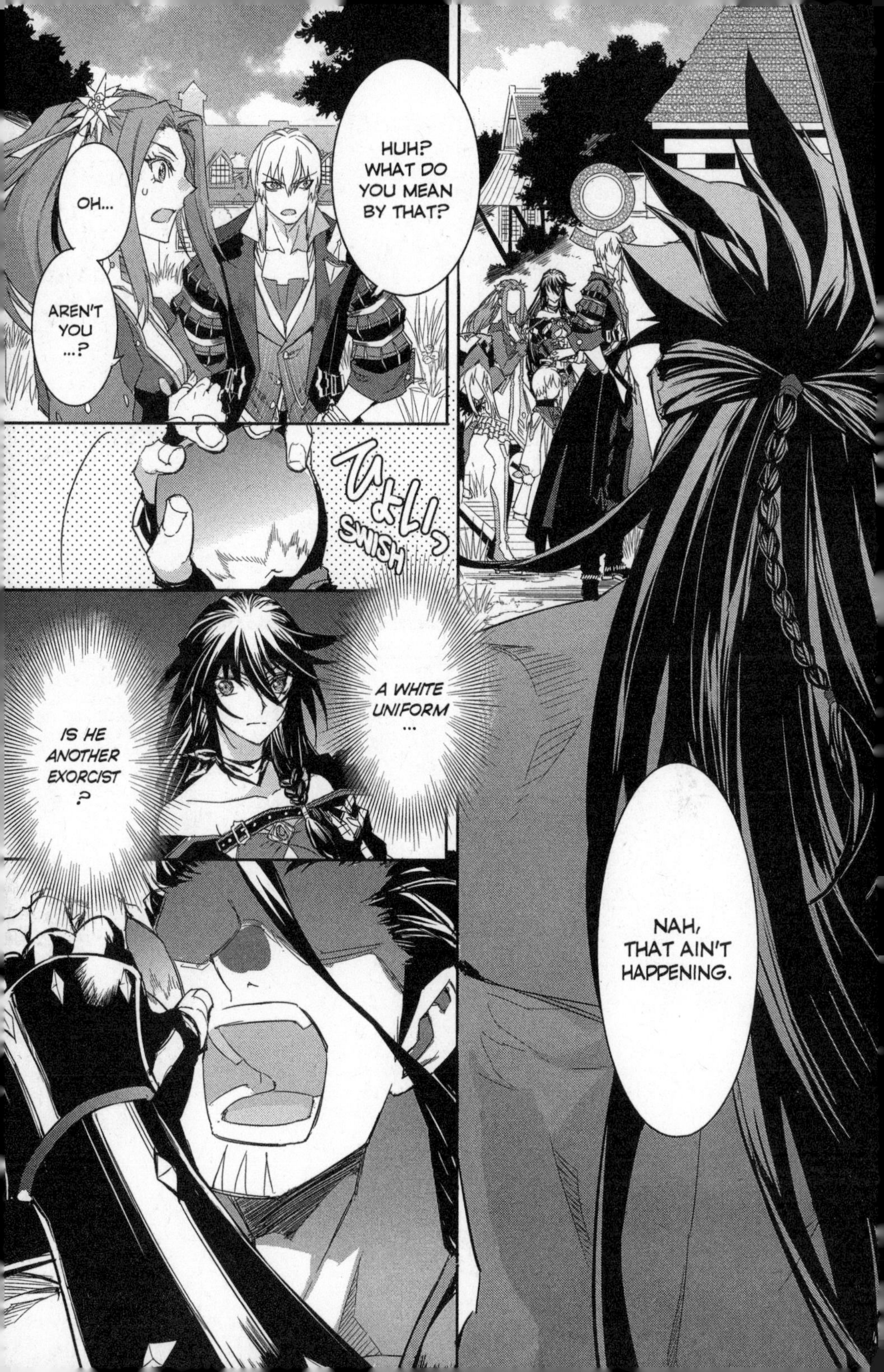
NAH, THAT AIN'T HAPPENING.
HUH? WHAT DO YOU MEAN BY THAT?
OH...
AREN'T YOU ...?
SWISH
A WHITE UNIFORM ...
IS HE ANOTHER EXORCIST ?

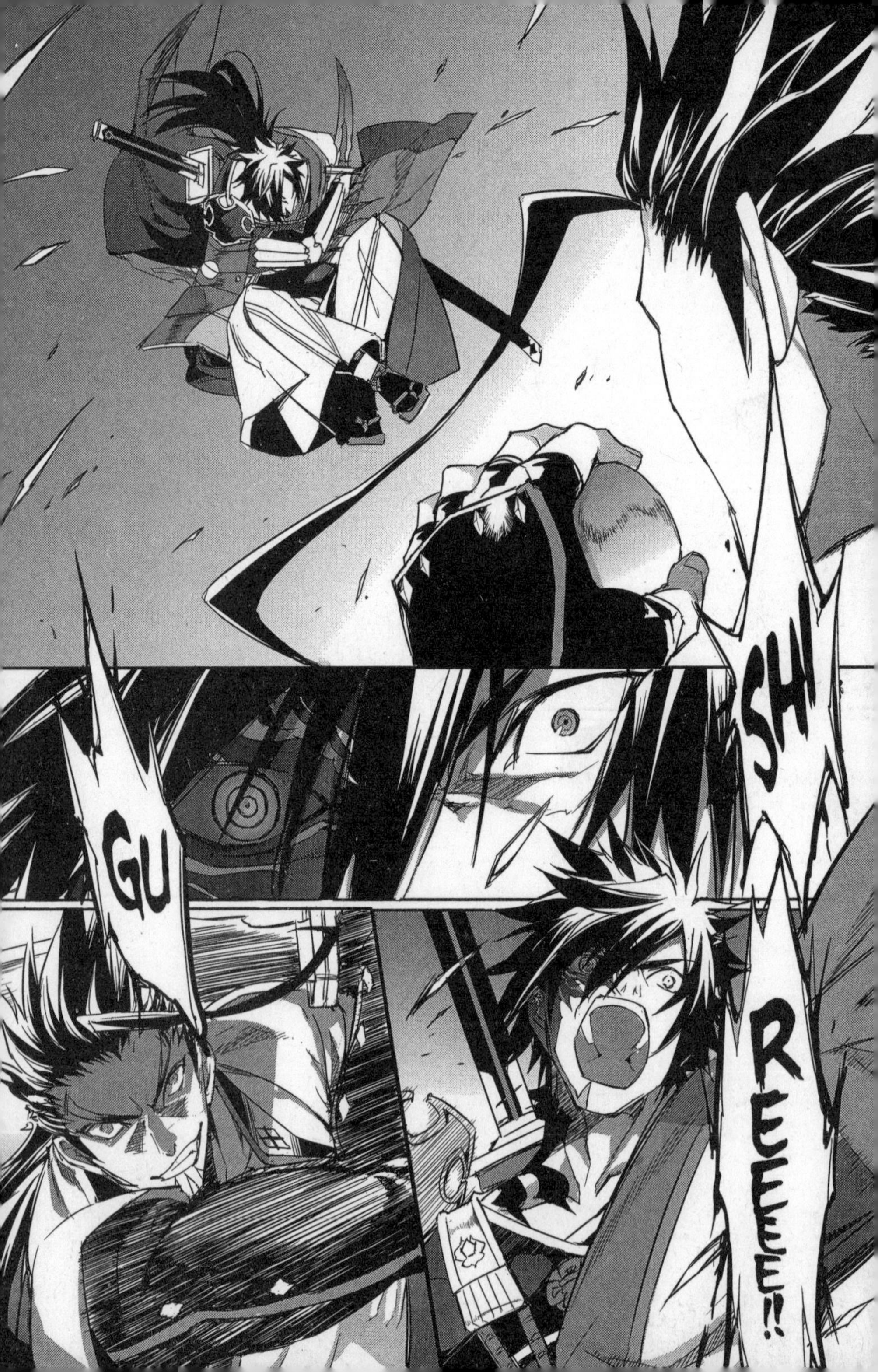
SHI
REEEE!!
GU

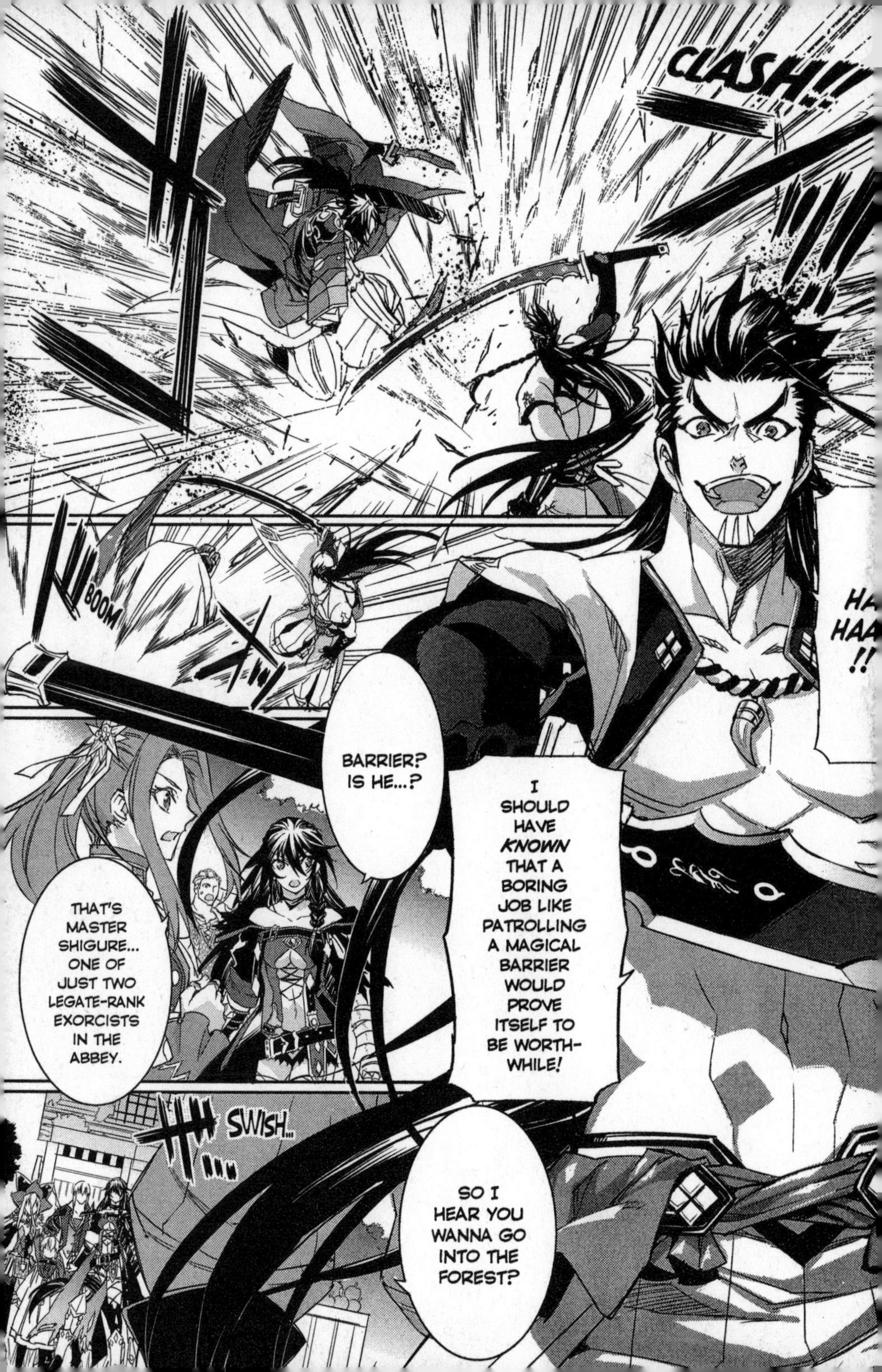

CLASH!!
HA HAA !!
BOOM
I SHOULD HAVE *KNOWN* THAT A BORING JOB LIKE PATROLLING A MAGICAL BARRIER WOULD PROVE ITSELF TO BE WORTH-WHILE!
BARRIER? IS HE...?
THAT'S MASTER SHIGURE... ONE OF JUST TWO LEGATE-RANK EXORCISTS IN THE ABBEY.
SO I HEAR YOU WANNA GO INTO THE FOREST?
SWISH...

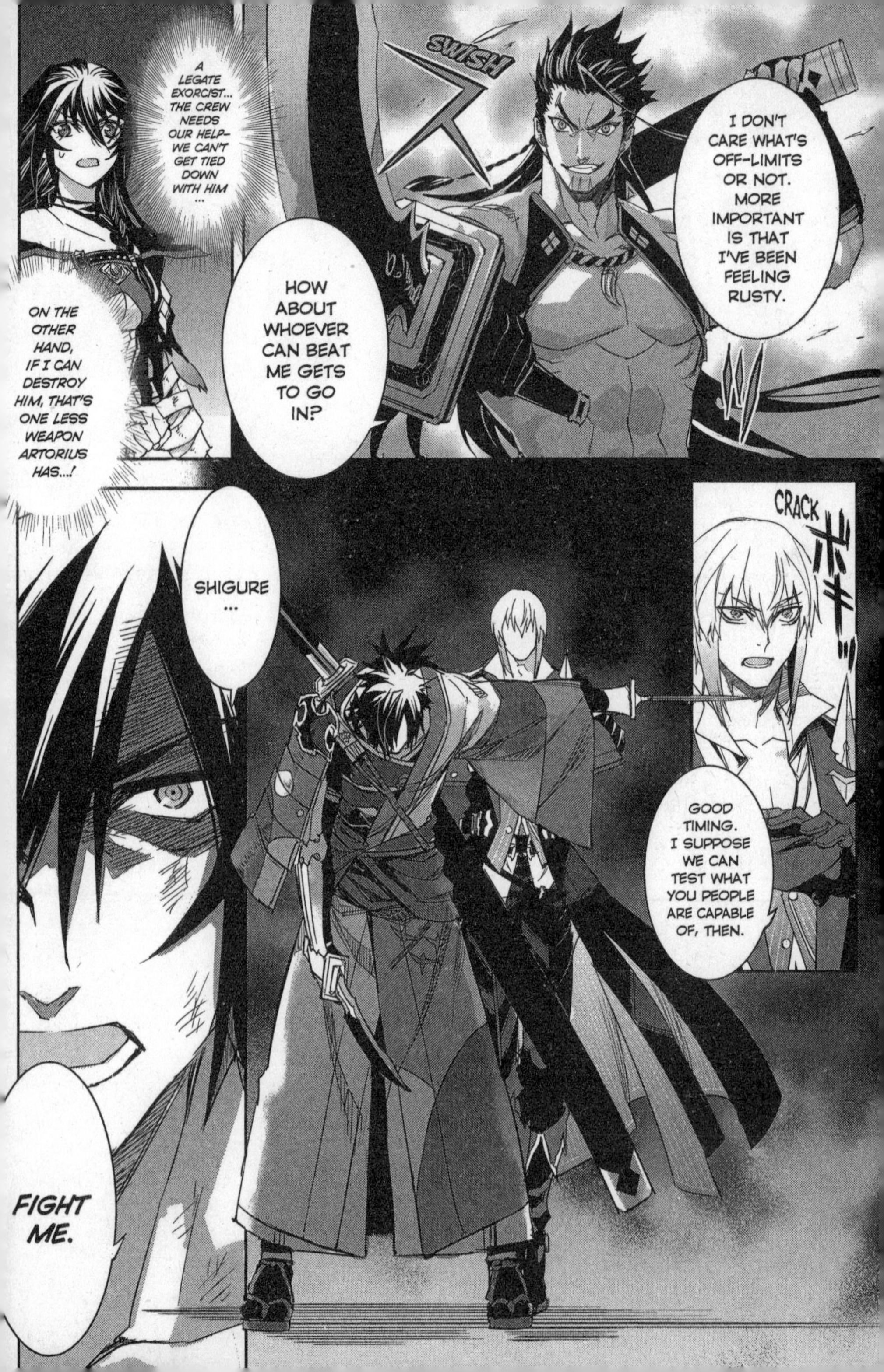
SWISH
I DON'T CARE WHAT'S OFF-LIMITS OR NOT. MORE IMPORTANT IS THAT I'VE BEEN FEELING RUSTY.
HOW ABOUT WHOEVER CAN BEAT ME GETS TO GO IN?
A LEGATE EXORCIST... THE CREW NEEDS OUR HELP- WE CAN'T GET TIED DOWN WITH HIM ...
ON THE OTHER HAND, IF I CAN DESTROY HIM, THAT'S ONE LESS WEAPON ARTORIUS HAS...!
CRACK
ボキ…
GOOD TIMING. I SUPPOSE WE CAN TEST WHAT YOU PEOPLE ARE CAPABLE OF, THEN.
SHIGURE ...
FIGHT ME.

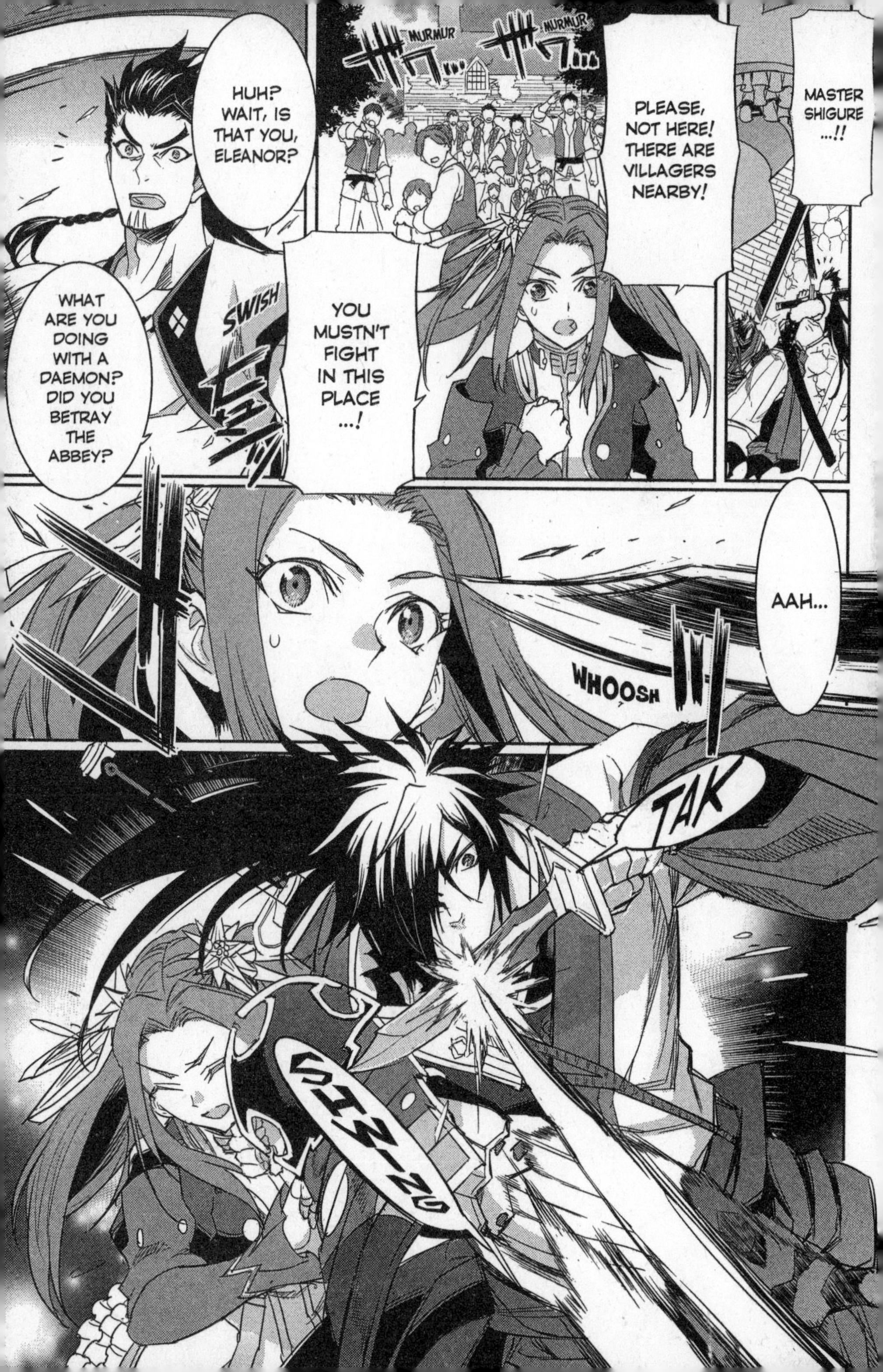
MASTER SHIGURE ...!!
MURMUR
MURMUR
PLEASE, NOT HERE! THERE ARE VILLAGERS NEARBY!
YOU MUSTN'T FIGHT IN THIS PLACE ...!
HUH? WAIT, IS THAT YOU, ELEANOR?
WHAT ARE YOU DOING WITH A DAEMON? DID YOU BETRAY THE ABBEY?
SWISH
AAH...
WHOOSH
TAK
SHIING

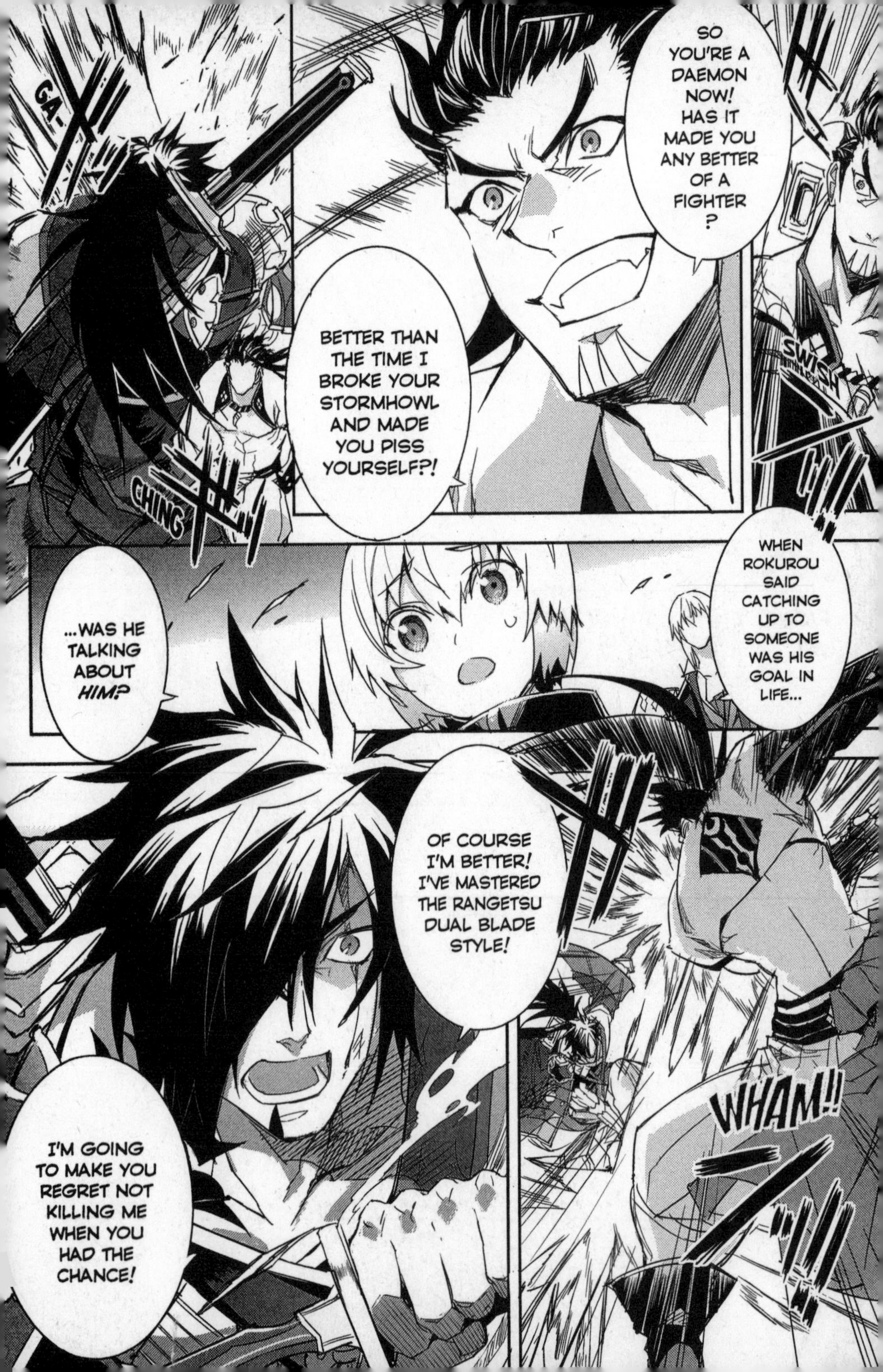
SO YOU'RE A DAEMON NOW! HAS IT MADE YOU ANY BETTER OF A FIGHTER?
SWISH
BETTER THAN THE TIME I BROKE YOUR STORMHOWL AND MADE YOU PISS YOURSELF?!
GA-
CHING
WHEN ROKUROU SAID CATCHING UP TO SOMEONE WAS HIS GOAL IN LIFE...
...WAS HE TALKING ABOUT *HIM?*
WHAM!!
OF COURSE I'M BETTER! I'VE MASTERED THE RANGETSU DUAL BLADE STYLE!
I'M GOING TO MAKE YOU REGRET NOT KILLING ME WHEN YOU HAD THE CHANCE!

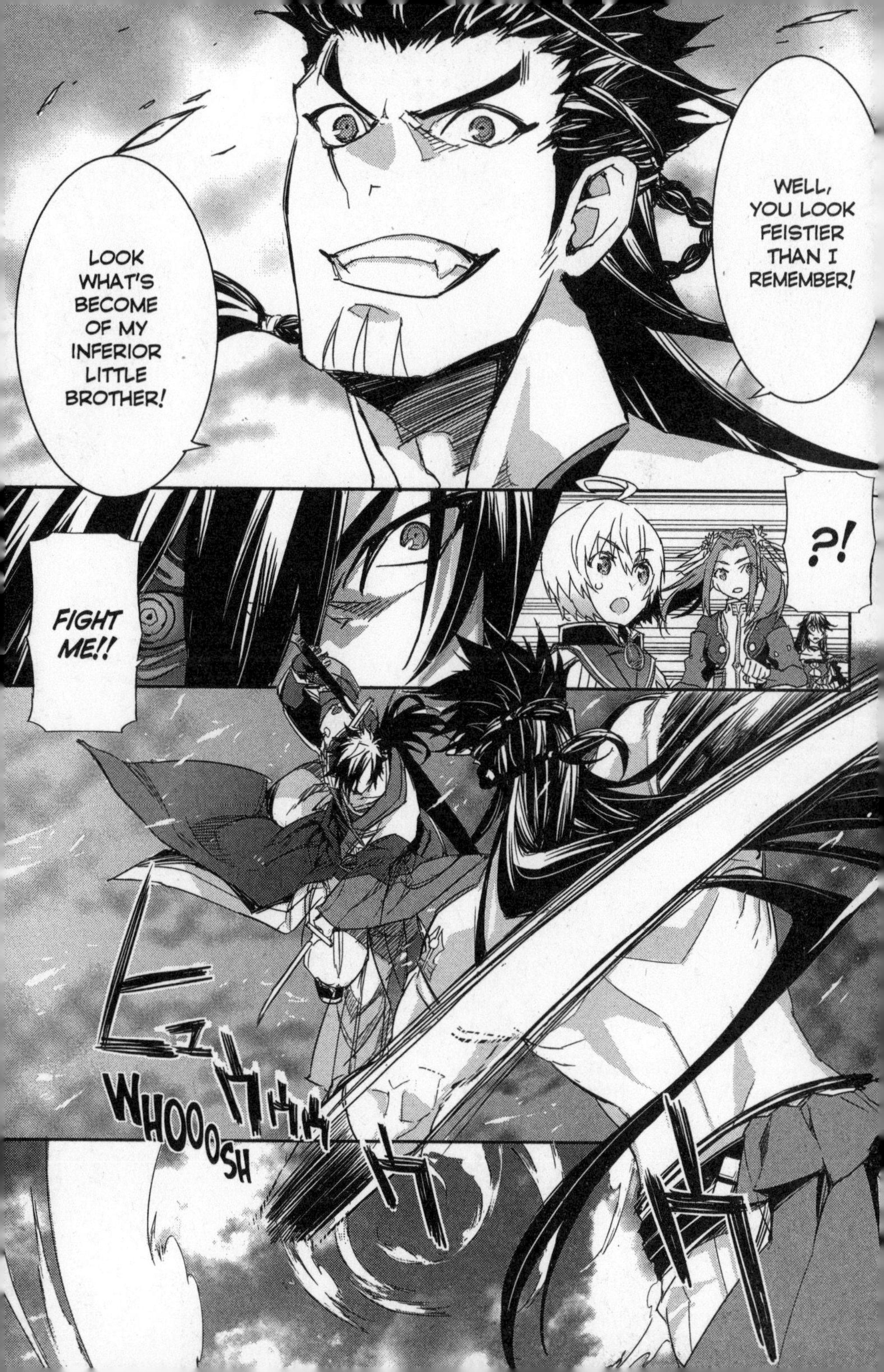
WELL, YOU LOOK FEISTIER THAN I REMEMBER!
LOOK WHAT'S BECOME OF MY INFERIOR LITTLE BROTHER!
?!
FIGHT ME!!
WHOOOSH

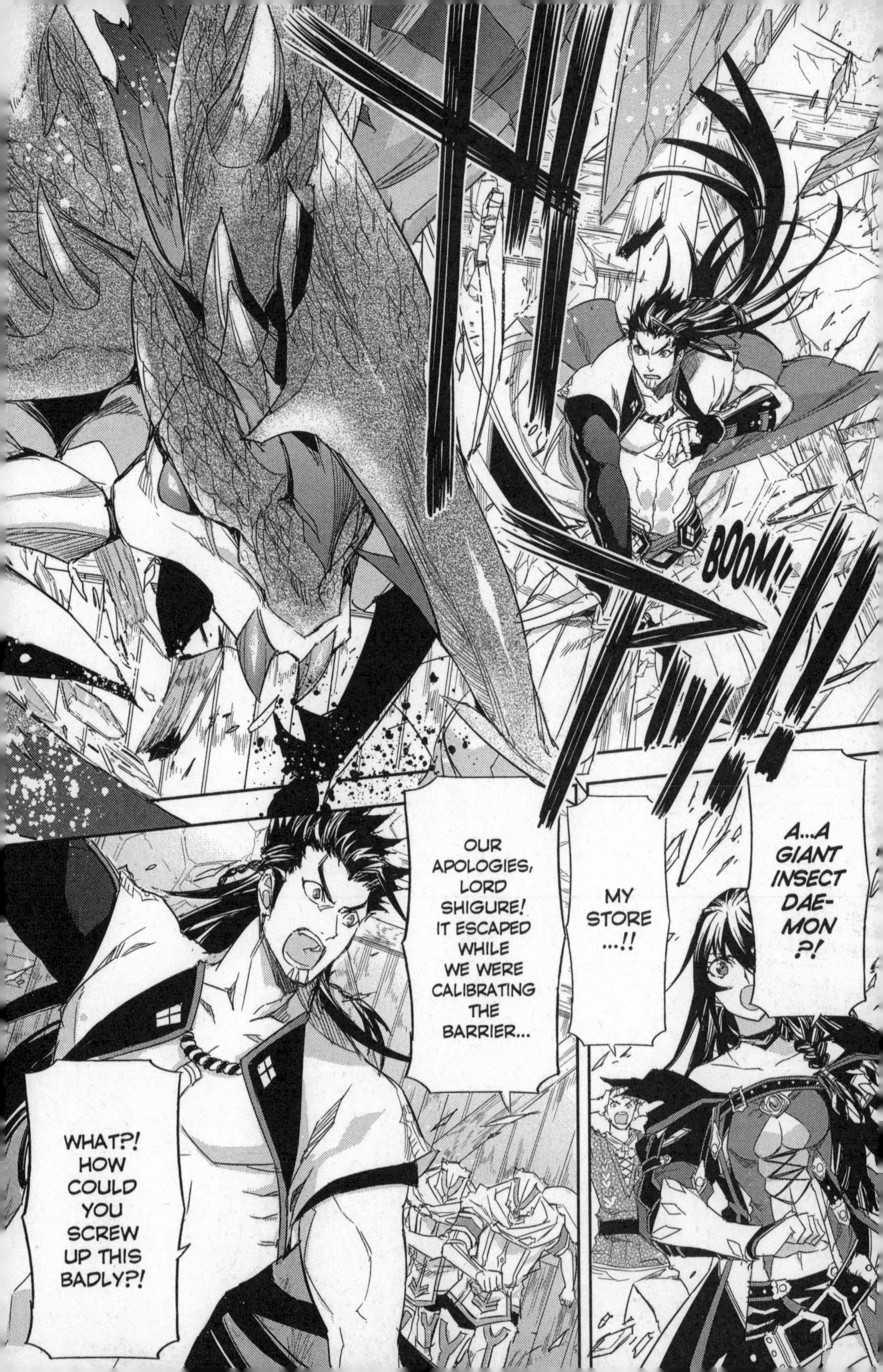
BOOM!!
A...A GIANT INSECT DAEMON?!
MY STORE...!!
OUR APOLOGIES, LORD SHIGURE! IT ESCAPED WHILE WE WERE CALIBRATING THE BARRIER...
WHAT?! HOW COULD YOU SCREW UP THIS BADLY?!

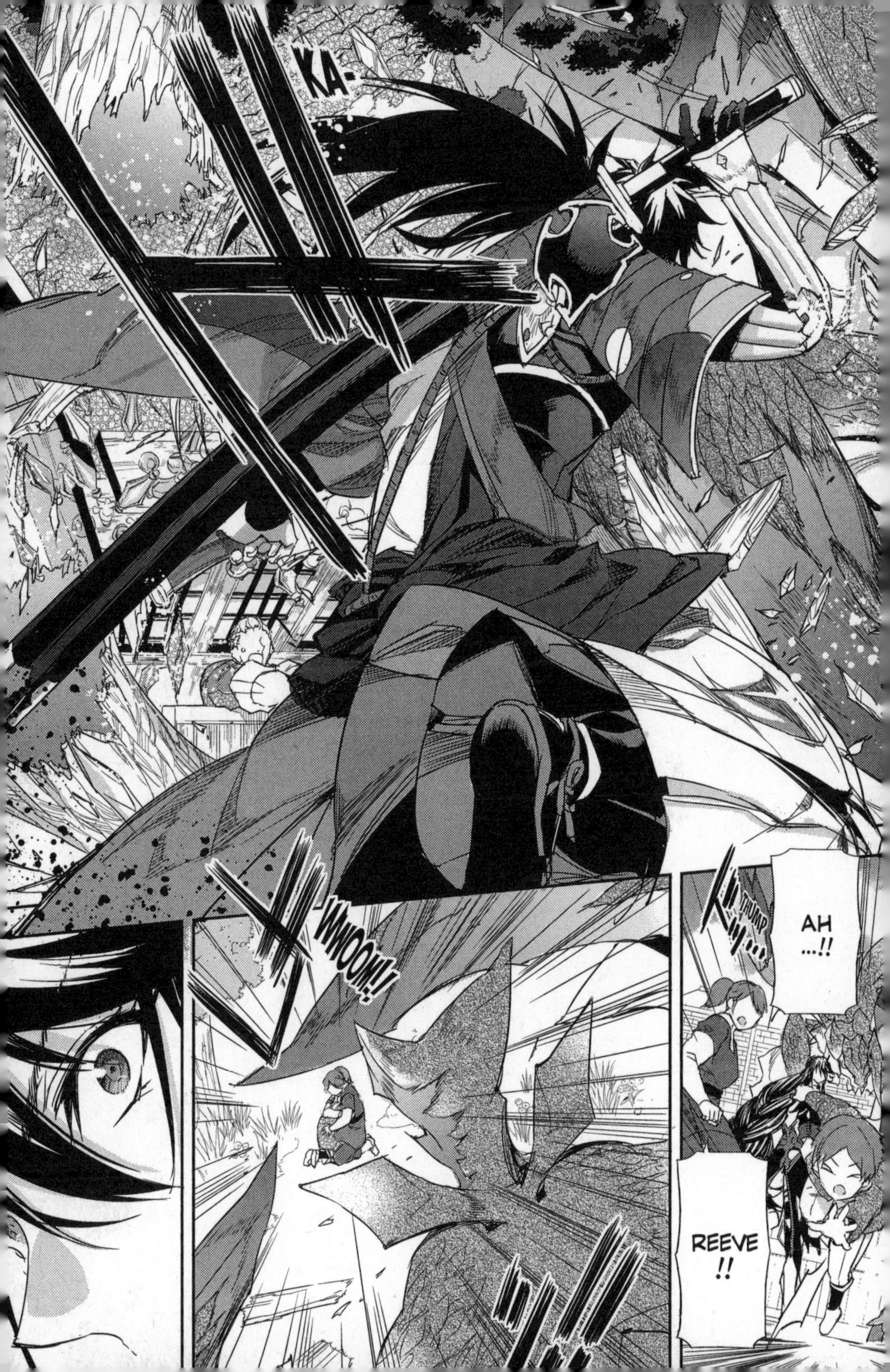
KA-
AH ...!!
THUMP
REEVE !!
VWOOM!!

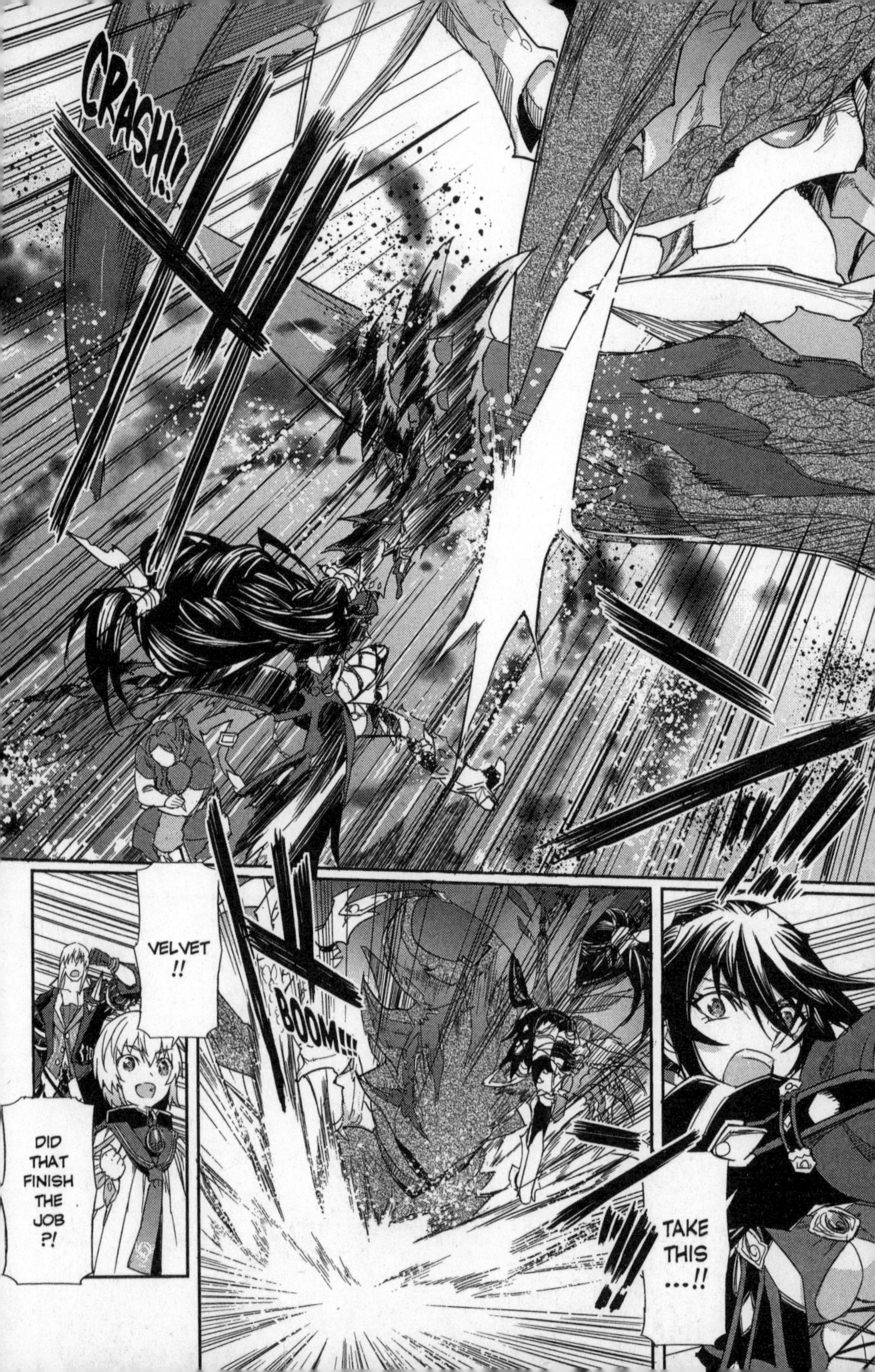
CRASH!!
TAKE THIS ...!!
BOOM!!!
VELVET !!
DID THAT FINISH THE JOB ?!

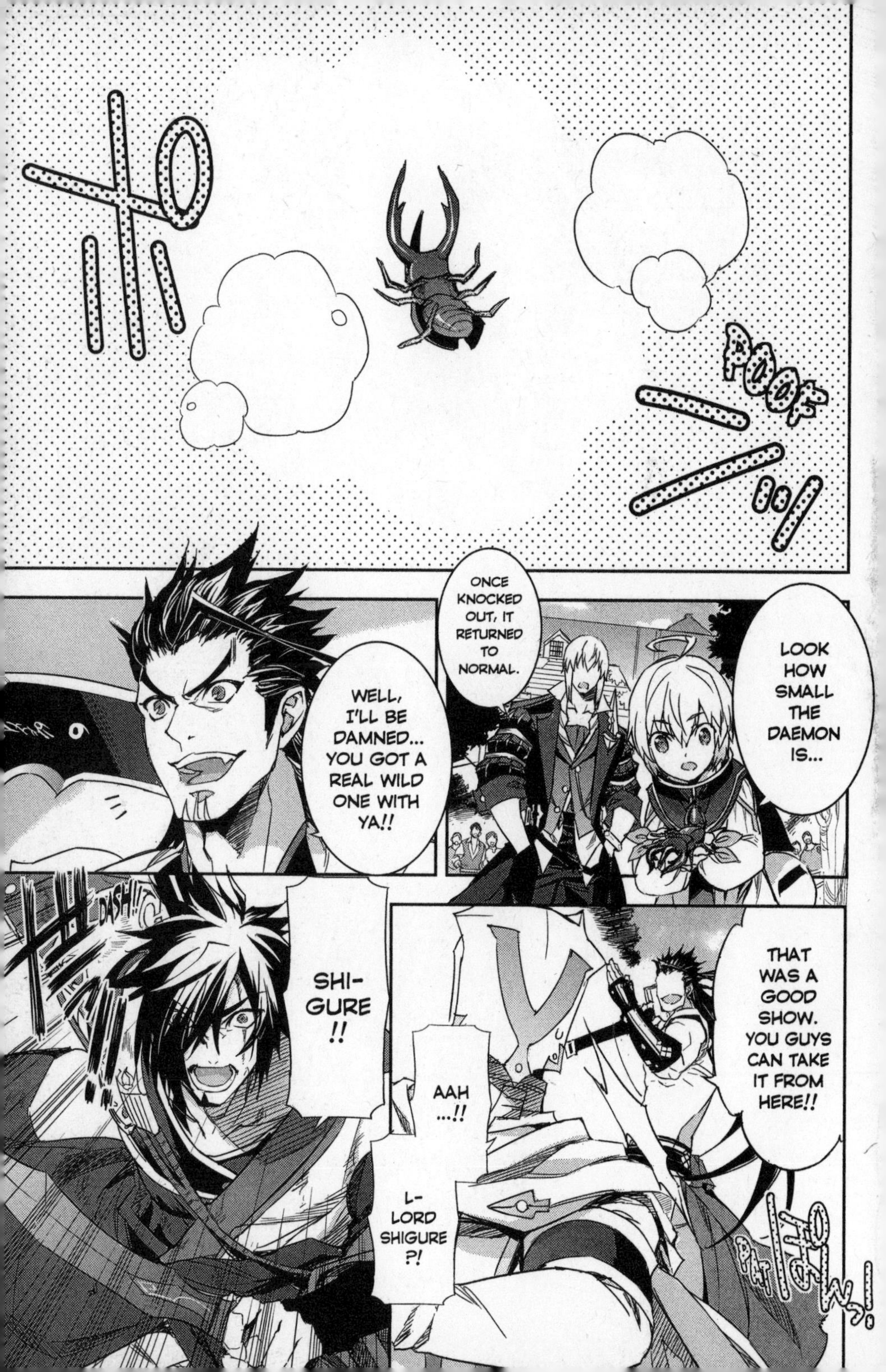
POOF
LOOK HOW SMALL THE DAEMON IS...
ONCE KNOCKED OUT, IT RETURNED TO NORMAL.
WELL, I'LL BE DAMNED... YOU GOT A REAL WILD ONE WITH YA!!
THAT WAS A GOOD SHOW. YOU GUYS CAN TAKE IT FROM HERE!!
PAT
AAH ...!!
L-LORD SHIGURE?!
SHI-GURE!!
DASH!!

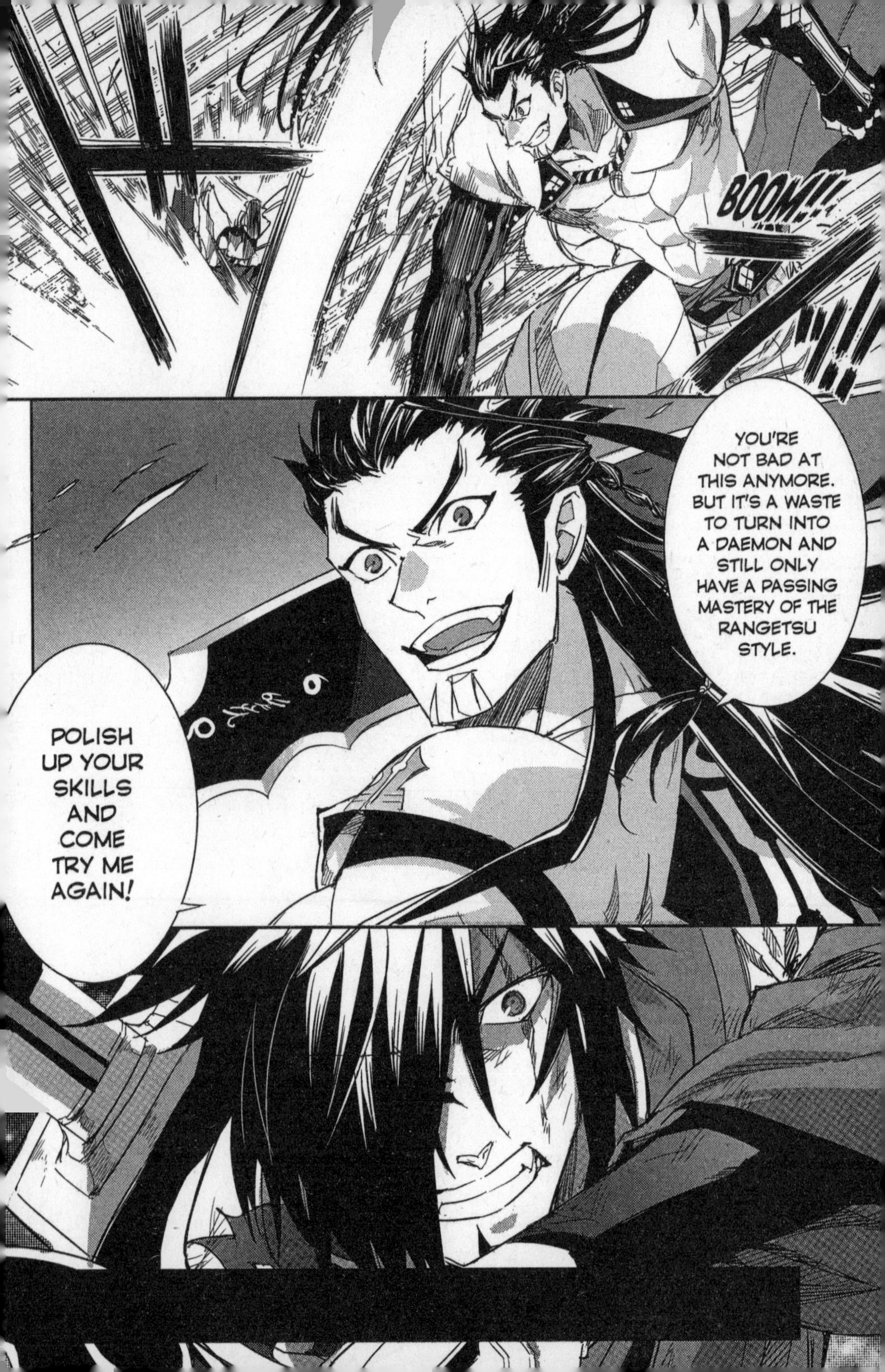
BOOM!!!
YOU'RE NOT BAD AT THIS ANYMORE. BUT IT'S A WASTE TO TURN INTO A DAEMON AND STILL ONLY HAVE A PASSING MASTERY OF THE RANGETSU STYLE.
POLISH UP YOUR SKILLS AND COME TRY ME AGAIN!

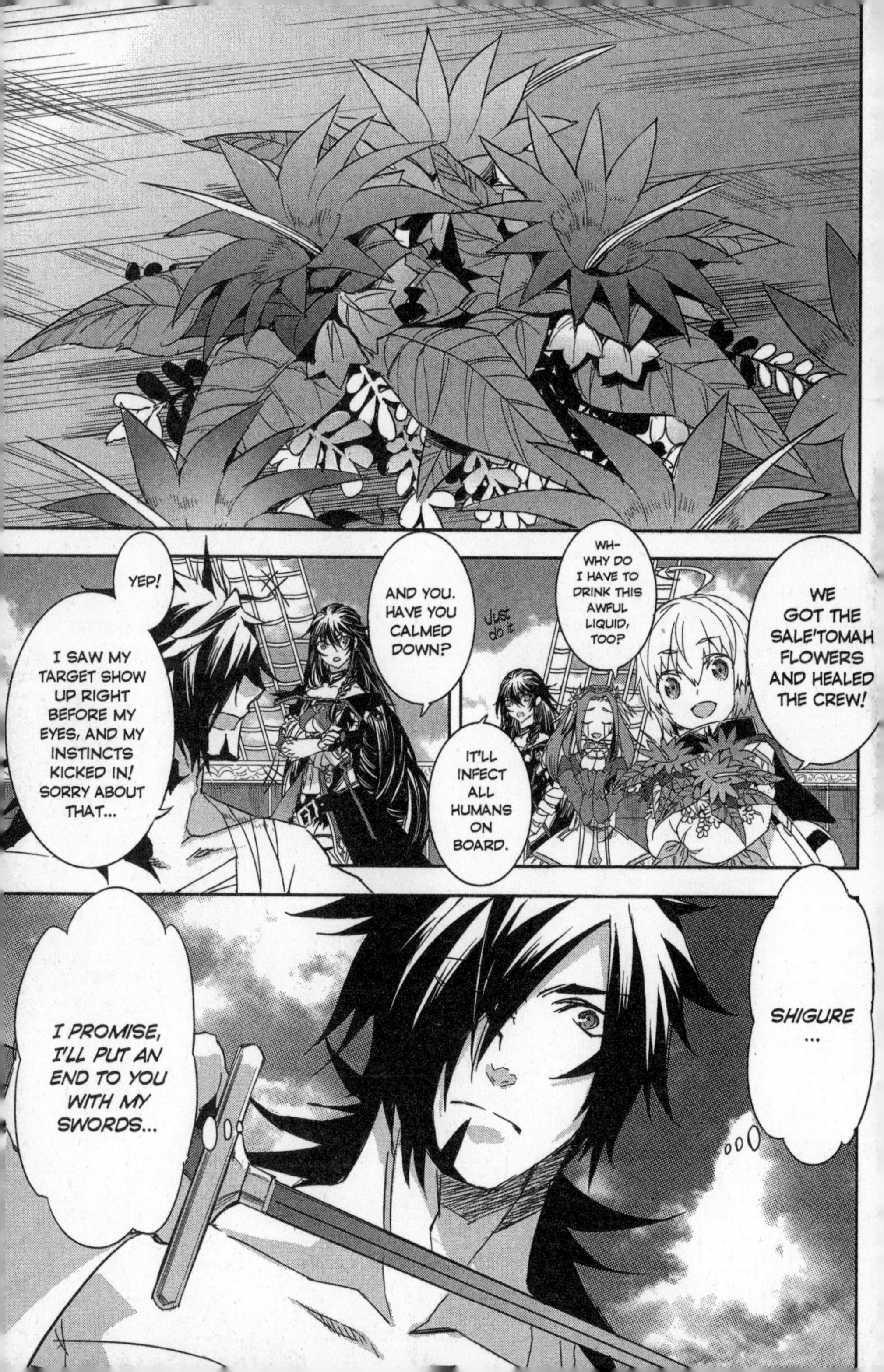
WE GOT THE SALE'TOMAH FLOWERS AND HEALED THE CREW!
WH- WHY DO I HAVE TO DRINK THIS AWFUL LIQUID, TOO?
Just do it
IT'LL INFECT ALL HUMANS ON BOARD.
AND YOU. HAVE YOU CALMED DOWN?
YEP!
I SAW MY TARGET SHOW UP RIGHT BEFORE MY EYES, AND MY INSTINCTS KICKED IN! SORRY ABOUT THAT...
SHIGURE ...
I PROMISE, I'LL PUT AN END TO YOU WITH MY SWORDS...

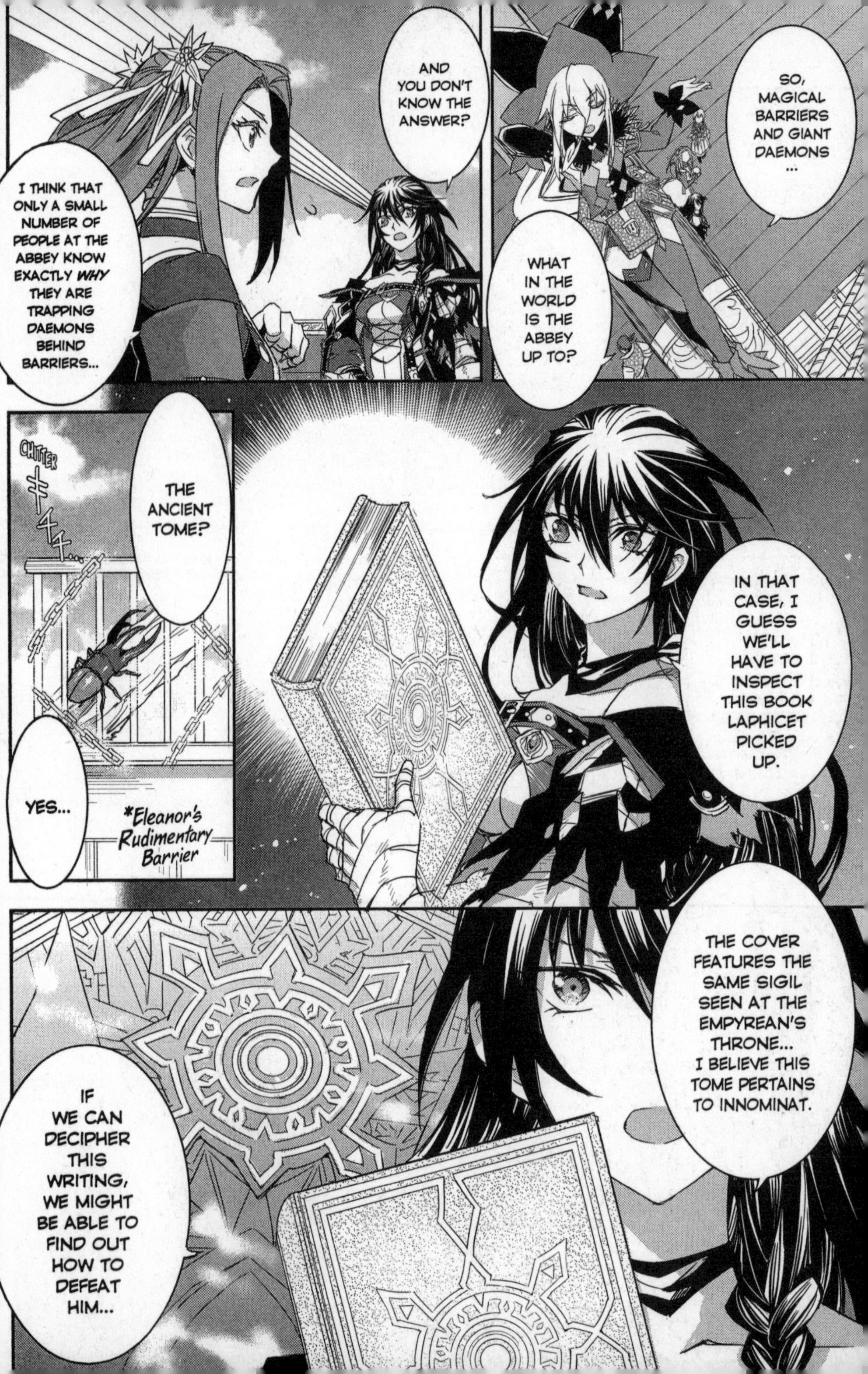

SO, MAGICAL BARRIERS AND GIANT DAEMONS ...
WHAT IN THE WORLD IS THE ABBEY UP TO?
AND YOU DON'T KNOW THE ANSWER?
I THINK THAT ONLY A SMALL NUMBER OF PEOPLE AT THE ABBEY KNOW EXACTLY *WHY* THEY ARE TRAPPING DAEMONS BEHIND BARRIERS...
IN THAT CASE, I GUESS WE'LL HAVE TO INSPECT THIS BOOK LAPHICET PICKED UP.
THE ANCIENT TOME?
CHITTER
YES...
*Eleanor's Rudimentary Barrier
THE COVER FEATURES THE SAME SIGIL SEEN AT THE EMPYREAN'S THRONE... I BELIEVE THIS TOME PERTAINS TO INNOMINAT.
IF WE CAN DECIPHER THIS WRITING, WE MIGHT BE ABLE TO FIND OUT HOW TO DEFEAT HIM...

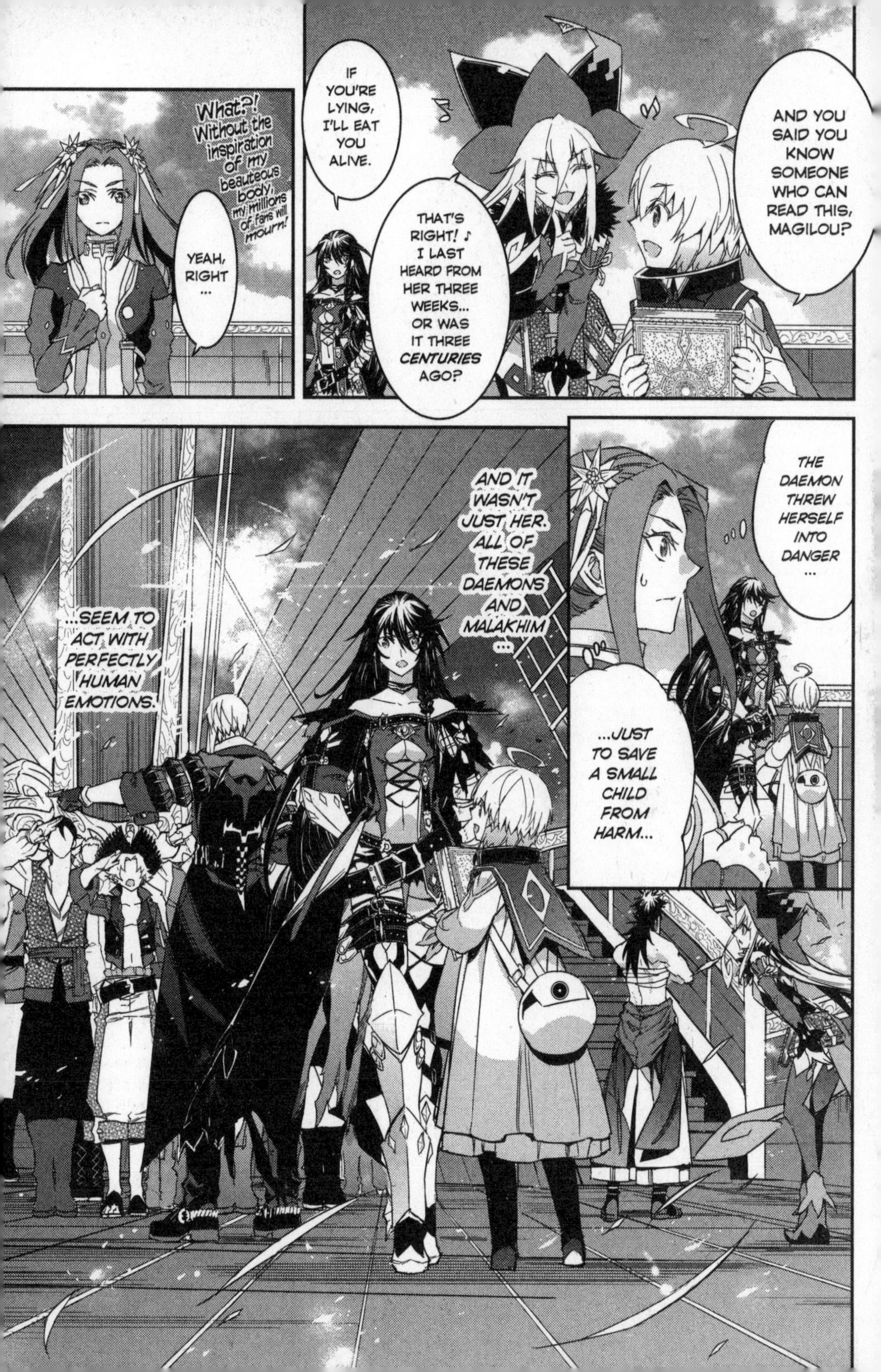
AND YOU SAID YOU KNOW SOMEONE WHO CAN READ THIS, MAGILOU?
THAT'S RIGHT! ♪ I LAST HEARD FROM HER THREE WEEKS... OR WAS IT THREE *CENTURIES* AGO?
IF YOU'RE LYING, I'LL EAT YOU ALIVE.
What?! Without the inspiration of my beauteous body, my millions of fans will mourn!
YEAH, RIGHT ...
THE DAEMON THREW HERSELF INTO DANGER ...
...JUST TO SAVE A SMALL CHILD FROM HARM...
AND IT WASN'T JUST HER. ALL OF THESE DAEMONS AND MALAKHIM ...
...SEEM TO ACT WITH PERFECTLY HUMAN EMOTIONS.

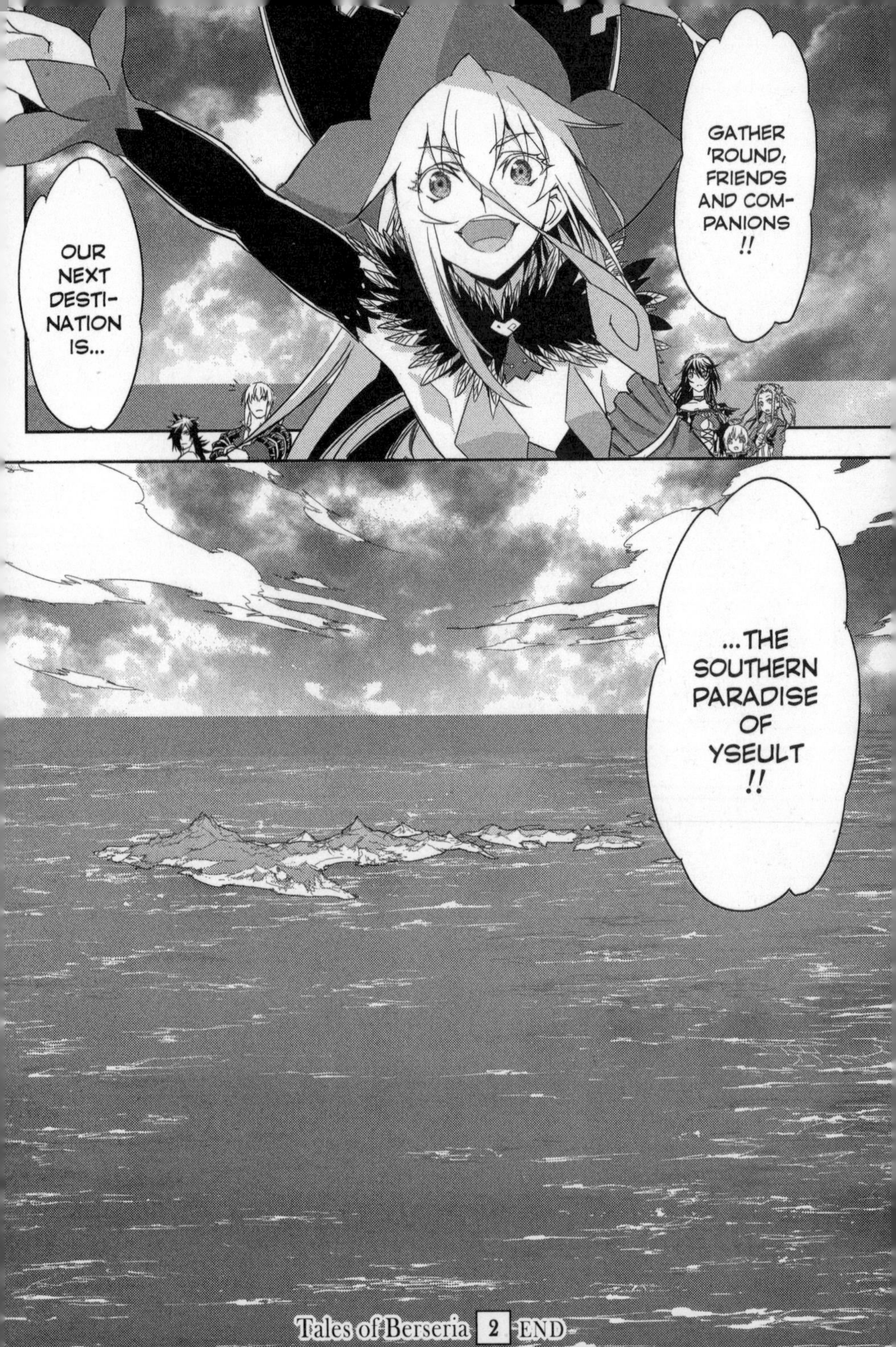
GATHER 'ROUND, FRIENDS AND COMPANIONS!!
OUR NEXT DESTINATION IS...
...THE SOUTHERN PARADISE OF YSEULT!!

Tales of Berseria 2 END

New Party Member!

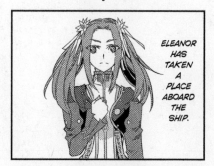

ELEANOR HAS TAKEN A PLACE ABOARD THE SHIP.
THANKS A LOT, MISS EXORCIST.
I'M GLAD YOU'RE FEELING BETTER.
I HEARD YOU WENT INTO THE SALE'TOMAH FOREST, MISS EXORCIST?
YES, BUT I WAS ONLY A PART OF THE GROUP. REALLY, I DIDN'T DO...
Oooh, so your name is Eleanor?
Do you mind if we call you Ellie?
SHE'S QUITE A HIT.
SHE MIGHT TAKE OVER YOUR SHIP.
CHATTER CHATTER
Um... excuse me...
...

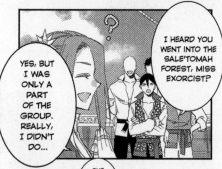

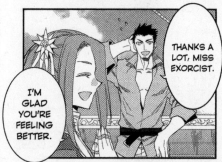

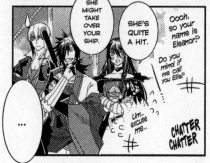

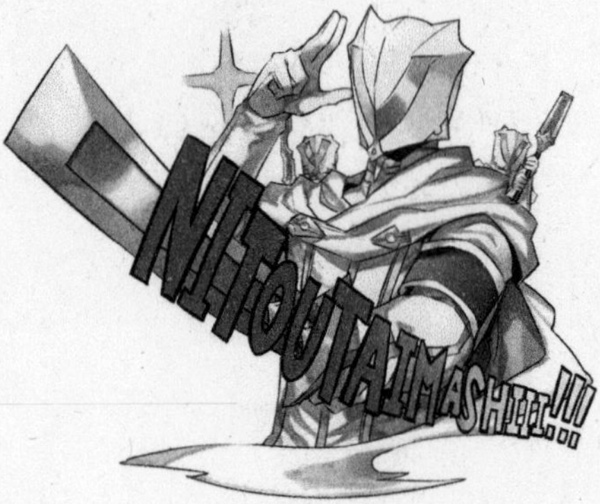
NI-TOUTAIMASHIII...!!!

Nobu Aonagi

Thanks to your support, here we are with Volume 2! The story of Velvet and her party is in the middle stages, but it's full steam ahead from here, so I hope you'll enjoy their adventures. And now, let the story begin...

ARTWORK: "Praetor-rank Exorcist!!"

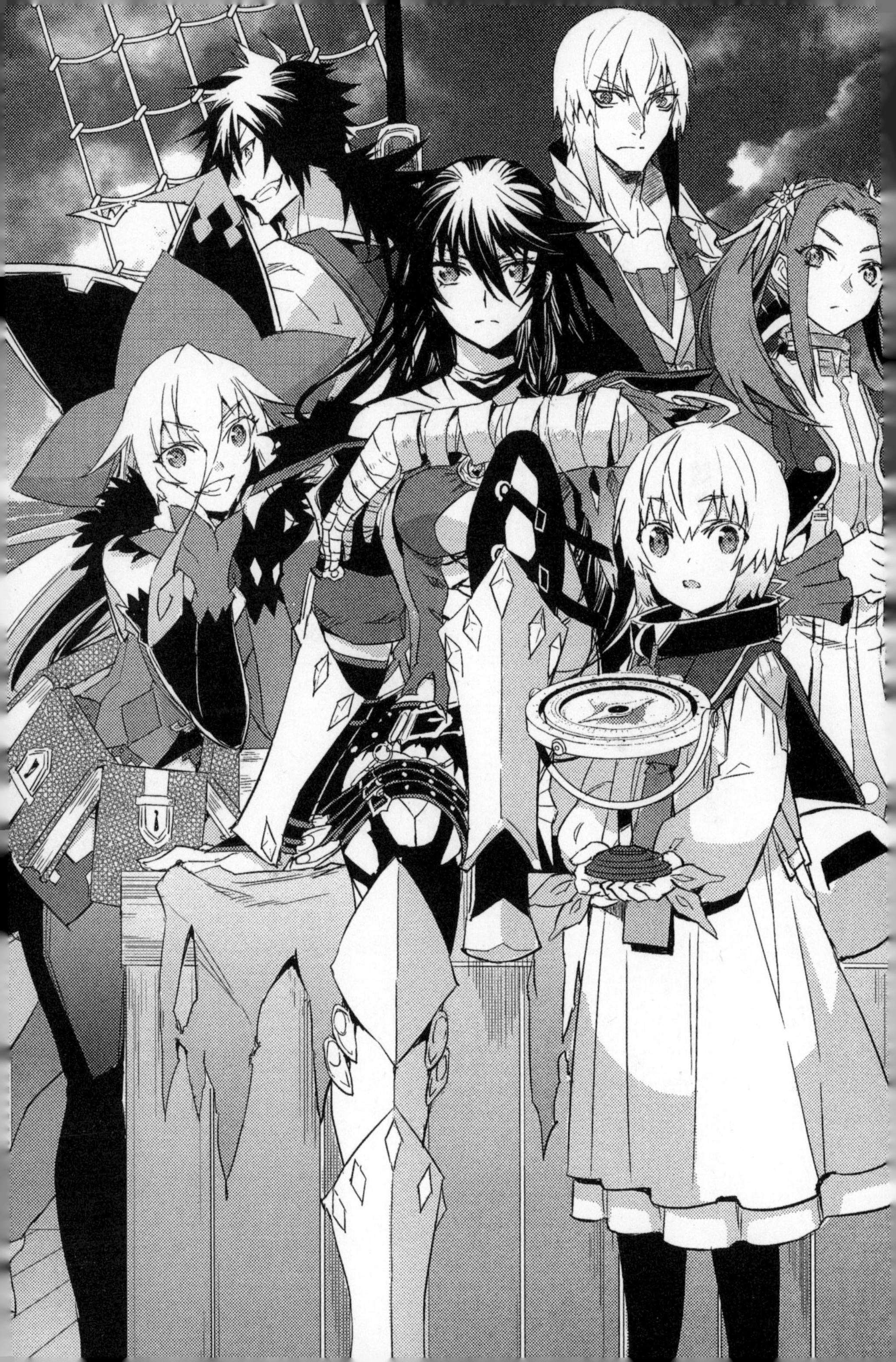

Eizen

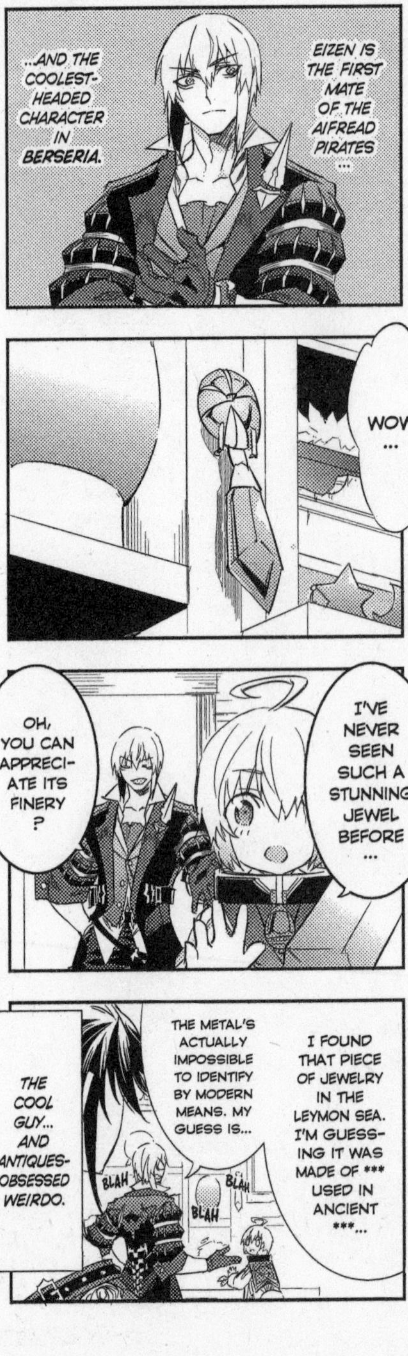
EIZEN IS THE FIRST MATE OF THE AIFREAD PIRATES...
...AND THE COOLEST-HEADED CHARACTER IN BERSERIA.
WOW...
I'VE NEVER SEEN SUCH A STUNNING JEWEL BEFORE...
OH, YOU CAN APPRECIATE ITS FINERY?
I FOUND THAT PIECE OF JEWELRY IN THE LEYMON SEA. I'M GUESSING IT WAS MADE OF *** USED IN ANCIENT ***...
THE METAL'S ACTUALLY IMPOSSIBLE TO IDENTIFY BY MODERN MEANS. MY GUESS IS...
BLAH
BLAH
BLAH
THE COOL GUY... AND ANTIQUES-OBSESSED WEIRDO.

Rokurou

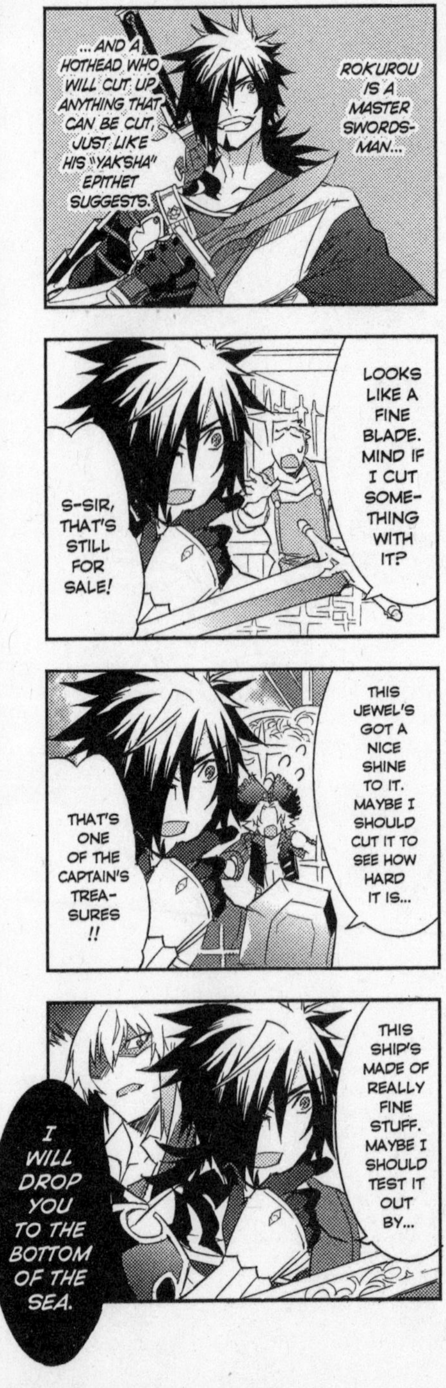
ROKUROU IS A MASTER SWORDS-MAN...
...AND A HOTHEAD WHO WILL CUT UP ANYTHING THAT CAN BE CUT, JUST LIKE HIS "YAKSHA" EPITHET SUGGESTS.
LOOKS LIKE A FINE BLADE. MIND IF I CUT SOME-THING WITH IT?
S-SIR, THAT'S STILL FOR SALE!
THIS JEWEL'S GOT A NICE SHINE TO IT. MAYBE I SHOULD CUT IT TO SEE HOW HARD IT IS...
THAT'S ONE OF THE CAPTAIN'S TREA-SURES!!
THIS SHIP'S MADE OF REALLY FINE STUFF. MAYBE I SHOULD TEST IT OUT BY...
I WILL DROP YOU TO THE BOTTOM OF THE SEA.

Tales of Berseria

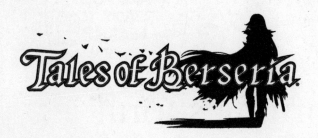

of Berseria

Tales of Berseria

Next Volume Preview

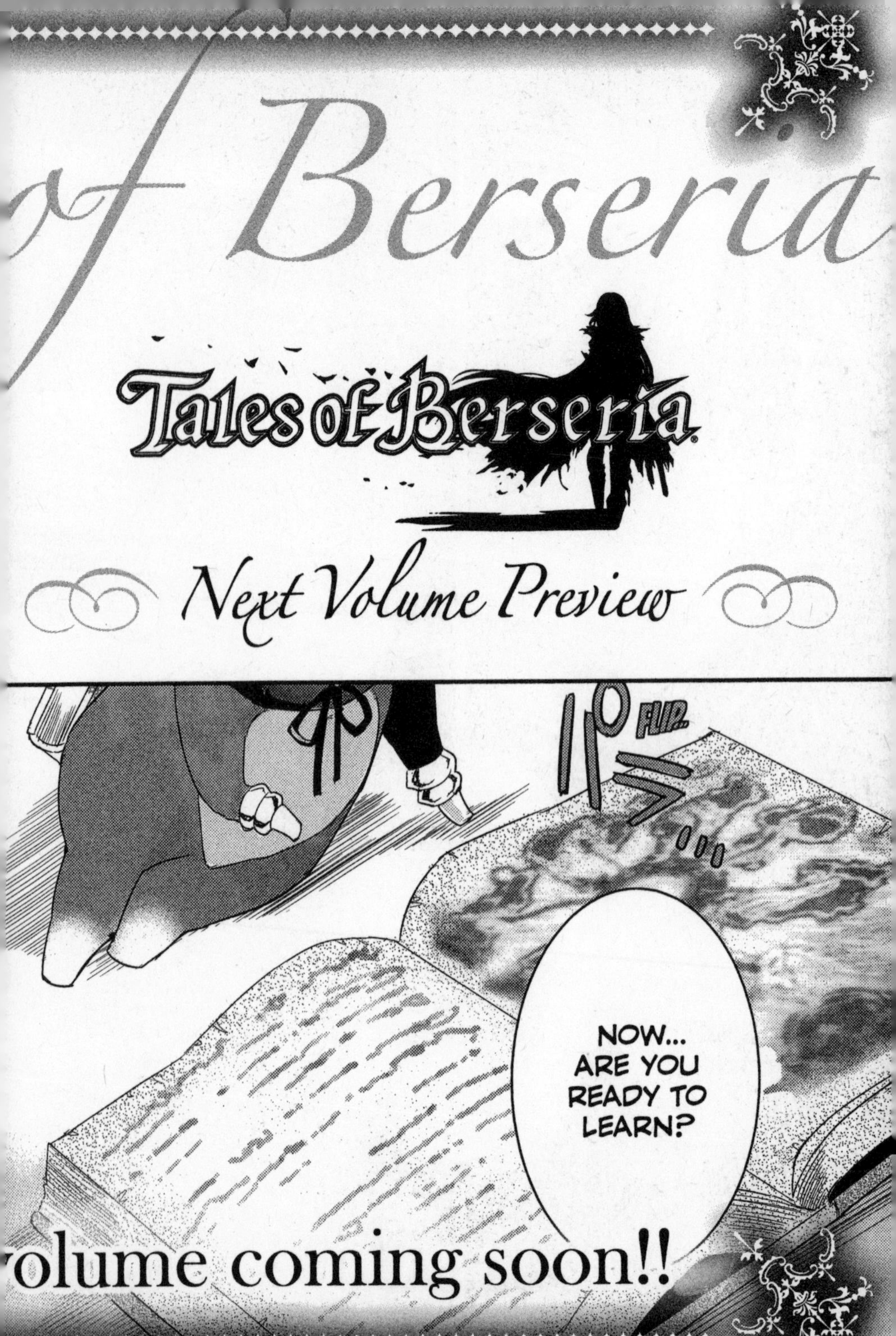
FLIP
NOW... ARE YOU READY TO LEARN?

olume coming soon!!

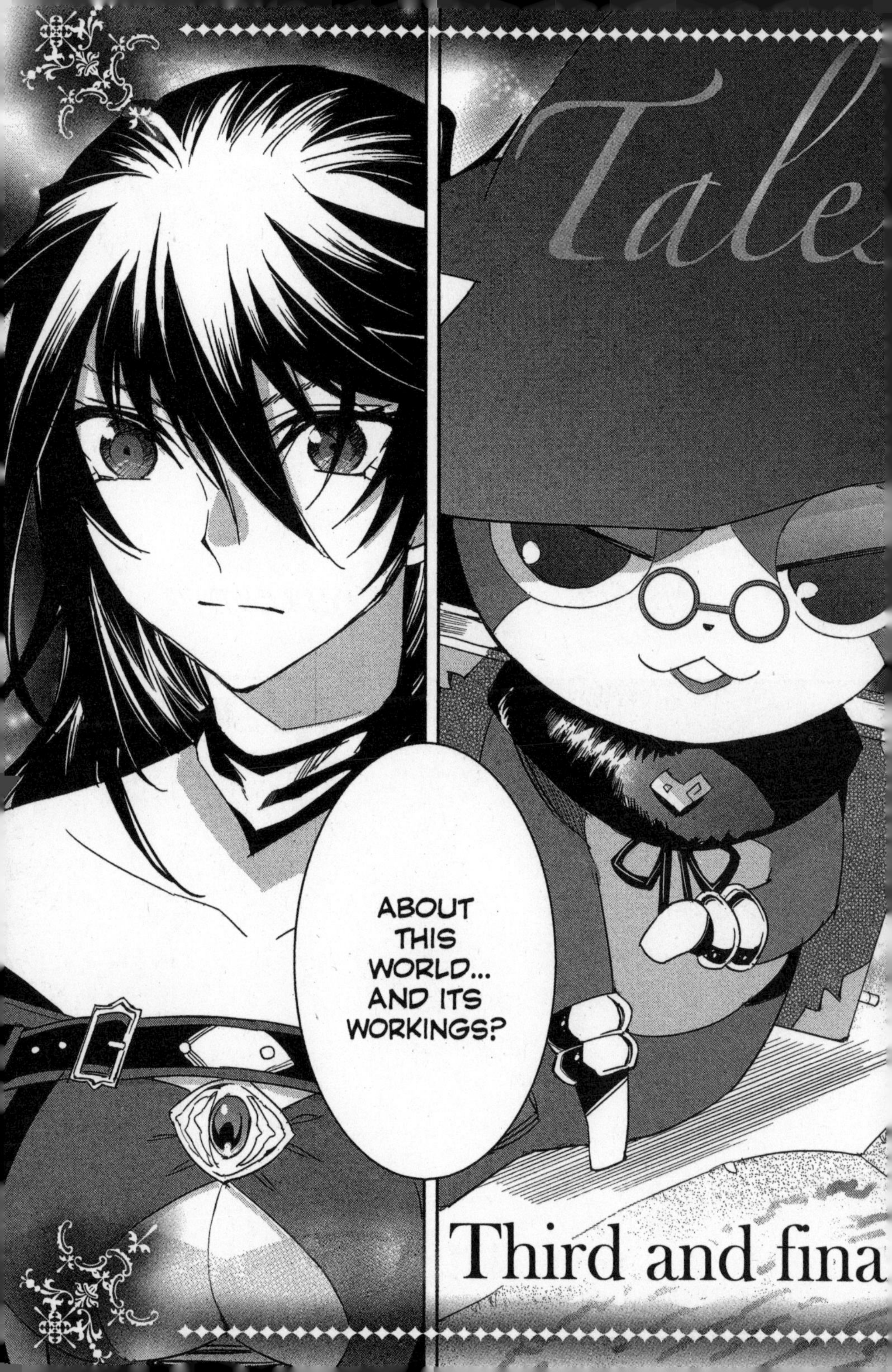
Tales
Third and fina
ABOUT THIS WORLD... AND ITS WORKINGS?

The slow-burn queer romance that'll sweep you off your feet!

10 DANCE

Inouesatoh presents

"A FANTASTIC DEBUT VOLUME... ONE OF MY FAVORITE BOOKS OF THE YEAR..."
— AiPT!

"10 DANCE IS A MUST-READ FOR ANYONE WHO'S ENJOYED MANGA AND ANIME ABOUT COMPETITIVE DANCE (ON OR OFF THE ICE!)."
—Anime UK News

Shinya Sugiki, the dashing lord of Standard Ballroom, and Shinya Suzuki, passionate king of Latin Dance: The two share more than just a first name and a love of the sport. They each want to become champion of the 10-Dance Competition, which means they'll need to learn the other's specialty dances, and who better to learn from than the best? But old rivalries die hard, and things get further complicated when they realize there might be more between them than an uneasy partnership...

KC KODANSHA COMICS

THE MAGICAL GIRL CLASSIC THAT BROUGHT A
GENERATION OF READERS TO MANGA, NOW BACK IN A
DEFINITIVE, HARDCOVER COLLECTOR'S EDITION!

CARDCAPTOR SAKURA
COLLECTOR'S EDITION
C L A M P

Ten-year-old Sakura Kinomoto
lives a pretty normal life with
her older brother, Tōya, and
widowed father, Fujitaka—
until the day she discovers a
strange book in her father's
library, and her life takes a
magical turn...

- A deluxe large-format
  hardcover edition
  of CLAMP's shojo
  manga classic
- All-new foil-stamped cover
  art on each volume
- Comes with exclusive
  collectible art card

KC
KODANSHA
COMICS

17 years after the original *Cardcaptor Sakura* manga ended, CLAMP returns with more magical adventures from a beloved manga classic!

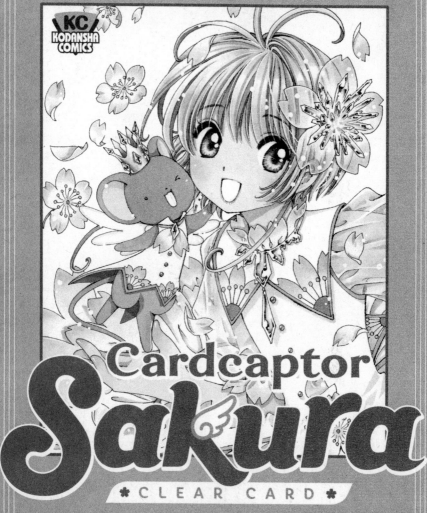

KC
KODANSHA
COMICS

Cardcaptor Sakura

❀ C L E A R C A R D ❀

Sakura Kinomoto's about to start middle school, and everything's coming up cherry blossoms. Not only has she managed to recapture the scattered Clow Cards and make them her own Sakura Cards, but her sweetheart Syaoran Li has moved from Hong Kong to Tokyo and is going to be in her class! But her joy is interrupted by a troubling dream in which the cards turn transparent, and when Sakura awakens to discover her dream has become reality, it's clear that her magical adventures are far from over...

EDENS ZERO
エデンズゼロ

HIRO MASHIMA IS BACK! JOIN THE CREATOR OF *FAIRY TAIL*
AS HE TAKES TO THE STARS FOR ANOTHER THRILLING SAGA!

A high-flying space adventure! All the steadfast friendship
and wild fighting you've been waiting for...IN SPACE!

At Granbell Kingdom, an abandoned amusement park, Shiki has lived his entire life among machines. But one day, Rebecca and her cat companion Happy appear at the park's front gates. Little do these newcomers know that this is the first human contact Granbell has had in a hundred years! As Shiki stumbles his way into making new friends, his former neighbors stir at an opportunity for a robo-rebellion... And when his old homeland becomes too dangerous, Shiki must join Rebecca and Happy on their spaceship and escape into the boundless cosmos.

KC KODANSHA COMICS

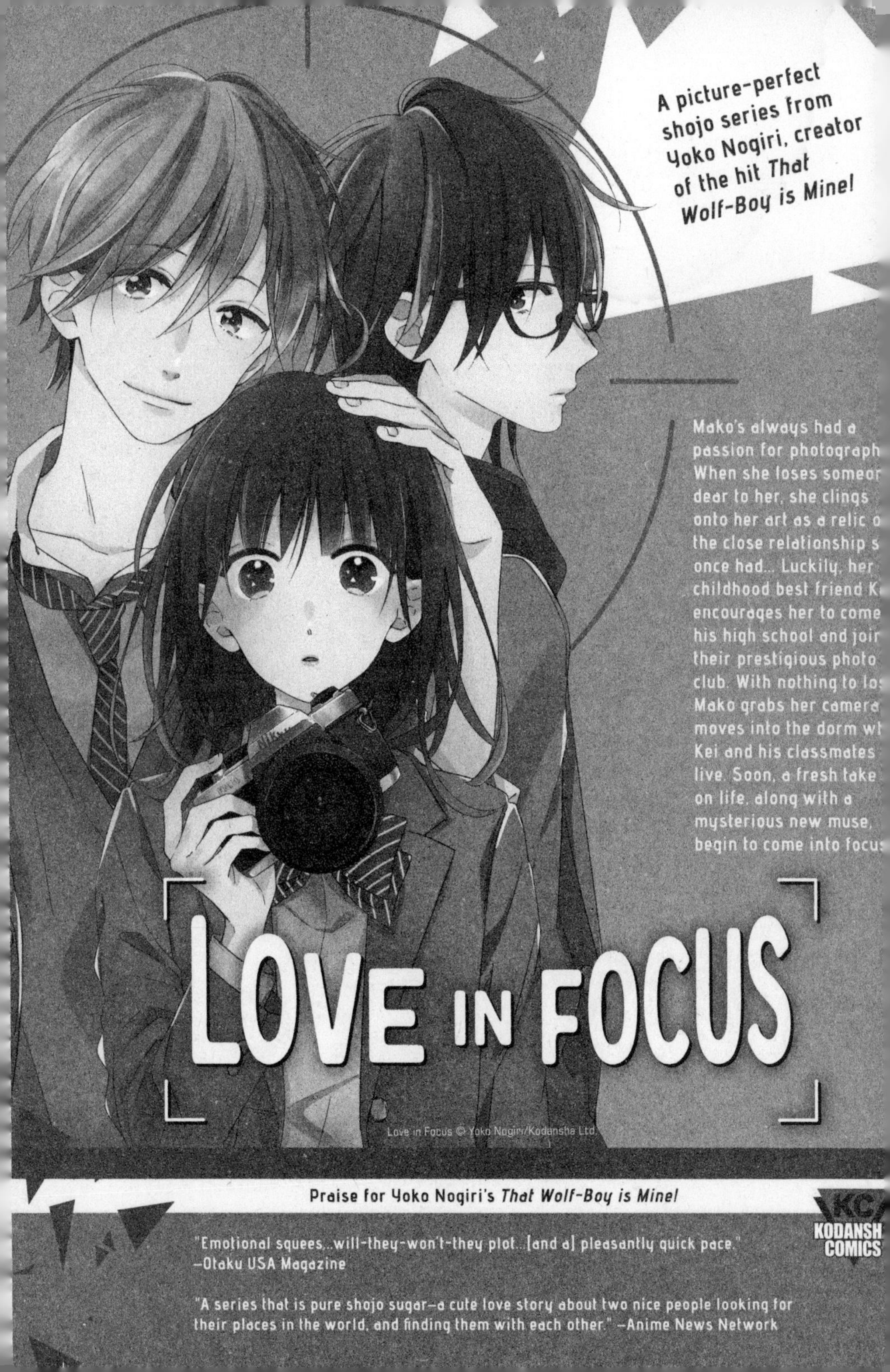

A picture-perfect shojo series from Yoko Nogiri, creator of the hit *That Wolf-Boy is Mine!*
Mako's always had a passion for photograph When she loses someor dear to her, she clings onto her art as a relic o the close relationship s once had... Luckily, her childhood best friend Ke encourages her to come his high school and joir their prestigious photo club. With nothing to los Mako grabs her camera moves into the dorm wi Kei and his classmates live. Soon, a fresh take on life, along with a mysterious new muse, begin to come into focu
LOVE IN FOCUS
Love in Focus © Yoko Nogiri/Kodansha Ltd.
Praise for Yoko Nogiri's *That Wolf-Boy is Mine!*
KC KODANSH COMICS
"Emotional squees...will-they-won't-they plot...[and a] pleasantly quick pace." –Otaku USA Magazine
"A series that is pure shojo sugar–a cute love story about two nice people looking for their places in the world, and finding them with each other." –Anime News Network

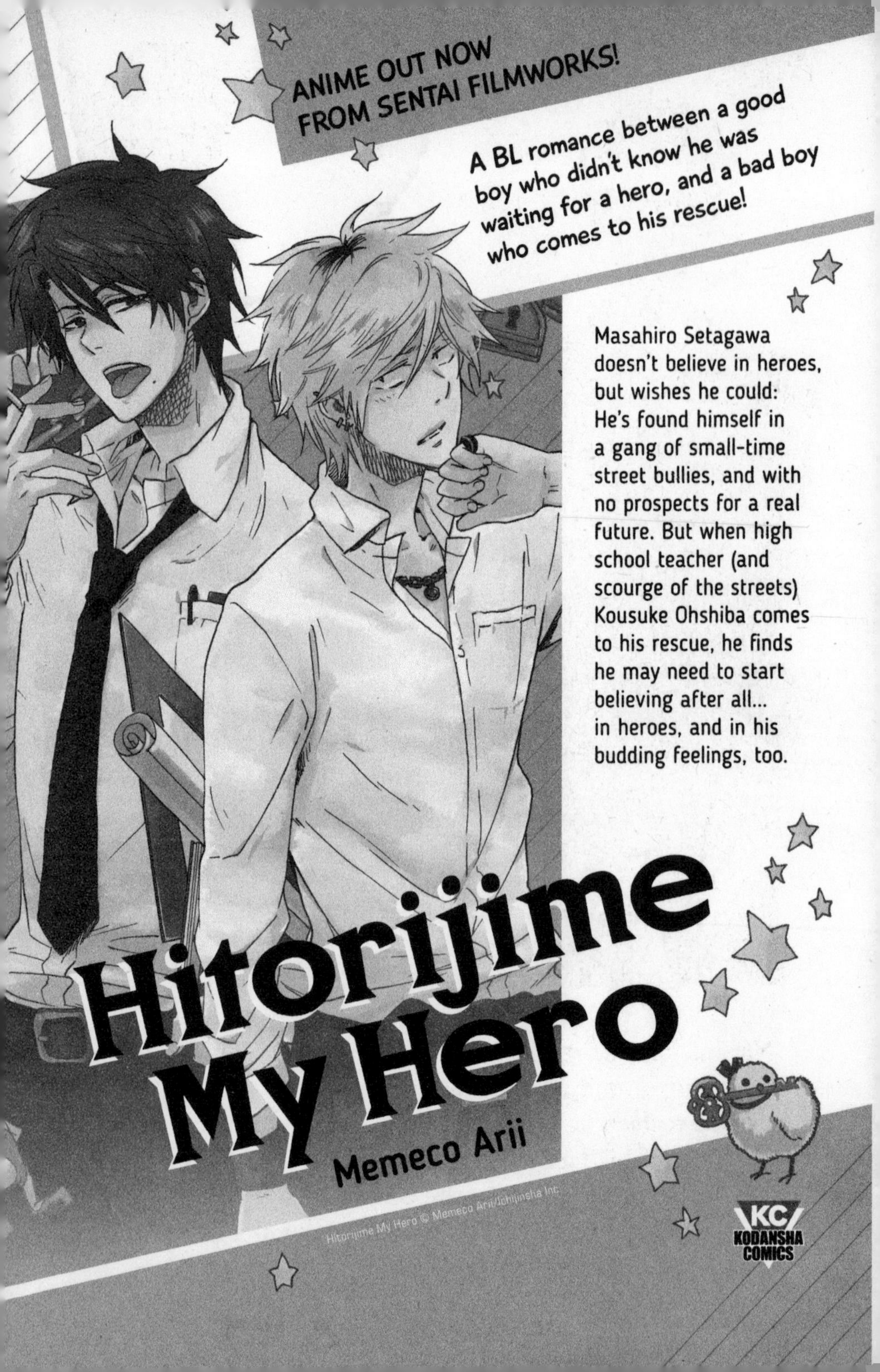
ANIME OUT NOW FROM SENTAI FILMWORKS!
A BL romance between a good boy who didn't know he was waiting for a hero, and a bad boy who comes to his rescue!
Masahiro Setagawa doesn't believe in heroes, but wishes he could: He's found himself in a gang of small-time street bullies, and with no prospects for a real future. But when high school teacher (and scourge of the streets) Kousuke Ohshiba comes to his rescue, he finds he may need to start believing after all... in heroes, and in his budding feelings, too.
Hitorijime My Hero
Memeco Arii
Hitorijime My Hero © Memeco Arii/Ichijinsha Inc.
KC KODANSHA COMICS

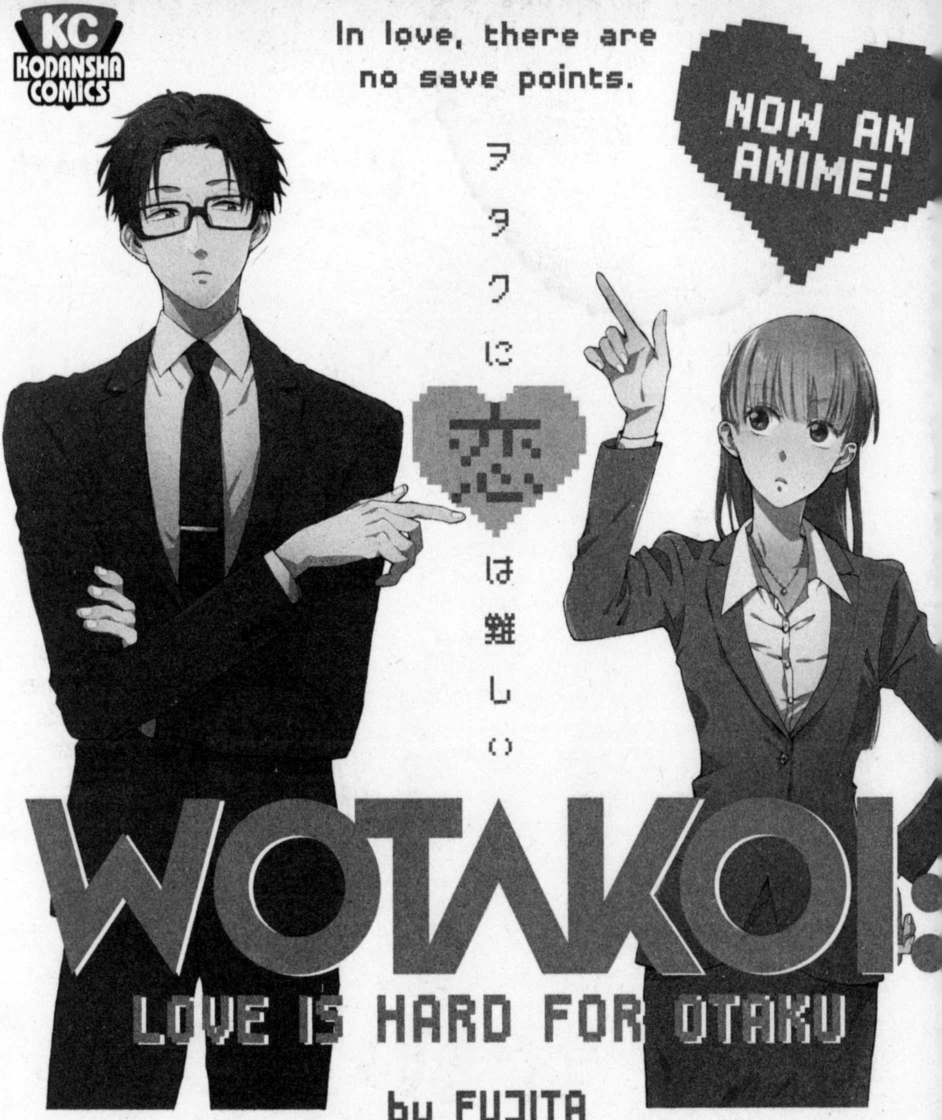
KC
KODANSHA COMICS
In love, there are no save points.
NOW AN ANIME!
ヲタクに恋は難しい
WOTAKOI:
LOVE IS HARD FOR OTAKU
by FUJITA

Narumi has had it rough: Every boyfriend she's had dumped her once they found out she was an otaku, so she's gone to great lengths to hide it. At her new job, she bumps into Hirotaka, her childhood friend and fellow otaku. When Hirotaka almost gets her secret outed at work, she comes up with a plan to keep him quiet. But he comes up with a counter-proposal: Why doesn't she just date him instead?

Magus of the Library

Mitsu Izumi

MITSU IZUMI'S STUNNING ARTWORK BRINGS A FANTASTICAL LITERARY ADVENTURE TO LUSH, THRILLING LIFE!

Young Theo adores books, but the prejudice and hatred of his village keeps them ever out of his reach. Then one day, he chances to meet Sedona, a traveling librarian who works for the great library of Aftzaak, City of Books, and his life changes forever...

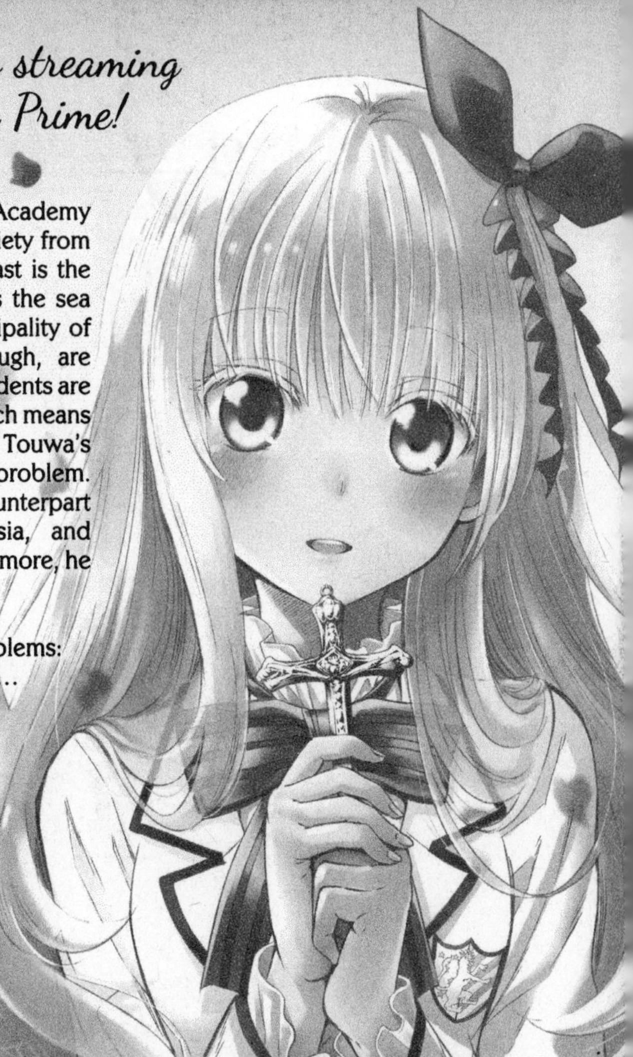

◆ KAMOME ▸
SHIRAHAMA

Witch Hat Atelier

A magical manga
adventure for
fans of Disney
and Studio
Ghibli!

Witch Hat Atelier © Kamome Shirahama/Kodansha Ltd

The magical adventure that took Japan by storm is finally here, from acclaimed DC and Marvel cover artist Kamome Shirahama!

In a world where everyone takes wonders like magic spells and dragons for granted, Coco is a girl with a simple dream: She wants to be a witch. But everybody knows magicians are born, not made, and Coco was not born with a gift for magic. Resigned to her un-magical life, Coco is about to give up on her dream to become a witch…until the day she meets Qifrey, a mysterious, traveling magician. After secretly seeing Qifrey perform magic in a way she's never seen before, Coco soon learns what everybody "knows" might not be the truth, and discovers that her magical dream may not be as far away as it may seem…

KC
KODANSHA
COMICS

THE HIGH SCHOOL HAREM COMEDY WITH FIVE TIMES THE CUTE GIRLS!

"An entertaining romantic-comedy with a snarky edge to it." —Taykobon

Futaro Uesugi i
a second-year
in high school,
scraping to get
by and pay off
his family's debt.
The only thing he
can do is study,
so when Futaro
receives a part-tim
job offer to tutor
the five daughters
of a wealthy
businessman, he
can't pass it up. Littl
does he know, these
five beautiful sisters
are quintuplets, but th
only thing they have i
common...is that they'r
all terrible at studying!

THE
QUINTESSENTIAL
QUINTUPLETS

negi haruba

ANIME
OUT NOW!

KC/
KODANSHA
COMICS

A Kodansha Comics Trade Paperback Original
Tales of Berseria 2 copyright
© 2017 Nobu Aonagi / Ichijinsha
© MUTSUMI INOMATA
© KOSUKE FUJISHIMA
© BANDAI NAMCO Entertainment Inc.

English translation copyright
© 2020 Nobu Aonagi / Ichijinsha
© MUTSUMI INOMATA
© KOSUKE FUJISHIMA
© BANDAI NAMCO Entertainment Inc.

Published in the United States by Kodansha Comics, an imprint of Kodansha USA Publishing, LLC, New York.

Publication rights for this English edition arranged through Kodansha Ltd., Tokyo.

First published in Japan in 2017 by Ichijinsha Inc., Tokyo as *Teiruzu Obu Beruseria,* volume 2

ISBN 978-1-63236-883-6

Original cover design by Misa Iwai (Banana Grove Studio)

Printed in the United States of America.

www.kodanshacomics.com

9 8 7 6 5 4 3 2 1
Translation: Stephen Paul
Lettering: Evan Hayden
Editing: Tiff Ferentini
Kodansha Comics edition cover design by Phil Balsman

Publisher: Kiichiro Sugawara
Managing editor: Maya Rosewood
Vice president of marketing & publicity: Naho Yamada

Director of publishing services: Ben Applegate
Associate director of operations: Stephen Pakula
Publishing services managing editor: Noelle Webster
Assistant production manager: Emi Lotto